Praise for *Dark Victory*

"Many readers will applaud Moldea for ferreting out these facts. Others will condemn him for his conclusions. But all should read *Dark Victory*."

—*The Dallas Morning News*

"Moldea's probing goes far in peeling away the facade of one of Hollywood's most powerful corporations."

—*Los Angeles Life, Daily News*

"A disquieting examination of the intricate network that binds business, politics, and the underworld"

—*Booklist*

"A smoldering indictment of the Hollywood entertainment industry's guilt-by-association ties to organized crime . . . Although, for the most part, MCA and Reagan have done nothing technically illegal (i.e. indictable) in their ruthless quest for power and success, they have used every means available, including mobsters and corrupt politicians and union officials. Sure to be controversial"

—*Library Journal*

"Moldea uses government documents to raise serious questions."

—*Publishers Weekly*

"There is much information that is fresh in this book, and through numerous interviews and previously unattainable federal documents, Moldea has woven myriad previously separated facts into a startling political pattern."

—*Los Angeles Times*

PENGUIN BOOKS

DARK VICTORY

Dan E. Moldea has specialized in organized-crime investigations since 1974. He has written for numerous publications and is the author of *The Hoffa Wars* and *The Hunting of Cain*. He lives in Washington, D.C.

DARK VICTORY

Ronald Reagan, MCA, and the Mob

DAN E. MOLDEA

PENGUIN BOOKS

PENGUIN BOOKS

Viking Penguin Inc., 40 West 23rd Street,
New York, New York 10010, U.S.A.
Penguin Books Ltd, Harmondsworth,
Middlesex, England
Penguin Books Australia Ltd, Ringwood,
Victoria, Australia
Penguin Books Canada Limited, 2801 John Street,
Markham, Ontario, Canada L3R 1B4
Penguin Books (N.Z.) Ltd, 182–190 Wairau Road,
Auckland 10, New Zealand

First published in the United States of America by
Viking Penguin Inc. 1986
This edition with a new afterword first published in Penguin Books 1987

ISBN 0 14 01.0478 X
(CIP data available)

Printed in the United States of America by
R. R. Donnelley & Sons Company, Harrisonburg, Virginia
Set in Times Roman

To Dad

Organized crime will put a man in the
White House someday—and he won't know
it until they hand him the bill.

RALPH SALERNO,
New York Police Department
1967

ACKNOWLEDGMENTS

This work could not have been completed without the encouragement of Washington journalists Jeff Goldberg and William Scott Malone. Goldberg and I co-authored a 1984 article on Ronald Reagan and MCA. Also essential were the help and guidance of David Robb, staff reporter for *Daily Variety; Los Angeles Times* reporter William K. Knoedelseder, Jr.; New York free-lance journalist Robert I. Friedman; Richard J. O'Connell and Betty Bosarge at the Washington Crime News Service; author Sheldon Tromberg; former *Sacramento Bee* reporter Dick Brenneman; Meloni Craig; Mary Moldea; and a variety of confidential sources who asked not to be identified for fear of professional reprisals.

Sincere gratitude is also expressed to Robert Evans of Cleveland, Ohio, who helped get this project started—as did Anne Zill and the Fund for Constitutional Government and Howard Bray and the Fund for Investigative Journalism.

And deep appreciation is extended to: Michael Allen, Merilou Baker, Dick Barnett, Ann Beattie, Dick Billings, Bob Borosage, Flip Brophy, Cristine Candela, Candy-O, Mark Carson, Isolde Chapin, Mae Churchill, Pat Clawson, Congressman John Conyers, Bob and Kaye Davis, Nancy Davis, Tim Davis, Neil Dignan, Janet Donovan, Ariel

Dorfman, Mike Ewing, Lou Farris, Rachel Fershko, Bob Fink, Carla Forero, Mike Fortun, Arthur Fox, John Friedman, Mike Gale, Sue Goodwin, Jim Hougan, Perdita Huston, Pam Johnson, Walter and Helen Johnston, Paulette Kernis, Mary King, Ron Koltnow, Alex Kura, Mike Lamonica, Saul Landau, Bob Lawrence, Rev. Lawrence Lazar, Paul Levy, Lt. Bill Lewis, Nancy Lewis, Bob Loomis, Myra MacPherson, Bob Manning, Janet Michaud, Ethelbert and Denise Miller, Kristy Miller, Marsha Moldea, Lt. Larry Momchilov, Sgt. Rich Munsey, Gary Nesbitt, Jo Nicholson, Noodles, Carl Oglesby, Tom O'Neill, Bob Pack, Ken Paff, Mark Perry, Dan Porter, Tom Raneses, Peter Range, Barbara Raskin, Mark Raskin, Carole Rebman, Barry Reighard, Bob Reiss, Rigo, Nick Roetzel, Ira Rosen, Tricia Rubacky, Ralph Salerno, Joe Schetzley, Curtis Seltzer, Carl Shoffler, Tony Shub, Georgiana Smith, John Sopko, Jeff Stein, Craig Stolz, Greg Stone, Joel Swerdlow, Jim Switzer, Marge Tabankin, Bill Thomas, Jonathan Toth, Dawn Trouard, Les and Judith Turner, Tom Victor, Tom von Stein, Jimmy Warner, Susan Waters, Danny Wexler, Herb White, Lee Wilson, Bob Zangrando, and Fred Zuch.

Also, in memory of: Ana Craciun, John J. Craciun, Charles Emery, Louis Gid, Richard Miller, Arthur Moneypenny, Paul Swerdlow, and John Toth.

Finally, I would like to thank my literary agent, Mel Berger, of the William Morris Agency in New York; my booking agents, Bob Katz and Jodi Solomon, of K & S Speakers in Cambridge, Massachusetts; my attorneys, George L. Farris of Akron, Ohio, and John Sikorski of Northampton, Massachusetts; my writing coach, Mrs. Nancy Nolte of Boulder, Colorado; Viking's Victoria Meyer, Rick Kurnit, and Anne Kinard; copy editor Ann Bartunek; and my patient editor at Viking, Daniel Frank, who believed in and fought for this project from the outset.

CONTENTS

Acknowledgments	xi
Frequently Mentioned Names	xv
Prologue	1
I. The Rise	9
II. The Fall	95
III. The Resurrection	217
Epilogue	305
Postscript	351
Notes	359
Bibliography	371
Index	379

Photographs appear following page 222.

FREQUENTLY
MENTIONED
NAMES

MCA's Sphere of Influence

Larry Barnett: MCA vice-president in charge of band-booking.

Laurence Beilenson: attorney for the Screen Actors and Screen Writers guilds who became legal counsel for MCA.

Arthur Park: Ronald Reagan's personal agent for *General Electric Theater*.

Ronald Reagan: president of the Screen Actors Guild; governor of California; president of the United States.

Taft Schreiber: MCA's first agent, head of Revue Productions, and MCA vice-president.

Sidney Sheinberg: Lew Wasserman's successor as president of MCA.

Jules Stein: founder of MCA, president of MCA, chairman of the board of MCA.

Allen Susman: general counsel for MCA.

Lew Wasserman: Stein's successor as both president and chairman of the board.

David "Sonny" Werblin: MCA vice-president and president of MCA-TV.

Union Officials

Roy Brewer: Hollywood representative of IATSE, the International Alliance of Theatrical Stage Employees Union.

George Browne: president of IATSE.

John Dales: executive secretary of the Screen Actors Guild.

James R. Hoffa: president of the Teamsters Union.

Robert Montgomery: president of the Screen Actors Guild.

James Caesar Petrillo: president of the American Federation of Musicians.

Jackie Presser: president of the Teamsters Union.

Herb Sorrell: president of the Conference of Studio Organizations.

Richard Walsh: Browne's successor as president of IATSE.

Organized Crime Figures and Associates

Anthony Accardo: head of the Chicago Mafia.

Gus Alex: member of the Chicago Mafia.

Willie Bioff: front man for the Chicago Mafia in Hollywood operations.

Morris (Moe) Dalitz: leader of Cleveland's Mayfield Road Gang; owner of Las Vegas casinos and the La Costa Country Club.

Allen M. Dorfman: fiduciary manager of the Teamsters pension fund.

James Fratianno: Los Angeles Mafia figure.

Sam Giancana: head of the Chicago Mafia.

Charles Gioe: the Chicago Mafia's operations man in Iowa.

Murray Humphreys: Chicago underworld figure.

Sidney R. Korshak: Chicago attorney, operating primarily out of Beverly Hills.

Johnny Roselli: overseer of the Chicago Mafia's operations in Hollywood.

Bugsy Siegel: overseer of the National Crime Syndicate's operations in Las Vegas.

Korshak's Sphere of Influence

"Colonel" Jake Arvey: Illinois National Democratic Party committeeman.

Greg Bautzer: Beverly Hills attorney.

Delbert Coleman: owner of the Parvin-Dohrmann Corporation.

Beldon Katleman: owner of the El Rancho Vegas hotel/casino.

Marshall Korshak: Democratic political figure in Chicago; brother of Sidney Korshak.

Eugene Wyman: Beverly Hills attorney.

Reagan's Sphere of Influence

Walter Annenberg: publishing mogul.

William Casey: CIA director under Reagan.

Ray Donovan: Secretary of Labor under Reagan.

Paul Laxalt: governor of Nevada; senator from Nevada; Reagan's campaign manager.

Nancy Reagan: Ronald Reagan's second wife; member of the board of the Screen Actors Guild.

Henry Salvatori: member of Reagan's Kitchen Cabinet.

William French Smith: Reagan's personal attorney; U.S. attorney general.

Holmes Tuttle: member of Reagan's Kitchen Cabinet.

Government Officials

Thurman Arnold: head of the Justice Department's Antitrust Division under Franklin D. Roosevelt.

Edmund (Pat) Brown: governor of California, 1959–1967.

Jerry Brown: Reagan's successor as governor of California, 1975–1981.

John Fricano: Antitrust Division attorney under Kennedy.

Barry Goldwater: senator from Arizona.

J. Edgar Hoover: FBI director.

Estes Kefauver: senator from Tennessee; chairman of the Kefauver Committee.

John F. Kennedy: president of the United States, 1961–1963.

Robert F. Kennedy: chief counsel of the McClellan Committee; U.S. attorney general under John Kennedy.

Lee Loevinger: head of the Antitrust Division under Kennedy.

Paul J. McCormick: judge in *Finley* v. *MCA.*

William C. Mathes: judge in *U.S.* v. *MCA.*

George Maury: Antitrust Division attorney under FDR.

John Mitchell: U.S. attorney general under Nixon.

Richard M. Nixon: president of the United States, 1969–1974.

Leonard Posner: Antitrust Division attorney under Eisenhower and Kennedy.

Charles Whittinghill: Antitrust Division attorney under Kennedy.

Corporate and Studio Executives

Barney Balaban: president of Balaban and Katz; president of Paramount Studios.

Charles G. Bluhdorn: chairman of the board of Gulf & Western, which owns Paramount.

Pat Casey: labor negotiator for the Motion Picture Producers Association.

Harry Cohn: founder and president of Columbia Pictures.

Bryan Foy: executive producer of Warner Brothers and Eagle-Lion Studios.

Howard Hughes: billionaire president of Caddo Corporation and RKO.

Kirk Kerkorian: majority stockholder in MGM/United Artists.

Carl Laemmle: founder of Universal Studios.

Louis B. Mayer: vice-president in charge of production of MGM.

Joseph Schenck: president of Twentieth Century–Fox.

Spyros Skouras: Schenck's successor as president of Twentieth Century–Fox.

Leo Spitz: legal counsel to the Producers Association; president of Universal-International Studios.

Joseph Vogel: president of MGM.

Jack L. Warner: president of Warner Brothers.

Darryl F. Zanuck: Schenck's partner in Twentieth Century–Fox; Skouras's successor as president.

Other Characters

Larry Finley: San Diego ballroom owner.

Jeff Kibre: leader of the IATSE progressives.

Robert Maheu: Howard Hughes's top aide.

Grant Sawyer: governor of Nevada.

Frank Sinatra: entertainer.

Kearney Walton, Jr.: bandleader.

Jane Wyman: actress; Reagan's first wife.

Paul Ziffren: California Democratic Party Committeeman; law partner of William French Smith; co-chairman of the 1984 U.S. Olympic Committee.

PROLOGUE

President Ronald Reagan's professional life—his acting career, his personal financial fortune, and his rise in politics—has been interwoven with and propelled by a powerful, Hollywood-based entertainment conglomerate named MCA. For nearly fifty years, Reagan has benefited both personally and financially from his association with this sixty-two-year-old company—formerly known as the Music Corporation of America—as well as from his close association with the firm's top executives: Jules Stein, Lew Wasserman, and Taft Schreiber.

Everyone involved has greatly profited from this relationship. MCA helped to make its client, actor Ronald Reagan, a multimillionaire; and the favors that were returned by Reagan, the former president of the Screen Actors Guild (SAG) and the former governor of California, have helped to transform MCA into a billion-dollar empire and the most powerful force in the entertainment world today.

Reagan and his closest friends have portrayed and defended the president's business transactions with MCA, which date back to 1940, as being totally above suspicion. But there remain numerous unanswered questions and allegations about the relationship between Reagan and MCA. These doubts raise delicate issues that involve possible personal and political payoffs—as well as links to major Mafia figures, particularly Beverly Hills attorney Sidney Korshak, who has been described by federal investigators as the principal link between the legitimate business world and organized crime.

In 1962, the Antitrust Division of the U.S. Department of Justice tried to resolve some of these questions, but their secret investigation was settled out of court before the evidence could be presented. The results of the probe were never made public, and no one close to MCA was ever indicted. However, through the Freedom of Information Act, many of these documents have been recovered and are excerpted in this book.

These records show that Reagan, the president of SAG and an FBI informant against Hollywood communists, was the subject of a federal grand jury investigation whose focus was Reagan's possible role in a suspected conspiracy between MCA and the actors' union. According to Justice Department documents, government prosecutors had concluded that decisions made by SAG while under Reagan's leadership became "the central fact of MCA's whole rise to power."

Over the past two decades, Ronald Reagan has refused to answer any in-depth questions about how he amassed his personal wealth—currently estimated at more than $4 million. In 1976, when he first ran for president, and again in 1980 and 1984, Reagan managed to avoid any intense scrutiny of his finances. His financial ties to MCA have been virtually ignored, relegated to the category of ancient history.

Nor has Reagan ever been asked about his personal, financial, professional, or political relationship with Sidney Korshak—who has repeatedly appeared to be involved with Reagan and several of his top advisers throughout their careers.

MCA first began to receive national attention in 1946, when a federal court in Los Angeles ruled against the company for antitrust violations. At the time, MCA was simply a talent agency, booking bands in nightclubs and actors in motion pictures. In rendering his decision, the presiding judge declared that MCA held a virtual monopoly over the entertainment business. This antitrust suit, one of many legal actions filed against MCA over the past fifty years, involved a San Diego ballroom operator who had accused MCA of demanding exorbitant prices from him to book bands for his dances—charging him much more than competing ballrooms were paying for their musical acts. The jury found that MCA's practices had restrained trade in the band-booking business, and it awarded the ballroom owner a $55,500 judgment.

In deciding against MCA, the judge called the talent agency "the Octopus . . . with tentacles reaching out to all phases and grasping everything in show business." The image of "the Octopus" remained and became MCA's nickname in both the Hollywood trade and the press.

Years ago, a motion picture executive commented, "A studio can't exist for any time without some contact with MCA. I would say it's impossible to operate without them. Jack Warner [the head of Warner Brothers] tried it. He couldn't hold out for long."

Today, MCA is still "the Octopus," even though it is out of the talent agency business and now the owner of the largest motion picture and television production companies in the United States, Universal Pictures and Universal-Television. Headquartered in the stark, imposing, black-steel and glass tower at Universal City on the edge of California's San Fernando Valley, the giant, two-billion-dollar conglomerate has offices in major cities all over the world and owns businesses in book and music publishing, a major record company, transportation systems, home video marketing, recreation services, a savings and loan company, real estate, data processing, mail-order purchasing, retail store merchandising, and cable television.

But, far and away, MCA's major business is show business. "They own it," comedian Jerry Lewis once quipped.

During the 1950s, MCA's then-television subsidiary, Revue Productions, became the world's most successful producer and distributor of television film series. Each week Revue supplied the television networks with some forty hours of programming, including such top-rated shows as *Wagon Train, Alfred Hitchcock Presents, The Jack Benny Show, Ozzie and Harriet, Dragnet, This Is Your Life,* and *Leave It to Beaver.*

After MCA bought Universal Studios and made plans to produce motion pictures as well as television programs, Revue became Universal-Television in 1962, creating such shows as *Marcus Welby, M.D., Columbo, McMillan and Wife, Kojak, The Six-Million-Dollar Man, The Rockford Files, The Incredible Hulk, Magnum, P.I.,* and *Miami Vice.* Under MCA, Universal Pictures has won three Academy Awards for Best Picture for *The Sting, The Deer Hunter,* and *Out of Africa.* And the studio has also produced such financial blockbusters as *Airport, American Graffiti, Jaws, E.T. the Extraterrestrial, On Golden Pond,* and *Back to the Future.*

For years, MCA has been viewed by its clients, rivals, and the business press as the General Motors of Hollywood. Despite the company's vast power within the entertainment industry, most Americans have never heard of MCA. Since the company was founded in 1924, it has cultivated an air of mystery about itself. In an industry that thrives on publicity, MCA's executives have thrived on anonymity. The guiding credo at MCA has always been that publicity is for the clients, not the company.

It is a show business legend that one of the ways MCA's agents tried to remain anonymous was to dress extremely conservatively—in black or dark-gray suits, white shirts, and dark, narrow ties. The top executives set the example, which everyone followed. MCA's management team was credited with bringing a correct, Ivy League dignity to a profession that had previously been characterized by plaid-jacketed, cigar-smoking agents who did nothing more than "peddle flesh." MCA believed agents should look, dress, and act like other businessmen and bankers. With the MCA dress code came the reputation for ruthless efficiency. During the 1950s, competitors derisively called MCA's aggressive agents "the black-suited Mafia."

The brains behind MCA was Jules Stein, a Chicago ophthalmologist who discovered that he could make more money booking bands. When Stein and an associate, Billy Goodheart, founded the Music Corporation of America in 1924, they began empire-building—with the help of James Petrillo, the head of the American Federation of Musicians, with whom MCA maintained a sweetheart labor-management relationship. According to Justice Department documents, Petrillo was paid off in return for favors to MCA. Taft Schreiber and Sonny Werblin were among the first two top MCA assistants, followed by Lew Wasserman, who was groomed as Stein's heir and was named president of the company in 1946; Stein then became MCA's chairman of the board.

The rise of MCA and its move to Hollywood paralleled the rise of the Chicago Mafia and its infiltration of the motion picture industry. While MCA was representing some of the top motion picture stars, Chicago mobsters took control of the International Alliance of Theatrical Stage Employees (IATSE), the major Hollywood labor union— through Willie Bioff, a small-time hood, who was supervised by Chicago mob lieutenant Johnny Roselli. The studios made payoffs to the underworld for labor peace—and to keep their workers' wages and benefits to a minimum. But when the studios' payoff man was caught for evading federal income taxes, he plea-bargained with the government, implicating Bioff, but not the Mafia, in the extortion scheme. Bioff was indicted and convicted—and then turned state's evidence against his cohorts, who were also convicted and sent to prison.

The Chicago Mafia's role in Hollywood did not end with the convictions; it simply changed. Chicago's new liaison in the motion picture industry became attorney Sidney Korshak, who had represented Bioff. Charles Gioe, a top Chicago Mafia figure, had told Bioff that Korshak was "our man . . . any message he may deliver to you is a message from us."

A close friend of Stein's and Wasserman's, Korshak quickly became one of the most powerful influences in the entertainment industry and in California politics. One of his key political connections was another former Chicagoan, Paul Ziffren, who at one point was California's delegate to the National Democratic Committee. (He would not seek reelection after his ties to major organized crime figures were exposed by a national magazine.) Korshak also associated himself with top Republican leaders to hedge his bets—and always have friends in power.

In the late 1940s Hollywood shifted its attention away from the Mafia's infiltration of the film industry to its infiltration by communists. Ronald Reagan, a young actor who was represented by Wasserman and MCA, was a star player during the investigation and hearings by the U.S. House Un-American Activities Committee (HUAC), serving as both an informant for the FBI and a friendly witness for the committee.

After his performance in the war against communism—which included support for IATSE, the union formerly controlled by Bioff that was still run by his same executive board—Reagan was rewarded by being elected as president of the Screen Actors Guild, serving for five consecutive one-year terms.

In 1952, during his fifth term, Reagan engineered a "blanket waiver," exempting MCA from SAG rules prohibiting a talent agency from also engaging in film production. Reagan's second wife, actress Nancy Davis, was also a member of the SAG board of directors at the time the MCA-SAG deal was made. MCA was the only such firm to have been granted such a favored status, giving it the ground floor in television production. It placed the company in a position where it could offer jobs to the actors it represented. Other talent agencies complained that this situation gave MCA an unfair advantage.

Soon after Reagan's tenure as SAG president ended, he found himself in serious financial trouble. With his film career on the skids, Reagan was saved by MCA with jobs in Las Vegas and on television. According to Justice Department documents, several government sources believed that the preferential treatment Reagan received from

MCA was a payoff for services rendered while Reagan was the president of SAG.

In 1959, the SAG membership reelected Reagan as president of SAG for a sixth term to lead an impending strike against the studios—despite the fact that Reagan had been producing episodes for *General Electric Theater*. According to SAG's by-laws, producers, even if they were primarily actors, are disqualified from serving on the SAG executive board. Previous board members faced with similar situations had resigned; Reagan refused to do so.

Although MCA and a handful of smaller studios made an early, separate peace with SAG and continued production, the major motion picture companies held out, causing the strike to last six weeks. In the end, according to the president of IATSE, Reagan's final settlement with the big studios came with the help of Sidney Korshak—with whom Reagan had allegedly been associated. The 1960 contract was so unsatisfactory to the SAG membership it has since been called "The Great Giveaway." Reagan resigned in midterm soon after the strike.

After several abortive attempts to investigate MCA for antitrust violations, the federal government—upon the election of John Kennedy as president and the appointment of Robert Kennedy as attorney general—began a concentrated probe into MCA's business affairs. The government had evidence that MCA had engaged in numerous civil and criminal violations of law and empaneled a federal grand jury to hear the specifics of its charges, which included restraint of trade, conspiracy with SAG to monopolize talent and film program productions, extortion, discrimination, blacklisting, and the use of predatory business practices. Among those called to testify was Ronald Reagan, who displayed a remarkable loss of memory while on the witness stand. Soon after, the federal income tax records of Reagan and his wife were subpoenaed for the years following the MCA-SAG blanket waiver.

In the midst of the grand jury's investigation, MCA purchased Universal Pictures and its parent company, Decca Records. The government immediately went to court, seeking to block MCA's takeover of the corporation. However, after lengthy negotiations between attorneys for the Justice Department's Antitrust Division and MCA, a consent decree was issued and the case was considered closed. The litigation forced MCA to choose whether it wished to be either a talent agency or a production company. Considering that its production efforts yielded nearly ten times more money than the talent agency, the decision was an easy one: MCA dissolved its talent agency.

Reagan has admitted that the government's breakup of MCA affected his political beliefs, inclining him toward a more conservative, antigovernment stance. Beginning with the Barry Goldwater presidential campaign in 1964 and then with his own bid for governor of California in 1966, Reagan's reactionary tone enhanced his image with other conservatives but nearly cost him his job with *General Electric Theater.* Among the guiding forces in the shaping of Reagan's political philosophy were MCA's Jules Stein and Taft Schreiber. According to law-enforcement authorities, several of Reagan's campaign financiers were close friends and associates of Sidney Korshak.

Stein and Schreiber—as well as Reagan's personal attorney, Los Angeles labor lawyer William French Smith—made several questionable financial transactions on Reagan's behalf, making him a multi-millionaire overnight. Once governor, Reagan made executive decisions that were greatly beneficial to MCA and other corporations with motion picture studio interests.

The same year that Reagan was elected governor of California, Paul Laxalt was elected governor of Nevada. Both Laxalt and Reagan had been heavily involved in the Goldwater campaign. The two men, as governors of neighboring states, became close friends while the latter tried to "clean up" Nevada's image. However, during Laxalt's tenure, a scandal broke out in Las Vegas over a corporation that owned several casinos. Korshak was the major target of the federal investigation that followed. Although Laxalt has been linked with Korshak's associates and clients, he has denied any association with Korshak.

Although Laxalt chose not to seek a second term as governor, Reagan did and was reelected. Laxalt returned to practicing law and then opened a gambling casino in Nevada—which failed. Laxalt then ran for the U.S. Senate and won. While serving as a senator, Laxalt ran Reagan's campaigns for the presidency in 1976 and again in 1980. Laxalt then became general chairman of the Republican National Committee.

Meantime, Stein removed himself as MCA's chairman of the board and was replaced by Wasserman—who was succeeded by the head of Universal-Television, Sidney Sheinberg. MCA grew enormously under Wasserman and Sheinberg. Its only major failure was an attempt to mass-produce a home entertainment system—consisting of video discs, containing motion pictures and other programs, which could be played on machines hooked up to standard television sets. However, MCA's idea was eclipsed by a similar product marketed by its rival RCA and another system developed by Sony, utilizing videocassettes that could do everything the MCA and RCA systems did as well as record television programs. Nevertheless, MCA continued to shatter box-office records with its blockbuster motion pictures while its television productions soared in the network ratings.

Wasserman also became increasingly involved in politics. He had supported President Jimmy Carter but then had a falling out with him after Reagan announced his 1980 candidacy. Korshak, a Democrat who had supported Reagan during his 1970 reelection bid for governor of California, had been the target of a four-part series in June of 1976 in *The New York Times*, which described him as "a behind-the-scenes 'fixer' who has been instrumental in helping criminal elements gain power in union affairs and infiltrate the leisure and entertainment industries." Although Korshak was not on record as supporting either Carter or Reagan in 1980, his close associate, Democrat Paul Ziffren, became a law partner of William French Smith, who later became Reagan's attorney general.

During the presidential campaign, Reagan met privately with known associates of organized crime and appointed others to his personal campaign staff. Several of these people were later given high positions in the Reagan administration after his election. President Reagan talked tough about the organized crime problem in the United States, while surrounding himself with many who were closely linked to those who have created it.

To illustrate this web of power and manipulation, this story has been organized chronologically, minimizing whatever reader confusion might result from the proliferation of names, events, and dates contained in the narrative. The common thread throughout this story is the corporation MCA. In tracing its history I have concentrated on the parallel and sometimes intertwining careers of Ronald Reagan, Lew Wasserman, and Sidney Korshak—and how these three men have affected political, business, and labor history in America.

I

THE RISE

CHAPTER ONE

NEAR THE END of World War I, the United States government built a naval base on the Mississippi River near the segregated Storyville neighborhood of New Orleans. The area, which covered thirty-eight blocks in the French Quarter, was a jazz musicians' paradise where townspeople jammed together on street corners every night, playing everything from boat whistles and washboards to open-bell trumpets and slide trombones into the early-morning hours. Known as "The District," Storyville stretched from Perdido and Gravier streets to Franklin and Locust streets and was the home of Ferdinand "Jelly Roll" Morton, the self-proclaimed "inventor" of jazz, as well as the home of a string of independent saloons, gambling joints, and brothels.

With the passage of the Volstead Act in 1919, the Prohibition Era began. The public drunkenness, crooked gambling, and open prostitution rampant in Storyville had earned it a reputation as Sin City, a reputation that had already reached Washington, D.C. The federal government needed little impetus to expropriate the land and permanently close down the area. Within days, thousands of people, packing everything they owned, left the city, looking for places to resettle.

"Closing the area meant the end of jobs for musicians, singers, and hundreds of other workers," said one observer. "But it was even more.

It was the coda for a fantastic era, and the termination of New Orleans as the world's hotbed of jazz."[1]

Most of the musicians—like trumpet players Joe "King" Oliver and Louis Armstrong—traveled north. Chicago became their new home and the new capital of jazz. King Oliver's Creole Jazz Band and Armstrong's Sunset Band worked at places like the Dreamland Café and the Royal Gardens on Chicago's South Side, as well as the Grand Theatre, the Colonial Theatre, and the North American Restaurant, all in and around the Loop, once again playing into the early-morning hours.

The Original Dixieland Jazz Band and the New Orleans Rhythm Kings were not among the first jazz bands, not even among the first all-white jazz bands, but their music—patterned after the rhythmic passion of Black rag and jazz—brought jazz to a larger, more cosmopolitan audience. These white bands quickly became known to audiences in places as distant as New York and London.

During the early 1920s, young South Side Chicago musicians—like Eddie Condon, Muggsy Spanier, and George Wettling—and West Side youths like Benny Goodman were influenced by the sound these groups produced. But Condon's and Goodman's music took on an identity of its own. It became known as "Chicago Style" or "White Chicago" because of its emphasis on Black off-the-beat rhythms and sharply defined notes, but with a new swing and aggressiveness. This variation of basic jazz, sometimes hard and harsh, seemed to epitomize the vitality of the Roaring Twenties and of Chicago, which had become a wide-open town.

The notorious Mafia leader Al Capone and his rival gangs had built their empires on illegal, bootlegged liquor, which brought them millions of dollars in unreported, untaxed income. When the Depression came, they were the only people with big money, so bankers, businessmen, and politicians often came to them for help. They usually received it—but always for a price. Massive violations of state and federal banking laws, the mob's infiltration of legitimate businesses, and political corruption became facts of life. Those who defied the system or double-crossed the people who paid them off were either personally destroyed or brutally murdered. Despite its more glorified Hollywood image, there was nothing glamorous about the real legacy of the Chicago Mafia.

Between machine-gun shootouts in the streets, the racketeers spent a lot of their dough in nightclubs and speakeasies, some of which they had built themselves. Juiced-up mobsters foot-tapped in time with jazz and Dixieland music played by one band or another in any number of clubs. Mafia members, who fantasized about playing a cool sax, befriended those musicians who could. Musicians—who dreamed about being rich and powerful, with plenty of dames around—allowed them to do so, usually making a few extra bucks, earning a little protection, and maybe even enjoying the favors of a mobster's moll.

Initially, music critics viewed jazz enthusiasts as "musical illiterates." But as a more commercial, toned-down form of jazz evolved, this relatively new innovation in music became more widely accepted. As a result, the band-booking business blossomed and the record industry boomed into a multi-million-dollar-a-year bonanza. In 1921 alone, twenty years after the pioneering Victor Talking Machine Company and the Columbia Graphophone Company were established, over $106 million in records were sold. Two years earlier, in 1919, New York's Radio Corporation of America (RCA) had been created.*

On October 7, 1922, WJZ, a Westinghouse radio station in Newark, New Jersey, hooked up with General Electric's WGY in Schenectady, New York, and broadcast the opening game of the World Series. The following year, AT&T's station in New York performed a similar feat, cabling radio signals to WMAF in South Dartmouth, Massachusetts. By 1924, twenty-five other stations were added to AT&T. Two years later, the National Broadcasting Company, NBC—which was owned and operated by RCA—took over AT&T's operations and became the first licensed radio network, broadcasting as far west as Kansas City to twenty-one cities.

The demand for musical entertainment on the radio was tremendous. In spite of the fear among some people that jazz and its variations would corrupt the public's taste in music, dance bands were in vogue. The radio made Eddie Condon, Benny Goodman, Duke Ellington, and Guy Lombardo household words. Increasingly, both well-known and lesser-known but up-and-coming bands needed managers to represent them professionally. Band members were musicians but not always businessmen, and most of them needed an agent to protect their financial interests.

The biggest talent bureau at the time was the New York–based William Morris Agency. It was founded in 1898 by Austrian immigrant Wilhelm Moses, who had changed his name to William Morris when

---

*President Woodrow Wilson encouraged the General Electric Company to form RCA because he feared that the technology for wireless radio transmissions would be controlled by foreign nations in the wake of World War I. GE was RCA's largest stockholder. Other investors included AT&T, Westinghouse, and United Fruit.

he came to the United States. Morris had retired in the early 1920s, turning the agency over to his son, William Morris, Jr., a scholarly man who had no taste for the business. Young Morris made Abe Lastfogel, a charming and popular man who had worked for the William Morris Agency since he was fourteen, the company's president. At that time, the agency numbered among its clients George Jessel, Jimmy Durante, Al Jolson, and Eddie Cantor.

Another prominent talent agency was the Associated Booking Corporation, run by Joseph G. Glaser. Glaser was Louis Armstrong's manager, as well as the exclusive agent for many of the top Black performers. A big Chicago White Sox fan who spent much of his time doing business at Comiskey Park, he had a reputation as a cold, crusty, hard-driving businessman. To ensure an edge in his business, he became a close associate of many of the top underworld figures in Chicago and New York, whom he had met through his band-booking agency.

In 1924, a small, soft-spoken, professorial-looking man named Julius Caesar Stein started the Music Corporation of America—MCA—in Chicago with a stake of only a thousand dollars—which included twenty-five dollars for the incorporation papers.

Born in South Bend, Indiana, on April 26, 1896, "Jules" Stein was the son of the proprietor of a small general store. His mother—who had bought him a mandolin as his first musical instrument—was an invalid whose care often drained the family's meager bank account. As a result, Stein, even as a child, was forced to make his own money. By the time he was twelve, Stein had saved enough money to see himself through prep school. He never returned home. Initially intrigued by the possibility of becoming a professional flyer, the black-haired, brown-eyed Stein, who had a sharply angular face with a pronounced chin and jaw, decided to move in a completely different direction and studied to be an ophthalmologist. (The year he founded MCA he published a respected, erudite treatise on "The Use of Telescopic Spectacles and Distil Lensen.")

But Stein had been smitten by show business. He began his entertainment career in Chicago shortly after leaving home. At the age of 14, he was leading an orchestra; his favorite song was "Alexander's Ragtime Band." As he worked his way through the University of West Virginia, graduating at eighteen, and medical school at the University of Chicago, he played in and booked dance bands, describing himself as a "schmaltzy" violinist and saxophone player.* During World War I,

---

*One of Stein's stints was in the backup band for Mae West's vaudeville show.

he served in the Army Reserve as a medical officer. After the war, he headed for Vienna to pursue postgraduate work. Stein had also found time to take a three-year correspondence course in business.

Returning to Chicago, he served a residency at Cook County Hospital and went into private practice, working as the assistant to Dr. Harry Gradle, one of the Midwest's most eminent eye surgeons. Soon after, Stein met an old college chum, William R. "Billy" Goodheart. A quick-tempered but accomplished pianist, Goodheart was viewed as the kind of guy who would slap around the newspaper boy for throwing the morning edition in the bushes. "Goodheart was known as a 'character,' " wrote one reporter. "He was said to sit in a raised chair so he could look down on his callers. When someone asked for two minutes of his time, he got just that—by a stopwatch. He carried pills for every ailment. He was a driver who demanded results and accepted no excuses."[2]

Goodheart shared Stein's interest in the music business. The two men became partners in Kenneworth Music. They soon discovered that they were shrewd businessmen and had a knack for organizing and promoting bands. Their principal business came from the mob-controlled nightclubs and speakeasies on Chicago's South Side, Capone's territory.

"I had a young assistant," Stein remembered, "and he'd ring up about bookings while I had a patient in the chair. I'd be saying, 'Can you read this, can you read this?' and all the while I'd be speaking [on] the phone. We had Hushaphones in those days, a box around the speaker so nobody could hear what you were saying, and I couldn't have done business without that."[3]

Stein recognized that he could make more money as a booking agent than anything else he could do. So Stein gave up his career with Dr. Gradle to found MCA with Goodheart. Overnight, Dr. Stein became simply Jules Stein. Working from a tiny, two-room office in downtown Chicago, Stein and Goodheart quickly began finding jobs for dance bands and other musical performers throughout the Midwest, as well as advising clients on their careers. In return, they usually took a ten-percent commission.

Stein was responsible for inventing the concept of "rotating bands" for the one-night stands and the week-long engagements. He convinced club owners that their businesses would grow if they frequently brought in new entertainers. Before that time, bands would play in one location for months, even years.

Stein and Goodheart also insisted that MCA be the exclusive agent of those bands and bandleaders it represented and later demanded that dance halls with which they worked hire MCA bands exclusively—a practice which had been unheard of previously. Once signed, MCA's clients and customers would then be offered MCA deals on automobiles and insurance policies. To secure bookings, MCA, according to several sources, occasionally resorted to intimidation. Some clubs that refused exclusive arrangements with MCA became the targets of "stink bomb" attacks, which would be launched during the acts of other agencies' bands.[4]

The dance band business meant an itinerant existence. Booking agents handled the details of getting acts from place to place and finding them places to stay. Many bands had to play nearly every night, traveling from city to city, state to state in order to make enough money to survive. Bands might consist of as few as five and as many as twenty musicians. MCA made sure they were taken care of. For many trips band managers, arrangers, and soloists might also have to be included. MCA had to provide for them as well. "Name" bands traveled in their own buses; "semi-name" bands had to lease or rent. MCA was also responsible for arranging radio broadcasts, as well as supplying publicity—posters, press releases, and newspaper ads. For its ten-percent commission, MCA took care of everything as part of its package deal, leaving the clubs with little to do.

MCA remained in constant touch with dance hall operators in the various states while its bands were on the road, trying to extend their tours or fill in open dates. Whenever possible, MCA tried to gain exclusives with the clubs and hotels, providing them not only with bands but with liquor, glasses, linen, and even confetti.

Stein and MCA handled themselves so professionally that bigger-name bands began to take notice and sought to be represented by them. Among others, Stein had penned a contract with the Coon-Sanders Kansas City Nighthawks, which played a softer variation of jazz. But Stein still did not have a big-name band and a way to crack the lucrative New York big-band market.

In 1928, MCA pulled its first big national coup by signing Guy Lombardo and his orchestra to an exclusive contract. Goodheart—whose goal was to make a million dollars by the time he was forty—first approached Lombardo while he was playing at the Music Box, a nightclub in Cleveland, Ohio. Lombardo rejected MCA's offer at first, insisting that he neither needed nor wanted an agent. But after Stein pulled strings to get him a long-term contract at the Roosevelt Hotel in New York, Lombardo signed, bringing in tow his close friend, pianist Eddy Duchin. Other major bandleaders followed in Lombardo's wake.

Goodheart left Chicago and opened the agency's New York office in the Paramount Theatre Building at 43rd and Broadway. MCA began to lock up bookings at New York's Waldorf-Astoria and many of the big, luxurious hotels and nightclubs in Chicago, New York, Miami, and Los Angeles.

By the mid-1930s—the Big-Band Era—MCA represented more than half of the major bands in the country, including those of Harry James, Tommy Dorsey, Kay Kyser, Xavier Cugat, Artie Shaw, and Gene Krupa. The agency booked them for one-night stands, as well as long-term engagements at dance halls, nightclubs, ice shows, county fairs, and big-city hotels. Stein, who had become a man-about-Chicago, was driving a Rolls-Royce and had purchased a beautiful French-style estate overlooking Lake Michigan.

With the growing popularity of musical programs on the radio—particularly on WGN in Chicago—Stein gained the support of his childhood friend, James Caesar Petrillo, the president of the Chicago local of the American Federation of Musicians (AFM).

Petrillo was the classical tough-guy labor boss. Born in 1892, the son of Italian immigrants, and a cornet-playing product of the Chicago slums, Petrillo had started as a union official for the Chicago local of the American Musicians Union in 1915. After losing his bid for president of his local in 1918, Petrillo abandoned the AMU and went to work for the AFM. In 1928, he became president of the AFM's Chicago local.

A small man, five feet six inches tall, with a fourth-grade education, a gruff style, rimless glasses, and monogrammed shirts, he spoke salty, ungrammatical English in a grating voice and rode around in a bullet-proof limousine. He was an extreme egotist and a shrewd and treacherous political infighter who ruled his union like a dictator. He loathed record companies, calling them "musical monsters which were killing employment" for live musicians, and eventually succeeded in making the companies pay artists for each record sold. He also forced the radio networks to pay their musicians at union scale regardless of whether the musicians were needed or not.

"If I was a good trumpet player," Petrillo said, "I wouldn't be here. I got desperate. I had to look for a job. I went into the union business."[5]

When he became national president of the AFM, union boss Petrillo became the most powerful figure in the music industry. He performed many favors for Stein. (Stein was given AFM's membership card number one and attended nearly all of its union meetings.) Petrillo used his clout to prevent other big-band talent agencies, in competition with

Stein, from obtaining licenses to operate, thereby helping to give Stein and MCA a virtual monopoly over the major bands in the music business. Whenever a dispute arose between a band and MCA, the executive board of Petrillo's union always sided with MCA. One source said he could not recall a single case before the AFM board that was won by a union member against MCA. "The fix was always in," he said. "Big-band leaders were pretty consistently voted down by AFM whenever they had a dispute with MCA."[6]

Petrillo also granted MCA an exclusive "blanket waiver," permitting Stein's firm to operate as both booking agent and radio production company—despite the fact that such an agreement was considered a conflict of interest and violated the AFM's by-laws. For instance, MCA, for as much as a thirty-percent profit, would package an entire radio program, complete with bands, singers, writers, directors, and producers, and sell it to the networks—even though all of the participants were represented by MCA. If a performer had a grievance, it would be difficult for him to complain to his agent, also his employer, who maintained a sweetheart relationship with his union.

With its association with Petrillo and AFM, MCA—along with its radio sponsor, Lucky Strike cigarettes—started producing network radio programs. MCA went to radio networks and told them, "We'll give you bands, but only if you give us remote radio lines." MCA agents then approached bandleaders, asking, "How would you like to be guaranteed forty weeks of employment during the year and to appear on radio every week on NBC's *Lucky Strike Hit Parade*?" What band could refuse such an offer? Finally, MCA would go to a prominent hotel owner and ask, "How would you like to have a big-name band, and have the band originate music from your hotel—with the hotel mentioned on a national radio hook-up every week?" The result was national exposure for MCA bands.

MCA followed the *Lucky Strike Hit Parade* with *The Magic Carpet* and later the *Camel Caravan*. All of these programs featured a rotation of MCA bands.

Because MCA had started to replace advertising agencies as the packagers of big-band music programs—while it continued its dual role as agent and producer as well—the growing corporation needed a great deal of cooperation and protection. Justice Department documents have charged that union officials, club owners, and bandleaders who cooperated with Stein often received "payola," in the form of cash, cars, and sometimes MCA stock options. "[I]t was well known that Petrillo took 'ice.'"[7]

The government also alleged that union leader Petrillo eventually became a millionaire—even though his yearly union salary reportedly never exceeded $26,000—as a direct result of his sweetheart relationship with MCA. Although the Justice Department uncovered evidence that Petrillo had received payoffs from MCA and other sources, he was never indicted.

CHAPTER TWO

THE MAFIA in Chicago was formed during World War I when "Big Jim" Colosimo, an Old World Sicilian racketeer, put together a loose-knit, mostly disorganized network of other Italian/Sicilian criminals to protect his brothels and other illegitimate businesses. Among those surrounding Colosimo was Johnny Torrio, a street-smart hood, who brought Al Capone into the organization in 1919. Capone had come from New York and was known as a ruthless assassin. He was also a cousin of Charles "Lucky" Luciano, who had been operating with Meyer Lansky and Benjamin "Bugsy" Siegel.

Torrio came to believe that Colosimo had little foresight and did not possess the imagination and strength to make his brand of disorganized crime organized. Consequently, Torrio contracted for Capone to murder Colosimo in 1920. Torrio succeeded him as the head of the Chicago Mafia, using Capone to systematically wipe out rival Irish and Sicilian gangs. By 1923, Capone had been named as Public Enemy Number One.

During Prohibition, Torrio changed the face of the underworld, particularly in Chicago, where he "made" or admitted criminals from other ethnic backgrounds into the traditional Italian/Sicilian crime group. Illegal money obtained through bootlegging, gambling, loan-sharking, and prostitution was channeled into legitimate businesses. But Capone quickly became too ambitious and tried to have Torrio executed. Even though Torrio survived, he decided to step aside for his younger protégé.

During the Capone reign of terror, the Chicago Mafia became the most feared crime organization in the United States. Disorganized crime became organized—with all the implicit degrees of control and discipline. By 1931, the Mafia had become "Americanized." The last of the Old World "Mustache Petes"—first-generation leaders of the American-Sicilian underworld—were slaughtered in September on the orders of Luciano, who retained the services of his associates Lansky and Siegel.

Four days after this bloody purge—which signaled the end of the "Castellammarese War"—a national crime syndicate was established. The United States was divided into twenty-four subdivisions, each controlled by the most powerful Mafia families in these various geographic areas. Nine of the leaders of these twenty-four crime groups were selected to sit on a national crime commission that would settle jurisdictional disputes.

This syndicate was created to frustrate the infighting among Mafia families that was interfering with the mob's primary goals to make money and to stay out of jail. With the increased stability and decreased exposure, mob financiers like Lansky were free to find legal and illegal money-making ventures, raise the necessary capital from participating crime families, launder funds through "friendly" banks, buy political protection, and oversee the fair distribution of profits from these activities.

By the time Capone began having his problems with the IRS, his enterprises were operating smoothly enough to survive his tax fraud conviction and imprisonment in 1931. Frank Nitti slid into power, backed by Capone's entire empire. Among Nitti's top associates was Jake "Greasy Thumb" Guzik, who was the Chicago underworld link to legitimate business and to the law-enforcement officials, judges, and politicians who walked around the city with their hands out, looking for someone to grease them.

Some politicians who opted to battle the Mafia found themselves in trouble. Chicago mayor Anton Cermak, a hardliner against the Chicago crime syndicate, was shot and later died from his wounds while campaigning with President-elect Franklin D. Roosevelt in 1933. Although it was widely thought that the assassin, Giuseppe Zangara, was really a nut gunning for Roosevelt, Cermak, before his death, insisted that he was the real target. Cermak added that he had been threatened because of his crusade against the underworld and had purchased a bulletproof vest—which he forgot to wear the day he was shot.[1]

Jules Stein's success in the band-booking business had been so complete that he attempted to get into areas peripheral to his own business, such as bootlegging. In doing so, he stepped on the toes of some powerful Chicago mobsters. The full story of Stein's dealings with the Chicago Mafia is fuzzy. There are conflicting accounts about the extent and true nature of his involvement with the underworld.

According to one version, the Chicago Mafia had watched Stein's successes with envy from the start and had tried to move in on him during the early 1930s, demanding a share of the action. In the midst of Prohibition, while he was booking bands into Chicago's speakeasies, Stein had also started bootlegging whisky and selling it to nightclub owners as part of the deals for his bands. According to Justice Department documents, his thriving sales crossed over into the jurisdiction of Chicago bootlegger Roger Touhy, an arch-rival of Capone.

Supposedly, Touhy had kidnapped Petrillo and held him for $50,000. Later, he threatened to do the same to Stein or his wife, Doris—whom he had married in 1928—if he failed to cooperate. Stein insisted later that he stood up to Touhy and took out a $75,000 insurance policy, covering him in the event of his kidnapping. "They tried to muscle in on me, and I never let them," Stein said. "I had the guts of a fool."[2]

Despite all the alleged threats, Stein continued to keep the company of numerous Chicago racketeers and was frequently seen with them at Henrici's Restaurant, the Home Drug Store, and the Palace Theatre, where such entertainers as Jack Benny, Sophie Tucker, and George Jessel performed.

Veteran Chicago crime investigators remained skeptical. "Both Stein and Petrillo made their deals with the major mob guys in this town," one of them said. "Touhy was nothing next to Capone and his boys, and that's where Stein and Petrillo's connections were. All the rest of that stuff about kidnappings was nothing more than high drama, well-contrived and acted out."

Whichever scenario is correct, it is clear that Stein had worked out some sort of accommodation or truce with the mob.

Jules Stein and James Petrillo had close ties to a paunchy little Chicago mobster named Willie Bioff. An ex-pimp and petty thief, the moon-faced and sleepy-eyed Bioff had been financially wiped out early in the Depression. "When things get bad," Bioff lamented, "there ain't no place for an honest pimp. The Johns are selling nickel apples and the broads are selling two-dollar cherries and who the hell needs me."[3]

According to Justice Department documents, Stein occasionally employed the services of a Bioff employee who specialized in disrupting the operations of theatres and nightclubs that refused to contract business with MCA. A law-enforcement official in Chicago identified the saboteur as Fred "Bugs" Blacker, who specialized in throwing stink bombs into target locations or infesting them with bedbugs.

Around 1931, Bioff met George Browne, the head of the Chicago local union of the International Alliance of Theatrical Stage Employees (IATSE). Together, Bioff and Browne tried to develop some scams. Their first enterprise was a soup kitchen. Bioff's friends in politics contributed money to a program in which Browne's working members could be fed for thirty-five cents a meal and their unemployed brothers could eat for free. Occasionally, a local celebrity or politician would drop by for a bowl of soup and an opportunity to be photographed with the common man. On their way out, they occasionally made donations, sometimes as much as fifty dollars. From the money donated, it was estimated by the Internal Revenue Service that at least seventy-five percent of it was skimmed by Bioff and Browne.

Through additional contributions to the soup kitchen from local theatre operators, Browne became personally acquainted with many of them and their employees. Using these contacts, Bioff and Browne tightened their grip on IATSE, offering workers job protection and more money—but also giving management a no-strike clause in their contracts.

Balaban and Katz, Inc., of Chicago, which owned the largest theatre chain in the country, was the first beneficiary of a Bioff and Browne sweetheart arrangement. Singer Barney Balaban and pianist Sam Katz had begun their business in 1916 by operating a string of nickelodeons. They offered Bioff and Browne $150 a week for the soup kitchen, in lieu of restoring a twenty-percent pay cut forced upon the workers. Bioff, who handled the negotiations, countered by demanding a lump-sum settlement. In the end, Bioff and Browne received $20,000 cash in return for labor peace. But very little of that money was spent for the soup kitchen.

Instead, Bioff and Browne went to a gambling casino owned by Nick Circella, a Capone mob member, and lived it up, throwing lots of money around. Their gay mood did not go unnoticed. A few days later Browne received a telephone call from Mafia kingpin Frankie Rio, who demanded fifty percent of whatever business they were in—"or else."

The Chicago underworld was deeply impressed with Bioff and Browne's scam and invited them to two meetings at the home of Frank Nitti, the heir to Al Capone, who was doing time in Alcatraz for income tax evasion.*

Nitti told his guests that he wanted Browne to run for president of IATSE, an American Federation of Labor union which operated in both the United States and Canada. In 1932, Browne had run for and lost the presidency of IATSE. This time, Nitti explained, Browne would go to the union's June 1934 international convention in Louisville, Kentucky, with the support of his people—namely, Capone's and Nitti's top musclemen, including Tony Accardo, Nitti's number-two man behind Paul DeLucia, as well as Louis "Lepke" Buchalter, Cleveland racketeer Morris Dalitz, and Abner "Longy" Zwillman of Newark, New Jersey, who was one of actress Jean Harlow's lovers and a familiar figure in Hollywood.

With support from his mobster backers, Browne was easily elected as president of IATSE. (Two of his rivals for the presidency had withdrawn from the race after receiving death threats.) After the IATSE convention, Tom Maloy, the business manager of the Motion Picture Operators Union Local 110 in Chicago, was found murdered gangland-style, as was Clyde Osterberg, a IATSE union dissident, who had earlier complained of Bioff's threats against him. Neither killing was ever solved, but the Chicago underworld had made it clear that it would accept no interference from anyone with regard to its takeover of the national IATSE union. Upon his election, Browne immediately appointed Bioff as his personal, full-power representative. In return, the Chicago Mafia was to receive two-thirds of whatever Browne and Bioff took or shook down.

Wasting no time, Bioff returned to Balaban and Katz, making big demands for better employment conditions and wages. The result was another large payoff—this time for $100,000. Bioff's shakedown scam also worked in New York and in other cities around the country.

The Chicago crime syndicate decided to hunt for bigger game. The new target was the film industry—a cash-rich business that promised fast and steady skim money. In late 1934, Bioff was sent to Hollywood, where IATSE had just lost a prolonged strike against the motion picture studios and, in the process, much of its membership.

---

*Also in attendance at the sitdowns were other Capone associates: Phil D'Andrea, Charles "Cherry Nose" Gioe, Paul "The Waiter" DeLucia, and Louis Campagna. A New York mob figure was present, too: Louis "Lepke" Buchalter, the head of Murder, Inc., who had been sent by Charles "Lucky" Luciano to represent the interests of the Eastern crime families.

The Depression had hit the film industry hard. Universal Studios, which had been built on a chicken farm by Carl Laemmle in 1912, had dramatically cut back its employment rolls, as had Warner Brothers, established by Jack, Harry, Sam, and Albert Warner in 1919. Such studios as Paramount, which had been founded in 1914 by W. W. Hodkinson and was operated by Adolph Zukor, and United Artists— a 1919 creation of actors Douglas Fairbanks, Sr., Mary Pickford, and Charlie Chaplin, and producer D. W. Griffith—had nearly been driven out of business.

The film industry was ripe for extortion. The Mafia knew that the studio moguls would cave in to its demands, trying to avoid future labor problems. As president of IATSE, the mob-controlled Browne, who was also a vice-president of the AFL, had the authority to order movie projectionists to strike throughout the country.

Mobsters Nick Circella and Johnny Roselli were sent to Hollywood by the Chicago Mafia to oversee its interests. Benjamin "Bugsy" Siegel was already in California, protecting East Coast underworld investments. It was time to achieve trade union dominion in Hollywood.

Bioff and IATSE met a jurisdictional dispute head-on. War broke out between IATSE and the rival United Studios Technicians Guild. Bloody battles were fought on Cahuenga Boulevard in Hollywood and at the gates of one of the studios on Pico Boulevard. According to one account, "The United Guild charged strong-arm tactics and ballot-box-stuffing by Bioff and hired its own 'heavies,' more than 150 longshoremen from the L.A. waterfront. The 'longies' waded into battle with Bioff's soldiers. . . . Heads were broken, blood spilled, and cars overturned and torched. . . . Bioff's routed the Guild's forces with clubs, gunbutts and fists." Bioff's forces—primarily professional thugs hired by Johnny Roselli—won easily.[4] Roselli had been in Hollywood for several years, working as an "undercover agent" for Pat Casey, a labor conciliator for the Motion Picture Producers and Distributors of America (MPPDA).

The head of the MPPDA was Will Hays, whom the Hollywood moguls had imported to be the moral "watchdog" of the motion picture business.

Hays had been the postmaster general under President Warren G. Harding and had been deeply involved in the Teapot Dome scandal, having taken a $260,000 bribe on behalf of the Republican Party. Ironically, the "Hays Office" had been created, in part, to survey the impact of gangster films on the American public. Nonetheless, mobsters continued to be portrayed as anti-heroes while the police were made to be shadowy figures who were generally as corrupt and violent as the targets of their investigations. Hays routinely hired gangsters to bust unions and break heads to avert strikes against the film industry.

"At that time," Roselli said, "I didn't have too much money. About 1933 or 1934 they had a strike in the [movie] industry, and the unions, that is the studios, were in difficulty. The unions were trying to get on to this, I don't know whether it was a demand for higher wages or recognition or what it was. I have forgotten what it was at the time. There was a little rough play around and the studios naturally didn't want it. They didn't want their workers hurt. They needed some cameramen to go back to work, and they had been threatened through some people. They had asked if I could help. I said, 'The only way to help is to fight fire with fire. You don't have to knock anybody on the head doing it, but you can just get enough protection for these fellows so no one will approach them with any rough play.'

"They asked me how much I would charge for this performance of duties. I said, 'I don't want anything, but I would like to get a job.' I said, 'You just pay the men that I will go out and hire to protect these people going to work in the studios, and later on . . . negotiate or [become an] assistant or something,' which later developed. He gave me some expenses. I said, 'You couldn't give me $100,000 to do this thing, but I will do it for nothing. I will help you all I can.'"[5]

In 1935—while the Mafia was playing ball with both the unions and the studios—Barney Balaban and Sam Katz moved to Hollywood, where they—along with Leo Spitz, who had negotiated the Balaban and Katz payoffs to Bioff and Browne in Chicago—became three of the biggest names in show business. Balaban was named as the president of Paramount; Katz became a vice-president of Metro-Goldwyn-Mayer; and Spitz became legal counsel for the MPPDA before becoming the president of the studios of Radio-Keith-Orpheum, RKO, which had been consolidated in 1928 by none other than Joseph P. Kennedy, Spitz's predecessor. Later, Spitz founded International Pictures and would be named as president of Universal by its new owners, Robert H. Cochrane and Nate J. Blumberg, who bought out Carl Laemmle in 1936.

By 1937, Bioff and the Chicago Mafia had started shaking down the major film studios, including Twentieth Century, Paramount, MGM, and Warner Brothers, for $50,000 a year each and the smaller studios —like RKO and Harry Cohn's eleven-year-old Columbia Pictures—for $25,000.[6]

Bioff told one studio executive, "I want you to know I elected Browne president, and I am his boss. He is to do whatever I want him to do. Now your industry is a prosperous industry, and I must get $2 million out of it."

Bioff later boasted, "It was like taking candy from babies. When I snapped my fingers, them producers jumped."

The middleman between Bioff and the studios was the president of the Motion Picture Producers Association, the lumbering, squinty-eyed Joseph Schenck, a former New York pharmacist who had moonlighted as an illegal drug dealer. In 1935, Schenck and former Warner Brothers executive Darryl F. Zanuck founded Twentieth Century, Inc., which merged with William Fox's Fox Film Corporation in 1938; the new company was Twentieth Century–Fox. Schenck—whose brother, Nicholas, had founded Metro-Goldwyn-Mayer and the Loew's theatre chain in 1924 with Marcus Loew*—had given Bioff a $100,000 payoff in return for guarantees of labor peace between IATSE and the studios. Schenck tried to disguise the extortion money as a loan.

The payoffs simply ensured that motion picture productions came off on schedule without problems from the 12,000 IATSE members, who were assessed two percent of their earnings by Bioff and Browne for no particular reason for forty-three weeks, beginning in December 1935. The total skim from the IATSE membership alone was over $1.5 million.

A top IATSE official recalled, "They got the two percent, and they never accounted for that. We agreed to give it to them on those terms, because we were in trouble. And we were being pushed around by big guys. And it took money, we knew, to save our union and to save our jobs."[7]

Some of the studio moguls tried to appear acrimonious, but they could see the figures: movie profits were up and unemployment was up with fewer people, now under tight union control, to pay. It was a perfect setup for management. The Internal Revenue Service estimated that by making the payoffs, the studio moguls saved $15 million that would have gone toward employee wages and benefits.

Bioff explained, "I've found that dickering with these picture producers goes about the same all the time. You get into a room with them, and they start yelling and hollering about how they're bein' held up and

---

*Nicholas Schenck and Marcus Loew had merged Metro Pictures and Goldwyn Pictures and named Louis B. Mayer as its head. When Loew died in 1926, Schenck renamed the company Metro-Goldwyn-Mayer.

robbed. That goes on and on. Me, I'm a busy man and don't get too much sleep. After a while it dies down, and the quiet wakes me up, and I say, 'All right, gentlemen, do we get the money?' "[8]

By 1937, with Bioff and Browne controlling IATSE, Petrillo cemented into power at AFM, and friends—like Balaban, Katz, Spitz, Cohn, and the Schencks—at the major studios, the Mafia had a stranglehold on the film industry.

CHAPTER THREE

In 1937, the same year that Bioff began shaking down the studios, Stein decided to challenge the William Morris Agency as the top talent agency in the country by creating an office in Beverly Hills. He placed a young agent, Taft B. Schreiber, in charge. Schreiber had walked into MCA's Chicago office eleven years earlier, looking for a job with a band, and was hired as Stein's messenger boy. "I had been a high school musician in Chicago," Schreiber said. "At the time there were only three people in MCA: Jules Stein, Billy Goodheart, and a secretary."[1]

Earlier, on December 16, 1936, Stein had hired Lew R. Wasserman, a Cleveland theatre usher and former candy peddler in a burlesque house. Born on March 15, 1913, Wasserman had moonlighted as the publicity director for the Mayfair Casino, a local nightclub in Cleveland. Although Wasserman had no more than a high school education, Stein made him MCA's national director of advertising and publicity. Wasserman's starting salary was $60 a week. Within two years—during which he wrote and handed out press releases—Wasserman was tapped as Stein's protégé and made a company vice-president.

Another early MCA employee, who would become a phenomenon in the entertainment business, was David A. Werblin. Born in Brooklyn in 1910, Werblin, a ruggedly good-looking former football player at

Rutgers University, had studied to be a journalist and had worked as a copy boy for *The New York Times.* At MCA, he started with a part-time job, working as Goodheart's office assistant in New York, performing menial chores for twenty-one dollars a week. Goodheart frequently taunted Werblin, calling him "Sonny boy." The nickname "Sonny" stuck, but the bad treatment did not. Werblin solidified his role as a "go-fer" when he became the band-boy for Guy Lombardo's orchestra; his jobs were primarily carrying instruments for the musicians and fetching coffee. But when Goodheart left MCA just prior to World War II, Sonny Werblin was selected to succeed his boss as head of the New York office.*

In California, Stein quickly moved MCA Artists, Ltd., into the business of representing general talent, not just musicians. He targeted Hollywood's most famous and established movie stars to become clients with his company. His first campaign was for actress Dorothy Lamour, but he failed to sign her until years later.

However, soon after, MCA scored its first big Hollywood triumph, signing actress Bette Davis, who had won the 1935 Academy Award for Best Actress for her role in *Dangerous.* (Her performance in *Jezebel* in 1938 would win her a second Oscar.) Stein had been so obsessed with landing Davis as a client that he placed her husband Harmon Nelson's best friend, Eddie Linsk—who for unknown reasons was nicknamed "Killer"—on the MCA payroll for two hundred dollars a week. Within a few weeks, Linsk had convinced Davis to switch agencies and join MCA.

More stars followed Davis's lead, among them Joan Crawford, John Garfield, Betty Grable, Bill Demarest, and Jane Wyman—just as bandleaders had followed Guy Lombardo to Stein a decade earlier.

During the early years of World War II, MCA continued to raid other agencies, stealing away clients. MCA had little interest in discovering new talent—it wanted big-name stars. If those stars were already represented by someone else, no problem; they could be bought off one way or another. Agent Jimmy Saphier lost bandleader David Rose when MCA offered Rose $20,000 cash to change firms and become one of its clients. Jules Stein also tried to woo Harry James's solo vocalist Kitty Kallen away from his band for a career of her own. The problem was that James was an MCA client—as was his wife, Betty Grable—and bad feelings resulted. Johnny Beck, the top agent with Associated

---

*Goodheart later became the vice-president of network sales at NBC.

Artists, was also bought out by MCA, and he was put in charge of MCA's motion picture division.

Perhaps the biggest losers during the early MCA empire-building days were the small, unknown groups. These bands were treated like common freight, haphazardly thrown onto shipping vessels and sent from one port to the next. MCA's common practice was to organize these groups and then ignore them, or to force them out of business to make way for someone else.

For example, Kearney Walton, Jr., was employed as an orchestra leader at the Biltmore Hotel in Los Angeles from 1936 to 1938. The hotel was owned by Baron Long, a tough businessman with long-standing ties to major Mafia figures. In 1938, an agent for MCA came to Walton and asked him to sign an exclusive contract. When Walton told Long that he had been approached by MCA, his employer told him that if he signed with MCA he would lose his job. Long simply did not want someone driving a hard bargain for his bands.

Walton didn't sign with MCA then, but soon he was sent to Omar's Dome, a nightclub owned by Long's brother-in-law. After several months, the MCA representative made him another offer. This time, with his engagement at Omar's Dome ending, Walton decided to sign. The MCA contract provided that Walton could not be represented by anyone else—but contained no guarantees for future work.

Walton did work, but not at clubs like the Biltmore. Instead, he played in small clubs in Laguna Beach and Pismo Beach—without any regularity. In the end, Walton "was starved out of the business." Ironically, soon after, Baron Long signed with MCA to ensure entertainment for the Biltmore.

In desperation, Walton wrote a letter to the U.S. Department of Justice, complaining that "MCA had monopolized the big-band business by forcing its representation on nearly all of the industry—via its contracts with hotels, resorts, dance halls, and night clubs, as well as with the bands themselves." In addition, Walton alleged that MCA had a sweetheart relationship with James Petrillo and the top officials of the American Federation of Musicians, who, in violation of AFM rules, permitted MCA to maintain exclusive contracts with hotels and nightclubs.

Walton's letter touched off a storm of investigations focusing on MCA that would last for decades. In 1941, acting on one of Walton's suggestions, George Maury, a special attorney for the Justice Department's Antitrust Division in Los Angeles, interviewed Lindsey "Spike"

Jones, the leader of a small, independent band. Jones, Walton had said, could be helpful to the government's investigation because of his own experiences with MCA.*

Formerly represented by MCA, Jones, like Duke Ellington and Count Basie, had left the agency in 1939 after Willard Alexander, a top MCA agent, had defected to the William Morris Agency. Jones told Maury that MCA controlled most of the big-name bands in America and Canada, and at least seventy-five percent of the entire band-booking business.[2]

"How has MCA become so successful?" Maury asked.

"They've devised a system of rotating bands in all these places they play," Jones replied. "The system's so perfect that without the MCA contract, a bandleader can't make enough bookings to make a living, and the clubs can't get bands unless they sign their contracts with MCA."

Jones charged that MCA engaged in a variety of "unethical practices" and would often "run down" and ridicule bandleaders not under its wing.

"What about Stein and the AFM?"

"Stein's a member of the union, its Chicago local, and he's present at nearly every AFM meeting."[3]

Jones concluded the interview by telling Maury that MCA had made its big move in Hollywood—in an attempt to launch its drive to represent stars in the motion picture industry. Its only competition would come from the William Morris Agency, the Myron Selznick Agency, the Hayward-Deverich Agency, and the General Amusement Company. Already, Jones said, many of the bands represented by these companies were trying to buy out their contracts so that they could sign with MCA.

Meantime, Assistant Attorney General Thurman Arnold had become concerned that radio broadcasters were not only broadcasting but were also involved in phonograph and record production, and the business management and representation of some of their own employees. As head of the Antitrust Division under President Franklin D. Roosevelt, Arnold was responsible for forty-four percent of all the antitrust actions that had been taken by the Justice Department since the passage of the Sherman Antitrust Act in 1891. Earlier, Arnold had forced General Electric and Westinghouse to sell its interests in RCA —and, thus, NBC. Arnold demanded that if these companies were

---

*Jones and his ragtag band, which included washboard and kazoo players, would later sell millions of copies of their first big hit, "My Two Front Teeth."

going to remain in the broadcasting business, they would have to compete with RCA and NBC.

Arnold authorized Victor Waters, another assistant attorney general, to call a meeting with the three principal radio networks—CBS, Mutual, and NBC—"to discuss various phases of chain broadcasting and the entire question of possible monopolistic practices on Saturday, October 25 [1941]."[4]

At the meeting with the network executives, Waters restated an FCC warning of the growth of conflicts of interest between broadcasters and artists, and "the unfair control by broadcasters over the supply of talent." The networks were also told that if they "did not divest themselves of their activities in the artists' management field the matter would be turned over to the Department of Justice for inquiry."[5] James Petrillo and the AFM agreed and pushed for action.

Of the three networks, only CBS agreed to relinquish its representation of artists, selling its rights to MCA for a reported $500,000. The others, NBC and Mutual, decided to ignore the FCC—although rumors were afloat that William Morris was going to bid for NBC.[6]

"[W]hat gave MCA its great impetus on bands was its deal with CBS when the AFM forced the [radio] networks to get out of the big-band business," a Justice Department memorandum reported. "MCA not only obtained all of the CBS bands, but also got access to CBS lines for radio broadcasts any time MCA wanted it. This meant that many of the bands gravitated toward MCA to get national exposure on CBS."[7]

The same week as the hearings with the networks, Tom C. Clark—the chief of the West Coast Regional Office of the Justice Department—following up on Maury's investigation, sent a letter to Thurman Arnold, citing the Walton letter and more information on the sweetheart relationship between Jules Stein and James Petrillo. Arnold replied to Clark two weeks later, asking him to monitor the MCA situation in California. But the Justice Department's investigation of MCA remained dormant for several months.

On April 3, 1942, another dissident MCA client brought the FBI into the act. Al Stone, representing the vaudeville team of Stone and Lee, wrote a letter to J. Edgar Hoover, the director of the FBI. Stone reported that he was in the midst of litigation against MCA, charging the talent agency with, among other things, breach of contract. Stone claimed that, although MCA had offered a settlement, he was going to fight the matter in court to draw public attention to MCA's tactics and attempts to monopolize the entertainment business.

Stone alleged that MCA and entertainer Danny Dare were involved in an exclusive representation contract with the *Danny Dare Review*. Stone and Lee were one of the acts in the show. While with the *Review,* they played for three and a half weeks at the El Cerrito and four weeks at the Ambassador Hotel in Los Angeles, followed by twelve weeks on the road with the comedy team of Laurel and Hardy in the summer and fall of 1940. According to Stone, MCA raked in all profits above the salary list at both the El Cerrito and the Ambassador, in addition to its ten-percent commission for Dare's show while it was on the road. Stone charged that the *Dare Review* received $7,000 for the El Cerrito engagement though the salary list was only $2,695, and $5,000 from the Ambassador while the salary list was $2,200.

When Stone discovered the extent of MCA's cut—in addition to its ten-percent commission—he and his partner said they would go to court. Consequently, Stone claimed, MCA threatened to keep them out of work. "That is another evil in show business," Stone wrote. "If an actor steps out of line with any of these big [corporate] agencies or bookers, they have enough influence to call the proper people and give the word . . . DON'T BOOK STONE AND LEE [emphasis Stone's]. This has been a common practice in show business for many years. . . . I am sure, Mr. Hoover, that if this organization was investigated you would find that they have nothing on an octopus."

Blackballed by MCA and back on the street, Stone and Lee had tried to file for unemployment compensation but were rejected. Deciding to take MCA to court, Stone and his wife sold nearly all their possessions and spent everything they had fighting MCA. Several of their colleagues, like Laurel and Hardy, who had also been hurt by MCA, feared similar reprisals and refused to testify on their behalf. Stone and Lee eventually lost their case and faded into obscurity.

Over a year passed after Stone's complaint to Hoover. Then, on April 30, 1943, Tom C. Clark sent a memorandum to the attorneys on his staff, advocating a government investigation of MCA. Antitrust attorney George Maury dissented, stating that only two witnesses, Kearney Walton and Spike Jones, had been interviewed, and no clear evidence showed a conspiracy between MCA and the AFM. In addition, Maury said, most of the big-name band members had joined the military in the midst of World War II.

"In view of the scantiness of the material and the almost impossibility of aiding the war effort by any such investigation at present," Maury wrote, "it is my best suggestion that any further investigation of this situation should be postponed for the duration of the war."[8]

CHAPTER FOUR

In 1938, Jeff Kibre, a studio craftsman and head of the IATSE progressives, filed a formal complaint with the National Labor Relations Board on behalf of the Motion Picture Technicians Committee. Based on information he received during an IRS audit of Joseph Schenck's 1937 income tax returns, Kibre charged that Willie Bioff and George Browne had taken a $100,000 payoff from Schenck, the president of the Motion Picture Producers Association, "in return for which the IA locals were turned into company unions which have been going through the motions of collective bargaining."[1]

A 1931 graduate of UCLA, Kibre came from a family of Hollywood set decorators. He had wanted to become a writer but went into the labor movement when he first became a studio craftsman. Kibre was viewed by nearly all who knew him as a good, honest, and dedicated man. Becoming more militant and aligning himself with leftist causes, Kibre was an easy target for those who disagreed with him—because of his politics. On at least one occasion, Bioff's goons came to Kibre's home and beat him up. Nevertheless, Kibre's charges—and the investigation that followed—shook Hollywood like an earthquake.

Others also went after Bioff. Arthur Ungar, the crusading editor of *Daily Variety,* began writing a series of exposés about Bioff, Browne,

Schenck, and the whole IATSE scam, which was now threatening the independence of writers, directors, and actors. The Screen Actors Guild (SAG) had also grown fearful of Bioff's pressure. It published a full-page ad in *The Hollywood Reporter,* * which stated, in part: "The IATSE is a very real menace. . . . Writers will find themselves in a boss-ruled union overnight if they stand alone. . . . IATSE can never take over writers if writers stand shoulder to shoulder with the actors' and directors' guilds. . . ."[2]

Former SAG president Robert Montgomery proposed that the Guild appropriate $5,000 to hire a private investigator to look into Bioff's background. That probe yielded details of Bioff's sleazy criminal past and associations.† Information was fed to Ungar, who, in spite of Bioff's threats against him, declared all-out war against the labor racketeer. But Bioff's problems were just beginning.

The break in the investigation came when federal investigators discovered that Schenck had received thousands of dollars in unreported cash through some of his investments and had been making payoffs to Bioff. Charged with income tax evasion and faced with stiff fines and a long stretch in prison if convicted, Schenck decided to talk and provided federal agents with details of the studios' $1.2 million in payoffs to Bioff and Browne. However, Schenck claimed that he was not aware of the extent to which Bioff and Browne were involved with the Chicago Mafia and could offer no information about it.

In return for Schenck's cooperation, the government dropped its tax evasion charges against him. Schenck pleaded guilty to one count of perjury. Sentenced to a year in jail, he was paroled after serving only four months and was later given a full pardon. He was, however, replaced as president of Twentieth Century–Fox by Spyros Skouras.

On May 23, 1941, Bioff and Browne were indicted on charges of extortion and racketeering by a federal grand jury. With Joseph Schenck's testimony, Bioff and Browne were convicted and sent to Alcatraz for ten and eight years, respectively. After being indicted, Bioff waved the American flag and told the press, "The unions on the West Coast are infested with communism. We expelled eighteen members during the last four years on charges that they were members of the Communist Party. We eliminate them as fast as we can. Our posi-

---

*Billy Wilkerson, publisher of *The Hollywood Reporter,* had previously made a deal with Bioff in which the trade paper would not publish news about studio–labor relations.

†Among the details of Bioff's past uncovered by *Daily Variety* and SAG was that he had not served his full jail term for an old pandering conviction. On April 15, 1940, Bioff was extradited back to Illinois, where he served six months in Chicago's Bridewell.

tion won't allow anything to stand in the way of the defense program [World War II]."

The U.S. government bought the story that the studio moguls had been subject to extortion and were the poor victims of Bioff—not that they had been co-partners in a conspiracy to keep employees' wages low and their union under tight control.

Two years later, government investigators in New York uncovered evidence of the Mafia's earlier plot to take over Hollywood through Bioff and Browne. Confronted with the information, Bioff decided to talk, implicating Frank Nitti, Johnny Roselli, Phil D'Andrea, Charles "Cherry Nose" Gioe, Paul Ricca, Nick Circella,* and Louis Campagna.

On the day the indictments were returned, Nitti, who had already done time for income tax evasion, shot and killed himself.†

Generally overlooked in press accounts during Bioff's testimony were his statements about a young labor lawyer he had been introduced to in 1939 at the Bismarck Hotel in Chicago by mobster Charles "Cherry Nose" Gioe. Bioff testified that, in very explicit terms, Gioe pointed to the lawyer and told Bioff, "[He] is our man, and I want you to do what he tells you. He is not just another lawyer but knows our gang and figures our best interest. Pay attention to him, and remember, any message he may deliver to you is a message from us."

The young attorney's name was Sidney R. Korshak.

Prior to Bioff's extortion indictment, Korshak—who was also a friend of Johnny Roselli—had called Bioff and asked to talk.

Bioff said that he and Korshak had a meeting in the attorney's room at the Ambassador Hotel in Los Angeles and "talked about everything in general." Bioff recalled, "He [Korshak] asked me about all these indictments [of Bioff and Browne]. I says, 'All I know about them at this time is what I have read in the newspapers.' He says, 'Well, are you prepared with your defense?' I said, 'No, not altogether.' He said, 'Well, Joe will be the next victim. Joe will be the man that you [gave] the money to, Joe Schenck'; that he [Korshak] had seen a transcript of

---

*According to author Ed Reid in *The Grim Reapers*, in an effort to silence Circella—who was thought to be a weak link and a possible future informant—syndicate killers broke into the home of his lover, Estelle Carey, "tied [her] to a chair in her apartment, poured gasoline over her, and set her afire. Her pet poodle, cowering in the corner of the room, was the only witness to the crime."

†Louis "Lepke" Buchalter, who was involved in the shakedown scheme, too, was not indicted but had already been convicted of murder; he was executed in New York's electric chair in 1944. Benjamin "Bugsy" Siegel was also not implicated, having spent less time in California and more time in Nevada—where gambling had been legal since 1931.

Schenck's [statement]; that there is enough material left there by the government to give any jury good reason to believe that I turned this money over to Joe Schenck [making Schenck the fall guy]. . . ."

"In other words, at your forthcoming trial you were to testify that way?" federal prosecutor Boris Kostelanetz asked.

"Yes."

". . . Sidney Korshak in this case deceived you, is that right?"

"Well, I don't know whether he deceived me. He advised me to lie."

Later, Bioff testified that Korshak—who had also represented George Browne after his conviction—had arranged for him to get $15,000 for his defense.[3]

Born on June 6, 1907, and raised on Chicago's West Side, Korshak was the son of Sidney and Beatrice Korshak, refugees from Lithuania. A basketball star in high school, he graduated from the University of Wisconsin, where he was a champion boxer. He earned his law degree in 1930 from DePaul University in Chicago.

At the time of Bioff's testimony, Korshak was in the U.S. Army, serving as a military instructor at Camp Lee, Virginia. Two months after entering the service, he ran into Bernice Stewart, a former model, dancer, and ice-skating star whom he had met in Los Angeles in 1941. Two years later, they were married at the Ambassador Hotel in New York City by a city magistrate. He was discharged from the service as a corporal two years later. Upon his return home, he and his brother Marshall—a graduate of John Marshall Law School in Chicago—set up a legal practice in downtown Chicago. Marshall was actively involved in the local Democratic Party. Both of them quickly achieved legitimacy, socializing with bankers, business executives, show people, sports figures, and politicians.

According to statements made to government investigators by Gioe —who had been sent by the Chicago underworld to run the mob's rackets in Iowa until 1939—he had met Korshak in or about 1933, three years after Korshak graduated from DePaul. Soon after, Korshak was formally introduced to the Chicago underworld by Gioe associate Gus Alex, a Greek member of the local syndicate who handled the mob's operations in and around the Loop. Alex was a favorite of Tony Accardo and Jake "Greasy Thumb" Guzik, who was in charge of making the Chicago mob's political payoffs.[4]

After Korshak's name came out in Bioff's 1943 testimony, FBI agents did a background check on Korshak but discovered nothing in their files; he had no criminal record. He had been arrested only once, in May 1931, along with his brother Ted, for starting a brawl in the

Show Boat nightclub in the Loop. When the police searched the Korshak brothers, a gun was found in Sid's pocket. Charged with carrying a concealed weapon, Korshak was held on $2,400 bond. At his arraignment, the charges were dropped.

Further inquiries made by the FBI revealed that Korshak, who lived in the mob-owned Seneca Hotel in Chicago, "had represented one George Scalise, who was at that time international president of the Building Service Employees with offices in New York City. In 1940 Korshak was receiving a $1,200-per-month retainer fee from Scalise to draft a new set of by-laws for the union that would enable him, among other things, to break up any union local into small units which he could reassemble as he saw fit. This would be a potent weapon against any recalcitrant local. Scalise was a New York hoodlum and ex-con and was indicted in New York City by Thomas Dewey for alleged extortion from hotels and contractors."[5]

Scalise, according to a confidential report of the Chicago Crime Commission, "allegedly drained the union treasury of an estimated $1.5 million in three years. After an investigation by the Cook County Grand Jury into the conduct of the Building Service Employees International Union and the manipulation of its finances by Scalise, who was ousted as president in April 1940, he was indicted by the district attorney of New York on charges of extorting more than $100,000 from hotels and cleaning contractors. It was alleged that on January 4, 1939, Scalise 'bought' some fifteen locals of the Elevator Operators Union. . . . The locals were handed over to Scalise's international by the International Union of Elevator Constructors, Operators and Starters in return for $10,000 drawn by Scalise from his treasury. Thereafter the dues of the locals flowed into Scalise's treasure chest."[6]

According to another government report, dated July 25, 1942, and developed by the intelligence division of the Internal Revenue Service during the aftermath of the Bioff/Browne trial, "Our informers have stated that Sidney Korshak, a lawyer in Chicago, Illinois, is often delegated to represent the Chicago gang, usually in some secret capacity. Since the conviction of Browne and Bioff on charges of racketeering, Korshak acts as Browne's attorney. He paid Browne's $10,000 fine and we are reliably informed that the gang [the Chicago Mafia], and not Browne, produced that money. . . .

"John Smith [the successor to Tom Maloy in Chicago's Motion Picture Operators Union Local 110] testified that about one year and a half ago, [an associate] telephoned him that George Browne had expressed the opinion that Local 110 should employ an attorney. Korshak subsequently appeared on the scene. Smith states that he was not employed or paid any money. He [Smith] did testify, however, with respect to the election of union officials on March 4, 1942."

Q: How much money did you draw to pay off the policemen?
A: About $1,000; made out a check for them.
Q: Made out to cash?
A: I don't know whether Pete cashed the check or I cashed the check.
Q: Did the police get the entire $1,000?
A: Yes.
Q: Was Sidney Korshak in the picture?
A: Well, he asked me if I wanted protection and I said no. At that time he thought I was going to hire him as attorney for the local and since there is trouble here I don't want no part of Korshak.[7]

According to federal investigators, one of those people who did turn to Korshak was Jules Stein, the president of MCA. "Korshak and Stein had met each other back in the early days of Chicago through the band-booking business," an FBI agent said. "They were introduced by Joe Glaser, a mutual friend who ran his own booking business [Associated Booking]. Stein knew that Korshak was connected [to the Mafia], and he went to him when he wanted to get a message to someone or wanted something done. . . . Korshak was also a friend of James Petrillo's."

CHAPTER
FIVE

ON MARCH 20, 1945, a major antitrust suit was filed against MCA by Larry Finley, who had leased the oceanfront Mission Beach Amusement Park and Dance Hall for three years from the city of San Diego, hoping to draw servicemen from nearby military installations and those returning home from the Pacific theatre. Finley had planned to operate Mission Beach six nights a week. Its dance floor was the largest and its sound system the best in San Diego. No alcohol was to be served, thereby guaranteeing civilized and well-behaved patrons. Both San Diego's mayor and the city council were impressed with Finley's credentials and his plans for Mission Beach. In addition, Finley had promised the city some $20,000 a year and a piece of the profits for the lease.

Finley—who had begun his career in the music business as a pianist and an orchestra leader fifteen years earlier in upstate New York—had obtained the Mission Beach lease in November 1944, at which time Larry Barnett, MCA vice-president in charge of band-booking, and MCA agent Harold Eames Bishop had pledged to supply him with a variety of name bands at market rates. To celebrate the opening of his dance hall, Finley planned a massive gala for early February 1945. But MCA failed to produce the big-name bands for the affair.

Asking for triple damages under Section 7 of the Sherman Antitrust Act in his $3.1 million suit, Finley charged that MCA, Jules Stein, Barnett, and Bishop had conspired to freeze him out of the entertainment business in San Diego. His evidence appeared to be overwhelming.

After Finley had initially threatened court action, MCA offered him the King Sisters for a two-day gig, February 10–11. This offer further infuriated Finley, because the King Sisters had just had a three-night stand at the Pacific Square Ballroom, located in downtown San Diego in the city's civic center, February 2–4. MCA also offered Jack Teagarden for two nights for a $2,500 minimum guarantee and fifty percent of the gross receipts, and Ted Fio Rito under the same terms. Finley insisted that MCA's scale was excessive and much higher than the fees charged other ballrooms.

Finley gave MCA the names of the bands he wanted for Mission Beach. But nearly all of those he named had been booked into the Pacific Square, owned and operated by Wayne Dailard, who had held the rights to Mission Beach before Finley outbid him in November 1944. Dailard, who had been an executive with RKO for thirteen years and was the former managing editor of the *San Diego Exposition,* had primarily booked Black and country-western bands—like Bob Wills and the Playboys—when he ran Mission Beach, hoping that Pacific Square would flourish as a result.[1]

Finley's attorneys obtained a copy of MCA's contract with Dailard, which had been drawn up while Dailard was operating Mission Beach. It provided that he had "first refusal on all orchestra bookings for the city of San Diego." In return, Dailard promised to accept "seventy-five percent of the orchestras offered . . . or a minimum of thirty-five orchestras per year."[2] Finley charged that MCA had similar exclusive arrangements with other operators around the country, like Jantzen Beach Park in Portland, Oregon. In these cases, MCA usually demanded that booking fees for other agencies bringing in acts be split with MCA when these non-MCA performers played at these exclusive clubs.

According to Barney McDevitt, a Finley public relations man, as soon as Finley brought suit, MCA offered him the exclusive band rights in Oakland, California, if he would drop the whole matter. Finley refused.[3]

Sparked by the Finley case, the Justice Department's Antitrust Division resumed its preliminary investigation of MCA, which had been dropped in 1943. Paul Fitting, another antitrust attorney in Los Angeles, interviewed Ralph Wonders, manager for the General Amusement Company in Hollywood, then one of the largest band-booking agencies. Among the bandleaders handled by General Amusement were Glenn Miller, Jimmy Dorsey, Charley Spivak, Cab Calloway, and Woody Herman. It also represented a variety of other artists and had booked several acts for Larry Finley at Mission Beach when his legal problems with MCA began.

Wonders told Fitting that he had seen the contract between Wayne Dailard and MCA, adding that it was the only such contract he had ever seen. "But," Wonders said, "a lot of the ballrooms have dealt with MCA exclusively. They knew that they could only get their bands if they dealt with them exclusively. . . . I know of one bandleader, who's represented by MCA, who owes them $19,000."

"Do any of the dance halls complain about MCA's tactics?" asked Fitting.

"Sure, lots of them do. But, until Larry Finley, no one had the guts to do anything about it. See, the problem is MCA's full-line forcing policy. The dance halls have to be willing to take the B- and C-grade bands, and then they'll get the bigger-name groups if they don't complain too much."

"What about bands splitting commissions [between MCA and a talent agency representing a band performing at a club with an exclusive contract with MCA]?"

"That's a common practice; it's sort of the general rule. Some of the bigger bands can put up a stink and avoid it. We had to split commissions with MCA on Stan Kenton and Spike Jones, but not on Jimmy Dorsey, Charley Spivak, or Woody Herman [who were all GAC clients]. I tell you openly that we split commissions on the Jantzen Beach Park Ballroom in Portland. That's the business."

"How have you fellows been able to break through the MCA stranglehold over the industry?"

"We've done all right in Chicago and at the New Yorker and the Pennsylvania hotels in New York. They used to be exclusively MCA; now they book General Amusement's bands. In the two New York hotels, the new managers are personal friends of mine and, during the war, there just weren't enough good bands available."

"What about in Los Angeles?"

"I can still get a good band in anywhere. MCA has about thirty-five percent more name bands than I do, and we're as big as William Morris —which represents Artie Shaw, Vaughn Monroe, and Duke Ellington, as well as Count Basie, Dizzy Gillespie, and Charlie Parker—and the

Frederick Brothers Agency, which runs fourth. But, for all of us, the big money is in the one-night stands. A good promoter can rent out large auditoriums for a night, book a big band, and make plenty for everyone."

"What about the unions? Who do you deal with? AFM?"

"Sure, we deal with AFM. We deal with the American Guild of Variety Artists. We deal with the Screen Actors Guild and the American Federation of Radio Artists."

"So what does the AFM do?"

"They appoint the booking agent as the exclusive agent, in return for commission of ten percent on steady engagements, and twenty percent on engagements of three days or less. The AFM obligates the booking agency, the bandleader, and the members of his band to stay in good standing with the union, and provides that the executive board of the American Federation of Musicians be the final arbiter of any disputes coming out of the contract."[4]

Fitting also interviewed Billy McDonald, who was in charge of bands for Frederick Brothers, the smallest of the four agencies representing name bands. It numbered among its clients Lawrence Welk and Wingy Manone. McDonald had been a West Coast bandleader, represented by MCA for nearly ten years. He told Fitting that he was still on excellent terms with the corporation but had a couple of complaints with its handling of his career. Mostly, he had been upset because MCA had refused lucrative bookings without consulting him.

As a booking agent, McDonald was among the first people Larry Finley turned to after his falling out with MCA. According to McDonald, Finley had had big problems trying to get bands for Mission Beach. "Finley got Henry Busse [a bandleader] from the William Morris Agency. In fact, the agent had to go through MCA to get him. Normally, Busse received something like $600–$800 a night and maybe $1,500 for two. Finley was forced to pay $2,750 for a two-night stand."[5]

Despite the antitrust investigation, MCA continued to expand.* And as MCA expanded, disgruntlement among some of the major bandleaders grew as well.

Did MCA work for them or did they work for MCA? Why did they feel completely dominated by their agency? Jack Teagarden recorded an album, "Jack Hits the Road," with the theme, "You won't see me

---

*By the end of World War II, the bandleaders represented by MCA included Jan Garber, Ted Fio Rito, Ted Lewis, Benny Goodman, Freddie Martin, Jack Teagarden, Bob Chester, Phil Harris, Skinny Ennis, Les Brown, Bernie Cummins, Al Donahue, Henry King, Harry Owens, and Tommy Tucker, among others.

for many a day, because I'm on the road for MCA." Tommy Dorsey had been quoted as saying, "They [MCA] make me so mad I could cut their throats, but I've got to play ball with them." When the term of Dorsey's contract with MCA ran out, he put a large ad in a trade paper, exclaiming: "Whew . . . I am finally out of the clutches of you-know-who."[6]

Two other bandleaders, Benny Goodman and Horace Heidt, had frequently protested—to no avail—against the bookings MCA had given them. Both musicians had even gone to the AFM and James Petrillo, seeking relief from their grievances against MCA, but were turned down by the AFM's executive board—which, each time, ruled in MCA's favor. As a result, both Goodman and Heidt actually disbanded their groups—and didn't play regularly again until their contracts with MCA expired in 1946. Until then, when Heidt did book his own act and perform, he was still required to pay MCA its ten-percent commission. During the interim Heidt lost his radio sponsor—which then backed another MCA show.

In April 1945, after three months of negotiations, MCA absorbed the prestigious Hayward-Deverich Agency of Beverly Hills, and the Leland Hayward Agency of New York. Both Leland Hayward and Nat Deverich were immediately named as vice-presidents of MCA Artists with ten-year employment contracts. Hayward—who had been pressured by his wife, actress Margaret Sullavan, to give up his business—also became a member of MCA's executive board.

Hayward had become an agent in 1930, joining the Myron Selznick Agency in New York. Soon after, he broke away and started his own firm. In 1937, Hayward and Deverich, who had been a vice-president of the Myron Selznick Agency,* became partners and started their own business in Hollywood.

Hayward-Deverich represented over three hundred clients, mostly playwrights and screenwriters, eighty of whom were based in Hollywood and ninety-two of whom were involved in Broadway productions in New York. Included among the actors were Greta Garbo, Ginger Rogers, Fred Astaire, Barbara Bel Geddes, Henry Fonda, Jimmy Stewart, Alfred Hitchcock, Ethel Merman, Laurence Olivier, Vivien Leigh, Barbara Stanwyck, Shirley Temple, Katharine Hepburn, and Gregory Peck. Hayward-Deverich also had represented the writers Arthur Miller, Dorothy Parker, and Dashiell Hammett.

MCA's domination of the top Hollywood talent was nearly complete.

---

*MCA had also raided the Myron Selznick Agency, taking such clients as Errol Flynn, Paulette Goddard, and Ingrid Bergman.

The big names meant bigger pictures, bigger salaries, and bigger commissions. According to a Justice Department document, "These top stars are the only ones who can be used as bankable credit—i.e., banks will loan money for financing a picture solely because a producer has one of these stars available. Without at least one of these stars, it is virtually impossible to get financing for a major motion picture."[7]

To federal attorneys, the major motion picture studios had always attempted to monopolize what the American people heard and saw at their local theatres. To the movie moguls, the American government had always tried to restrict their ability to participate in the free-enterprise system.

As early as 1938, the Justice Department's Antitrust Division had filed suit against the eight big motion picture companies—Paramount, Loews, RKO, Warner Brothers, Twentieth Century–Fox, Columbia, Universal, and United Artists—for "combining and conspiring to restrain trade in the production, distribution, and exhibition of motion pictures," in violation of the Sherman Antitrust Act. Essentially—in what became known as simply "the Paramount case"—the federal government wanted to prove that the studios had tried to control the production, distribution, and exhibition of all motion pictures. Five of these companies—Paramount, Loews, RKO, Warner Brothers, and Twentieth Century–Fox—owned their own strings of theatres and, of course, gave them the first opportunities to offer Hollywood's best films. Consequently, the government claimed that the major motion picture companies were engaged in block-booking, forcing independently owned theatres to accept the bad, low-grossing films in order to get the occasional blockbusters. Through this practice of block-booking, the studios began to control more and more of the first-run theatres.

Columbia, United Artists, and Universal owned no theatres but were linked with the five major studios because of allegations of price-fixing and illegal trade practices.

Thurman Arnold, the head of the Antitrust Division, charged that the motion picture business had become "an industrial dictatorship and distinctly un-American," insisting that such concentrations of power were a threat to democracy, as well as an unfair tax on the people. Arnold said, "The danger in this country is the private seizure of power. It is subject to no checks and balances, it is subject to no elections every four years, it is subject to no criticism and no attacks because no one even knows about it." He added that he was interested in "abolishing all monopolistic practices in the motion picture industry." By October

1940, a settlement had been reached, although few changes were made. Many theatre operations remained under the control of the big studios.

In August 1944, the Justice Department asked for a new trial. This time, treading lightly on the alleged antitrust violations, the government pushed for "divorcement"—to divorce theatre interests from the studios' production and distribution enterprises. As the trial started on October 8, 1945, the motion picture companies, in their defense, insisted that strict obedience to federal antitrust laws would destroy the film industry—to which the government replied that the studios needed to petition Congress to obtain exemption from the Sherman Antitrust Act.

The trial lasted nearly three months. When the court decision was read on December 31, 1945, the studios were cleared of violating federal antitrust laws and were permitted to keep their theatres. However, the court struck down many of the abuses the studios had engaged in at the local theatre level, such as price-fixing and other questionable trade practices. Even though the lower court's decision gave both sides "victories," the government immediately announced that it would appeal to the U.S. Supreme Court, while the studios announced that they would counter-appeal.

CHAPTER
SIX

THE FINLEY ANTITRUST CASE against MCA went to trial on January 29, 1946, in Los Angeles. F. Filmore Jaffe, Finley's attorney, set out to prove arguments that MCA's exclusive arrangement with Wayne Dailard in San Diego had constituted a monopoly, thus creating an illegal restraint of trade against Finley and his business. Jaffe produced evidence of alleged unethical practices employed by MCA, such as forcing other talent agencies bringing dance bands into the San Diego area to split commissions with MCA.

Jaffe had obtained an internal memorandum from the Frederick Brothers Agency that gave evidence of coercion and intimidation by MCA. The memo discussed the dilemma of Jerry Jones, the owner of the Rainbow Rendezvous, a dance hall in Salt Lake City, Utah. A top official with Frederick Brothers wrote that Jones had "said on the phone that he is forced to take nothing but MCA attractions and cannot possibly do business with us in the future unless MCA cannot give him a suitable attraction for his open date. During his recent trip here, [MCA vice-president] Larry Barnett, [MCA agent] Eames Bishop, and Taft Schreiber said it would have to be this way or else they would give T. R. Covey [the owner of the Cocoanut Grove Ballroom, also of Salt Lake City] two name attractions a week, and if such happens Jerry said it would murder his business, as his spot is small and he counts on a steady nightly trade."[1]

MCA's lawyers, Frank P. Doherty and Harold F. Collins, in response to Finley's charges that the MCA enterprise constituted a monopoly operating in an unethical manner, insisted: "The evidence affirmatively shows without conflict that MCA does not 'control' any bands. It is clear that MCA at all times acts only as the employment agent of the bands which it represents, and that the bandleader with whom contracts are made is the principal and acts on behalf of himself and the musicians who comprise the band, all under rules and regulations zealously kept and made effective by the American Federation of Musicians. MCA is not the principal, only the agent. . . . Any conspiracy which is claimed or asserted was solely that existing between Bishop, Barnett, and [Pacific Square operator Wayne] Dailard. . . . The Los Angeles office of MCA and not any other office in any other state is alleged or proved to have been involved in the alleged conspiracy."[2]

Jules Stein's deposition dissected MCA's corporate empire, which at the time included the band-booking agency, Music Corporation of America; the motion picture actors' agency, MCA Artists, Ltd.; the radio performers' agency, Management Corporation of America; and the California Movie Company.

Stein* explained that his East Coast talent was handled by MCA's New York offices; the Chicago bureau was in charge of the Midwest; and the Los Angeles and San Francisco offices shared MCA's West Coast operations. "Cleveland handles Ohio and perhaps part of Michigan," he said, "and they interlock with some in Chicago and New York. I think they go as far as Pittsburgh in the East. Dallas handles Texas and goes as far up as Kansas City. There is no sharp demarcation."[3]

After ten days of trial arguments and testimonies, the Finley antitrust case against MCA went to the jury. After only a few hours of deliberation, the jury returned to the courtroom and announced in favor of Finley, awarding him $55,500 in damages from MCA. Later, U.S. District Judge Paul J. McCormick, who presided over the trial and had earlier dismissed the charges against Stein, awarded Finley another $9,092 for costs and fees. In his final statement to the court, Judge McCormick called MCA "the Octopus . . . with tentacles reaching out to all phases and grasping everything in show business."

Judge McCormick added that he had found "that there is ample and

---

*In 1945, Jules Stein and his family purchased a two-story, semicircular Mediterranean villa, built on two acres on Angelo Drive in Beverly Hills. The mansion had been designed by Wallace Neff, a famous architect. Stein's neighbor across the street was Greta Garbo.

substantial evidence to support and sustain the implied finding of the jury that the defendants have conspired to restrain interstate commerce and to monopolize interstate commerce in that portion of the business of musical entertainment involving bands, orchestras, and attractions furnishing dance music at places of public entertainment. . . ."

Jules Stein was incensed. "The jury, by this decision, has in effect censured the efforts of our company in behalf of our clients in seeking the best places of employment for the maximum wages consistent with the furtherance of the artists' careers," he told the press.

Within a month of the verdict, rumors of a major MCA shakeup circulated on both coasts. Sonny Werblin, the New York MCA chief and second in command to Stein, and M. B. Lipsey, the head of the Chicago office, flew to Palm Springs for a series of meetings with their boss. Most talk centered on Stein, who was thought to be considering stepping down as president in favor of Werblin.

But after the first week of meetings, the only changes made were the reshuffling of several second-level personnel and the elevation of Larry Barnett as "coordinator of all orchestra and recording activities for MCA." During the second week of meetings, Leland Hayward, Taft Schreiber, and Lew Wasserman were summoned. Despite MCA's statements that "no other changes would be made," the Hollywood trade publications continued to speculate that Stein was stepping down.

After meetings during the second week in March, MCA continued playing its game with the press, still insisting that no major changes would be made. But in reality changes *were* being planned. Stein was not stepping down, he was stepping up—to become MCA's chairman of the board. And the new president was not Werblin—who had suffered a near-fatal heart attack a few years earlier—or even Taft Schreiber. Instead, Stein said he was going to name vice-president Lew Wasserman as MCA's new president and chief executive officer, saying of his thirty-three-year-old protégé, "Lew was the student who surpassed the teacher."

As of April 26, 1946—Stein's fiftieth birthday—Stein slowly eased himself out as the key day-to-day operator of MCA, and Wasserman began to assume the mantle of one of the most powerful executives in the entertainment business. The move became official on December 16, 1946, at MCA's annual meeting. Wasserman's formal promotion came ten years to the day after he joined MCA.

The tall, lanky, soft-spoken Wasserman presented a sharp contrast to the usual image of the glitzy, high-pressure Hollywood agent. He always wore the clothes that he made MCA's trademark: plain dark suits, white shirts, and skinny dark ties. Competitors called MCA's agents "the black-suited Mafia." Like Stein, Wasserman fanatically shunned all forms of personal publicity. With the moral support of his wife—Edith Beckerman, whom he had married in 1936—he worked seven days a week, sixteen hours a day in his plush Beverly Hills office. Impatient with inefficiency, cold and brusque when angry, he was a ruthless, hard-nosed negotiator. A self-admitted high-stakes gambler, he was considered an incisive thinker who made decisions quickly.

Wasserman preferred to dispense with paperwork, rarely writing memoranda or keeping personal records. Without any advanced education, he had made himself an expert at finance, taxes, law—and especially sales. For all of his business ferocity, even his most critical Hollywood rivals considered him a smooth, charming, likable, and honest man who had a natural tendency to understate his own considerable accomplishments. Every project he touched seemed to become successful—though shrouded in secrecy.

CHAPTER SEVEN

THE JUSTICE DEPARTMENT had watched the Finley case closely, as part of its continuing scrutiny of the monopolistic practices within the entertainment industry. At the same time, it was doing battle on another front with James Petrillo and the AFM.

In 1946, the U.S. Congress passed the Lea Act, best known as the "Anti-Petrillo Act," which prohibited the AFM from forcing broadcasters to hire more musicians than they needed.* Soon after the law was passed, the AFM contested its legality in Chicago's U.S. District Court, which ruled it unconstitutional. In their appeal to the U.S. Supreme Court, government attorneys stated that the Lea Act "represents the deliberate judgment of Congress as to the existence of an evil affecting the broadcasting system of the nation and as to the best method of remedying such evil." The Supreme Court overturned the lower-court decision, stating that the Lea Act was indeed constitutional.

As part of its antitrust investigation, Justice Department attorneys interviewed Charles Wick, a top executive of the William Morris

*The Lea Act was passed by Congress in 1946 after Petrillo attempted to compel radio station WAAF in Chicago to employ three persons not needed.

Agency, the first band-booking agency on the West Coast. Wick had at one time been a musician with his own orchestra, as well as a composer and arranger. For a short period, he was the administrator for Tommy Dorsey's orchestra.

Wick alleged that aside from MCA's talent agency and similar business ventures, "They also sell liquor to hotels to whom they sell orchestras." He estimated that MCA's bands grossed $15 million a year and that MCA's cut was at least 12.5 percent of that, or $1.8 million. Wick told the attorneys that at least three bandleaders—Tommy Dorsey, Harry James, and Kay Kyser—each grossed a million dollars annually. He also admitted splitting commissions with MCA when singer Vaughn Monroe played at the Pacific Square in San Diego. Monroe had since left William Morris and joined MCA.

"Do you know of any affiliation between MCA and the American Federation of Musicians?" one of the antitrust lawyers asked.

"That is very explosive ground. I know of none. I've heard of rumors. I don't say I entertain that view."

"Wherein would there be some connection between MCA and AFM, if there's any?"

"Well, this is only academic. If I may not refer to MCA, I could say that the likely affiliation between a union and an agency of this sort, if such existed, and which I have no reason to believe exists, would come whereby various strict union rules governing the coordination of the agency and the artists in relation to the union and the various entertainment purchasers might be released or overlooked or specially construed in a fairly moot situation in favor of the agency."

Later, when Wick was asked why MCA was so successful, he replied, "The main factor of MCA's dominance is the fact that they can force a particular [dance hall operator] to accept an MCA orchestra, because MCA wants to play the band at that particular point at that particular date because of a matter of good routing for their orchestra."

The government attorney asked, "How is MCA able to force them to do that? What pressures can it bring?" Wick then told a story about Gordon Coffey, a dance hall operator in several California towns. "[Let's say] he [Coffey] wants one of our bands and MCA wants to knock it out. If he doesn't take the band they [MCA] want, they can say 'We'll give our bands to someone else in your territory and you will get none, and that'll break you.' They can do that. That is another form of coercion: the law of supply and demand. . . ."

"Do you think that these same efforts of pressure are exerted in other parts of the United States?"

"Very definitely."

"Your organization runs into it frequently?"

"Yes. It is generally known in the field, even by musicians. They can also pressure hotels and nightclubs . . . in the same manner to take the bands they want to give you. They say, 'If we give you Mr. X box-office, we want you to take Joe A and Joe B no-draw. . . .'"

"What pressures could MCA bring upon its own bands to, more or less, make them play where they wanted them to?"

"Well, if their band is of top quality, they usually, in their personal relationships, act as diplomatically as possible, and therefore, with a top band, they would not bring any kind of direct pressure, because a top band is not solicitous of their good favor. However, a band that is not top, they can bring all kinds of pressure just, more or less, by intimidation, because they can tell him that only so-and-so may be available to his group in the way of bookings. . . . "

"Do you know of any instances where MCA had undertaken to do some pirating [stealing of clients]?"

"Oh, yes. Although I will say, in all fairness, that all agencies sandbag their opponents, although personally I will say—not professionally—that MCA's business tactics and scruples are highly questionable. That is a personal view, and I was very surprised when I came [to William Morris at] the amount of integrity and ethics they try to maintain in the face of pretty stiff competition."[1]

A few days after the Wick interview, Holmes Baldridge, special assistant to the U.S. attorney general, sent a memorandum to Fred Weller, special attorney for the department's antitrust office in Los Angeles. Baldridge concluded that MCA's activities—in its representation of actors, entertainers, and musicians, along with its subsidiary holdings—were nationwide rather than confined to the West Coast area. He added that most of MCA's name bands broadcasted over networks covering much of the United States, and that "this fact should strengthen the commerce phase of the case [against MCA]."

In his response, dated March 22, 1946, Weller replied: "If the facts developed are consistent with our present information, this looks like a good case. We are anxious to expedite it as much as possible."

Weller and government antitrust lawyer Herman Bennett tried once more to intiate a full-scale federal investigation of MCA. In the detailed memorandum, they outlined their case against the talent agency, again requesting an FBI investigation. Using the Finley case and the conduct of its original defendants—Jules Stein, Larry Barnett, and Eames Bishop—as evidence of MCA's antitrust violations, Weller and Bennett wrote: "It is believed that an FBI investigation will disclose that other individuals, affiliates of MCA, and other corporations are implicated in the conspiracy and that such investigation will also disclose facts that warrant a grand jury investigation."[2]

Specifically, they charged that MCA had "exerted pressure" on those with whom it did business for the following purposes:

1. It has compelled promoters to agree to take only MCA bands or that a great percentage of bands used by them be MCA bands.
2. In setting up their schedules, promoters have been compelled to take bands which they did not want.
3. Promoters have been prevented from using bands under contract with other agencies.
4. Other booking agencies have been forced to split commissions with MCA on receipts of bands under contract with other agencies.
5. MCA has compelled promoters against their will to accept an MCA band merely because MCA wanted to play the band at a particular time and place. This is sometimes done even when the promoter has other commitments with other agencies or other bands.
6. Bands have been pressured to play at certain places.
7. It has compelled bands to refuse to play at certain places and for certain promoters.

Weller and Bennett continued: "For a thoroughly complete investigation for the purpose of uncovering the entire MCA setup with all of its affiliates, interests and tentacles, its financial setup and its control of other phases of the entertainment industry, it would seem necessary to have a grand jury investigation in order that the books, records, correspondence, and office memoranda of MCA could be called for evidence.

"For the time being, a Bureau investigation covering certain cities and more or less confined to band-booking agencies, bandleaders, hotels, nightclubs and the larger ballroom operations should disclose substantial evidence of the illegal practices of MCA and a monopoly and restraint of trade in 'name' and 'semi-name' bands."

During the spring of 1946, the antitrust office in Los Angeles formally requested that the U.S. attorney general order an FBI investigation of the corporation. Specifically requested were probes of the relationship between MCA and the AFM and their sweetheart relationship; MCA's takeovers of the CBS Artists Bureau and the Hayward-Deverich Agency; and the subsequent takeovers of such businesses as the Mike Falk Agency and the William Meiklejohn Agency. Further, the FBI was asked to investigate the practice of commission-splitting and a variety of devices of coercion and intimidation against bands and dance halls utilized by MCA.

On June 24, U.S. District Court Judge Paul J. McCormick, who had presided over the *Finley* v. *MCA* case, upheld the final verdict but overturned the jury's decision on the damages awarded to Finley, indicating that, upon reconsideration, "the jury's fixation of the damages for the inquiry to the plaintiffs by reason of defendants' wrongdoing does not conform to the yardstick of certainty required by the decisions of the courts of the United States."[3]

Ironically, just the previous month, Larry Finley—who ended up winning only his attorney's fees—had booked his first MCA band, Tiny Hill and his orchestra, into Mission Beach for a two-week stand. All communications and contracts between Finley and MCA were handled by mail, and not a word about the booking was breathed to Pacific Square, which, by then, had been sold by Dailard.

The court's equivocation in the Finley case quickly put a damper on the whole MCA investigation in Washington. In the Justice Department's rather condescending August 12 reply to the Los Angeles office's request for the FBI investigation, George B. Haddock, special assistant to the U.S. attorney general, wrote: "The attorney general has expressed a personal interest in this investigation. . . . [But] at most it would appear that MCA is monopolizing the business of placing name bands, or, stated otherwise, the business of supplying name band entertainment. . . . The trouble here is the fact that bands are not fungible, and it would be an extremely difficult thing to draw any distinction between name bands and non-name bands on the basis of merit of the entertainment they produce. The non-name band of today becomes the name band of tomorrow. Usually, where we attempt to charge monopolization, we have involved a commodity capable of specific definition on some basis other than the price which is being paid for it as of the time the complaint is filed."

Haddock concluded his letter by telling his West Coast colleagues that before the Justice Department "can proceed intelligently with further investigation, it will be necessary to outline with greater clarity the theory upon which the investigation is based."[4]

The Los Angeles Antitrust Division was buoyed by a four-part story about MCA that appeared in the *Saturday Evening Post* in August 1946. Entitled "Star-Spangled Octopus," it was written by David G. Wittels.

According to a former top official at MCA, the agency had been approached by Wittels early in his investigation. He gave its executives the option of cooperating and allowing their version of the facts to be known—or not cooperating and letting the chips fall where they may. "At first," the MCA executive said, "the decision was made to give him the runaround, send him to the PR department and the general counsel's office, that type of thing. Then, Stein decided to open up to the *Post*. As things turned out, we probably came out of it a lot better. The story probably did us a lot of good. . . . The only bad thing was that people got wise to our operations and saw how we worked."

Much of Wittels's information appeared to come from the reports prepared by the Justice Department's Antitrust Division, except that Wittels was able to go further with detail and piece together the story of Frank Sinatra's experience with MCA.

Sinatra had originally been a vocalist for Harry James, who became an MCA client. Later, Sinatra went with Tommy Dorsey, who was also under contract with MCA. But, although Sinatra was a big hit with both James and Dorsey, MCA never offered him a personal contract. Finally, in 1942, Sinatra left Dorsey and went out on his own.* However, there was a price for his freedom. Sinatra had to give one-third of his future earnings to Dorsey—and another ten percent to Dorsey's manager.

However, Mafia leader "Lucky" Luciano wrote in his memoirs that he was instrumental in the rise of Sinatra's career. "When the time came when some dough was needed to put Frank across with the public," Luciano wrote, "the guys put up. . . . He needed publicity, clothes, different kinds of special music things, and they all cost quite a bit of money—I think it was about fifty or sixty grand. I okayed the money and it came out of the fund, even though some guys put up a little extra on a personal basis. It all helped him become a big star and he was just showin' his appreciation by comin' down to Havana to say hello to me."[5] Sinatra has denied any contact other than meeting Luciano once.

The following year, Sinatra was signed by the General Amusement Corporation and became a huge success. At that point, MCA approached Sinatra, telling him that MCA could do a better job for him than GAC. Sinatra tried to get out of his contract with GAC, but GAC refused. The singer then pretended that he had a bad throat and

---

*Sinatra was allegedly helped in his departure from Dorsey's band by New Jersey mobster Willie Moretti, a neighbor of Sinatra's. According to published reports, Moretti supposedly made Dorsey an offer he could not refuse, forcing the bandleader to cancel the contract at gunpoint. Sinatra has denied this story, and Moretti was murdered in a gangland-style slaying in 1951.

couldn't sing. The MCA agent went to GAC and told its executives that Sinatra was unhappy with them, and that MCA was going to start booking Sinatra for no commission. Still, GAC refused to relent.

"Above all, there was the matter of the 33⅓ percent to Dorsey, ten percent to Dorsey's manager, and now ten percent to the booking agents," Wittels wrote. "That made a total of 53⅓ percent before taxes —not counting what he [Sinatra] was paying a press agent, writers, and Alex Stordahl, a crack arranger who had left Dorsey to follow him. The money was rolling in beyond his wildest dreams, but he was practically broke."

Sinatra then threatened to go to his union, the American Guild of Variety Artists (AGVA), the vaudeville union. Under union rules, if a performer can show that his agent is not getting him work, he can demand his release from the agency. GAC's dilemma was clear: if it battled Sinatra in front of the AVGA and lost, they would lose Sinatra and a lot of money. If GAC won, Sinatra might still refuse to perform, and GAC would still lose.

MCA's squeeze of GAC worked.

Screaming "foul," GAC finally capitulated and gave Sinatra to MCA —with the proviso that GAC would receive a cut of Sinatra's future business. "In return for relinquishing its client, General Amusement gets half of MCA's ten-percent commissions on Sinatra until November 30, 1948, the expiration date of the old contract. If Sinatra signs again with MCA after that, General Amusement is to get one quarter of MCA's commissions as long as he remains an MCA client."[6]

However, the Antitrust Division's investigation of MCA could not be saved by the Wittels series. Once again, the case remained dormant.

Meantime, earlier that summer, Tom C. Clark, who had become U.S. attorney general,* gave a speech before the Chicago Bar Association, announcing that the United States was the target of "a sinister and deep-seated plot on the part of the communists, ideologists, and a small group of radicals." Adding that he had received evidence of a conspiracy to take over labor unions, to provoke workers to strike, and to challenge civil authorities, he attacked those lawyers who offered their legal services to those involved.[7]

Clark's comments signaled a call to arms, one which would deeply affect Hollywood in the years to come.

---

*In 1949, Clark was appointed as an associate Supreme Court justice by President Harry Truman.

CHAPTER EIGHT

THE SCREEN ACTORS GUILD (SAG) was founded on June 30, 1933, as a result of demands by the motion picture studios the previous March that all contract and free-lance actors accept a fifty-percent and twenty-percent cut, respectively, in wages. In response, the actors/organizers held a series of secret meetings in secluded locations. Such safeguards were taken because previous attempts to form an actors' union were received with actor blacklists drawn up by studio executives.

The first SAG board of directors was composed of Leon Ames, Clay Clement, James Gleason, Lucille Gleason, Boris Karloff, Claude King, Noel Madison, Ralph Morgan, Alan Mowbray, Bradley Page, Ivan Simpson, Alden Gay Thomson, Richard Tucker, Arthur Vinton, and Morgan Wallace. Ralph Morgan was selected as SAG's first president; Kenneth Thomson—who was later accused of being "a friend of the mob" but was credited with having a hand in driving Bioff out of Hollywood—was appointed its executive secretary; and Laurence Beilenson, the attorney for the Screen Writers Guild—which had also been created in 1933—became its general counsel.

Within months of SAG's creation, other actors joined, including Edward Arnold, Ralph Bellamy, James Cagney, Eddie Cantor, Gary

Cooper, Miriam Hopkins, Groucho Marx, Robert Montgomery, Paul Muni, George Raft, and Spencer Tracy. By the end of its first year, SAG had nearly 2,000 members.

In the midst of its efforts for recognition from the studios, SAG became a member of the American Federation of Labor in 1935. Two years later, on May 7, 1937, a mass information meeting of actors was held at the Hollywood Legion Stadium; earlier, ninety-eight percent of the membership voted to strike if the studios failed to negotiate a contract with the new union. Dramatically, as in a scene from a movie, Robert Montgomery, who had succeeded Eddie Cantor as SAG president in 1935, walked up to the podium and read a letter from the studios to the large crowd. "We wish to express ourselves as being in favor of the Guild shop. . . . We expect to have contracts drawn between the Screen Actors Guild and the studios before the expiration of this week." The letter was signed by Louis B. Mayer and Joseph M. Schenck. Montgomery declared that the moment was "the victory of an ideal."

From the outset, SAG fought hard for its membership, particularly those who had not achieved star status. In its first contract, which was signed by thirteen producers, minimum-pay rates were set and continuous employment guaranteed, as well as the establishment of an arbitration clause. Before this contract, some actors were making very little money with no benefits, amidst slave-like working conditions. If these lower-paid actors complained about their long hours of work and the cavalier treatment of them by the studios, they could easily find themselves back out on the streets, ending their dreams of Hollywood stardom.

The Guild was not a typical labor union. It was run at the top by mostly wealthy, established stars—who were largely politically conservative—while the majority of the rank and file was comprised of struggling or out-of-work actors, who were generally far more liberal.

Ronald Reagan joined the Screen Actors Guild soon after receiving his first movie contract with Warner Brothers in 1937. Although he was then supposedly a moderate, he had come to SAG at first only with reluctance. "I must admit," Reagan said, "I was not sold on the idea right away. I was doing all right for myself; a union seemed unnecessary. It was Helen Broderick, that fine actress, who nailed me in a corner of the commissary one day at Warners, after I'd made a crack about having to join a union, and gave me an hour's lecture on the facts of life. After that I turned really eager and I have considered myself a rabid union man ever since."[1]

Born in Tampico, Illinois, on February 6, 1911, Reagan was the son of Jack Reagan, a hard-drinking, first-generation Irishman, and Nelle Reagan, a kind and sensitive, well-read woman of Scotch and English descent. In 1920, the Reagan family moved to Dixon, ninety miles from Chicago. A football star in high school, Reagan received his undergraduate degree from Eureka College, a Christian church school in southern Illinois. An athlete and an actor in school plays, Reagan—nicknamed "Dutch"—began working as a radio announcer with station WOC in Davenport, Iowa, and then later with WHO, a 50,000-watt station in Des Moines, Iowa, as a sports announcer. On Saturday nights, Reagan sometimes hosted WHO's popular barn dance, which featured dance bands and other entertainment. In his free time, Reagan frequented Si's Moonlight Inn and, on occasion, "he visited the nearby Club Belvedere, which had a casino,* [but Reagan] didn't gamble."[2]

Reagan's entry into the film industry came quite innocently. One night Reagan met Joy Hodges, a former WHO employee who had gone to Hollywood and started a singing career with Jimmy Grier's orchestra. She encouraged him to look her up in Los Angeles when he went on spring training with the Chicago Cubs. Later, she introduced him to talent agent William Meiklejohn, who thought he had discovered another Robert Taylor and set up a screen test for him at Warner Brothers.

Warners hired him at two hundred dollars a week. In his first film, *Love Is on the Air,* he played Andy McLeod, a radio announcer who was trying to expose the mob's control of local politicians.

Reagan's executive producer at Warners was Bryan Foy, a former Democratic ward politician from Chicago. Known to have business and social contacts with Chicago Mafia figures, including Johnny Roselli and Willie Bioff, Foy produced the first one-hundred-percent-talking

---

*According to an Iowa law-enforcement official, the gambling operations of the Club Belvedere were conducted "by the Chicago Mafia. . . . The man who ran things for the Capone people in this state at the time was [Charles] 'Cherry Nose' Gioe [later convicted in the Bioff/Browne/Schenck scandal]." According to a government report, Gioe, a close friend of Sidney Korshak, had interests in hotels and restaurants in the Midwest. In 1928, he became the Chicago mob's representative in Iowa, "bootlegging liquor into Iowa from Wisconsin," according to the report. After Prohibition, Gioe remained in Iowa until 1939 to oversee the Chicago underworld's gambling interests at such places as the Club Belvedere. There is no evidence that Reagan and Gioe were acquainted, although it was well known that Chicago underworld figures operating in Iowa "had a special interest in college athletes and sports writers," according to a Chicago law-enforcement official.

Among those writers approached was crime reporter Clark Mollenhoff, who worked for Iowa's *Des Moines Register* and later won a Pulitzer Prize. Mollenhoff said that he was approached by one man, who he did not know was a Mafia figure, who "offered to pick up the tab for me for a weekend 'you won't forget' in St. Louis or Chicago. I am sure now that I never would have forgotten that weekend; I wouldn't have been permitted to do so. But at the time it seemed like a generous offer made by a nice fellow who was misunderstood by the Chicago police."[3]

movie, Warners' *Lights of New York,* in 1928 and later became known as the "King of the Bs," because of his money-making, second-rate movies. He was the eldest son of Eddie Foy and part of the family vaudeville act, the Seven Little Foys.*

"I soon learned," Reagan said, "that I could go in to Brynie and tell him that I had been laid off, but couldn't take it at the moment because of all my expenses. He would pick up the phone, call a couple of his henchmen, and actually get a picture going on four or five days' notice —just to put me back on salary."[4]

Reagan starred in thirty-one movies between 1937 and 1943, and became known as "the Errol Flynn of the Bs." His most heralded roles were in *Brother Rat* in 1938, *Dark Victory*† in 1939, and *Knute Rockne, All-American,* portraying the tragic George Gipp, in 1940. With his role in the 1942 production of *King's Row*—playing a man whose legs have just been amputated and who exclaims, "Where's the rest of me?" —Reagan achieved a degree of star status.

During the first four years of his acting career, when his earnings rose from eight hundred dollars a month to $1,650 a week, Reagan had been represented by William Meiklejohn. In 1940, MCA bought out Meiklejohn's agency and absorbed his clients—who included Reagan, Jane Wyman, and William Demarest. Meiklejohn then became head of MCA's studio talent department, and Lew Wasserman became Reagan's principal agent. Based on the success of *King's Row* in 1942, Wasserman renegotiated Reagan's contract with Warner Brothers, obtaining a deal that paid Reagan $3,500 a week for seven years. The deal gave Reagan the distinction of being Wasserman's first "million-dollar client."

MCA executive Taft Schreiber explained that Reagan had possessed an unusual quality, which had endeared him to the MCA management team from the start. Unlike many other actors, Reagan accepted MCA's career guidance without a fuss. "He had only this one agency," Schreiber said. "This was it. It wasn't the agent's fault if things didn't go well. Most actors blamed their agents. He understood. He had a very sound grasp of the situation."[5]

Reagan spent most of his time during World War II serving his

---

*Foy's younger brother, Eddie Foy, Jr., was featured in three of Reagan's movies: *Going Places, Code of the Secret Service,* and *Murder in the Air.*

†*Dark Victory*—a drama about a wealthy young woman who develops a brain tumor, goes blind, and then dies—was based on an unsuccessful Broadway play starring Tallulah Bankhead. Using her influence with Jack Warner, Bette Davis convinced him to allow her to star in the movie. The movie was beaten out for Best Picture by *Gone With the Wind.* Vivien Leigh won over Davis for Best Actress. In *Dark Victory,* Reagan plays Davis's young and charming but rarely sober friend.

military tour of duty stateside. Reagan explained, "Lew Wasserman of MCA reminded me of a war that was going on, of Hollywood stars like Jimmy Stewart who had already been drafted, and of my own reserve-officer status. He said, 'We don't know how much time you have—let's get what we can while we can.' "[6] Because of bad eyesight—which disqualified him from combat—he was stationed at Fort Mason in San Francisco as a liaison officer before being transferred to Hollywood by the Army Air Corps to narrate military training films. He served as a lieutenant in the First Motion Picture Unit of the Army Air Corps, located at the nine-acre studio in Culver City once owned by producer Hal Roach and thus nicknamed "Fort Roach" and "The Culver City Commandos." His commander was Albert Paul Mantz, the famous movie stunt pilot who was later killed while performing. Other stars, like Alan Ladd, Clark Gable, Gig Young, and Van Heflin, joined Reagan in filming morale-boosting movies for the army.*

On August 8, 1946, after Reagan returned from the service, Billy Wilkerson, the right-wing publisher of *The Hollywood Reporter*, who had admitted his working relationship with Willie Bioff, wrote an editorial, calling the American Veterans Committee, of which Reagan was a member, "fronters," a euphemism for communists. Reagan defended the AVC, saying, "At the recent AVC National Convention in Des Moines, Iowa, a tentative pink infiltration was met and dealt with in true democratic fashion. . . . Of course, to deny that there are some 'commies' aboard would be ridiculous as those guys inkle [*sic*] in just about every place."

The following week, an anonymous letter from "A Wounded Marine" was published in *The Hollywood Reporter* as a cheap-shot reply to Reagan. "I remember during the war how Reagan, as a Cutting Room Commando at Fort Roach, so bravely fought the war from the polished nightclub floors of Hollywood, while some of us wallowed in the blood and guts of a dark South Sea Island front. . . . I went to a couple of meetings of AVC and if that isn't loaded with Molotov vermin then Joe Stalin is getting ready to become a minister."

On August 22, actors/combat veterans Eddie Albert, Douglas Fairbanks, Jr., Melvyn Douglas, William Holden, and Congressional Medal of Honor winner Audie Murphy, among others, wrote in *The Hollywood Reporter*, "The attack on Ronald Reagan is an attack on all in

---

*During the war, the 3,503 members of the Screen Actors Guild made 25,925 free appearances in support of the Allied war effort; 150 SAG members participated in front-line USO camp shows; and 1,574 Armed Forces Radio broadcasts were made by members. Aside from the work done by Reagan and his colleagues at Fort Roach, thirty-seven short films were distributed to 16,000 theatres.[7]

our community who served during the war in work for which their valuable motion picture training fitted them, work which had to be done at home."*8

In the midst of this fracas, the Screen Actors Guild held nominations for its executive board. Robert Montgomery, who had been SAG president from 1935 to 1938, was elected to replace outgoing president George Murphy, who had served since 1944. Ronald Reagan was nominated to serve as SAG's third vice-president.

Reagan had become increasingly involved in union politics through his first wife, actress Jane Wyman, who was a member of the SAG board and convinced its members to appoint him to a vacant alternate seat in 1941.†

Prior to his election as third vice-president of the SAG board, Reagan had been appointed as an alternate board member on two other occasions. In February 1946, he was named alternate to actor Rex Ingram, and the following month he became Boris Karloff's alternate.

Reagan has always maintained that he volunteered his services to SAG for totally unselfish motives. However, some of his critics, including some SAG board members, have charged that, under the surface, he viewed the Guild as a source of power and status. "Undoubtedly, Reagan's film career shows," one observer said, "that he went into politics only when he was washed up as an actor."9

---

*Wilkerson later apologized to Reagan.

†Reagan and the twenty-four-year-old Wyman had met in 1938 after being cast as sweethearts in the film *Brother Rat*. They were married two years later, on January 26, 1940. It was Reagan's first marriage and Wyman's second; she had earlier been married less than a year to a Los Angeles businessman. Hollywood gossip columnists—particularly Louella Parsons, who was from Reagan's hometown, and who had announced their engagement and held their wedding reception at her home—called their relationship "one of the great romances of the century." Hollywood hype aside, Reagan and Wyman starred together in three undistinguished movies in 1940: *Brother Rat and a Baby, An Angel from Texas,* and *Tugboat Annie Sails Again,* as Warner Brothers and Bryan Foy tried to cash in on their all-American couple.

CHAPTER NINE

THE HIGHLIGHT of Reagan's early years on the SAG board was his role in the power struggle between the 16,000-member International Alliance of State and Theatrical Employees (IATSE) and the Conference of Studio Unions (CSU).

Despite IATSE's claims that it had reformed itself from the days the union was controlled by the Mafia, the same seven members who had sat on its executive board during the Bioff-Browne reign remained in place—including its new New York–based international president, a forty-five-year-old Irish-American, Richard Walsh, who had been a vice-president under Browne. Consequently, there were numerous charges that the gangsterism within IATSE had not been removed, only replaced. The new IATSE response to such attacks was identical to Bioff and Browne's: that their critics were obviously communists. Asked about the situation in his union, Walsh replied, "That's a problem I don't talk about at all. . . . A good president never takes responsibility for anything."[1]

A big, tough Nebraskan, Roy Brewer was appointed as the union's international representative in March 1945 and sent to Hollywood. Born in 1909 in Nebraska's Cairo Hall County, Brewer had attended Baptist College in Grand Island for one semester and studied law through LaSalle Extension University. In 1926, he started working as a projectionist in a local theatre, and, the following year, was elected secretary of the Grand Island Central Labor Union, as well as vice-president of the Nebraska State Federation of Labor. In 1933, at twenty-three, he was elected president of the federation, a post he held until 1944. Briefly, in 1935, he worked with Tom C. Clark as a compliance officer under the National Recovery Administration—which worked in cooperation with the Justice Department when NRA codes were violated. While working in the Office of Labor Production of the War Production Board, he received his Hollywood assignment from IATSE.

Instead of trying to rid the union of its gangster image and all remnants of mob control, Brewer was obsessed with eliminating "the communist influence" within the union and the movie industry in general. "When Browne [and Bioff] went to jail," Brewer insisted, "that ended any connection with the mob in the IATSE." When pressed on his claim that the Mafia no longer existed in Hollywood, Brewer replied, "When Walsh was beginning to deal with these problems—he had an awful fight to save Hollywood and to convince the government, too, that he was not tainted with this, really—he went along with them [the Mafia], he did some things." Without elaborating, Brewer said, "Walsh had done a good job of cleaning up the mob. . . ."

Shifting his attention away from the problem of the Mafia's infiltration of his union, Brewer continued, "The truth is, [the communists] had this town in the palm of their hands; they were calling the shots. . . . They had 360-some people who have been clearly and positively identified as dues-paying members of the Communist Party. We had other [information] that top stars, top directors, and top producers [were involved], and they were kicking in five percent of their salaries to the Communist Party's coffers. And they were making salaries of up to $5,000 a week."[2]

Along with several members of Hollywood's ultraconservative community—such as producer Walt Disney; actors Robert Taylor, Gary Cooper, and John Wayne; columnist Hedda Hopper; and Hollywood Teamsters leader Joe Tuohy—Roy Brewer was an officer of the Motion Picture Alliance for the Preservation of American Ideals, which was allied with the studios and heavily supported by newspaper mogul William Randolph Hearst. According to the group's "Statement of Principles," the Alliance was created because "in our special field of motion pictures, we resent the growing impression that this industry is made up of, and dominated by, communists, radicals and crackpots. . . . We pledge to fight, with every means at our organized command, any effort of any group or individual to divert the loyalty of the screen from the free America that gave it birth."

Jeff Kibre, the leader of the IATSE progressives, had proven to be instrumental in the final downfall of Bioff, Browne, and Joe Schenck. However, after the Schenck confession and the Bioff-Browne convictions, Kibre, who had performed so heroically against the mob but was an admitted communist, was immediately blackballed by, among others, the studios, the Alliance, and IATSE. Unwelcome in the Hollywood community, Kibre eventually became an organizer for the United Auto Workers and later helped organize the fishermen's union.

Jeff Kibre's legacy of pro-union, anti-corruption militancy fell upon Herb Sorrell, a stocky former boxer with a flat nose. A former business agent with the Hollywood painters' union, Motion Picture Painters Local 644, Sorrell, in 1942, created the Conference of Studio Unions, "a coalition of five dissatisfied AFL locals (the Screen Cartoonists Guild, the Screen Office Employees Guild, Film Technicians Local 683, Machinists Local 1185, and Motion Picture Painters Local 644)." By 1945, CSU had added the carpenters' union and three other locals to the fold.[3]

Sorrell continued to denounce the ongoing corruption and Mafia influence within IATSE. As CSU became bigger and more popular, Brewer and the Alliance began to view him as a serious threat. Brewer attacked the CSU as "communist-dominated" and claimed Sorrell "followed the Communist Party line."

"We were fighting for our lives," said Brewer. "It's either the communists or us."

Using the red-baiting line, Brewer, IATSE, and the Motion Picture Alliance began waging a public relations war against CSU.

Although Sorrell had supported a variety of left-wing causes and received support from Harry Bridges, the militant president of the International Longshoremens and Warehousemens Union, he always denied throughout his career that he was or ever had been a communist. Unsophisticated in many ways, Sorrell was still viewed by most of the Hollywood community as being a dedicated and honest union man who operated a clean, honest, and democratic labor organization.

In March 1945, Sorrell called a CSU strike in Hollywood as a result of a jurisdictional dispute between CSU and IATSE over the representation of Hollywood's skilled, behind-the-camera workers. A three-member arbitration committee from the AFL had supported the United Brotherhood of Carpenters, a member of the CSU coalition of trade unions, over IATSE's newly formed "set-erectors union." However, both IATSE and the motion picture studios had ignored this and other pro-CSU judgments by the AFL, even when its president, William Green, personally intervened.

"The relationship with the employers and [IATSE] has always been a close one," Brewer said. "We fought each other, but the point is that we lived in an industry, and we had the industry and its welfare in common. Our leaders have always understood that if they [the studios] didn't make money, we wouldn't get it. So you had to help them make money to get it."[4]

On October 5, 1945, hundreds of CSU members picketing outside the gates of Warner Brothers were pelted by tear gas thrown by pro-IATSE goons and strikebreakers—who then used chains, rubber hoses, and blackjacks to attack the CSU partisans. While the fire department turned their hoses on them, knocking them off their feet, police officers moved in and beat the protesters with their clubs.[5]

In other incidents, Brewer and Hollywood Teamsters leader Joe Tuohy packed buses with union goons and sent them crashing through the CSU picket lines. Those strikers who interfered were pummeled by the legbreakers or arrested by the police, who clearly supported IATSE, the Teamsters, and the studios. Later, Tuohy—who had defied a membership vote not to cross the CSU picket lines—was hired by Joe Schenck as an "industrial relations director" for Schenck's National Theaters. In his new position, Tuohy made a four-hundred-dollar-a-week salary, a raise of $275 a week over what he made as a union official.

Brewer admitted soliciting the Teamsters to break the CSU picket line. "Well, there was some Teamsters thing that was questionable," Brewer said, "but they were on our side and, as far as I was concerned, I was with fellows who were trade unionists. They were our allies."[6]

Brewer continued, "We took the people through. I was there. We got the buses, we made the arrangements. The studios were reluctant, but they cooperated. We ordered our men to go in and make the sets. . . . We had a riotous condition." But, Brewer insisted, "We never engaged in any violence . . . the police were cooperating with us."[7]

Reagan agreed with Brewer—that CSU was behind the violence. "[A] thousand strikers had massed at Warners," Reagan said. "Three autos had been overturned, clubs, chains, bottles, bricks, and two-by-fours were used freely. Now various homes of the IATSE members were bombed by night; other workers were ambushed and slugged."[8]

Father George H. Dunne, a Roman Catholic priest, had been commissioned by *Commonweal,* a liberal Catholic weekly, to make an investigation of the labor dispute in Hollywood. Dunne's report suggested a different story:

"The producers and the IATSE leadership have always reacted very sensitively when the Browne-Bioff era has been introduced into the discussion of Hollywood's labor disputes. They pretend it has nothing to do with the present. They would like the public to think that there has been a complete change since those days. . . . Actually little has changed.

"The men who made the deals with Browne and Bioff, and through them with the notorious Chicago gang, still run the industry. The same men who sat in council with Browne and Bioff as heads of the IATSE still run the union. . . .

"Browne and Bioff, thanks to the government, have gone. The other people are the same. Their methods are the same.

"The record is clear. It is a shameful record of collaboration between the producers and the leadership of IATSE, first to betray the interests of the IATSE members themselves and, in the later period, to destroy the opposition of democratic trade unionism represented by the Conference of Studio Organizations."[9]

Reagan brushed Dunne and his report off, saying, "George Murphy [SAG president from 1944 to 1946] and I decided he must be the victim of a snow job."[10]

Referring to his close ties to IATSE and the Teamsters during the strike, Dunne had also been critical in his report of Ronald Reagan, "whose Rover Boy activities helped mightily to confuse the issues."[11]

In 1946, the National Labor Relations Board—which Brewer claimed "was completely under the control of the communists"—again ruled in favor of CSU over IATSE in another jurisdictional dispute over Hollywood decorators. IATSE and the studios ignored that decision as well. Again, CSU struck in July 1946 for three days in protest. The strike was effective—as SAG helped to negotiate a short-lived peace agreement called "The Treaty of Beverly Hills," which provided for a twenty-five–percent wage increase. But CSU's success was to be short-lived.

By September 1946, during the third and final CSU strike—which began after Walt Disney red-baited his cartoonists, who were also CSU members—the studios turned the work stoppage into a lock-out of nearly all of the CSU membership, especially the carpenters and the painters, most of whom would later be blacklisted. After initially remaining neutral in the CSU strike, the SAG membership, persuaded by Montgomery, Murphy, and Reagan, voted to cross the CSU picket lines.

In his condemnation of CSU, Reagan said, "What the communists wanted to do in terms of the CSU strike was to shut down the industry, and when everybody was angry and dissatisfied with their unions for their failures, the communists would propose one big union for Hollywood. . . ."

Reagan said that in the midst of the final CSU strike, the SAG leadership was, on occasion, protected by IATSE members. Reagan even hired his own armed bodyguard and carried a .32-caliber Smith & Wesson pistol as he crossed the CSU picket line on his way to work at Warner Brothers. He claimed that he had received an anonymous telephone call threatening that "a squad was ready to take care of me and fix my face so that I'd never work in pictures again."[12]

He has since said and resaid that "a handful of Teamsters" protected him from bodily harm when SAG and IATSE were engaged in pitched combat with the "communists." He never has given any further details about the incident.

Recalling the violence in the IATSE-CSU dispute, Reagan said, "None of us yet believed that what a few anonymous people wanted was exactly what was happening in Hollywood—a state of chaos. . . . Pat Casey, the producers' labor negotiator, said the situation was 'explosive.' "[13]

Casey, who had been working to settle labor disputes with the Motion Picture Producers and Distributors Association, had been directly involved in the IATSE-CSU dispute, protecting the interests of the studios. Supporting the IATSE-SAG faction because of its long-term ties with MPPDA, Casey remained in the background of the dispute. Among Casey's employees had been Johnny Roselli, who previously served as an "undercover agent" with the firm.

Was the Mafia in any way involved in the Hollywood violence? Academy Award–winning producer Irving Allen, who had no sympathy for the communists, said, "When there was a labor problem in the studios—and they were always coming up then—the studios would go to Sidney Korshak [a long-time Roselli associate] and hire him as their lawyer. And he was always able to solve them. He was very good. He was able to solve . . . most of the problems in this town.* And, from my point of view, he earned his fee."[15]

When asked whether Korshak was involved in the studios' and IATSE's war with CSU, Brewer was less than direct: "He didn't have much to do with it. . . . I don't know what he did, if he did anything. He may have appeared, but he wasn't a major factor. Maybe I did know him, but I can't remember everybody. I don't want to take anything from him or give him anything. He may be very well informed . . . but I don't know him."[16]

On March 10, 1947, the Screen Actors Guild selected Ronald Reagan to complete the unfinished term of Robert Montgomery, who, among other board members, had to resign as president because he was also a film producer and, thus, according to SAG's by-laws, not permitted to hold office in the Guild.

According to the SAG board minutes of that March 10 meeting: "Four resignations from members of the board of directors were presented: Robert Montgomery, president; Franchot Tone, 1st vice-president; Dick Powell, 2nd vice-president; and James Cagney. These letters of resignation explained that each of the actors now has a financial interest in the production of the pictures in which they appear, and that while their primary interest will always be that of actors, they do not feel that they should hold office in the Guild while their present status in the industry continues, particularly in view of the fact that the Guild will soon be going into negotiations for its new contract.

"At this point, John Garfield, Harpo Marx, and Dennis O'Keefe stated that they were in approximately the same position as the above-named officers, and, therefore, each of them offered his resignation as of this date and left the meeting."

That same month, a U.S. House Special Subcommittee on Labor

---

*At the time, the Los Angeles–based Korshak was heavily involved with labor unions, either defending them or buying them off, depending on who was paying his fee. In 1946, he was retained by Joel Goldblatt, president of a chain of department stores in Chicago, who had become the target of extortion demands in return for labor peace. "Mr. Korshak acted as an intermediary between Mr. Goldblatt and the union officials," *The New York Times* reported, "resolving the company's labor difficulties and relieving Mr. Goldblatt of the need to be personally involved in payoffs."[14]

By 1947, Korshak had started representing several other large Chicago companies and manufacturers, including Spiegel, Inc., the mail-order house. However, most of Korshak's time was spent helping these companies avoid legitimate union organizing.

Among Korshak's clients was the vice-president of the First National Bank of Chicago, Walter Heymann—who was also Goldblatt's banker. Korshak helped First National and other banks with their labor problems. Heymann later became a member of MCA's board of directors.

began to investigate the IATSE-CSU situation. However, Pennsylvania Republican Carroll D. Kearns,* who chaired the subcommittee, made a deal with IATSE and the studios before the hearings began in which no testimony would be heard about charges of the Mafia's influence on IATSE. According to Father Dunne's report in *Commonweal,* "He [Kearns] was visibly pained by any remark, however indirect, that called into question their [IATSE's and the studios'] sincerity, integrity, and good faith. He seemed to regard these men who for years connived with the filthiest elements of the underworld as paragons of virtue."[17]

Just before Kearns arrived in Hollywood, Sorrell was kidnapped and beaten by three men—one of whom was wearing a police officer's uniform. The battered Sorrell was then dropped in the desert.

At the same time, Brewer and an array of politicians and studio executives prompted the House Un-American Activities Committee hearings investigating the film industry. The first round of HUAC hearings began that October, and the Brewer partisans hoped to destroy the CSU and the left-wing artists who supported it once and for all. Chaired by J. Parnell Thomas, a New Jersey Republican—and with Representative Richard M. Nixon of California on the panel—HUAC subpoenaed forty-one witnesses, nineteen of whom were considered "unfriendly" and unwilling to testify. Thirteen of "The Nineteen" were Jewish, prompting charges that the investigation had anti-Semitic overtones.

Among the friendly witnesses who testified were SAG president Reagan, former SAG presidents Montgomery and Murphy, SAG board member Robert Taylor, and Roy Brewer. Reagan told the committee, "There has been a small clique within the Screen Actors Guild which has consistently opposed the policies of the Guild Board and officers of the Guild, as evidenced by votes on various issues. That small clique referred to has been suspected of more or less following the tactics we associate with the Communist Party." At the end of his testimony, however, Reagan upheld the rights of others to free speech and their participation in the electoral process. "I detest, I abhor their [the Communist Party's] philosophy, but . . . ," Reagan said, "I never as a citizen want to see our country become urged, by either fear or resentment of this group, that we ever compromise with any of our democratic principles through that fear or resentment [*sic*]."

On November 24 and 25, 1947, motion picture executives met at the Waldorf-Astoria Hotel in New York to decide how the studios were

---

*Representative Kearns, a musician and a music teacher, had been an active member of the Petrillo-led American Federation of Musicians.

going to deal with communists in the film industry and, in particular, those who defied HUAC. The executives decided to sacrifice ten Holly-wood artists—eight writers and two directors who had been charged with contempt of Congress by the committee. The Hollywood blacklist had been born.

"The producers, meeting en masse in New York, put out what was called the 'Waldorf Declaration,' " Reagan said in his defense of the action. "They agreed none of them would knowingly employ commu-nists or those who refused to answer questions about their affiliations. The communists were among those who reacted in Hollywood by distorting any facts they got, claiming they were victims of a 'blacklist' —when they were actually working members of a conspiracy directed by Soviet Russia against the United States. In war, that is treason and the name for such is a traitor; in peace, it is apparently martyr. It is easy to call oneself a 'political party' and hide other motives behind it: the Mafia can do it, so can a Chicago mob of gangsters. My own test for the time when the communists may call themselves a legitimate politi-cal party is that time when, in the USSR, an effective anti-communist political party wins an election. At that time, I shall withdraw my objections to labeling communists 'political.' "[18]

Consequently, before the Kearns subcommittee—which had surpris-ingly criticized IATSE's close association with the studios—and HUAC had adjourned their hearings, Herb Sorrell and the CSU were fired from their jobs. The CSU simply dematerialized. The Hollywood Ten were convicted of contempt of Congress and imprisoned, leaving Brewer, IATSE, and their allies with a closed shop, in firm control of Hollywood.*

The battle to rid Hollywood of all suspected communists was the bond that continued to cement the alliance between the Reagan-led SAG and the Brewer-controlled IATSE, even after the CSU had been purged. During these postwar years, Reagan became a close friend and associate of Brewer—who became the keeper of the Hollywood black-list and continued to turn his back on the Mafia's involvement in the film industry.

HUAC returned to Hollywood in March 1951. Forty-five "un-friendly witnesses" were immediately subpoenaed, as the committee sought to force those testifying to name names of those they knew or thought to be communists.

---

*Ironically, HUAC chairman J. Parnell Thomas was later indicted and convicted for taking kickbacks, and sent to Danbury Penitentiary—while two members of the Hollywood Ten, Lester Cole and Ring Lardner, Jr., were imprisoned there.

During these hearings, thirty members of the Hollywood community —in desperate, and often unsuccessful, attempts to save their jobs— named nearly three hundred of their colleagues as members or former members of the Communist Party. With communism appearing to be rampant in the film industry, the studios panicked and began cranking out anti-communist movies—which mostly contained old gangster movie plots, except that the gangsters were now replaced by communists who machine-gunned patriotic Americans and then sped off in fast cars. Two movies, Richard Widmark's *Pickup on South Street* and George Raft's *A Bullet for Joey,* actually portrayed the Mafia teaming up with the police to fight zombie-like communists.

Arthur Miller had earlier been approached by director Elia Kazan to write a movie about the Mafia on the waterfront and had already drafted a screenplay, entitled *The Hook,* that was to be produced by Columbia—which then withdrew from the project. "The reason, according to Miller, [was] that Harry Cohn, Roy Brewer, and the FBI all suggested that Miller should substitute reds for racketeers as the force terrorizing the waterfront workers. When Miller said no, Cohn fired off a telegram to him which said, 'Strange how the minute we want to make a script pro-American, Miller pulls out.' "*[19]

Cheering on HUAC once again was the Motion Picture Alliance for the Preservation of American Ideals—with John Wayne as president and IATSE's Roy Brewer and the Teamsters' Joe Tuohy on its executive committee. Credited with "cleansing" the communists from Hollywood's labor unions, Brewer had remained the Alliance's chief enforcer and the keeper of the growing Hollywood blacklist.

In the end, HUAC blacklisted or "graylisted" nearly two thousand artists in the motion picture, radio, and television industries. Roy Brewer insisted, "The communists created the blacklist, themselves— or they brought it on themselves by making a record. And, first of all, they blacklisted the anti-communists to whatever extent that they could. . . . There never would've been a blacklist if the communists hadn't come in here and seduced these people and got them to pay money to further the cause of the Soviet Union and to discriminate against the people who didn't like it."[20]

Soon after the HUAC hearings, Brewer, who had been Hollywood's most powerful union force, went to work for the studios of Allied Artists, employed as the "manager of branch operations." Brewer's

---

*Kazan later directed Budd Schulberg's anti-Mafia, pro-informer screenplay *On the Waterfront,* and Miller later wrote the anti-Mafia but anti-informer *A View from the Bridge.*

responsibilities included the handling of labor relations, except that this time he sat on management's side of the table.

With his departure from the union, Brewer was honored by a story appearing in *The Hollywood Reporter* stating: "It was Brewer who was responsible for the restoration of labor peace in Hollywood; it was he who was responsible for the routing of communists in the motion picture industry. . . . It was he who was mainly responsible for the creation of a public relations program which did so much to make of Hollywood what Rep. Donald L. Jackson recently said was 'without doubt the cleanest industry in the United States and in the world. . . .'"[21]

Meantime, the Reagan-led Screen Actors Guild joined the "Crusade for Freedom," a counterattack against "communist lies and treachery." Reagan, saying that SAG would not defend those actors who defied HUAC, told his SAG colleagues, "It is every member's duty to cooperate fully." SAG, following the James Petrillo–controlled American Federation of Musicians, passed a resolution in March 1951 that it would not take any action against those studios which would deny jobs to any actor whose "actions outside of union activities have so offended American public opinion that he has made himself unsalable at the box office." Two years later, SAG would force its membership—and those applying for membership—to sign loyalty oaths, saying, "I am not now and will not become a member of the Communist Party nor of any other organization that seeks to overthrow the government of the United States by force or violence."

MCA had remained passive while clients like Arthur Miller were red-baited and blacklisted in the entertainment industry. Talent agents, like just about everyone else in Hollywood, were busy finding cover. Instead of threatening to withhold all of their clients' services if one of them was blacklisted, they sat back and played HUAC and the Alliance's dangerous game. MCA was known to have asked for contract releases from their blacklisted clients, such as screenwriter Nedrick Young. Another screenwriter, Milton Gelman, who was also a former agent, said, "If MCA had gotten together with William Morris and said, 'We're going to pull all our shows off the air,' they could have broken the whole goddamn operation to begin with. The sponsors would have had nothing to show. But everyone ran scared."[22]

Reagan's experiences with HUAC, blacklists, and red-baiting, and his battles against the CSU, transformed his political outlook from that of a self-proclaimed liberal to a conservative anti-communist. From that point on, he began allying himself more and more with the interests of the businessmen, the producers, and the studios, moving away from the working actors. He began to associate increasingly with the powerful studio executives, like Jack Warner and Louis B. Mayer; with the stronger anti-communists within SAG, like Robert Montgomery and George Murphy; and with other politically conservative Hollywood businessmen, like MCA executives Jules Stein and Taft Schreiber.

CHAPTER TEN

As RONALD REAGAN'S political career became increasingly involved with the Screen Actors Guild, Jane Wyman's acting career took off in a big way. She received rave reviews for her performances in *The Lost Weekend* in 1945 with Ray Milland—who was the only non-MCA client among the top stars in the film—and *The Yearling* in 1947. Reagan spent more time at SAG meetings than he did with his family, which now included a daughter and an adopted son.

In June 1947, while Reagan was in the hospital with a severe case of viral pneumonia, Wyman gave birth to their third child. The baby was four months premature and died soon after delivery. The Reagan-Wyman marriage was never quite the same. Reagan became more deeply entrenched in politics, while Wyman started work on *Johnny Belinda,* in which she played a deaf mute.

The celebrated couple separated on December 14, 1947—a month after Reagan was elected to a full term as president of SAG. Charging Reagan with "extreme mental cruelty," Wyman filed for divorce and later disclosed in court that her husband's work with the Screen Actors Guild had led to the demise of the marriage. Even though Wyman had once been a member of the SAG board, she no longer shared her husband's interest in the union. When she was occasionally asked her opinion about an issue, she felt that her ideas "were never considered important. Most of their discussions were far above me. . . . Finally, there was nothing in common between us, nothing to sustain our marriage."[1]

Reagan received most of the sympathy in the Hollywood trade press. He bemoaned his state, saying with chagrin, "Perhaps I should have let someone else save the world and have saved my own home." Wyman needed little sympathy. While she and Reagan were separated, she won the 1948 Academy Award for Best Actress for her performance in *Johnny Belinda*.

Nine days before the separation, Reagan's name appeared on an FBI report entitled "Communist Infiltration of the Motion Picture Industry." Reagan was identified as FBI confidential informant "T-10," according to a story first reported in the *San Jose Mercury News*.[2]

The first known reference to Reagan's name in an FBI file had been made on September 17, 1941. An FBI agent wrote a memorandum to Hugh Clegg, the assistant special agent in charge of the FBI's Los Angeles Division. The G-man wrote that he had become "intimately acquainted with the following persons who might be of some assistance to the Bureau." Among the names listed was "Ronald Reagan, Warner Brothers Studio, Hollywood, California."

Reagan was first contacted for information by the FBI on November 18, 1943, according to a Justice Department document. At the time, he was in the military, stationed at "Fort Roach." During this first known FBI interview with Reagan, the actor told a special agent that he had nearly been in a fistfight with a German sympathizer who had made some anti-Semitic remarks during a party in Los Angeles.

The FBI report stated, "Reagan and [name deleted] became involved in a conversation about the conduct of the war. . . . Specifically subject [name deleted] stated that the Jews involved in shipping were glad of the sinkings of Allied vessels by German submarines because they profited thereby through an insurance racket. . . . Due to the nature of the remarks made by subject, Reagan became highly incensed and withdrew from the conversation. He said that he almost came to blows with subject, although he emphasized that considerable drinking had been done by all persons involved."[3]

On April 10, 1947, Reagan and Wyman were visited by the FBI and interviewed about the Hollywood Independent Citizens Committee of Arts, Sciences and Professions (HICCASP), which Reagan had quit in 1946 because of suspected communists among its leadership. Also, during this interview, Reagan gave the FBI an outline of his duties as

SAG president, and both he and Wyman provided the government with "information regarding the activities of some members of the Guild who they suspected were carrying on Communist Party work."

The FBI report continued, "Reagan and Jane Wyman advised [that] for the past several months they have observed during Guild meetings there are two 'cliques' of members, one headed by [name deleted] and [name deleted] which on all questions of policy that confront the Guild follow the Communist Party line.[4]

"T-10 advised Special Agent [name deleted] that he has been made a member of a committee headed by [Louis] B. Mayer [the head of MGM], the purpose of which allegedly is to 'purge' the motion picture industry of Communist Party members, which committee was an outgrowth of the Thomas Committee hearings in Washington and the subsequent meeting of motion picture producers in New York City. . . . T-10 stated it is his firm conviction that Congress should declare, first of all, by statute, that the Communist Party is not a legal party, but is a foreign-inspired conspiracy. Secondly, Congress should define what organizations are communist-controlled so that membership therein could be construed as an indication of disloyalty. He felt that lacking a definitive stand on the part of the government it would be very difficult for any committee of motion picture people to conduct any type of cleansing of their own household."[5]

The interlocutory judgment for the Reagans' divorce decree was granted on June 29, 1948, after a property settlement the previous February. The divorce became final on July 18, 1949. According to civil records in the Los Angeles Hall of Records, Wyman kept custody of their two children and their principal residence on Cordell Drive in Los Angeles. Represented by SAG attorney Laurence Beilenson, Reagan agreed to pay five hundred dollars a month in child support. The couple had also purchased an eight-acre property—they named it "Yearling Row" after their best movies, *The Yearling* and *King's Row*—in the San Fernando Valley. Reagan kept that, as well as his membership in the Friars Club, a Los Angeles men's club whose members included Mickey Rooney, Johnny Roselli, Groucho Marx, and Sidney Korshak.

In the meantime, Reagan's acting career had taken a nosedive. After a string of losers, he was passed over by Warner Brothers for the lead in *Ghost Mountain,* which eventually starred Errol Flynn. Reagan was angered when Warners was publicly critical of his role in *That Hagen Girl,* a box-office disaster he never wanted to do, in which he starred with a grown-up Shirley Temple. Consequently, Reagan threatened to sabotage his next film with Warners. Lew Wasserman and MCA came to the rescue.

"Lew had foresight and a more practical approach," Reagan said. "My contract [with Warner Brothers] had three years to go. Lew rewrote it to read one picture a year for three years, at a salary for that one picture equal to half my yearly income, and full rights to do outside pictures. In other words, I was at last a free lance. My face was saved and the studio wasn't hurt because every studio in town was really trying to unload contracts. . . . One week later Lew added a five-year, five-picture deal at Universal, and I bellied up to the bar like a conquering hero ordering drinks for the house. You could hardly see my wounded ego under all those $75,000 plasters."[6]

Reagan's escape from his contract with Warners was facilitated by the 1948 U.S. Supreme Court landmark decision in the Paramount antitrust case. The court held that the eight Hollywood studios had violated federal antitrust laws and thus, among other actions, were forced to "divorce" their companies from their theatre holdings. The decision immediately caused tremendous financial problems for the established film industry. Production lots were sold, and many actors' contracts were dropped. However, top actors were then in a position to demand a cut of a picture's gross—which guaranteed them money, even if a picture did poorly at the box office.

The Paramount case also dramatically affected the actual financing of motion pictures. Prior to the decision, the studios were assured of the distribution of their films because of their ownership of local theatres. In fact, before World War II, the major motion picture production companies financed their own projects. Because the studios were forced to divest themselves of these theatres, banks were reluctant to loan money for film production without full security. Banks would even take a mortgage on the motion picture—after the production company approached the bank with a complete package, which included the script, director, and stars. With the financial crunch felt by the Hollywood establishment, independent movie producers began increasingly doing their own films, obtaining financing from their private sources.

Television was the new rage, and box-office revenues began to drop dramatically. Instead of trying to jump into television in its infancy, most of the studios preferred to ignore it. One exception was Barney Balaban at Paramount, influenced by stockholder Jules Stein, who viewed television as a means of "advertising and promoting the Hollywood product."

In his *Saturday Evening Post* series on MCA, David Wittels had revealed that Jules Stein was the second-largest stockholder in Paramount Studios, with 20,000 shares. The reporter concluded that MCA "is the biggest and most powerful booking agency in the history of show business," but that "MCA controls too many jobs with its intricate tie-ups throughout the entertainment industry, its package deals with its exclusive contracts with outlets for talent."

Regarding Jules Stein's purchase of Paramount stock, a Justice Department document alleged that after the acquisition, MCA "began to feed its clients to Paramount. This was done partly in order to enhance the value of the stock. . . . Through the purchase of this stock, Paramount was made a captive market by MCA for its talent."[7]

Despite his newfound free-lance status, Reagan was still badly shaken after his divorce. According to the trade publications, he appeared to be devastated. Reagan moved into a small apartment and became a bachelor again, looking for a way out of his personal and professional problems. However, he did find time to help Nancy Davis, a twenty-eight-year-old actress whose name had appeared on Communist Party mailing lists.

Nancy Davis was the daughter of stage actress Edith Luckett and the stepdaughter of Dr. Loyal Davis, a prosperous Chicago neurosurgeon who had adopted Nancy when she was very young. A 1943 graduate of Smith College, Nancy Davis had been deeply influenced politically by her stepfather, who was an ultraconservative anti-communist. After college, she came to Hollywood and in 1949 was cast in her first film, *Shadow on the Wall,* which starred Zachary Scott and Ann Sothern. She then made a brief appearance in *The Doctor and the Girl,* with Glenn Ford and Janet Leigh. Davis had gone to her producer at MGM, Mervyn LeRoy, a close friend of Sidney Korshak and later the president of the Hollywood Park Racing Association, who advised her to talk to the president of SAG about the Communist Party mailings she was receiving.

"I told Mervyn how upset I was," Davis remembered. "Mervyn made my problem his—he is that kind of man. He told me he knew the man who could fix this thing, the president of the Screen Actors Guild, and would speak to him about my problem. . . . Mervyn assured me that Ronnie was a nice young man and I was a nice young woman, and it might be nice if we met."[8]

LeRoy also recalled the incident, adding, "I called Ronnie and explained the problem. I said he ought to talk to the girl, because the whole thing had her so upset.

" 'Besides,' I said, 'you're single and she's kind of cute and you should meet her.'

"So Ronnie said, okay, send her down. . . . I always say that's the one and only thing we can thank the communists for—if it hadn't been for their propaganda material, Nancy and Ronnie Reagan might never have met."[9]

Later, it was determined that another Hollywood Nancy Davis had been politically active, and that the two were confused. MGM's Nancy Davis was "cleared," and she and Reagan started dating. Soon after, she was appointed to fill a vacant seat on the SAG board of directors —where she could be closer to her new boyfriend and help him with his work.

CHAPTER ELEVEN

As Reagan left Warner Brothers, so, too, did his producer, Bryan Foy, who had had a falling out with Jack Warner, the president. Foy was then appointed as executive producer at Eagle-Lion Studios, run by Arthur B. Krim, who later bought out United Artists. As one of his first acts in his new position, Foy named Chicago Mafia figure Johnny Roselli as an Eagle-Lion producer. The appointment came just as Roselli was released from Atlanta Penitentiary, where he had served less than half of his six-year sentence for his role in the Bioff-Browne-Schenck scandal.

Three other convicted conspirators in the scandal were also released around the same time. In 1947, Tony Accardo, who had become the boss of the Chicago Mafia after Nitti's suicide, visited Paul Ricca, Louis Campagna, and Charles Gioe at Fort Leavenworth Penitentiary. Accardo, who was accompanied by Chicago attorney Eugene Bernstein, had illegally assumed the name of another lawyer, Joseph Bulger.*

Soon after, according to a government report, "the three mobsters

---

*Accardo and Bernstein were later indicted—as a result of Accardo's use of a false name—but both were later acquitted. However, Campagna and Ricca had been told that their paroles would not be granted until their combined tax debt to the IRS, totaling nearly $470,000, was paid. Bernstein came to the rescue, settling the two mobsters' accounts with the government by offering a $190,000 combined settlement. Bernstein said he received the money, in cash, from "persons unknown." Soon after the payment was made, Campagna and Ricca were released.

were released on parole after serving a minimum period of imprisonment although they were known to be vicious gangsters. . . . A prominent member of the Missouri bar [Paul Dillon, who had been Harry
Truman's campaign manager in St. Louis in 1934] presented their
parole applications to the parole board, which granted the parole
against the recommendations of the prosecuting attorney and the
judge who presided at their trial. . . . [T]his early release from imprisonment of three dangerous mobsters is a shocking abuse of parole
power."[1]

The Chicago Crime Commission stated that "during the congressional hearings in September 1947, Harry Ash [director of the Illinois
Crime Prevention Bureau] testified that in May 1947 he received a letter
from a parole authority in the penitentiary in Leavenworth, Kansas,
inquiring as to whether he would be willing to serve as a parole adviser
for Charles "Cherry Nose" Gioe. About the same time that the message
was received, attorney Sidney R. Korshak, who had formerly represented Gioe, called Ash on the telephone and requested him to act as
parole adviser for Gioe. Ash did write a letter, in which he stated that
he had known Gioe since 1915 and considered him a satisfactory subject for parole."[2]

Ash had been Korshak's law partner since December 1939.

Johnny Roselli's real name was Filippo Sacco. He was born in Es-
teria, Italy, on June 4, 1905, and came to the Boston area when he was
six. Moving west as a teenager, he settled in Chicago and became a
bootlegger and a gambler, working for the Capone gang.

Roselli was sent to Los Angeles about 1930 and worked in the illegal
gambling wire service operated by Moses Annenberg, the former circulation manager for the Hearst newspapers who also had supplied information to bookmakers across the country. Annenberg owned several
publications, including *The Philadelphia Inquirer, The Daily Racing
Form,* and two raunchy magazines, *Baltimore Brevities* and *Click,*
which was banned by the Canadian government.

Annenberg was indicted by a federal grand jury in August 1939 for
income tax evasion, along with two associates and his son, Walter
Annenberg, who was charged with aiding and abetting the income tax
evasion of his father. The following year, the elder Annenberg plea-
bargained, agreeing to admit his guilt if the charges against his associates and son were dismissed. The government agreed to Annenberg's
terms. He was required to pay $9.5 million in back taxes and penalties

and sentenced to three years in Lewisburg Penitentiary in Pennsylvania. Two years later, while out on parole, Annenberg died, and Walter Annenberg took over his father's publishing empire.

When Annenberg's wire service ended, Roselli was working for Pat Casey, MPPDA's labor negotiator, and was officially on Casey's payroll when he was indicted for extortion in 1943. Roselli once told his friend, Southern California Mafia leader James Fratianno, "The best years of my life were when I was a producer with Brynie Foy. I liked being with those people. I knew half the movie people in this town on a first-name basis. Jack Warner, Harry Cohn, Sam Goldwyn, Joe Schenck, Clark Gable, George Raft, Jean Harlow, Gary Cooper. Shit, I even knew Charlie Chaplin. I knew them all and enjoyed their company."[3]

But Roselli's profile loomed too large for him to go back to his old ways. Even though no one complained about his reentry into Hollywood—not Ronald Reagan, Roy Brewer, the studio producers, or the Motion Picture Alliance for the Preservation of American Ideals— Roselli was no longer the Chicago Mafia's eyes and ears in Hollywood.

Also gone from the scene was Benjamin "Bugsy" Siegel, who had come a long way from his boyhood roots on New York's Lower East Side, where he, Meyer Lansky, and Charles "Lucky" Luciano created the strongest criminal triumvirate in modern American history. While operating in Hollywood, Siegel had been introduced to the local elite by George Raft. The mobster dined with Mary Pickford and Douglas Fairbanks, Jr., and lived in the same neighborhood as Humphrey Bogart, Judy Garland, and Bing Crosby. The stars seemed to enjoy having the friendship of a gangster; it was their version of a walk on the wild side. Jack Warner frequently boasted about his friendship with the mobster.

Siegel, with the help of Del E. Webb Construction, had built the first big-time Nevada hotel/casino, the Flamingo, near two other establishments, the Last Frontier and the El Rancho Vegas, along Highway 91 in Las Vegas. The Flamingo quickly became a weekend resort on "The Strip" soon after it officially opened on March 27, 1947. Through the friends he made in Hollywood, Siegel always had top stars perform in his floor shows. However, Siegel lived too high and managed to get himself badly in debt. As a result, he skimmed perhaps as much as $3 million from the Flamingo's treasury—and was caught.

While staying at the Beverly Hills mansion of his lover, party-girl Virginia Hill, on June 20, 1947, Siegel was killed by Frankie Carbo, who emptied the nine-bullet clip of his .30-caliber army carbine through an open window in the house. The murder had been ordered by Siegel's long-time friends Lansky and Luciano, who wanted to demonstrate what would happen to those who stole from the mob.[4]

With Roselli overexposed and Siegel dead, the Mafia needed a new face to run its operations in Hollywood. The man selected for the job was Sidney Korshak, who had allegedly been involved in the battles between IATSE and CSU. He had the legal background, the necessary contacts in the film industry, and the full support of the Chicago Mafia.

Consistent with a 1942 IRS report which stated that Korshak was "often delegated to represent the Chicago mob, usually in some secret capacity," a law-enforcement official in Los Angeles said, "Korshak wasn't the kind of guy who formally represented the Chicago mob. He was more valuable in the shadows, with plenty of insulation. They needed a face that wasn't too familiar, and a name that wasn't too notorious. They also wanted a guy without the overt connections, someone who could appear legitimate."

In fact, according to an FBI document based on wiretap information, Chicago mobster Leslie "The Killer" Kruse "had been instructed by the 'outfit' never to personally contact Sidney Korshak, hoodlum attorney."[5]

By January 1948, Korshak had taken a home at 1711 Coldwater Canyon, just outside Beverly Hills, and had another house at 17031 Magnolia in Encino, an exclusive area in greater Los Angeles, while keeping his residence and law practice in Chicago.[6]

Labor lawyer Sidney Korshak, who had been operating in California since the early 1940s, had really arrived in Hollywood. A new, more ambitious and sophisticated era of the Mafia's penetration of the film industry had begun.

CHAPTER TWELVE

THE SENATE Special Committee to Investigate Organized Crime in Interstate Commerce began its work in May 1950. Chaired by Senator Estes Kefauver, a lanky, homespun Democrat from Tennessee, and with Rudolph Halley as chief counsel, the five-member Kefauver Committee intended to travel from city to city and hold hearings, investigating the extent of the Mafia's influence in the United States. In the process, Kefauver was walking on political eggshells, since most of the big-city mobs, at that time, were working with the local Democratic Party machines. His sidekick was Senator Charles W. Tobey, a Bible-thumping Republican who usually wore a copyreader's visor during the hearings.

Nearly twenty million people would view the live, televised coverage provided by NBC and CBS as some of America's top underworld figures appeared before the Senate panel and network cameras. However, most of the mobsters called refused to answer even the simplest of questions, preferring instead to take the Fifth Amendment.

New York mob boss Frank Costello insisted that his face not appear on television—so the cameras focused on his wringing hands throughout his testimony. A close friend of Jack Warner's and George Wood's (Wood was a vice-president of the William Morris Agency), Costello was among those who talked but didn't say very much. He was well connected in Hollywood and had earlier helped Warner with some "labor problems."[1]

Philip D'Andrea, one of the Chicago Mafia members convicted in the Bioff-Browne-Schenck scandal and the former editor of a newspaper for Italian-Americans, was in California when he was subpoenaed to testify before the committee. When asked whether he had heard of the Mafia, he claimed that he really didn't know much about it.

"Would you say it would be unusual for any man of your age who was born in Sicily to say that he knew nothing about the Mafia?" asked George S. Robinson, the committee's associate counsel.

"Yes, I would think so," D'Andrea replied. "If he was born in Sicily, I would think so, because, as I say, years ago it was a byword in every family. People were scared to death of having a little home, for fear somebody would come over and blow it up, or for fear that they would get a letter. That was the condition here about twenty years ago, that I recall."

"What would you say were some of the other concepts or principles of the Mafia that you recall from your childhood, having heard talked about in the family?"

"One of the concepts was that it would be a good idea to keep your mouth closed."[2]

Also testifying was former MPPDA "investigator" Johnny Roselli, who said that he had been employed by Eagle-Lion Studios, under Bryan Foy and Robert T. Cain Productions. He also said that he had financed and produced two movies, but that he was then unemployed because Foy had gone back to Warner Brothers. Counsel Halley replied, "Mr. Foy hasn't dumped you. He phoned me in a very nice way. He asked for no favors, but he told me he wanted me to know that in his opinion you were going straight, that you have had a lot of unnecessary trouble. He asked for nothing, but he felt he ought to give you that character backing."

Roselli had also been instrumental in the war between Harry Cohn and his brother, Jack, in 1932, when the two men were battling for control of Columbia Pictures. When a third partner offered to sell his shares to the highest bidder, Harry Cohn turned to Roselli, who obtained the money from New Jersey crime boss Abner "Longy" Zwillman. At one time, Cohn, a former New York pool hustler, reportedly had gambling debts as high as $400,000 while with Columbia. And, again, Roselli helped bail him out. As a gesture of their friendship,

Cohn proudly wore a star sapphire ring Roselli had given him as a gift. With Roselli around, Cohn felt protected when Bioff and IATSE threatened Columbia with a strike.

Before the Senate committee, Roselli was then asked how he first became involved with Bioff and the studios.

"I represented, we might say, the picture industry. I worked for Pat Casey, who was a labor conciliator for the industry. I was with him for several years, and along about 1941 or 1942 I was indicted with the rest of them. I met Browne and Bioff along [sic] fifteen, sixteen, or seventeen years ago. In their negotiations out on the West Coast, Mr. Bioff was running the industry to his own liking, with others. I would discuss this with Pat Casey, and there were wild and woolly rumors about this man [Bioff] getting money. I was very friendly with Harry Cohn, on whom Bioff called a one-day strike. I was successful in getting the strike called off."

"How did you do that?" asked Halley.

"At this time Mr. Cohn was at Palm Springs. He called me on the telephone and told me about the strike being called in the studio. He knew that I had known Browne and Bioff. How he knew it was either through—Mr. Cohn and I used to go to the races, and one day Browne and Bioff stopped by Mr. Cohn's box and knew him and me. We talked and walked away. So he [Cohn] said, 'I know you know this fellow [Bioff]. Would you like—' he knew that I was around Pat Casey, doing some work for him. 'Would you try to make a contact with Bioff to find out what this thing is?' I said, 'Why don't you have Mendel Silverberg, who was the attorney, or Mr. Casey do it?' He said, 'Well, no one seems to find them here this morning.'

"I said, 'You mean you want me to go represent you?' He said, 'Yes.' So I talked it over I think that day with Pat Casey. I asked him if he knew what violations there were at this studio. He said that he didn't think there were any. I asked him if he tried to get hold of Bioff that day, and he said he couldn't find him. I went to the telephone. I stopped and had lunch—this was around eleven-thirty or twelve o'clock—at the Vendome on Sunset Boulevard and tried to get Bioff on the telephone. He told me he wasn't around, that he wasn't available. I knew I had this thing to do for Mr. Cohn, who was my friend. Of course, I didn't think it was the right thing. I didn't think there was any violations there. I went to his [Bioff's] office. The girl tried to stop me and I stepped over the railing. There was a low railing there. I went back to his office. He was sitting behind his desk I think with his hat on. He may have had a topcoat. I remember the picture very well. He had a gun on his desk. I said, 'I just called you up. What is the idea of your not answering the telephone?'

"Who is this you were calling on?" asked Kefauver.

"Bioff. He said, 'Well, I think I know what you want.' I proceeded to call him names. The reason I did that was because I knew this man was a vicious man. I saw this gun on his desk, but I was on the right side, I guess. I might as well say that. I asked him what the idea was of calling the strike on Cohn. He said, 'Well, I found there were violations, and it is not my fault.' He said, 'Browne ordered me to do it.'

"I said, 'You get Browne on the telephone and I will talk to him.' I think he did. In fact, I know he did. I talked to Browne and Browne told me on the phone, he said, 'Listen, that is not my doing. That is his [Bioff's]. Don't let him kid you.'

"I hung up and said, 'If there are any violations you talk to Harry Cohn and get it straightened out.'

"He said, 'All right.' I think we called Harry Cohn at Palm Springs, and Bioff talked to him. We later made an appointment at my apartment. Oh, at that point Bioff said, 'Well, you know, [former Chicago Mafia boss] Frank Nitti is my friend.'

"I said, 'To hell with you and Nitti.'

"He said, 'Well, I am going to have to tell him.'

"I said, 'I don't care who the hell you tell. If you have a violation on this studio, you go ahead and call us." Of course, I used some choice language which I wouldn't want to repeat in front of you gentlemen. I was mad enough to use it at the time.

"He [Bioff] met Harry Cohn at my apartment that afternoon, that evening. I sat there with him a few minutes, and we had some words. He [Bioff] said he found the violations. He wouldn't state the violations that he found, but he said the men could go back to work that evening."

"What respect did you command with respect to Bioff and Browne?" Halley asked.

"I didn't command any respect from Browne but I was going to command it from Bioff that day."

"How?"

"If he didn't have a violation, I knew that there were rumors around that this man was doing things in the industry which I didn't think were just right and I knew he was getting money somewhere. I didn't know he was getting money, but there were rumors that he was, and he wasn't going to do that to a friend of mine."

"How were you important enough that they cared what you thought?"

"He didn't seem to care. He called the strike, and I was just showing their hand, I guess. They probably didn't want things to tumble on top of them maybe."[3]

Forty-six-year-old Charles "Cherry Nose" Gioe also testified.* He insisted that all he knew about the Mafia was "what I read in the newspapers." Gioe was then asked about his relationship with Sidney Korshak. "I have known Sidney a long time, just as friends," Gioe replied.

"How long have you known him?" Kefauver asked.

"I would say I knew Sidney maybe sixteen or seventeen years."

"You were not in school with him?"

"No, sir."

"How did you get to know him?"

"Through some fellows on the West Side when he just opened his office. He had just finished school and opened an office, I believe, about that time."

"What fellows?"

"Oh, some kids he knew around there that I just happened to know. It was just a casual acquaintance at the time when I met him, just as a lawyer. That is all. I think he handled a deal for them in regard to a café or something. That was the first time I met him."[4]

Korshak—whose brother Marshall was elected to the Illinois State Senate—had been the first person to be subpoenaed for the Senate panel's public hearings in Chicago. However, he was never called as a witness before Kefauver and the members of his committee left Chicago. What happened? According to *The New York Times*, "Ironically, the Kefauver Committee's 1950 hearings on organized crime provided Mr. Korshak with an opportunity to enhance his reputation. . . .

"One trusted Korshak friend and business associate recalled in an interview that shortly after the committee's visit Mr. Korshak had shown him infrared photographs of Senator Kefauver in an obviously compromising position with a young woman.

"Mr. Korshak explained, the friend said, that a woman had been supplied by the Chicago underworld and a camera had been planted in the Senator's room at the Drake Hotel to photograph her with Mr. Kefauver.

---

*Gioe had once been arrested with James de Mora—alias Jack "Machinegun" McGurn—who had ordered vaudeville actor Joe E. Lewis' throat slashed in November 1927. On another occasion, Gioe had been arrested with Tony Accardo for carrying concealed weapons.

" 'Sid showed it to me,' the friend said. 'That was the end of [the] hearings, and this also made Sid a very big man with the boys. Sid was the guy responsible.' "[5]

In the midst of the hearings, Lester Velie, a crime reporter for *Collier's,* described the Chicago Mafia as being "as strong today as the United States Army." In discussing Korshak, Velie wrote that he "seems to transact much of his practice while traveling, for he is out of his office about half the time—shuttling between Chicago, New York, Florida, and the West Coast. . . . Korshak seems to commit little business to paper and keeps few files."[6]

At the end of the committee's investigation in 1951—which included 52,000 miles of travel to fifteen cities—the panel concluded, "There is a sinister criminal organization known as the Mafia operating throughout the country with ties in other nations. . . . The Mafia is the direct descendant of a criminal organization of the same name originating in the island of Sicily. . . . The membership of the Mafia today is not confined to persons of Sicilian origin. The Mafia is a loose-knit organization specializing in the sale and distribution of narcotics, the conduct of various gambling enterprises, prostitution, and other rackets based on extortion and violence. . . . The power of the Mafia is based on a ruthless enforcement of its edicts and its own law of vengeance, to which have been creditably attributed literally hundreds of murders throughout the country."[7]

In its 1,400-page final report, the Kefauver Committee recommended to the full Senate that wiretapping be legalized for federal agents to combat organized crime. It also proposed that witnesses against the mob be given immunity from prosecution in return for their testimonies against their more dangerous bosses. Both proposals were rejected by the Senate.

On the motion picture front, Associated Press Hollywood correspondent James Bacon credited MCA's Lew Wasserman with saving Universal Pictures by getting his client Jimmy Stewart to play the lead in the 1950 Western drama *Winchester 73.*

"In those days, Bill Goetz was head of the studio and it was in financial trouble," Bacon wrote. "There were no star names on the roster, just seventy-five-dollar-a-week contract players like Rock Hudson and Shelley Winters. Goetz cast Rock and Shelley in the movie but needed a star name to sell the picture. Wasserman sensed this and demanded—and got—a fabulous deal for Stewart that netted him fifty percent of the profits.

"The movie was a blockbuster at the box office. Jimmy got rich. Goetz got blasted by all the other studio heads for ruining the industry. Percentage deals for stars were practically unheard of in those days."[8]

As the giant talent agency began to turn its attention to television, the Justice Department's Antitrust Division in Los Angeles received a letter from Assistant U.S. Attorney General Herbert A. Bergson, notifying its staff that the government had "recommended against the FBI investigation [of MCA]. Our file in this matter [is] accordingly closed. . . ."[9]

MCA was spared once again.

II

THE FALL

CHAPTER THIRTEEN

ALTHOUGH TELEVISION technology began as early as 1923, network programming really didn't start until 1946. General Electric, an early pioneer in the new medium, began telecasting in Schenectady, New York, in 1928, while NBC and CBS had created primitive television stations in New York City in 1930 and 1931, respectively. By 1938, NBC was broadcasting scenes from the Broadway play *Susan and God,* as well as occasional on-the-scene news events. The following year, NBC televised the opening ceremonies of the 1939 World's Fair in New York, featuring President Franklin D. Roosevelt delivering the keynote address. At the time, television viewing was so limited that NBC maintained a list of everyone who owned a television and sent them directly a weekly schedule of programs to be aired.

By 1941, NBC and CBS had several shows to offer their New York viewing audiences. Working with General Electric, NBC had developed the first network, telecasting the same programs to its station in New York, General Electric's station in Schenectady, and a Philco station in Philadelphia. That same year, both NBC and CBS became the first commercially licensed television broadcasters.

After the war, while the motion picture industry was having its best time ever—grossing over $2 billion in 1946 alone—network television started to take off. The Depression was over, and people had money. With this money, they could get married, buy homes, and raise families. Leisure time became premium family time. And, to those who could afford a television, family time started to revolve around the TV sets in their living rooms. Advertisers viewed television as a revolutionary new means of reaching consumers. Producers, directors, writers, technicians, and actors discovered a new medium to exhibit their talents.

On May 9, NBC unveiled the first entertainment series, *Hour Glass,* an hour-long variety show, sponsored by Chase and Sanborn Coffee and Tender Leaf Tea. *Hour Glass* was followed by such NBC programs as *I Love to Eat,* a cooking show, and *Gillette Cavalcade of Sports.* NBC's *Kraft Television Theater* followed in 1947 with low-budget dramatic productions.

Not yet competitive in the new market, CBS was already trying to revolutionize the industry by making color television the standard—and thereby making the other networks' black-and-white telecasts obsolete. But CBS's technology was not ready. After NBC broadcast the first televised World Series in 1947, CBS jumped into the black-and-white market. By 1948, CBS was coming on strong with *Arthur Godfrey's Talent Scouts* and *Ed Sullivan's Toast of the Town.*

In August 1948, ABC received its first New York station and began programming sports shows, news shorts, and old movies.

MCA watched the growth of television carefully. Jules Stein said, "There is nothing so permanent as change. Had I stayed in the radio business, I'd be out of business today. We went into television when the movies could have taken over the television business. In the early days of television, the movie business could have owned the stations. But those men [the studio owners] were too sure of themselves. They were too smug."[1]

In the midst of the near-extinction of the big bands—caused by the popularity of individual singers and the rise of bop—seven major record companies—Capitol, Columbia, Decca, London, Mercury, MGM, and RCA—remained in business, recording more solo artists and smaller musical groups.

As television eclipsed the popularity of radio, it also started to challenge the motion picture industry, which was in the midst of a deep recession and had turned to such gimmicks as "3-D," "Natural Vision," and "Cinerama" in hopes of revolutionizing the film business.

The boost that sent Jules Stein, Lew Wasserman, and MCA rocketing into the world of television occurred during Reagan's final months as the president of the Screen Actors Guild in 1952.

MCA had already started producing earlier that year. MCA vice-president Karl Kramer first suggested forming Revue Productions for a television show called *Stars Over Hollywood*. Kramer was given the go-ahead to find a commercial sponsor. Armour, the meat packer, obliged; thus, Revue Productions, MCA's new television production company, was born. MCA rented space at Eagle-Lion Studios for its early production ventures.

In 1939, SAG had amended its by-laws to read that no agents could engage in theatrical film production without a waiver from the Guild. According to SAG's by-laws, "[The] Screen Actors Guild may issue waivers at its discretion . . . but any such waiver shall be without prejudice to any claim by an actor that the agent's production activities have interfered with the proper representation of the actor by the agent or to the agent's defense thereto."

Any violation of this rule would be classified as a conflict of interest since agents would be representing their clients in negotiations with their own production companies. In other words, instead of an actor employing the agent, the agent would remain the agent but also become the employer. However, the SAG by-laws had not been updated to specifically include television production.

Reagan and the SAG board were involved in negotiations with the Alliance of Television Producers over the issue of paying actors when TV programs were rerun, which the producers had refused to do. The Guild postponed a threatened strike to negotiate further. On June 6, 1952, former SAG legal counsel Laurence Beilenson—who had become exclusively an attorney for Revue Productions and had previously represented Reagan in his divorce from Jane Wyman—met with members of the SAG board to discuss a possible solution to the deadlock in the negotiations.

"MCA had been trying to get me for years," Beilenson explained. "And I always told them that I wouldn't take them as long as I was representing the Guild. So I resigned from the Guild . . . in 1949. After I resigned, Wasserman called me and said, 'What's holding you now?' And I said, 'Nothing.' "

Beilenson added that he went with MCA-Revue with the proviso that "I not take part in any negotiations with the Guild or unions, because, when I was representing the Guild, I wouldn't represent agents or producers. I felt that would constitute conflicts of interest."[2]

Nevertheless, soon after joining the MCA-Revue team, Beilenson was thrust into the middle of the SAG-ATP dispute. Beilenson suggested a formula whereby the producers could rerun a program once for free, with a minimum royalty schedule for all future reruns.

Because it was thought that other Hollywood unions would be affected by any ultimate agreement, SAG and the producers agreed to bring IATSE's national president, Richard Walsh, into the discussions. Walsh met with SAG's executive committee at the home of SAG board member Walter Pidgeon. Walsh told the committee that IATSE would support a SAG-sponsored strike. James Caesar Petrillo, the president of the American Federation of Musicians, was also brought into the negotiations and pledged his union's support to SAG's cause.

The following week, according to SAG's official minutes of the June 16, 1952, meeting of the SAG board of directors, "[D]iscussions were held with Revue Productions, which is in the rather peculiar position of being on both sides of the fence inasmuch as they are agents for actors as well as being producers." MCA was indeed engaging in production without a SAG-approved waiver.

As the negotiations between SAG and ATP progressed, the producers relented somewhat, indicating that, according to the minutes of the June 30th board meeting, "[T]hey want that second run without any additional payment. They will agree to repay fifty percent of the actor's salary for the third and fourth run, twenty-five percent for the fifth run, and a single twenty-five-percent payment for the sixth and all subsequent runs."

SAG still wasn't ready to settle. Then, the SAG minutes continued, "Further discussion was had with Mr. Beilenson, representing Revue Productions, who stated that if a deadlock exists, they would still be willing to help break it. In connection with the negotiations with Revue, it was pointed out that this [is] a wholly-owned subsidiary of MCA and that the pattern of agents' interests in production in television, as in the radio field, is well established. Consequently, it appears desirable to recognize the right of agents to engage in TV film production and package-show operation, subject to reasonable regulation by the Guild."

Once the contract between SAG and ATP was made final, Lew Wasserman immediately wanted to get MCA into the television production business on a larger scale. In order to gain authorization for this dual status, MCA had to convince SAG to approve an exclusive "blanket waiver" of its rules. The only previous exceptions had been for the Myron Selznick Agency and Charles Feldman, an agent for Famous Artists, who also made an occasional movie. Selznick and Feldman received temporary SAG waivers on a case-by-case basis and under strict union control.

According to SAG guidelines, the process for obtaining a waiver was quite simple. The agent telephoned the SAG office, saying he wanted to produce a show. He would be told to submit a letter to the union, applying for the waiver. Upon receipt, a SAG committee would determine whether or not to grant the request.

In July 1952, there was a series of meetings between certain members of the SAG board and MCA, including Wasserman, Schreiber, Beilenson, and Kramer. No record of these private meetings was kept.[3]

At the conclusion of these talks, Reagan and SAG national executive secretary John Dales—working in concert with Beilenson—managed to engineer a "special arrangement" between the union and the giant talent agency. However, a Justice Department document stated that "Wasserman and Schreiber could sell SAG anything" because of their relationship with Reagan.[4]

The unprecedented deal granted MCA permission to operate in the profitable field of television production with its talent agency, MCA Artists, and its new television production company, Revue Productions, headed by MCA executive Taft Schreiber. Nothing like it had ever been approved by the SAG board before.

According to the official minutes of the July 14th meeting of the full SAG board*: "A report was made on a special agreement which has been drawn up between Revue Productions, Inc., a wholly-owned subsidiary of MCA Artists, Ltd., and the Guild in connection with television production. . . . The board indicated at its last meeting that it understood and agreed that agents would be interested in the television field as they are in radio. Therefore, further meetings were held with Laurence W. Beilenson, representing Revue Productions, and an agreement was reached which permits MCA to enter and remain in the field of film television during the life of the present Agency regulations but prohibits them from charging commission to any of their clients who appear in their television films."

According to SAG board member George Chandler, "MCA asked [the] Screen Actors Guild for assurances that if it signed and continued in television film production, it would not have to cease such production when [the] Screen Actors Guild should later regulate agents in the television film field. The Screen Actors Guild Board of Directors, after

---

*Aside from the president, Reagan, present for all or part of the July meeting were SAG board members Leon Ames, Edward Arnold, Gertrude Astor, Richard Carlson, George Chandler, Nancy Davis, Rosemary de Camp, Frank Faylen, Wallace Ford, Paul Harvey, Robert Keith, Grafton Linn, Philo McCollough, Walter Pidgeon, George Sowards, Kent Taylor, Regis Toomey, Audrey Totter, and Rhys Williams.
Only a handful of these actors were actually represented by MCA.

consideration, granted this request, agreeing that if in the future it should adopt agency regulations in the television film field which prohibited agents from engaging in television film production, it would grant MCA a waiver of such prohibition for the term of the regulations. The agreement was made by Screen Actors Guild to stimulate employment of actors in television films at a time when motion picture employment was generally at a low ebb."[5]

Walter Pidgeon made the following motion, seconded by Leon Ames: "RESOLVED, that the special letter agreement with Revue Productions, Inc., and MCA Artists, Ltd., copy of which is attached hereto, be and it is hereby approved and ratified."

According to the minutes of the meeting, the motion carried unanimously.

John Dales, an attorney who had been SAG's executive secretary since 1943, recalled that the SAG board felt that the studios were threatened by television, so the board decided, " 'Here's a chance for these guys [MCA] to really go and bring this business to Hollywood and keep it there.' We were concerned about potential conflict. So we went back to them [MCA] and said, 'If we franchise agents—and we think we will—we will give you a waiver to produce, but with all kinds of restrictions: you can't take any commissions from any of your actors that you put in those pictures. Secondly, you must give them not less than the amount they customarily receive—in fact, not less than their highest salary for comparable work. And there was to be a fiduciary relationship [between agent and actor], which 'we will be the judge of as to whether or not you're carrying [it] out.' In other words, everything the agent does with respect to the actor must be in the best interest of the actor."[6]

In his July 23, 1952, letter to MCA, Reagan wrote, "At the present time you are engaged in the motion picture and television film agency business and in the television film production business; you expect to continue in both. You have explained to us your reasons for so doing.

"We agree that for a period commencing with the date hereof and expiring October 31, 1959, if any contract rule or regulation made by us prevents your engaging in both businesses we hereby give you waiver thereof for such period. . . ."

Revue Productions, after receiving the SAG waiver, immediately "began to sell reruns of *Stars Over Hollywood* directly to local stations and advertisers, and soon after produced its first syndicated show, an anthology called *Chevron Theatre*."[7]

MCA had simply employed the same tactic it used with James Petrillo and the AFM to begin its fast rise in the band-booking business and in radio production—with the same result. And like the MCA-AFM blanket waiver, the MCA-SAG blanket waiver was exclusive; other agencies could not get it. Among those who complained the loudest was the William Morris Agency, which represented Sophia Loren, Deborah Kerr, Kim Novak, Natalie Wood, Jack Lemmon, and Steve McQueen. Herbert Siegel, chairman of the General Artists Corporation, screamed, "I've never run across anything like this in all my years in the business. MCA and we are playing in the same ball game, but there is one set of rules for them and quite a different set of rules for everyone else."

The Justice Department's Antitrust Division later reported, "The MCA-SAG arrangements, in effect, have placed MCA in a highly favorable competitive position over other talent agencies and television producers. It alone has been in a position to use its unique dual position as a lever to induce talent to be represented by it and to use such talent in its own television productions. This has served to restrain the competitive efforts of other talent agencies and television film producers."

An FBI report also charged that "any blanket waiver granted to MCA would give MCA a competitive advantage in that they have available to them increased job opportunities and, therefore, have more to offer in this respect to their prospective clients." The FBI also insisted that the waiver would "have the effect of deterring any MCA client from discharging MCA."[8]

The Justice Department later received information that "until the granting of the blanket waiver, MCA . . . was merely another competitor. But with the granting of the waiver, the battle took on a one-sided aspect. Since MCA had the right to make as many television shows as it wanted, it could always guarantee talent work in television. Therefore, the talent left the other talent agencies in droves. Moreover, MCA got not only a huge new pool of talent but the right to use it in television shows. This increased the salability of the television shows, and more and more production resulted. The central fact of MCA's whole rise to power was undoubtedly the blanket waiver. This gave it the real jet-speed boost."[9]

But, as with the AFM waiver and the relationship between Petrillo and Jules Stein, rumors circulated around Hollywood about the SAG waiver and a possible deal between Reagan and Wasserman. Actor Dana Andrews, who later became president of SAG, said, "Ronald Reagan's a very affable fellow. Of course, it's a lot of bullshit, but it works. I don't think he's a vicious man, but I think if it would get him a job, he would kiss ass anytime. But he'd do it pleasantly. He's always looking out for himself. . . .

"Being president of SAG doesn't mean you can make deals, but you do have more influence. I was in the Guild in 1952, but I wasn't on the board when SAG gave MCA the waiver to produce for television. . . . I remember that the government man was looking into that, and he wanted to know if I knew if a secret deal had been made. . . . He said that he was going to continue to look into it. Later, he told me that there had been no proof that there had been such an arrangement. And if there was such a thing, I didn't know about it. . . .

"But I'll tell you one thing, Lew Wasserman . . . gets what he wants, one way or the other. He had enemies all over town, and he still does. But people respect him because he has power."[10]

When Wasserman was asked whether a secret deal had been made with Reagan, the MCA president replied, "That's outrageous. It's absolutely untrue. . . . Did we bribe anyone? My answer is no!"[11]

A federal law-enforcement officer, who was well-acquainted with Hollywood during the early 1950s, said, "If there was a secret deal between a major production company and a labor union, there was one man they'd go to to cut it: Sidney Korshak." Although he admitted that he had only heard rumors about Korshak's possible role in the MCA-SAG blanket waiver, he insisted that "Korshak was all over the place back then, doing his work for the Chicago mob."

Korshak's name did crop up in a Hollywood investigation at about the same time as the MCA-SAG arrangement and the 1952 purchase of Universal Pictures by Decca Records. A group of investors had made a $7 million–plus bid to purchase the RKO Pictures Corporation from Howard Hughes. Hughes had earlier owned a movie company, the Caddo Corporation, which was responsible for such films as *The Racket, Hell's Angels,* and *Scarface.* Hughes had developed a fascination for gangsters and their life styles.

Among the new RKO investors were Ralph E. Stolkin, a thirty-four-year-old Chicago millionaire; his father-in-law and partner in his mail-order business, Abraham Leonard Koolish; and Ray Ryan, a wealthy oilman.

A key player in the negotiations was Korshak, who initially introduced Stolkin to Arnold Grant, a young attorney who—if the deal went through—was to succeed Hughes's business associate, Noah Dietrich, as RKO's chairman of the board. Korshak was slated to handle RKO's labor problems.

On October 16, 1952, soon after the RKO purchase was announced,

The Wall Street Journal carried a detailed story about it, as well as its new owners, charging that Stolkin, Koolish, and Ryan had all been involved with "organized crime, fraudulent mail-order schemes, and big-time gambling." Stolkin had been connected to the distribution of punchboards, "a yokel gambling device"; Koolish was linked to "an Illinois insurance fraud scheme"; and Ryan, it was discovered, was a heavy gambler and a business partner of New York Mafia boss Frank Costello. The report also described Korshak as the "catalytic agent" for the deal.

Within days after the *Journal*'s series, the RKO purchase deal collapsed, and Korshak resigned as the studio's labor lawyer. "Temporary" control of RKO was later given back to Hughes,* who kept the Stolkin group's $1.5 million down payment.

A former Hughes employee said, "Howard Hughes knew the kind of people he was dealing with; he always did. He knew their backgrounds, and he knew their associations. That was the way he operated. In the case of the Stolkin group, he took their down payment and then waited. At the right time, he leaked the story to the press."

---

*On July 18, 1955, Hughes—the first person to be the sole owner of a major motion picture company—sold RKO and all of its remaining properties for $25 million to Thomas F. O'Neil, the heir to the General Tire and Rubber Company in Akron, Ohio. Hughes had made a final profit of $6.5 million.

CHAPTER FOURTEEN

AT THE JUSTICE DEPARTMENT, there was deep and open suspicion that there had been some sort of illegal tie-in—or even a payoff—between MCA and Reagan in return for the MCA-SAG blanket waiver. As Justice Department records noted, "It was thought . . . that SAG might have purposely favored MCA for some illegal consideration." Although it may never be proven that Reagan or any other SAG official pushed through the SAG special arrangement with MCA and then received a suitcase filled with cash, it is clear that, within months of the deal, Reagan benefited personally, financially, professionally, and politically from his relationship with MCA.

Ronald Reagan had been faced with mounting debts, including a large back-tax assessment from the Internal Revenue Service. On March 4, 1952, Reagan married Nancy Davis. Her career was quickly put on hold when she became pregnant. Reagan was worried about mortgage payments on the 290 acres of rocky but scenic property in Malibu Canyon that he had purchased in 1951, using Yearling Row as a down payment. Reagan had paid $85,000, or about $293 per acre, for property that was situated on the corner of Mulholland Drive and Cornell Road in Agoura, California, outside of Los Angeles. Furthermore, the Reagans had purchased a three-bedroom, ranch-style home

—where they spent most of their time—in Pacific Palisades, a beautiful area near the ocean between Santa Monica and Malibu.

In 1953, the forty-three-year-old Reagan turned for help to MCA president Lew Wasserman and Arthur Park, whom Wasserman had hand-picked as Reagan's new day-to-day agent. A one-time musician and tennis pro, Park had been hired for seventy-five dollars a week by Taft Schreiber in 1936 and became an MCA vice-president eleven years later. Among his other clients at MCA was Reagan's ex-wife, Jane Wyman.

Speaking of the differences between Reagan's two wives, Park said, "The styles of Jane and Nancy are totally different. I had to continue handling Jane and Ronnie when they were divorced, and I must say one thing for Jane Wyman—I never heard her criticize Ronald Reagan ever. And I don't remember Ronald Reagan saying anything downgrading Jane, either.

"But Nancy's a very ambitious woman—just take it from there. Ambitious women do anything to meet their ends. It's obvious. She's been promoting Ronald Reagan's activities politically from the time she married him. . . . Jane and Ronnie were really two separate entities. Nancy, as an actress, really didn't get anyplace, let's face it. She had ambitions, but when she married Ronnie, she backed off. So she was never in competition with him. She always played her part, happily and well, as his wife."[1]

Reagan refused to perform on television, fearing overexposure, or in a risky stage production on Broadway, so he, along with Wasserman and Park, decided to give Las Vegas a try. If nothing else, Reagan would be sure to make some big money. For two weeks' work in Vegas, he could make as much as he had for his last movie.

Through MCA, he signed a contract with Beldon Katleman, the owner of the El Rancho Vegas hotel/casino in Las Vegas. Reagan had known Katleman—a Los Angeles–based parking-lot mogul who was the nephew-in-law of Columbia's Harry Cohn and a close, personal friend of Sidney Korshak—from the Friars Club, which had held a testimonial dinner in Reagan's honor in 1950. Reagan was assigned to emcee a low-budget nightclub act that would be featured in Katleman's showroom. As the master of ceremonies, Reagan was to tell jokes, dance, and sing, as well as introduce the other performers.

"Art Park phoned to say Beldon wanted to move our date up to Christmas," Reagan said. "I needed the booking and certainly the money, but something inside me rebelled at the idea of hearing 'Silent Night' in Las Vegas—and we said no. [Katleman's] next call was a demand that I appear as master of ceremonies at one of his regularly scheduled shows, and the show he had picked headlined a stripper. I'm sure the stripper* was a nice girl—the kind you might even take home to Mama—but try as I would, I couldn't come up with an idea of how we could work together, in front of people. . . . The El Rancho [deal] ended up a mutual cancellation."[2]

Twenty minutes after the El Rancho deal fell through, Reagan was booked into the Last Frontier hotel/casino for two weeks, February 14–28, 1954—where Johnny Roselli was on the payroll as a "public relations consultant." Reagan served as emcee for a show featuring several comedy, song, and dance teams, including the Continentals, the Honey Brothers, the Blackburn Twins, and the Adorabelles.

After the engagement, Reagan recalled, "We had a wonderfully successful two weeks, with a sellout every night and offers from the Waldorf in New York and top clubs from Miami to Chicago. It was a great experience to have and remember, but two weeks were enough. Nancy was with me and sat through every show, and when it was over we couldn't wait to get back to the Palisades. . . . When we were back home, we thought of it as just so many more weeks we'd bought that we could hold out in our waiting game."[3]

Returning to Hollywood, the unemployed Reagan was saved once again by his friends at MCA. The vehicle, this time, would be network television.

In one of MCA's first deals to produce television programs, Wasserman had obtained an agreement with the General Electric Company to sponsor an anthology series of weekly, half-hour dramas, *General Electric Theater.* The show was the "flagship" program of MCA's new entry into the production business, made possible by the 1952 SAG waiver. *GE Theater* premiered on February 1, 1953, alternating on a week-to-week basis with *The Fred Waring Show,* a musical variety show. After five years on the air, the Waring program broadcast its last show on May 30, 1954.

Consequently, General Electric made plans to buy a weekly show, and Wasserman offered to give the company an established star to be the host and to represent GE's corporate image.

The actual pitch to GE had come from Ben Duffy, an executive at

---

*Despite Reagan's insistence that he not be seen with strippers, he was later photographed inside the showroom at Katleman's El Rancho Vegas. Caught unaware, Reagan was sitting at a crowded table in the audience, directly under a trapeze, during the bawdy act of Lili St. Cyr, the most famous stripper of that era in Hollywood and Las Vegas. A smiling Reagan, apparently thoroughly enjoying himself, was captured in the picture as he watched the sexy St. Cyr slip out of her scant costume from the trapeze.

the Batten, Barton, Durstine and Osborn advertising agency and a close friend of Taft Schreiber's. BBD&O had done extensive business with MCA for years and had been the Republican National Committee's advertising firm since 1952. BBD&O also represented United States Steel, DuPont, Revlon, and the American Tobacco Company, and later became responsible for finding sponsors for *The $64,000 Question.*

Schreiber went right to Reagan—who no longer feared television overexposure as much as unemployment. "When Schreiber wanted to give Ronnie a proper test for the new *GE Theater,*" according to one report, "he simply gave him the lead in an episode of another MCA-produced television series, *Medallion Theater.* After the live program was finished, Henry Denker, the co-producer, remembered that 'the cameras were kept running while two MCA guys got Reagan up against a gray background. They filmed an opening, middle break and closing as if he were host on a series.' "[4]

Wasserman offered Reagan the job as host, program supervisor, and occasional star of MCA's *GE Theater.* The deal called for Reagan to receive a large salary from GE of $125,000 a year, or $2,500 per show, plus a generous expense account. Art Park later said that MCA's Revue Productions, the show's producer, had also paid Reagan "a very fancy sum," but this amount was never disclosed. Over the next five years, Reagan's salary graduated to $169,000 a year, and GE also later installed a $5,000 all-electric kitchen in Reagan's home.

Arthur Park recalled, "I was sitting on pins and needles because this was a hell of a contract. Not only did MCA have Reagan on *GE Theater* as a performer, but we also produced the show. So it was a very, very large commission for our company."[5]

Reagan did not need long to decide whether to take the job. "The real extra, however, and the one that had drawn me into the picture," Reagan said, "was MCA's idea to hang the package on some personal appearance tours, in which for a number of weeks each year I'd visit GE plants, meeting employees and taking part in their extensive Employee and Community Relations Program. I had been tagged because of my experience in the Guild and the speaking I'd done in the industry's behalf along the 'mashed potato' circuit."[6]

Appearing in the prime-time, 9:00–9:30 P.M. Sunday slot on CBS, immediately after the MCA-represented *Ed Sullivan Show,* Reagan finally became an established star.*

Even though he was no longer the president of the Screen Actors

---

*Reagan also continued his career as a free-lance motion picture actor, making two movies for RKO in 1954: *Cattle Queen of Montana* and *Tennessee's Partner.*

Guild, Reagan continued to serve on its board while his wife, Nancy, also remained an active board member. During the spring of 1954, SAG completed negotiations amending a 1949 agreement with the Artists' Managers Guild, which represented SAG members' talent agents, including MCA, in both motion pictures and television. Prior to the original agreement and as a result of a 1937 law passed by the California State Legislature, the permissible duration of an agent/actor contract was seven years, with no escape clause as long as the actor received one day of work every four months. Under the 1949 agreement, the agent/actor contract lasted one year if it was a first contract and three years if the contract was being renewed. An actor could fire an agent if he did not receive a minimum of fifteen days of work every ninety days or if the agent had a conflict of interest in representing the actor. The SAG-AMG contract stated that agencies representing SAG members would have to apply and pay one hundred dollars or more simply for an agency "franchise" from the SAG board, as well as a permit from the state.

The 1954 agreement also prohibited talent agencies from producing television shows without a limited SAG-approved waiver—except MCA, which had received its blanket waiver in 1952. After 1954, several agents requested production rights and were granted limited waivers, such as the Saphier Agency, Ashley-Steiner, Art Rush, the Tom Somlyo Agency, GAC, the Mitchell J. Hamilburg Agency, Orsatti and Company, Famous Artists, the Lester Salkow Agency, Jerome Hellman Associates, Frank Cooper, and the John Gibbs Agency. However, none of these agents or agencies received an MCA-type waiver.[7]

In April 1953, Lew Wasserman and Karl Kramer had requested and received a pro forma, nonexclusive waiver from the Screen Writers Guild in a letter signed by its then-president, Richard L. Green. Laurence Beilenson, MCA's counsel, had previously represented the Screen Writers Guild as well as SAG. MCA never approached the Directors Guild for such a waiver.

As a result of its blanket waivers, MCA literally began to take over the entertainment industry. In 1954, the first year that MCA published its financial records, the company reported a sizable $6 million profit from its MCA Artists, Inc. By comparison, MCA's profit from its television and film production and rentals had already soared to an additional $15 million annually.

The Justice Department's Antitrust Division in Los Angeles had continued to observe the MCA situation, but still it received no support from official Washington.

In 1954, Justice Department attorney Maurice Silverman conducted a lengthy interview with a source from Hollywood about the new phase of MCA's "package deals." The source indicated that he would be "a dead duck" if it became known that he was cooperating with the Justice Department. The source, according to Silverman's report, stated that: "MCA has a representative stationed at every studio. [It] acquires information about the stories of pictures scheduled for production, the casts required, and the directors needed. If artists they represent are engaged for a picture they inquire about the director. If a director is proposed whom they do not represent they indicate that their artists are not going to like that director and in the end one of MCA's directors gets the job. This technique is repeated with respect to the writers needed. This, of course, makes it advantageous for directors and writers to be represented by them rather than by other agencies and furthers the preservation of their dominant position."

The source added that all producers were "at MCA's mercy. . . . Impasses are always developing between MCA and producers at crucial times of which MCA takes full advantage. . . . It takes many weeks of preparation to get a picture ready for actual shooting. The scenery and costumes are made up, the location is gotten ready, and the sets are put in place. Commitments are made for cameramen, personnel, and directors. When shooting time comes any delays are enormously expensive; each day's shooting time [costs] many thousands of dollars. Just as everything [is ready] to begin the actual shooting MCA is in the habit of asking for changes in contractual arrangements made for the services of the people it represents. It has the power to call its artists off and because all producers must depend to a very great extent on MCA for talent . . . it can force such changes. Although this is true with respect to both the major studios and the independent producers, the independent producer is at a very much greater disadvantage, for the major studios have some talent directly under contract to it for a definite period of time. However, the tendency in recent years has been for the major studios to have fewer and fewer contract players as this cuts down their overhead."[8]

Assistant U.S. Attorney General Stanley N. Barnes, replying to Silverman's report, advised that the matter "be kept highly confidential."

In an important antitrust case involving the producing, booking, and presenting of legitimate stage attractions in interstate commerce, the U.S. Supreme Court ruled on February 14, 1955, in *U.S. v. Shubert*, that antitrust laws were applicable to these business activities. During the case, the defendants—several New York theatre owners—tried to make a distinction between the interstate distribution of film and the interstate distribution of "live entertainment." In the majority opinion, Chief Justice Earl Warren, ruling against this contention, wrote: "The defendants seek to distinguish the motion picture cases [*U.S. v. Paramount*] on the ground that the product of the motion picture industry is 'an article of trade . . . an inanimate thing—a reel of photograph film in a metal box—which moves into interstate commerce like any other manufactured product'; on the other hand, according to this argument, a legitimate theatrical attraction is 'intangible and evanescent, unique and individual . . . an experience of living people. . . .' Congress can regulate traffic though it consists of intangibles." Warren added that the matter was "clear beyond question that the allegations of the government's complaint bring the defendants within the scope of the Sherman [Antitrust] Act even though the actual performance of a legitimate stage attraction 'is, of course, a local affair.' "[9]

Blaming the producers for allowing the agencies to get away "with murder," Indiana theatre operator Roy L. Kalver, in delivering his keynote address to the national convention of theatre operators in November 1956, said: "Don't the producers have the courage to strike back with vigor and not resort to shabby and shameful actions of a few years ago when they swooned supinely when threatened by the beetle-browed Mr. Bioff and the [mendacious] Mr. Browne . . . ? It is evident that the producers have created their own monster which is threatening to devour them. When television first threw them into a panic, one of their first moves was the elimination of their contract players, their own reserve of players and artists, both for the present and the future. Today they are almost completely dependent on these talent agencies and not only are they desperate for personalities for the current needs, but are without the means to develop new talent, the new faces, the stars that our industry so greatly depends upon for its continuation."[10]

Inspired by the Supreme Court decision, Senator Warren Magnuson sent a letter to U.S. Attorney General William P. Rogers, complaining that the Justice Department's Antitrust Division in Washington had failed to do anything with "a stack of information about the monopolistic practices of a handful of companies which included the networks that have already put out of business more than two-thirds of the TV producers." Rogers immediately forwarded Magnuson's letter to the Justice Department's Antitrust Division, where it was assigned in March 1955 to Bernard M. Hollander for a status report.

Completing his survey, Hollander noted that Magnuson's "stack of information" consisted "entirely of clippings from *Variety, Broadcast-*

ing, Billboard, and other trade papers." Hollander added that MCA, the principal alleged antitrust violator, was being watched closely by the Antitrust Division. He also mentioned that a young attorney named Leonard Posner had been assigned to the case on a part-time basis.[11]

Two months later, the Screen Actors Guild came under investigation by the Antitrust Division. The probe was touched off by a complaint from an irate agent who challenged the legality of the 1954 SAG–Artists' Managers Guild agreement, which stated that talent agencies representing SAG members had to apply for and pay $100 or more for a "franchise" from the SAG board. The letter was sent to attorney Stanley Disney, of the Los Angeles office of the Antitrust Division, who later stated, "I believe the arrangement violates the antitrust laws of the United States. . . . Even without proof that the SAG has misused the power that this restriction gives it, I believe the restriction illegal. The SAG, including as it does virtually all screen actors, does not have the right to establish a 'white list' of agents with whom its members can deal, when the right of being entered upon such list is controlled by the SAG."[12]

Disney's boss, James M. McGrath, consented to a "limited preliminary investigation" four days after Disney's request.[13]

The following day, May 18, Herman D. Hover—the owner of Ciro's in Hollywood, who had had trouble with MCA in the past*—filed a triple-damages, $1.7 million antitrust suit against the talent agency/ production company, charging that he had lost $526,500 because "MCA defendants failed to permit name acts to be booked into Ciro's, and as a result Ciro's was forced to operate without name acts. . . ."

Using most of the arguments about MCA's tactics cited by Larry Finley in his suit against the corporation, Hover added, "The MCA defendants have employed or are employing the combined power which they have, arising from their control of the booking of name acts, name bands, name singers, top producers, directors and writers, together with the predominant position in the field of packaging deals for motion pictures, filmed and live television presentations, stage and floor shows for theatres, hotels, cafés, nightclubs and other entertainment outlets, their predominant position in the distribution of films for television and their position in television production, together with their position of exclusive booker of entertainment attractions into numerous hotel, café

---

*In April 1950, five nightclubs in Pittsburgh agreed to boycott MCA after one of the clubs refused to succumb to MCA's demands to accept a lesser-known band in return for the chance of a bigger-name band at a later date. Hover and Ciro's joined the protest. That June, MCA and the six nightclubs settled their dispute—after the clubs promised to request MCA clients and MCA promised to be fair.

and nightclub entertainment outlets, to force and coerce name acts, name bands, name singers and other entertainment attractions to make an MCA defendant their exclusive representative and agent."[14]

In his brief to the court, Hover's attorney, pointing to the recent Supreme Court decision in the *Shubert* case, wrote, "The correctness of Chief Judge McCormick's ruling in the *Finley* [v. *MCA*] case has, of course, now been completely vindicated. . . ."[15]

The case was later settled, with the terms undisclosed.

MCA's *General Electric Theater* had become a big hit among television viewers in America. Already among the top twenty shows in the Nielsen ratings during the first year with Reagan as its host, the program had featured the television debuts of such stars as Joseph Cotten, Alan Ladd, Fred MacMurray, James Stewart, and Myrna Loy, among others.

Continuing on the SAG board of directors, with his wife still a board member, Reagan decided to broaden his experience by becoming a producer for *GE Theater*. According to SAG's by-laws, any SAG member who was also a producer was ineligible to be a member of the SAG board. In fact, Reagan had become president of SAG in 1947 when Robert Montgomery was forced to resign because of his activities as a producer.

Reagan's first production for General Electric in 1955 was *Seeds of Hate,* a drama concerning racial prejudice against American Indians in the Old West. Written by Gerald Drayson Adams and directed by Sydney Lanfield, both MCA clients, *Seeds of Hate* starred Charlton Heston, Steve Cochran, and Diana Douglas, who were also represented by MCA.

Reagan was so thrilled by his new role that he wrote a brief op-ed piece—which dealt with politics as much as television production—for the twenty-fifth anniversary issue of *The Hollywood Reporter,* saying, in part: "I have for the past months been . . . combining television and motion pictures chores. This manifold job has taught me one thing for sure: never again will I allow myself to get into a position where I must make a choice between a seat in Congress and a comfortable position in the arms of my leading lady.

"Actors are citizens and should exert those rights by speaking their minds, but an actor's first duty is to his profession. Hence, you can rest assured that I will never again run for mayor of anything but head man in my own household.

"You may remember a few seasons back when I was honorary mayor of Thousand Oaks. . . . It was then that someone seriously approached me with the suggestion that I run for Congress.

"That proved to be the last straw!

"I realized then that I was becoming a Dr. Jekyll and Mr. Hyde, and the two characters were competing to control me. I selected the Jekyll character—an actor without self-competition. . . .

"Now I am getting the biggest chance of my entire career. My *General Electric Theater* bosses have permitted me to produce *Seeds of Hate* for their series. It's an exciting challenge and I'll have a chance to blame only myself if it doesn't pan out. At least I won't be able to do what many producers are prone to do—blame the cast if the picture fails to pan out."[16]

At the time, Reagan was technically an employee of Batten, Barton, Durstine and Osborn, *GE Theater*'s advertising agency. Filmed at the studios of Revue Productions, *Seeds of Hate* went into production on September 29, 1955, for three days, after two days of rehearsals, and was aired on December 11.[17]

Even when the program aired—and *Variety* announced that Reagan had produced the program—no one from the SAG membership challenged Reagan's eligibility to remain on the SAG board.

CHAPTER FIFTEEN

DURING THE EARLY 1950s, Sidney Korshak purchased $25,000 worth of stock in the Union Casualty Company of New York, owned and operated by Chicago labor racketeer Paul "Red" Dorfman, who had been the head of the Chicago Wastehandlers Union, and his stepson, Allen M. Dorfman. A few years earlier, Union Casualty had become the insurance company for the Teamsters Central States Health and Welfare Fund by decree of then-Teamsters international vice-president James R. Hoffa of Detroit. Allen Dorfman, who had had no previous experience in the insurance business, was appointed its manager.

During the first eight years of fiduciary management by Union Casualty, the Dorfmans made more than $3 million in commissions and service fees. In one instance, Allen Dorfman took $51,462 in premiums and simply deposited it in a special account he had opened with his mother. There were no complaints from Hoffa and the Teamsters.

An FBI intelligence report stated that "the labor racket's web had as its center Sidney Korshak and around him were Murray Humphreys, Gus Alex, Joey Glimco, and Jake Arvey" as well as three local attorneys.

Alex had been Korshak's long-time friend. Humphreys, nicknamed "The Camel," was identified as one of the top leaders of the Chicago mob. Glimco, a corrupt trustee of Chicago Cabdrivers Local 777 and a close friend of Hoffa, had been arrested thirty-six times—twice for murder. Arvey was a member of the National Democratic Committee and had allegedly been introduced by Korshak to associates of New York Mafia don Frank Costello in New Orleans.*

Korshak had also moved into the band-booking business. The listed owner of the Associated Booking Corporation was Joseph G. Glaser, who represented, among others, Louis Armstrong. In its 1946 request for an FBI investigation, the Justice Department's Antitrust Division in Los Angeles wrote a memorandum to Washington, suggesting a probe into the close ties between Associated Booking and MCA. According to a subsequent FBI report unrelated to the MCA investigation, "A rundown of the corporation does not reveal [Korshak's] name; however, he is reported to be a principal in the Associated Booking Corp., who are booking agents for many of the top entertainers and orchestras. This corporation has offices at 445 Park Avenue, New York City, with branches in Chicago, Beverly Hills, Miami, Dallas, and Las Vegas. This puts him close to many of the top Hollywood set."[1]

Korshak and his associates in Paul and Allen Dorfman's Union Casualty Insurance Company experienced another windfall in 1955, during union-management negotiations for the 1955 National Master Freight Agreement. Jimmy Hoffa, the chairman of the Central Conference of Teamsters, introduced an innovation in workmen's benefits: the pension fund. According to Hoffa's plan, employers under Teamster contracts would contribute two dollars per week per employee to the Central States, Southeast, and Southwest Areas Pension Fund. Intended to provide a ninety-dollar-a-month pension to supplement Social Security benefits for eligible union members, Hoffa's Central States Pension Fund was placed in the care of Korshak's friend, Allen Dorfman, who had already been stealing money from the Central States Health and Welfare Fund.

According to FBI documents, Korshak "had been doing work for Hoffa and the Teamsters" at the time of the creation of the Central States Pension Fund. The nature of the work was unknown. However,

---

*On August 8, 1954, long-time Korshak associate Charles "Cherry Nose" Gioe was machine-gunned to death, and his body was stuffed into the trunk of a car. The police had no clues. Just the previous month, according to the FBI, Gioe had allegedly asked Korshak to make arrangements for the naturalization of Paul Ricca, another member of the Chicago mob convicted in the Bioff-Browne-Schenck Hollywood scandal. Ricca was another close associate of Hoffa's.

it was known that Korshak and "labor consultant" Nate Shefferman*
had been negotiating contracts together between the Teamsters Union
and the Englander Corporation, a large furniture manufacturer. According to federal investigators, these negotiations resulted in "sweetheart contracts," in which Englander made a covert arrangement with
the negotiators at the expense of the workers' future salaries and benefits. Shefferman, alone, made over $76,000 for his role in bargaining
talks.

It is not known what Korshak—who rarely put anything in writing
or appeared in court—thought about Willie Bioff after the Hollywood
extortionist testified against his co-conspirators in 1943. In his testimony, Bioff cited Korshak's role with and importance to the Chicago
Mafia. Korshak suddenly found himself in a spotlight at center stage.
Bioff not only exposed Korshak but sent several members of the Chicago mob to jail. Bioff wisely dashed off somewhere after his court
appearance and hid. He moved to Phoenix and assumed the name
"William Nelson."

After spending a few anonymous years in Arizona, Bioff became
friends with Gus Greenbaum, another Chicago hoodlum and bookmaker who was pals with Tony Accardo and Jake "Greasy Thumb"
Guzik. After Bugsy Siegel was murdered in Beverly Hills, Greenbaum
had been tapped to be Siegel's successor as the manager of the Flamingo
hotel/casino. Greenbaum was a success in the gambling business, making friends with his underworld bosses as well as a few other people in
legitimate businesses. One of his political friends was Barry Goldwater,
then a Phoenix city councilman, who was a frequent guest at the casino,
along with Goldwater's brother, Robert, who had a reputation in Las
Vegas as a high-roller.

After a series of illnesses, Greenbaum retired and returned to Arizona, where Goldwater, a Republican, had become a United States
senator. While Greenbaum and Bioff were becoming fast friends, Bioff
met Goldwater. Goldwater and Bioff were frequently seen together at
a variety of social and political functions. Bioff gave Goldwater campaign contributions and accepted the use of Goldwater's private airplane on occasion when he needed to get somewhere quickly.

Meantime, Accardo and Guzik placed pressure on Greenbaum to

---

*Nate Shefferman was the owner of the Chicago-based firm Labor Relations Associates, which
the Sears, Roebuck Company and its subsidiaries employed for union-busting activities. Shefferman, like Korshak, was a close friend of both Hoffa and Teamsters president Dave Beck and "had
received $85,000 in union funds from Beck to purchase a variety of items for him wholesale."[2]

return to Las Vegas to operate their new casino, the Riviera. Green-baum reluctantly accepted—after his sister-in-law was killed under mysterious circumstances—and took Bioff along with him, naming him as the Riviera's entertainment director.

When Accardo heard that Greenbaum had hired Bioff in 1955, he dispatched Marshall Califano—a prime suspect in no less than ten syndicate murders—to protest Bioff's employment on behalf of the casino's "investors." Korshak was allegedly among those with a financial interest in the Riviera. Despite Califano's efforts, Greenbaum refused to fire Bioff.

Two weeks after Califano's visit, Bioff returned to Phoenix with Senator Goldwater in his private plane. On November 4, 1955, Bioff stepped into his car and turned on the ignition, detonating a bomb under the hood. He was killed instantly.

When Goldwater was asked why he had been hanging out with Bioff, he denied knowing that "William Nelson" was really Willie Bioff. When challenged on specifics, Goldwater retracted his initial story and said that he "was making a study of the labor movement, and that Bioff was helping him explore union racketeering."[3]

Shortly after, Greenbaum and his wife were found dead in their home with their throats cut. Goldwater attended both Bioff's and the Greenbaums' funerals. The murders of Bioff and the Greenbaums have never been solved.

On January 30, 1957, the U.S. Senate Select Committee on Improper Activities in the Labor or Management Field was created. Chaired by John L. McClellan, an Arkansas Democrat, the committee consisted of four Democrats: McClellan, John Kennedy of Massachusetts, Sam Ervin of North Carolina, and Pat McNamara of Michigan; and four Republicans: vice chairman Irving Ives of New York, Joe McCarthy of Wisconsin, Karl E. Mundt of South Dakota, and Barry Goldwater of Arizona. Senator Kennedy's brother Robert Kennedy—who had convinced McClellan to do the investigation—was selected as the Senate Rackets Committee's chief counsel.

As with the Kefauver Committee, Sidney Korshak was the first among those associated with the Chicago underworld pursued by the McClellan Committee. Robert Kennedy and staff investigator Pierre Salinger visited Korshak at his office in Chicago and asked him questions about the sweetheart contracts he negotiated in concert with Nathan Shefferman and Labor Relations Associates, Inc. Of course,

Korshak denied any wrongdoing. Salinger, in his background report on Korshak to Kennedy, described him as having "a reputation of being extremely close to the old Capone syndicate."[4]

On October 30, 1957, Korshak appeared before the full committee. The questioning of the witness was conducted entirely by Robert Kennedy. Aside from the Shefferman arrangement, Kennedy asked Korshak about a labor dispute he had settled for Max Factor, the Hollywood-based cosmetic company. The union organizer during the campaign was Michael Katz, who had identified himself during his appearance before the committee as an organizer for Processing Fabricators Union Local 802 and "a communist exterminator."

"I believe I was in the Friars Club in California," Korshak explained. "I received a telephone call from Mr. Katz. He met me in front of the place. He told me that he was organizing the company, and that he was having difficulty getting together with management. He understood that one of the Factors was from Chicago. He asked if I would arrange a meeting with management."

"Which Factor was that?" Kennedy asked.

"This was a Mr. John Factor ["Jake the Barber"]. Mr. John Factor was in the club at this particular time. I asked Mr. Katz to wait. I walked in and told Mr. Factor what I had just learned from Mr. Katz. Mr. Factor said that the only one that he knew at the plant was his half-brother, and that he was in Europe at the time, so he couldn't or wouldn't talk to anyone else. I went out and communicated that to Mr. Katz. . . ."

"As a matter of interest, is he the one who was kidnapped by [Chicago mobster and Capone nemesis] Roger Touhy?"

"That is correct. . . ."

"What was his half-brother's name?"

"I believe that would be Max Factor."

Korshak said that he could not recall having anything further to do with the matter, even after Kennedy confronted him with his own telephone toll-call records, showing an eighteen-minute, nine-second call from Korshak to Katz.

"A great deal of my business is transacted on the telephone," Korshak replied. "I would be hazarding a guess if I said other than I can't recall. Was that telephone call, Mr. Kennedy, around the same time that the Max Factor Company was being organized?"

"That is correct," Kennedy responded.

"Then if I guessed, I would say that I called him to tell him—he may have tried to reach me. He may have wired me, or attempted to reach me. I may have been returning the call. I am sure that it would have to do with the Max Factor Company. I am sure that I would have told him that I have no interest whatsoever in the Max Factor Company, and that John Factor wasn't interested in the Max Factor Company."[5]

Sidney Korshak had become closer to Chicago mobster Gus Alex. The two men had become business partners in several ventures. Alex had applied for a Chicago apartment and used Korshak as a personal reference. Korshak, according to the files of the Lake Shore Management Company, described Alex as "a man of excellent financial responsibility whom he could recommend as an excellent tenant."[6]

Their wives, Bernice Korshak and Marianne (Ryan) Alex, were inseparable friends. A confidential FBI report stated that in 1958, "Gus Alex had moved up to an important position in the crime syndicate of Chicago. . . . Sidney Korshak, well-known Chicago attorney, was the person who advised top racketeers in Chicago insofar as their legitimate enterprises were concerned. . . . Gus Alex was the hoodlum closest to Korshak and . . . this was the basis for the belief that Alex had moved into a high echelon of the syndicate."[7]

During the spring of 1958, Gus Alex disappeared—after he had been subpoenaed to testify before the McClellan Committee. While U.S. marshals searched for Alex, Korshak provided Alex with a temporary home in Palm Springs, as well as the use of his automobile. Soon after, the Chicago FBI went to Korshak and asked him what he knew. "Korshak advised that he did not represent Alex as an attorney but through his wife, Bernice's, friendship with Alex's wife, he knows Alex as well . . . ," the FBI report of the interview stated. "At that time Korshak indicated that he would attempt to get word to Alex that he should accept the subpoena. In July 1958, when attempts were made [by the FBI] to contact Korshak's wife, Korshak contacted the Chicago Office [of the FBI] and advised that his wife was in California and was having dinner that night in Beverly Hills with Peter Lawford [John and Robert Kennedy's brother-in-law]. . . . In July 1958, Alex was served with a subpoena in Chicago by a representative of the Senate Rackets Committee."[8]

When Alex appeared before the committee, he took the Fifth Amendment thirty-nine times, refusing to answer whether he had been Jake "Greasy Thumb" Guzik's bodyguard, whether he had been the Capone mob's top enforcer, whether he was involved in the Dome, a Chicago gambling casino, or even whether his sister was married to mobster Joey Glimco's brother.

With Senator McClellan's patience wearing thin, he chided Alex.

"You stated that you were an American citizen. Do you have enough love and respect for your country that you would in any way and to any degree cooperate with your government and those who are trying to preserve the very freedoms you exercise and now enjoy . . . ?"

"Under the Fifth Amendment to the Constitution of the United States," Alex replied, "I decline to answer on the grounds that my answer may tend to incriminate me."[9]

CHAPTER
SIXTEEN

In 1957, the Antitrust Division of the Justice Department once again became interested in possible litigation against MCA. On April 16, 1957, Walter K. Bennett of the division's Los Angeles office wrote a memorandum to Richard B. O'Donnell, chief of the New York office, stating: "It will be recalled that Music Corporation of America has been the subject of a number of complaints; the last one considered, according to our records, was dated February 8, 1954, and consisted of a charge by an independent motion picture producer who claimed that MCA had a monopoly on entertainment talent which it built up and maintains by predatory practices.

". . . Previous inquiries conducted by this office indicate that MCA has bought out other agencies and that it has had artists under exclusive contract, as well as writers. Complaints by independent producers of motion picture and television shows suggest an attempt to monopolize these businesses. The claim has been made that MCA, with another agency, the William Morris Agency, controls at least seventy-five percent of the top writers, directors, and artists. Dependent on the results of . . . interviews in Boston, you may care to recommend that the investigation closed in 1954 be reopened."

Nine days later, Leonard Posner, a government antitrust attorney who had been working part-time on the case, assumed the role of point man in the day-to-day preliminary investigation. Posner's initial probe was two-pronged; he wanted to investigate both MCA and the William Morris Agency, both of which represented artists as well as packaged and distributed shows. A package for either a motion picture or television show could simply be an idea or a script. It would usually be generated by a writer. Sometimes it would be a joint effort of several artists with various talents or a unilaterally owned package. Occasionally, a package could be a finished film.

When a talent agent received a package, it usually required at least a final editing or, at most, the selection of the right studio, a budget, insurance, the necessary copyrights, financing, and the physical production of the program.

MCA would receive a ten-percent commission on the sale of the package from first exhibition over a national television network; twenty percent from any network rerun; thirty percent for runs on regional networks; forty percent for runs on local television stations; and fifty percent for foreign distribution.[1]

Posner's interest in MCA was greater because, unlike William Morris, MCA was involved in production. Although William Morris packaged programs for such production companies as Four Star, Lou Edelman, Sheldon Leonard, and Danny Thomas, the agency only took its ten-percent commission from those individual artists they packaged.

The focus of Posner's investigation was the "tie-in" device by which a producer was forced to take an entire package rather than selected individuals. "If scripts are copyrighted (as they probably are)," Posner wrote, "the 'tie-in' may well be a 'per se' violation of the antitrust laws. Even when there is no copyright involved, the argument could be made that both scripts and performers . . . are highly unique and, in effect, represent monopolies. Even assuming that monopoly is not involved, the restraints may be unreasonable."

In February 1958, MCA's subsidiary, Management Corporation of America, bought the television distribution rights to over 750 pre-1948 feature films from Paramount for a guaranteed $35 million—$10 million in cash and payments of $2.1 million a year for twelve years. MCA agreed to pay Paramount as much as $15 million if rentals exceeded $51.25 million prior to 1974. At the time the deal was made, Stein was still Paramount's second largest stockholder.

Of the films purchased, sixty-four were "dogs" and were immediately dropped, and 430 were considered "C" pictures, defined as "poor" or "unsuitable." Since it would be difficult to find sponsors for these films, they were primarily used for "fringe time" viewing, or for bargaining for the rest of the package.

MCA's intent was to sell television stations as many films as possible through its wholly-owned subsidiary, the EMKA Corporation. As in a catalogue, each film had a price and stations could order the films from any of dozens of MCA salesmen who would come calling. The cost of distributing these movies varied. If MCA was distributing numerous films simultaneously, its salesmen blanketed local television markets and offered a large selection of films at a lower price than a smaller distributor with fewer films. Consequently, smaller distributors had a higher distribution cost. If a station bought one movie at a time, it would have to decide whether it wanted to pay, for instance, $5,000 for a lesser movie for five viewings over seven years or whether it would be better to purchase a better film, like the 1944 Academy Award–winning production *Going My Way,* for $5,000 for two runs over three years. As a general rule, the first station in a particular local market that offered to buy the entire film package would get it. Usually these stations would have to take the 430 "C" pictures in order to get the other "A" and "B" movies. This practice of "block-booking" had been outlawed by the U.S. Supreme Court in the Paramount case in 1948. MCA, in attempting to sell its newly acquired films, was accused of this practice.

Other companies had purchased other film companies' backlists. Screen Gems, for example, bought 998 pre-1948 and 372 post-1948 films from Columbia; and Seven Arts purchased fourteen pre-1948 and 326 post-1948 motion pictures from Warner Brothers and Twentieth Century–Fox in 1956. A year earlier, Desilu, a new production company formed by Desi Arnaz and Lucille Ball (*I Love Lucy* had begun in 1951), bought out the RKO studio and its entire backlist of 740 films. Desilu's vice-president for public affairs was former SAG president George Murphy.

MCA's acquisition of Paramount's film library prompted Assistant Attorney General Victor R. Hansen of the Antitrust Division to write Jules Stein a letter, saying in part, "While we do not mean to imply that such acquisition necessarily violates the antitrust laws, it does raise certain questions under those laws." Those questions revolved around the legality of MCA's multiple role as agent, producer, and, now, distributor. Hansen then asked for MCA to provide the federal government with all information pertaining to the sale.[2]

The FBI's routine public-records search with Dun and Bradstreet, the corporate financial analysts, yielded little. "This company," the respected firm concluded, "is not actively engaged as a seeker of mercantile credit. However, it is reported to be prompt and satisfactory for payment of purchases on credit terms." Dun and Bradstreet also noted that MCA had "declined to release financial information, and financial statements have been obtained from industry sources."[3]

Soon after the purchase of the Paramount film library, Charles Whittinghill, also of the Antitrust Division, requested the authority "to empanel a grand jury in the Southern District of New York to investigate possible violations of the Sherman Act arising out of alleged tie-in sales by NBC and CBS of network time and network-produced shows." Among the tie-ins Whittinghill hoped to investigate were those of MCA because of its "extremely close relationship with NBC, to which it supplies numerous 'live' properties."[4]

A Justice Department document stated that "NBC is being completely 'snowed under' by CBS in the program ratings. . . . NBC's personnel are far inferior to CBS's in caliber and cannot turn out the quality product. Because of this, NBC is forced to rely on MCA's stable of stars and upon MCA's show production facilities. Hence, NBC sticks close to MCA and to MCA's 'Revue Productions.' "[5]

MCA's program packager was attorney and talent agent Henry Jaffee, who also represented Robert Sarnoff, the chairman of the board of NBC, and had previously represented former NBC president Sylvester "Pat" Weaver. Because of these relationships, Jaffee allegedly kept down the price of talent sold to NBC.

Further, there was a sweetheart relationship between MCA vice-president Sonny Werblin, who was in charge of television sales, and NBC vice-president Robert Kintner, who later became network president and stated during the spring of 1957 in the presence of Sarnoff and others, "Sonny, look at the [NBC] schedule for next season; here are the empty spots, you fill them in."[6]

Werblin did so, rearranging the NBC prime-time schedule and replacing set programming while the NBC programmers watched with their hats in their hands. When the NBC programming bloodbath was completed, MCA had fourteen shows on the air—eight and a half hours of MCA-produced programs on prime-time television. Among MCA's programs were *Wagon Train, Wells Fargo,* and *M Squad.* However, the rest of the NBC-MCA schedule was filled with clinkers.

Kintner, a former newspaper columnist with recognized strengths as a news programmer, denied that the meeting ever took place. He may have had reason to do so. An ex–MCA agent told how Kintner became president of NBC. "They began with Manny Sacks," he explained. "He was a former MCA man who moved over to Columbia Records. MCA took him out of Columbia and put him in at RCA [NBC's parent company]. Then they cultivated Kintner, who was head of ABC, and sold him to Sacks. They said, 'Listen, Manny, what you need as president of NBC is a man with vision, a Kintner, or somebody like him. You take him and we'll give you all our goodies.'"[7]

Shortly after Kintner took over at NBC, he was invited to Lew Wasserman's "birthday party" in Hollywood. "On the night appointed," recalled an industry source, "Kintner came in his best bib and tucker, and there he found every big star on MCA's roster. . . .' In the midst of this glittering assemblage, Wasserman stood up and announced to the multitude, 'This is not a birthday party for Lew Wasserman. This happens to be a surprise party for my good and true friend Robert Kintner to celebrate his having taken over the throne at NBC.' "[8]

In the midst of NBC's love affair with MCA, the William Morris Agency protested to the network, "We're being discriminated against; you're locking us out."[9]

Former NBC president Pat Weaver, who had been responsible for the network's special programming and "spectaculars," said that to accept the fact that MCA had an exclusive deal with NBC in which the network was forced to take all of MCA's product, "one would have to assume either that Bobby Sarnoff was dumb or that Kintner is crooked." Weaver said that he could not believe either theory. Weaver contended that Kintner was a "newspaperman" and knew little about entertainment. When he went to his friend Sonny Werblin, he was talking to someone who did.[10]

Nevertheless, MCA's production income jumped from $8.7 million in 1954 to a $49,865,000 gross in 1957. MCA's talent agency, which had earnings of $8.8 million in 1954, remained the same in 1957.*

In 1957, William Morris reported its revenues to be $41,371,000 and nearly $4 million in commissions.†

Within MCA, business had become extremely competitive. According to an MCA agent, "We were supposed to be battling for commissions with the William Morris Agency, the General Artists

---

*MCA's top television clients included Art Linkletter; Robert Cummings; Ozzie and Harriet Nelson and their sons, David and Ricky; Fred MacMurray; Donna Reed; Phil Silvers; George Gobel; Alfred Hitchcock; Jack Benny; George Burns; Betty Furness; and Ernie Kovacs and his wife, Edie Adams.

†William Morris's television and motion picture clients included Sammy Davis, Jr., Danny Kaye, Lloyd Bridges, Anita Ekberg, Jean Simmons, Barbara Stanwyck, Spencer Tracy, Melvyn Douglas, Glenn Ford, Barry Nelson, Laraine Day, and Frank Sinatra, who had left MCA in a huff.

Corporation, and other talent agencies, but I found that my most ruthless enemy was the man in the next office at MCA. I'd go to an advertising executive and sell him a TV show, and then a fellow MCA man would go to him and say, 'Why do you want to buy that piece of junk? The show *I* represent would be much better for you.' We were pitted against each other by the nature of the agency, and it was like living in a snarling, cannibalistic, primitive society where your survival depended on your brutality and guile. We got comparatively small salaries plus a big Christmas bonus which we received at the end of the year. The bonus was based on what you had sold during the year to contribute to the profits of the company, and it could amount to as much as fifteen or twenty thousand dollars. Thus we were all out scrambling for the bonus, and if you had to assassinate one of your colleagues to up your bonus, you assassinated him. Spying, memo-stealing, eavesdropping were all common practice. Once I was talking to an executive at Metro-Goldwyn-Mayer about a deal. Two minutes later, I got a call from my superior at MCA, berating me about what I had said to the Metro man. He had the conversation almost verbatim. Later, I learned that my colleague in the next office had flattened himself against the wall outside my door and had listened to every word of my conversation with the MGM executive. Then he had reported it to my boss."[11]

Even Wasserman was beginning to feel the heat. During a meeting with CBS executives in New York, focusing on "a deal for purchasing Paramount pictures for all of CBS's O & O [owned and operated] stations, Wasserman called in from the West Coast and insisted that they break up the meeting, because he was afraid to do business with a station group as such. Merle Jones [a CBS executive] asked sarcastically, 'Is it all right if we stay for a cocktail?' The meeting took place in MCA's suite in the Hotel Pierre."[12]

"You have to understand," explained a former top MCA executive. "We knew that the antitrust people in Washington and Los Angeles were starting to breathe down our necks. We were doing everything we could do to avoid antitrust problems. It was something we were sensitive to. Wasserman was aware of it, and he made sure we were, too."

After not receiving a reply to the government's request for detailed information about the Paramount backlist purchase, federal antitrust lawyer John Sirigano, Jr., requested on July 10, 1958, that the Federal Communications Commission supply the government with data on MCA filed by those television stations doing business with the firm.

"At about 4:30 P.M., August 5, 1958," Sirigano wrote in an internal

Justice Department memorandum, "I received a long-distance call from Mr. [Cyrus R.] Vance of Simpson, Thatcher of New York City, who stated that he was representing MCA and was aware of our request to the FCC and stated that MCA was perturbed over the possibility that confidential information regarding MCA operations might be available [to a competitor]."

Sirigano replied that the Justice Department was within the law requesting the information under the "Federal Reports Act," but that Vance and MCA would be better served to appeal directly to the FCC. "Mr. Vance stated that to avoid any controversy MCA would offer to supply us with any information relevant to their activities in film distribution on a voluntary basis if we would withdraw our request to the FCC to examine MCA reports. I stated that as a matter of policy we could not make an exception for MCA."

After the Sirigano-Vance conversation, MCA notified the FCC "that while it believed that disclosure by the FCC of material supplied by MCA to [the Justice Department] was unauthorized it was waiving any objection to such disclosure."[13]

CHAPTER SEVENTEEN

ON NBC's popular, big-money quiz show, *Twenty-One*, contestants went head-to-head, answering questions in a variety of categories with degrees of difficulty ranging from a rating of one to eleven and trying to get a total score of twenty-one. Any contestant, for instance, answering a question with an eleven rating and a second with a ten rating was guaranteed a tie. To heighten the drama, as well as the visuals, contestants stood in isolation booths on stage. The winner from each show kept returning the following week until defeated by a challenger. Among the early winners was Herbert Stempel, who in 1958 enjoyed a long run on the show. Stempel's reign was ended by Charles Van Doren. After tying Stempel three times, Van Doren finally defeated him during the fourth week and became an overnight sensation in America. A year later, while Van Doren—who was then represented by MCA, as had been the producers of *Twenty-One,* Jack Barry and Dan Enright—was filling in on NBC's *Today* show for host David Garroway over the summer, Stempel charged that *Twenty-One* was fixed and that Van Doren had been given answers to questions in advance of the show.

In the wake of allegations against other quiz shows—NBC's *Dotto,* and CBS's *The $64,000 Challenge* and *The $64,000 Question*—a special committee of the U.S. House of Representatives* subpoenaed Van Doren. He confessed that he had been fed answers by a producer of the show, because the knowledgeable Stempel was too good and couldn't be beaten but had become unpopular with *Twenty-One*'s audience.

TV Guide later ran an editorial entitled "Now Is the Time for Action." In part, *TV Guide* stated: "Now that television's dirty quiz linen has been washed in public, it might not be amiss for the industry itself to clean out the rest of the hamper. Why wait for a few months until the quiz matter dies down and then be subjected to more headlines and investigations and public resentment on other dubious practices that could just as readily be aired and corrected now?

"Item: Talent agencies control—directly or indirectly—more than forty percent of nighttime network TV. With the networks so dependent upon MCA and William Morris and a few smaller talent agencies, it is possible for the agencies to sell them routine shows on the basis of special deals, talent tie-ins, or just a good 'in'. . .

"At the heart of the matter is the question of exactly who is to control the medium."[1]

On December 16, 1958, MCA and Revue Productions purchased the run-down 367-acre backlot of Universal Pictures—which had been merged with Decca Records in February 1952—for $11,250,000. The buildings on the property were of solid steel, brick, and stucco construction and included sixteen sound stages, as well as a variety of geographic and historical set designs. As part of the purchase agreement, Universal was to pay MCA $1 million a year for ten years for leasing rights to the property. Previously, Revue had owned the one-acre lot at Republic Pictures, which had stopped producing films. MCA sold its Republic property for a reported $9 million. Soon after the contract was signed, Universal received a glut of MCA-represented clients for its motion pictures. It was another incredible deal for MCA.

Wasserman authorized an enormous rehabilitation program for Revue's new home, ultimately costing $110 million. "Very few companies in the industry had spent money on capital-improvement programs," Lew Wasserman said. "The theory had been 'don't spend any money you can't charge off to a film.' I'm not going to say we can walk on water, but we were defying conventional thinking."[2]

---

*Also, during 1950–60, Congress investigated the "payola" scandal in which deejays were accused of accepting bribes to play record companies' music. Actually, the deejays were scapegoats for a wider range of corruption in the industry. The payola scandal had its roots in the longstanding war between the American Society of Composers, Authors, and Publishers (ASCAP) and Broadcast Music, Inc. (BMI), which were competing for the lion's share of the recording market. (See Steve Chapple and Reebee Garofalo, *Rock 'N' Roll Is Here to Pay.*)

An industry source reflected that "MCA made a big mistake when it bought the Universal lot. When they did this they went into a different business. Thus MCA got away from its function of representing talent. Jules Stein always used to tell the MCA salesmen: 'Never forget that what we began with was representation of talent; that is our main function and it must remain so. . . .' MCA had forgotten this admonition of Stein's and [had] now made production its main function."

On January 8, 1959, the U.S. Justice Department finally authorized a full-field FBI investigation of MCA. The formalities were included in a letter from Assistant Attorney General Victor R. Hansen of the Antitrust Division in Washington, D.C., to FBI director J. Edgar Hoover. Hansen wrote that "MCA may be restraining trade (a) by refusing to book its artists in productions competing with those under MCA control, (b) by compelling producers to hire writers and directors in order to obtain [acting] talent, (c) by compelling producers to hire talent in order to obtain scripts, writers or directors, (d) by obtaining representation of talent through predatory practices, (e) by refusing to book talent at terms satisfactory to the talent but not to MCA (which practice may be accomplished by failing or omitting to inform talent of offers), or (f) by monopolizing the talent agency and the booking business."

Included in the letter to Hoover was another addressed to MCA, requesting "the examination of the books, records and files of the Music Corporation of America."

While Hoover and the FBI began their work, the Antitrust Division received information about the power MCA wielded during the casting of the Twentieth Century–Fox production of *The Young Lions.* According to an industry source, Marlon Brando, Montgomery Clift, Maximilian Schell, and Tony Randall had been slated for the leads of this World War II drama, based upon Irwin Shaw's best-selling epic novel. Directed by Edward Dmytryk, the only member of the Hollywood Ten who had recanted and named names before HUAC, in 1951, *The Young Lions* filming was delayed when MCA asked its producers to change a member of the cast for one of its clients. When Twentieth Century–Fox protested, MCA threatened to pull Brando and Clift, both MCA clients, out of the movie. The studio ultimately capitulated to MCA, removing Tony Randall from the cast and adding MCA's Dean Martin, who had just split up with his comedy partner, Jerry Lewis, and was looking for work.

MCA Artists was making a ten-percent commission from its clients; Revue Productions received twenty percent of its shows' profits from the networks; and MCA-TV, Ltd., the corporation's distribution company, received another ten percent for distributing MCA's film library. MCA took all of its fees off the top, leaving fewer dollars to be divided among program producers and stars who negotiated ownership interests in the shows they worked.

Although the William Morris Agency, as well as MCA, had been the subject of the federal investigation, the Antitrust Division backed off from William Morris and concentrated on MCA. According to a Justice Department memorandum, "William Morris, MCA Artists, Ltd.'s, principal competitor, deducts any fees the owner of the show must pay to a distributor for reruns before it computes the fee. . . . Some of the stars represented by William Morris own a certain percentage of the film for rerun purposes. In no case does William Morris take more than ten percent of the show's profit, as contrasted with . . . MCA."[3]

CHAPTER EIGHTEEN

DURING 1959, Sidney Korshak was still working with the Teamsters Union, and he and his brother Marshall were often seen with the president of the Teamsters Union, Jimmy Hoffa, who had been elected in 1957. Sidney had kept his clout in the labor movement and was known to have also been doing work for the United Steelworkers Union upon request of its president, of whom Korshak was a close friend. The Chicago attorney was representing the Hotel and Restaurant Workers and Bartenders Union Local 450 in Cicero, Illinois, as well as Chicago's liquor salesmen. According to a confidential IRS report, "Korshak is a man with many influential friends and can make peace in many disputes through his friendships in the fields of labor, management, and government."[1]

In May 1959, the FBI received reliable information that Korshak had negotiated a contract between Chicago's Premium Beer Sales, Inc., and local Mafia boss Tony Accardo, in which Accardo was hired as a "salesman" and given a $65,000-a-year salary.* Korshak had appeared before a federal grand jury investigating the connection between Ac-

---

*Accardo's daughter was a secretary in Korshak's Chicago law office.

cardo and Premium but "denied that he had drawn up the original contract between Premium and Accardo, stating that [an executive of Premium], whom he had known for many years, had contacted him and presented a contract, asking for Korshak's legal opinion as to whether it was a good contract or not. Korshak stated he studied the contract, suggested some revisions, and returned the contract. . . ." Korshak added that he had been given five hundred dollars for his services.[2]

The FBI had also learned that Korshak and his brother Marshall were attorneys for American Distillers. American Distillers was also represented by Paul Ziffren, another Chicago attorney who was a close friend of both Korshak and Lew Wasserman.

Paul Ziffren was born in Davenport, Iowa, on July 18, 1913. He received both his undergraduate and law degrees at Northwestern University. He attended law school with a scholarship from the Pritzker Foundation. In 1938, he was admitted to the Illinois bar. His first job was in the office of the chief counsel for the IRS in Chicago. There Ziffren worked on the successful income tax evasion case against Moe Annenberg. He later became an assistant U.S. attorney and head of the tax division in the U.S. Attorney's office. On March 22, 1941, Ziffren resigned from government service and became a member of the law firm Gottlieb and Schwartz, specializing in corporate law.

Ziffren left Chicago and came to California in 1943, when he was thirty years old. In May 1944, he was admitted to the California bar and spent less than a year with a Los Angeles firm. He then opened a partnership—Schwartz, Ziffren, and Steinberg—in downtown Los Angeles while he simultaneously maintained a legal partnership with his political mentor, Jake Arvey, the mob-connected head of Chicago's Democratic Party and a long-time friend of Korshak's. According to several sources, Ziffren "was like a son" to Arvey.

Ziffren was also a close friend and associate of Alex Louis Greenberg, a reputed front man for Chicago Mafia boss Frank Nitti, and a business partner of Arvey. Ziffren and Greenberg, according to income tax records uncovered by the Kefauver Committee, were partners in a real estate interest, Store Properties, Inc., located in San Bernardino, California, which had holdings in several states, including Arizona, California, Colorado, Florida, Illinois, New York, Oklahoma, and Utah. The president of their firm was Samuel Genis, a known front for Greenberg, who had been previously arrested for embezzlement and for passing bad checks. Genis was not convicted on either charge. He was also a known associate of underworld figures Abner "Longy" Zwillman, Frank Costello, and Meyer Lansky. At one point, Ziffren loaned Genis—who was killed in a car accident in 1955—$93,000 for their business.*

By 1950, Ziffren had opened his own office in the Heyler Building of Beverly Hills. That same year, he became the chief fund-raiser for Helen Gahagan Douglas, the Democratic nominee for the U.S. Senate, whose Republican opponent was Richard Nixon.

Despite Douglas's defeat, Ziffren remained involved in California politics. During the early 1950s, an attempt was being made to recall the mayor of Los Angeles, who had been clamping down on the local Mafia. During the campaign, the intelligence division of the Los Angeles Police Department learned that the crusade was being engineered by close associates of the Chicago underworld. The hotel from which the recall operation was being run was owned by close associates of the Capone mob who were closely linked to Ziffren.†

In 1953, Ziffren, a respected liberal with a strong record in support of civil rights and civil liberties, became California's elected member of the Democratic National Committee, on which he sat with Arvey, who held the same position in Illinois.

Two years later, on December 18, 1955, Greenberg was shot four times in his left arm, head, chest, and groin in an obvious gangland slaying—after his autobiography, "My 46 Years with Chicago Gangsters," appeared in *The Chicago Tribune*. At the time of his murder, Greenberg was the owner of the Canadian Ace Brewing Company in Chicago, which reportedly grossed $10 million annually.

During Ziffren's term as California's representative on the Democratic National Committee, California's Democratic Party enjoyed great success: Pat Brown, the first Democratic governor since 1940, was elected in 1958,‡ and both houses of the California State Legislature

---

*Ziffren was divorced in 1947 from his first wife, Phyllis, who was also a Los Angeles attorney. According to a Los Angeles Police report, Ziffren paid his ex-wife five hundred dollars a month in alimony and another $250 a month in support for their two children. Greenberg personally intervened on Ziffren's behalf, trying unsuccessfully to save the marriage. Soon after Ziffren married his second wife, Genis paid back his loan. Ziffren deposited the interest in the names of his second wife and mother-in-law for unknown reasons—although no law was broken by doing so.

†"One partner who was listed on the hotel liquor license with Ziffren," said one report, "was the wife of Fred Evans, a Capone money adviser and fence who was executed in a gangland killing in 1959. Another had been an officer in an investment company that converted underworld loot into real estate and other assets." This setup, the report continued, was the first disclosure of "a momentous money migration: Chicago underworld cash was flowing into California and was putting solid, legitimate enterprises secretly into some of the uncleanest hands in America."³

‡During the gubernatorial race, Ziffren's underworld ties were repeatedly questioned by the Republican candidate, California senator William F. Knowland. During the campaign, Brown distanced himself from Ziffren, saying, "I am the architect of my own campaign. Paul Ziffren has no connection with it. Mr. Ziffren needs no defense from me. He is perfectly capable of taking care of himself."

were captured that same year for the first time since 1885. Lauding Ziffren, Paul Butler, the chairman of the Democratic National Committee, said in 1960, "Paul Ziffren has been the greatest single force and most important individual Democrat in the resurgence of the Democratic Party in California."[4]

Thought by many to be the heir-apparent to Butler, Ziffren cut his public political career short after the 1960 Democratic National Convention in Los Angeles. However, his hand was forced when reporter Lester Velie, who had earlier written a revealing story about Sidney Korshak, published a story in *Reader's Digest,* chronicling Ziffren's long-standing ties to major organized crime figures.*

In April 1959, Korshak accompanied Mary Zwillman, the widow of Zwillman, to Las Vegas, where Korshak was helping her dispose of her husband's interest in the Sands hotel/casino. Her husband, facing a long stretch in prison for income tax evasion, had been found hanging from a water pipe in the basement of their mansion. Although law-enforcement authorities ruled Zwillman's death a suicide, others were not so sure. There was nothing nearby—no box or platform of any kind —from which he could have jumped.

According to a confidential report of the Los Angeles Police Department, "In 1959 Korshak had an interest in the American National Bank of Chicago. Held 1500 shares in Merritt, Chapman & Scott Co. [a large building contractor]. Had shares in the City National Bank of Beverly Hills and had an oil partnership with Roy Huffington, Inc., 2119 Bank of the Southwest, Houston, Texas."[6]

During an FBI investigation in June 1959, Korshak was interviewed by FBI agents. At that time, according to the FBI report, Korshak indicated "that he and his law partners maintain on a permanent basis Room 2001 in the Essex House in New York City. He also advised at this time that he always maintains permanent rooms in the Beverly Hills Hotel in Beverly Hills, California, and that he maintains permanent space in the Ocotillo Lodge in Palm Springs, California. Since the purchase of his home at 10624 Chalon Road in Bel Air, Korshak no longer maintains residence at the Beverly Hills Hotel on a permanent basis. . . . Information available indicates that Korshak also maintains residences in New York, Las Vegas, and a summer home in Paris, as well as residences in Los Angeles and Chicago."[7]

---

*Regarding Sidney Korshak, Ziffren said, "My relationship with Sid is essentially a social relationship. I consider him a friend of mine, but he never discusses his business with me, nor do I with him."[5]

Korshak also told the FBI agents that his law practice "consists largely of representing labor unions and theatrical people."

In 1959, Joan Cohn—the widow of Columbia Pictures mogul Harry Cohn, who died in 1958—married shoe manufacturer Harry Karl in Korshak's Chicago apartment. According to a confidential FBI document, "After about three weeks, Joan Cohn Karl filed divorce proceedings against Harry Karl in Los Angeles Superior Court. At that time information was received by the Los Angeles office that possibly the marriage was a sham engaged in for the financial convenience of people behind the principal [Korshak]. The speculation was that Harry Cohn was fronting for Chicago investors in Columbia Pictures and when he died his estate went into probate and the marriage of Karl and Cohn was contrived as a method through which the real investors in Columbia Pictures could regain title to their property without disclosing themselves on public records."

At the conclusion of the FBI interview, Korshak told the agents that he, his wife, and their two teenage sons "were taking off with Dinah Shore, television entertainer, and her oldest child, for a two-month tour of Europe. Concerning his associates, Korshak advised that he has been linked with many people and has become friendly with many people because he will not 'back away from anyone or repudiate anybody.' "[7]

CHAPTER NINETEEN

In November 1959, in anticipation of a battle with motion picture and television producers over actors' residuals for the broadcast of old movies and a badly needed actors' pension and welfare fund, Ronald Reagan was elected to an unprecedented sixth term as president of the Screen Actors Guild. He was unopposed and generally considered SAG's strongest voice within the Hollywood community.

At first, Reagan recalled, he did not want to be SAG president again. But to help him make a decision as to whether to become head of the labor union, he asked management for its advice. "Finally," Reagan explained, "I called my agent, Lew Wasserman—who else? I knew that he shared my belief that my career [in films] had suffered. To tell the truth, I was positive he'd reiterate that belief and I could say 'no' with a clear conscience. Well, I pulled the ripcord and the chute didn't open. Lew said he thought I should take the job. It was still a satisfactory answer because down inside me there was a certain knowledge that I wouldn't like me very much the other way."[1]

Within a month of his election, Reagan became the target of controversy within the guild because of his activities with *GE Theater*. Although *GE Theater* had fallen from third in the Nielsens in 1956–57 to twenty-third in 1959–60, the show was still secure in its Sunday-night prime-time slot. Because of the show's earlier success, Reagan's new contract gave him more responsibility for program production. As a result of charges that Reagan had an ownership interest in the MCA-Revue program and was producing shows, *Screen Actor,* the official voice of SAG, said in its December issue that Reagan, who had been an official with the union for the past thirteen years, had been the subject of "vile and unscrupulous tactics" and "false rumors" having no basis in truth.

Screen Actor continued, "Members are being told that Ronald Reagan, president of the Guild, produces and has an ownership interest in the television series, the *General Electric Theater.* . . . Ronald Reagan is a contract employee of the advertising agency Batten, Barton, Durstine and Osborn. Under this contract he is required to appear as an actor, as a master of ceremonies, and to make personal appearances. He is paid a weekly salary. He has no ownership interest, percentage, participation or otherwise in the *General Electric Theater,* or any other picture or series. He is not the producer of the series and he has no voice in the selection or approval of the actors employed."

The primary grievance of the Screen Actors Guild was the millions of dollars its members felt they were owed by the various production companies for old movies sold to the television markets. Since 1948, vocal SAG members had been demanding that the union negotiate an agreement with movie producers so that actors could be paid when their movies left the theatres and began running on television. By 1960, MCA's shrewd 1958 purchase of Paramount Pictures' backlist of pre-1948 films for $50 million had already grossed MCA an incredible $60 million. The actors felt that some of that money—as well as money from all movies made prior to 1960—belonged to them. "That's why Reagan was elected president of SAG again in 1959," said a SAG board member. "We knew how close he was to MCA and thought he could get us our best deal."

MCA stood to be among the biggest losers if SAG struck against the industry and bargained hard for residuals. MCA quickly joined with a handful of smaller production companies to settle quickly with SAG, opting "to agree to agree with whatever was settled" between SAG and the larger studios, according to the SAG board member. But the major studios—which were led by Spyros Skouras of Twentieth Century–Fox —refused to negotiate on the pre-1960 movie rentals.

The quick settlement between MCA and other smaller companies with SAG provoked charges by some SAG board members that Reagan was conducting selective bargaining. Powerful forces in the industry came to Reagan's rescue. Frank Sinatra held a press conference and, with Reagan standing by his side, announced that he had authorized his film production company to sign a collective bargaining agreement with SAG. Sinatra's company, Dorchester Productions, which had been filming *Ocean's Eleven* at Warner Brothers, agreed to a five-percent actors' residual after the film was released. Like MCA, Sinatra continued production. Sinatra then appealed to the other studios "to do a little compromising," adding that "the Screen Actors Guild has already compromised greatly from its original contract demands."[2]

After Sinatra's company had signed the agreement, "the roof fell in," according to Reagan. "Richard Walsh of the IATSE moved in—issuing an ultimatum to Frank and all other independents who had shown signs of going along. . . . Walsh's act could hardly be excused. He [already] had a signed contract [with the producers] with months to run. We resented the effect it had of interfering with our negotiations."

Reagan then contacted George Meany, president of the AFL-CIO; Meany talked to Walsh. At a subsequent meeting, Reagan remembered that he called Walsh "a lousy, damn strike-breaker."[3]

When asked about these events as chronicled by Reagan, Walsh simply replied that they were "not told as they happened," refusing to challenge Reagan's statement specifically.

However, when pressed, Walsh sharply replied, "Korshak's involved in that whole proposition you're talking about there, and it would tie back into Reagan. . . . Reagan was a friend of, talked to Sidney Korshak, and it would all tie back together. That's the whole thing that was going on at the time you're talking about. . . . I know Sidney Korshak. I know where he comes from, what he is, and what he's done. He's a labor lawyer, as the term goes."[4]

Pressed for more details about the relationship between Reagan and Korshak, particularly during the 1960 SAG negotiations, Walsh refused further comment.

Earlier, Milton Rackmil—a close friend of Korshak and the president of Decca-Universal, which had become increasingly dependent on MCA talent—told Reagan, during a private meeting, of a split among the producers. Breaking ranks, Rackmil agreed to give six percent of the post-1948 movies and seven percent of the post-1960 films to the actors, as well as a five-percent employee-paid contribution to the proposed SAG pension and welfare fund. When the other major studios refused to follow suit, the SAG membership voted to strike on March 7, 1960.

Several weeks into the strike, Reagan and SAG national executive secretary John Dales met at the Beverly Hills Hotel—where Korshak, by coincidence or not, conducted much of his business—again in private, with long-time Loew's company man Joe Vogel, the president of MGM. At that meeting, the two sides reached a tentative agreement.

The final settlement, reached on April 18 after a bitter six-week strike —which superseded the SAG–Universal agreement—was later termed "The Great Giveaway" by the Hollywood acting community. The contract, which Reagan recommended, required the actors to forfeit all of their claims to residual payments for television showings of movies prior to 1960. In return for this huge concession, the studios promised to create a pension and welfare plan for actors with a one-time initial contribution of a mere $2.65 million. In the future, actors would be entitled to six percent of all future gross sales of theatrical movies to television—after the producers deducted their distribution costs, which sometimes were as high as forty percent.

The SAG membership approved the settlement. The SAG leadership, especially Reagan, assured their members that the best possible deal had been negotiated. The actors had also been warned that several of the studios could close permanently if the strike continued much longer. John Dales—SAG's chief negotiator, along with Reagan, during the strike—defended the settlement and Reagan's performance. "We came out of the 1960 strike with ninety percent of what we asked for," he said. "We got substantial raises, an unheard-of pension and welfare plan at the time. . . . Some members were beginning to get destitute as the strike wore on. It was Ron's judgment and mine that we should take the deal."[5]

Older actors, who lost thousands of dollars when the pre-1960 pictures were sacrificed, were far less charitable about Reagan's skills during the strike. One veteran television actor and SAG member said, "We spent twenty years correcting the Reagan contract. In no way did we win that strike—we lost it. Reagan was a conservative, management-sweetheart union president, and he ran SAG like a country club instead of a militant labor union."[6]

Even Bob Hope, one of Reagan's closest friends, was deeply upset about the 1960 settlement. "The pictures were sold down the river for a certain amount of money," Hope said bitterly, "and it was nothing. . . . See, I made something like sixty pictures, and my pictures are running on TV all over the world. Who's getting the money for that? The studios. Why aren't *we* getting some money . . . ?

"We're talking about thousands and thousands of dollars, and Jules Stein walked in and paid $50 million for Paramount's pre-1948 library of films and bought them for MCA. . . . He got his money back in about two years, and now they own all those pictures."[7]

As the 1960 strike wound down, charges against Reagan's dual actor-producer role, particularly with regard to his status with *General Electric Theater,* again became an issue.

The negotiation of his contract with GE in 1959 had given Reagan twenty-five-percent ownership of the program, in addition to his salary. Reagan was technically no longer an employee of the BBD&O advertising agency. Instead, he had become an employee of Revue Productions and MCA.

When Wasserman was asked about the discrepancy between Reagan's denials that he had not been producing and what was already on the record, the MCA president simply forgot. He said he could not recall whether or not Reagan had produced any GE shows. "I wouldn't know how to draw the line between producing and being the host," Wasserman said. "Being a host was kind of a combination."

Wasserman also contended that he could not remember what ownership interest Reagan had received in 1959 when he renegotiated his GE contract. "I'm sure [Reagan] made the best deal his people were capable of making," Wasserman said, distancing himself from his own performance on Reagan's behalf. "No, I don't know what he received."

Finally, when Wasserman was asked to comment on whether there had been any conflicts of interest between Reagan's close ties with MCA and the subsequent SAG strike, he replied, "I am certain there was never any conflict of interest."[8]

As the 1960 strike ended, Reagan left no doubt as to which side of the line he was on between actor and producer. On June 7, 1960, after serving only seven months of his twelve-month term, Reagan resigned as SAG president to become a partner in a joint production venture with MCA and Revue Productions.

In his July letter of resignation to SAG, Reagan stated: "The Guild has commenced negotiations with television producers. Up to now I have been a salaried employee with no interest in profits. Now I plan to change that status by becoming a producer with an interest in profits. Therefore, with deep regret, I tender my resignation as president and member of the board of directors of the Guild."

At least one member of the SAG board was happy to see Reagan leave. Actor James Garner, who had been appointed to the board by Reagan, said, "[W]hen I was vice-president of the Screen Actors Guild when he was its president, we used to tell him what to say. He can talk around a subject better than anyone in the world. He's never had an original thought that I know of, and we go back a hell of a lot of years."[9]

In the midst of the SAG strike, a major movement was initiated to merge two of the most powerful unions in the entertainment industry. While SAG had grown from 7,338 to 13,403 members since Reagan's 1952 presidency, the American Federation of Television and Radio Artists (AFTRA)—which represented live TV and radio performers as well as record artists—had also swelled from 8,500 to 14,000 members during the same period of time. Two previous attempts to consolidate the two unions had been unsuccessful, primarily because of the conservative SAG leadership, which had had jurisdictional disputes with AFTRA over television actors. In several appeals to the National Labor Relations Board, SAG had been winning the battle for control.

The difference in 1960 was that a professional consultant was retained by both groups. His job was to carefully examine and predict the impact of the proposed merger, and to recommend whether it should happen.

In his final report to both union boards, consultant David L. Cole advocated the merger, stating that such a move would give the performers tremendous bargaining power when negotiating with the various production companies. He added that the union would effectively end the jurisdictional disputes and streamline their administrative procedures. Also, since many members of SAG were also members of AFTRA, and vice versa, pension and welfare plans could become uniform.

Cole proposed that the name of the newly merged union be the Television, Radio, and Screen Actors Guild. He recommended that its headquarters be in Hollywood, because of the heavier concentration of members in California.

Reagan had always openly admitted his opposition to the general idea of one big performers' union to negotiate with management. As to Cole's 1960 plan, he told actor Walter Pidgeon, "Walter, I agree with you completely—I'm going to keep an open mind. I'm going to read his plan before I vote no."[10]

The proposed merger failed.

CHAPTER TWENTY

ON SEPTEMBER 1, 1959, MCA underwent a corporate reorganization, bringing all of its companies under one corporate structure, now called MCA, Inc. On October 9, it became a publicly owned corporation, listed on the New York Stock Exchange and offering 400,000 shares at $17.50 a share. Its new board of directors included Stein; Wasserman; Walter M. Heymann, the vice-chairman of the First National Bank of Chicago; Charles Miller, Stein's brother-in-law; and Leigh M. Battson, the president of Union Oil of California.

In the July 1960 issue of *Fortune,* reporter Edward T. Thompson wrote a penetrating story about MCA entitled "There's No Show Business Like MCA's Business." Thompson reported that MCA, which employed 3,000 people, had a $15 million revolving loan with the First National Bank of Chicago, but that the company's working capital was $31 million. He added that Jules Stein personally owned 1,430,000 shares of MCA stock, which was selling for thirty-three dollars a share during the spring of 1960. Wasserman "holds 715,000 shares, and seven other officers own more than 30,000 shares apiece. In all, the officers and directors own at least seventy-five percent of the company."

Thompson's story only gave the Justice Department's Antitrust Division further reason to pursue its on-and-off-again investigation of

MCA. MCA seemed to take the high road with the Antitrust Division by pledging in a letter from its legal counsel, Cyrus Vance, on February 29, 1960, to Charles L. Whittinghill, chief of litigation for the Antitrust Division, that it would "cooperate fully" with the government's investigation. MCA did limit the government's discovery to the years 1957 and 1958, and excluded all documents referring to foreign acquisitions. The information submitted would include MCA's six major divisions: National Television Sales, Revue Studios, Syndicated Sales, Pre-1948 Paramount Features Sales, MCA Artists, and the Industrial Show and Fair Division.

The Antitrust Division, in their response to Vance, insisted that there be no limits to the scope of its request. However, they did allow MCA to eliminate listing the acquisition of foreign agencies.*

A clearer indication of MCA's willingness to cooperate with the federal government came in October 1960 when the FCC subpoenaed MCA vice-president Taft Schreiber to testify during its hearings on network programming. The FCC also requested a list of all television programs produced by MCA and Revue in which they had a financial interest as well as a list of those television shows which MCA or Revue had packaged or for which they had received a percentage of the selling price.

Schreiber, during his appearance before the commission, refused to comply with the subpoena and when pressed on the witness stand simply stood up and walked out of the hearing. The FCC's presiding officer ruled that Schreiber's actions were contumacious. Schreiber appealed but was overruled and again ordered to testify. FCC commissioner Frederick W. Ford had earlier complained, "It seems as if you can't even go to the bathroom in Hollywood without asking MCA's permission. What upsets me most is the way people tell me that MCA says, 'Nobody in Washington can touch us.' "

While MCA made feeble, somewhat cosmetic attempts to comply with the Antitrust Division's requests, the FBI was conducting an array of interviews. For the most part, those interviewed were primarily outside MCA's sphere of influence. Those inside who were interviewed were not asked very penetrating questions for fear that interviewers would tip off MCA to the government's case in the event that a grand jury was convened and prosecutions brought about. Nearly all of those interviewed demanded total confidentiality for fear of reprisals from MCA or one of its subsidiaries.

---

*The FBI also learned that MCA had fourteen U.S. subdivisions, two Canadian subdivisions, and twelve foreign subsidiaries, all of which were wholly owned.

One industry source told Antitrust Division attorney Leonard Posner, "MCA is the biggest single power in television today. Its power and 'tentacles' are such that both networks and motion picture companies have to bow down before it."[1]

Posner told another source that the government believed that "MCA has engrossed the largest part of the top talent in the motion picture and television industry. This they have used as leverage to obtain a powerful foothold in the programming production industry. MCA uses this unique talent (which is a kind of copyright or patent) as the source of leverage to enable it to gain a foothold in the markets in other areas. They use predatory practices such as blacklists, and they use tie-ins to require other parties to take certain talent, show facilities, or other production components that the other party did not want." When Posner finished his summary, his source said, "That's MCA. You have just described MCA; that's the way they work."[2]

FBI special agent Carter Billings filed his report on the Bureau's findings after its search of MCA records. According to Posner, "Billings said that inspection of the MCA files took place in MCA offices. The files were brought to the FBI in a separate room. The FBI was not given direct access to the files. No personal files of Wasserman or Stein were produced. [MCA's house legal counsel Morris] Schrier claimed they did not have any.

"Billings said that the FBI first began looking into MCA files on July 1, 1959. They finished examining files in December 1959. There was an average of three men per day employed almost continuously in examining these files. The total examination took approximately six months."

One problem the FBI found was the destruction of records by MCA. For instance, "the records retained in [William] Meiklejohn's office were all destroyed," according to one FBI report. "This was apparently done upon the recommendation of a business efficiency survey concern which was then engaged in a survey of the studio operations."[3]

The FBI found several of MCA's responses to be "unsatisfactory," particularly when they concerned MCA's and Revue's activities in the packaging and ownership of network television programs. Nevertheless, the FBI determined that MCA controlled "approximately fifty to seventy-five percent of the top motion picture, television, and radio talent," which it had, for the most part, obtained through "predatory practices." The FBI, among other things, questioned MCA's relationship with NBC and its president, Robert Kintner, calling the network a "captive market for MCA's television shows."

One source interviewed by the FBI stated that "MCA would immediately agree to a [civil settlement] if one were filed. On the other hand . . . they will resist 'to the end of time' any criminal allegations against them."[4]

As Posner continued his interviews, he was told, "MCA will do anything in its power to keep an independent producer like David Susskind [who was a former MCA agent] from getting some of its talent to use in an independent production—this, despite their fiduciary relationship, which should require MCA to try to get employment for its actors. But MCA also considers the fact that Susskind is competition when it comes to program production. Hence they will do everything in their power to book their talent elsewhere when Susskind wants some of them, even going to the extent of building a pilot show to keep the star out of circulation. . . . They would rather 'break the leg' of one of their stars than allow independent producers to use them on shows competitive to MCA."[5]

A pro-MCA source told Posner that "MCA was benevolent. It was good to its employees, it set up trust funds for them, and when it represented a star, that star got the best representation that money could buy. He said that it is a brilliant organization. He also said: 'You will not be able to prove your case against MCA, because . . . MCA has been extremely careful not to do anything overtly which could be construed as illegal.' "

Yet another MCA admirer told the FBI, "Jules Stein, Lew Wasserman, and Taft Schreiber are three of the smartest, most intelligent businessmen in the world today and so superior to the guys running agencies that they make them look sick. In principle, that is the reason why they are a big success. [They are] just smarter, shrewder, have more talent, and they were tough and did things within the law they were entitled to do."[6]

When Posner broached the subject of the relationship between MCA and Paramount, his source replied, "[I]f you are talking about links, what about the one between Universal and MCA?" The most obvious was MCA's purchase of Universal's backlot, but the source added that "MCA now had working for them at least two or three of the big stars [at] Universal, such as [Burt] Lancaster, Tony Curtis, and Janet Leigh."

Posner's source said that there must have been some sort of a tie-in deal there in order for MCA to get these stars. The source added, "Perhaps that was part of the consideration for MCA's paying so much for the Universal lot. Another example of such a tie-in . . . is the Alfred Hitchcock picture *Psycho*. The picture was produced on the Universal lot by MCA. . . . Financing for the picture came from the company that is going to distribute the picture—Paramount. . . . In other words, MCA represented Hitchcock and told Paramount that if it wanted to finance and release the Hitchcock picture, it would have to be produced on the Universal lot so that MCA could get its cut from the below-the-line facilities. This arrangement was made in spite of the fact that Paramount had a lot that was half empty at the time. Obviously, Paramount would have preferred to have had the picture made on its own lot, so that it could have gotten some of its money back toward overhead."[7]

Since 1955, *Alfred Hitchcock Presents* had followed Ronald Reagan's *General Electric Theater* on Sunday in the 9:30–10:00 P.M. slot on CBS. Although Hitchcock "owned" his program, it was made by MCA's Revue Productions—as was *The Jack Benny Program,* which in 1959 followed *GE Theater* and *Alfred Hitchcock Presents* at 10:00 P.M. In September 1960, MCA switched Hitchcock's mystery anthology from CBS to NBC, leaving a gap in the CBS Sunday-night schedule. All of this seemed mundane to most viewers, except the Antitrust Division.

CBS wanted to move Benny's show up a half hour to fill the void left by *Alfred Hitchcock.* However, with a star of Jack Benny's stature, a network could not make such a move unilaterally; Benny had to agree to the change. MCA, Benny's representative, decided, according to the Justice Department, to flex its muscles with CBS. MCA allegedly told CBS and the Benny show's sponsor, Lever Brothers, that if they wanted to move, and even keep, *The Jack Benny Program,* they would have to take two other MCA productions, *Checkmate,* an hour-long private-eye series, and *Ichabod and Me,* a situation comedy. Both shows were owned by Benny's company, J & M Productions.

CBS reportedly complied, placed *Checkmate* on Saturday nights, and received permission to move *The Jack Benny Program* up a half hour to follow *General Electric Theater* on Sunday nights. Later, when Benny was having income tax problems, MCA bought his company for one percent of MCA stock, worth $2,745,000.

Speaking of the deal, Benny said, "What happened when MCA began representing me? Well, I got into business. They helped me set up a corporation, Amusement Enterprises, and then they advised me to dissolve it by selling the shares and keeping most of the money as capital gains.

"Then they helped me form J & M. They put me in a position where I could pay terrific taxes and still keep some money for myself. That was one of the attractions of MCA. They call it giving an actor an 'estate.' "[8]

According to a Justice Department document, "MCA's switch of *Alfred Hitchcock Presents* from CBS to NBC came shortly after the failure of [Revue executive producer Hubbell] 'Hub' Robinson's *Ford Star Time Show.*" The Hitchcock program, according to the report, "might have been a sop to Ford because of the failure of *Star Time.* The Justice Department suspected that the Hitchcock switch released Ford from paying for the costs of nine *Star Time* episodes not aired and that MCA also had a proviso with NBC to take other lesser MCA shows, such as 'Hub' Robinson's *Thriller,* in return for Hitchcock."

The report also said that the *Star Time* deal with Ford had begun before Robinson had become its executive producer. "MCA had an advantage over other independent package producers by virtue of its being able to go to J. Walter Thompson, the advertising agency which represented Ford, and say, 'We'll give you a lot of stars. We'll give you [Alec] Guinness, Ingrid Bergman, and many others [including Marilyn Monroe, Sir Laurence Olivier, and playwright Arthur Miller].' Ford swallowed the bait and signed the contract. MCA, however, did not deliver all the stars [except Guinness and Bergman]. But . . . it was by virtue of using the leverage inherent in the monopolies represented by these unique and irreplaceable stars that MCA was able to make the sale of the package (before it was produced) to Ford."

"MCA would not explicitly tell outside packagers," one source told Posner, "that it would never give them Guinness or Bergman. But let an outside producer try to get them. They would not allow an outside producer to use these stars. Part of the reason is due to the fact that these stars should not appear on television. They are too big and important. They are paid per exposure, and their price for exposure in motion pictures is about $750,000 per film. In television, Bergman would receive only about $100,000 for the exposure. Hence, since such exposure would serve to dilute her [public image as a motion picture star], she would never have been used on television. The only reason she was used on television was because it redounded to the benefit of MCA, if not Bergman."

Posner added his own comment on his source's statement, writing, "Bergman gets $750,000 per picture. Hence, if MCA merely sold Bergman to MGM, [MCA] would get ten percent of $750,000, or $75,000 commission. But when it sells Bergman as part of an overall package involving $160,000 per show, it gets ten percent of the gross price of the show, i.e., thirty-nine [episodes] times $160,000 or $6,240,000 gross, which nets MCA $624,000. In such a case, MCA is glad to sacrifice Bergman's interest for MCA's own interest. That is why MCA will put

Bergman on television in an MCA package. But MCA will never permit such stars to do television shows for an independent producer. In such a case, since MCA would get nothing out of the sale of the overall package, it would merely obtain . . . ten percent [in a single commission]."[9]

The *Ford Star Time* case illustrated how MCA manipulated sponsors and advertising agencies to get good *and* bad shows on the air. According to a Justice Department report, "MCA will sell a 'bomb' [a bad show] to an advertising agency. The agency buys it in good faith and hopes that it will be a good show. After the MCA show proves its lack of worth, the agency approaches MCA to cancel the contract after thirteen weeks. MCA will say: 'We'll let you out of the "bomb" after thirteen weeks, but in order to do so you will have to take this other new series,' which [MCA] touts very highly. The result is that MCA gets deeper and deeper into the advertising agency's budget. The trouble with this tie-in proposition is that in order to obtain its release from a bona fide contract, the advertising agency agrees to take another show."

Sources told Antitrust Division attorneys that the advertising agencies involved would never admit to falling for MCA's scheme—because it would also be an admission that they purchased a "bomb" in the first place, which would anger their sponsor. An example of this was the MCA-Revue–produced *Johnny Staccato,* which appeared on NBC in 1959 and proved to be a loser. *Johnny Staccato* was sponsored by Reynolds Aluminum, which was represented by the William Esty Agency. According to a Justice Department document, "In order to get out of its commitment to *Johnny Staccato,* Esty had to take another show."[10]

According to an industry source interviewed by Posner, director Blake Edwards had earlier gone to his MCA agent with a new program idea, called *Peter Gunn.* "This show was then copied by MCA in an almost Chinese-copy style and the facsimile was called *Johnny Staccato,*" wrote Posner.* "In spite of its fiduciary obligations to Edwards, MCA then sold the show. When Edwards protested and sought his release from an MCA representation contract because of this incident, MCA refused to let him go. . . . MCA was seeking to keep him in bondage."[11]

The parade of charges continued. One source said that he "would gladly shoot several of MCA's officers if he had the chance." Another

---

*Edwards's original *Peter Gunn* was produced as well, and ran for two years beginning in September of 1958.

charged that MCA had become an "Iron Curtain" organization because of its secrecy and bunker mentality during the antitrust investigation. One person even charged MCA with corporate espionage, charging that its executives regularly placed secretaries from their typing pool in studios all over Hollywood, so that it could "get copies of scripts virtually immediately." Another source charged that some actors were forced to kick back part of their salaries to MCA. Someone else charged that MCA "was a bad influence on the industry because it puts out programs of violence and sadism and sex which help to create juvenile delinquents." Yet another said that MCA had engaged in "commercial bribery" and even made "use of women to entice executives of buying organizations." Someone else warned that MCA "was a tough, vindictive outfit. If you go after them too hard, watch out for the concrete shoes." There was even a charge that MCA had helped to destroy RKO by refusing to give the studio its talent.

MCA's tactics had affected its relationship with Warner Brothers, which was also in television production and had provided ABC with some of its top shows, including *Maverick, Cheyenne,* and *Sugarfoot.* Matters between the two companies had deteriorated so badly that the studio refused to permit MCA personnel on its lot. The dispute between MCA and Warner Brothers occurred during the early 1950s when Warners had offered a young, unknown stage actor named Charlton Heston a standard studio contract and wanted him to play the lead in *Ethan Frome.* However, MCA, Heston's agent, persuaded him to do *Dark City* with producer Hal Wallis at Paramount instead. Warners executives were so angry that they declared war on MCA. In fact, the situation had become so intense that "William Morris was representing the talent for MCA on the Warner Brothers lot."[12] However, peace between MCA and Warners came about when MCA later negotiated for Heston to star in three Warner Brothers films.

MCA also allegedly used cash and gifts to induce prospective clients to sign an exclusive-representation contract. For example, Rock Hudson refused a home in Bel Air to leave the Henry Wilson Agency and sign with MCA. Jayne Mansfield did switch agencies after she was offered and accepted $50,000 in cash to do so. Another allegation was that Dean Martin and Jerry Lewis, before their split, were similarly offered money by MCA—if they would leave their agent, Abner Greshler, and become MCA clients.

In another case, MCA was overprotective of one of its top clients. Stanley Kramer was producing the Abby Mann classic *Judgment at*

Nuremberg, a moving drama about the Nazi war crimes trial, and wanted Montgomery Clift to play a small part in the film. For this twelve-minute part, Kramer offered Clift $75,000 for one week of shooting. MCA refused the offer, saying that Kramer had to give Clift his usual $300,000 a movie. Kramer could not afford to pay that much and looked for someone else to play Clift's part. But, soon after, Clift called Kramer and offered to do the part for no salary, asking for only travel and hotel expenses. Kramer happily agreed to Clift's terms.

When Clift was asked why he was willing to work for free, he replied sarcastically, "So that when the picture is over, I can take a big, empty paper bag, tie a blue ribbon around it, and send it to MCA with a note saying, 'Your commission is inside.' "[13]

Some of those interviewed defended MCA with enthusiasm. One recalled how a Hollywood uproar over the hiring of Dalton Trumbo— one of the blacklisted writers of the Hollywood Ten—to write the screenplay for Stanley Kubrick's 1960 super-spectacular, *Spartacus,* was averted when Wasserman approved of and protected Trumbo.

Interviewed by the FBI, Ed Sullivan defended MCA, saying that he "never had any difficulty with regard to the acquisition of MCA talent." He added that "MCA was an extremely efficient organization and that . . . many of the complaints [against MCA] were misunderstandings."[14]

Another story revealed Cary Grant's angry departure from MCA. With television still in its infancy, many of the top Hollywood stars simply refused to do television, thinking that it could compromise and tarnish their images in motion pictures. They preferred the public to pay to see them rather than get them for free. During a meeting with Grant, MCA executives told him, according to a Justice Department document, "that he should appear in a television series. Grant immediately became hostile. He asked again whether they really believed that he should appear on television and MCA replied in the affirmative. He asked who would produce the series. They replied, 'MCA.' Grant then stood up and said, 'Our contract is over as of now,' and he left MCA never to return."[15]

Frank Sinatra, who had gone through so much to change talent agencies and come to MCA, also left angrily. According to another Justice Department report, "Sinatra has had a great deal of trouble with MCA. . . . Sinatra had climbed to heights and then his career had declined precipitously. Sinatra was at that very time very irritated at the way MCA was representing him. . . ." The rift between Sinatra and MCA eventually culminated in an open breach in 1952. Then MCA did something unparalleled in the industry: the talent agency took a full-page ad in *The Hollywood Reporter* and *Daily Variety,* stating that it was releasing Sinatra unconditionally.[16]

Sinatra then went to the William Morris Agency, as did several other MCA clients, including Gloria DeHaven, Jan Murray, and Eddie Fisher. Soon after, Sinatra won the part of Maggio in *From Here to Eternity,* for which he received the 1953 Oscar for Best Supporting Actor.

Ironically, according to FBI documents in 1962, "Sinatra's crowd, [known as] the 'Rat Pack,' is reported to have boasted that they already have 'killed' the government's antitrust investigation of MCA."[17]

The "Rat Pack" had also come up the previous year—in an FBI electronic surveillance operation. Chicago Mafia boss Sam Giancana was having a conversation with Johnny Formosa, one of his lieutenants, about their feelings of betrayal at Sinatra's inability to "deliver" favorable treatment from his friend President Kennedy. During this discussion, they also talked about the "Rat Pack."

"Let's show these fuckin' Hollywood fruitcakes that they can't get away with it as if nothing's happened," Formosa said. "Let's hit Sinatra. Or I could whack out a couple of those other guys. [Peter] Lawford and that [Dean] Martin, and I could take the nigger [Sammy Davis, Jr.] and put his other eye out."

"No . . . ," Giancana replied, "I've got other plans for them."

Soon after this bugged conversation, Sinatra, Martin, and Davis performed at the Villa Venice, a nightclub in Chicago, adjoining an illegal gambling club operated by Giancana's mob. The receipts for just one month, according to wiretaps, were $3 million. Although Sinatra admitted performing at the Villa Venice, he denied that he knew Giancana was in any way connected with the club. FBI agents later asked Davis why he had agreed to perform at the nightclub. "Baby, I have to say it's for my man Francis." And for Frank's friends? "By all means." Like Giancana? "By all means."[18]

CHAPTER
TWENTY-ONE

JOHN F. KENNEDY was inaugurated as president of the United States in January 1961 and had already appointed his brother, Robert F. Kennedy, as attorney general. Under Kennedy, the U.S. Justice Department pledged that among its top priorities would be prosecutions of the nation's top Mafia leaders, their associates, and antitrust violators.

On March 8, 1961, the FCC subpoenaed Taft Schreiber once again to testify at its hearings. As before, Schreiber refused to testify except in a secret session. He was asked several preliminary questions, like which television programs MCA packaged, and again refused to answer, even after being directed to do so by the commission. According to a former top MCA executive, "There was something really awful about the whole FCC thing. Our total defiance was viewed by nearly everyone as nothing less than a reckless disregard for the process of government. You want to know something? We were scared. That's right, scared. We were scared of that goddamn Antitrust Division. Whatever was said in front of the FCC was going right into the case file being built over at Justice. We knew they were starting to breathe down our necks; we could feel it."

Two weeks later, Robert Kennedy was formally notified by Lee

Loevinger, the head of the Antitrust Division in Washington, that "MCA is now being investigated by the General Litigation Section of the Antitrust Division. If the evidence warrants, a request will be made . . . for grand jury authority. . . . The investigation is expected to result in either a criminal or civil case, or both."[1]

That same day, March 21, the chairman of the FCC sent Kennedy a letter, requesting a conference "on the possibility of bringing a criminal action against Taft Schreiber, vice-president of MCA." Three days later, attorneys representing Schreiber charged that the FCC "has not shown that the information sought to be subpoenaed is necessary or appropriate for the discharge of any statutory authority conferred upon it by Congress," adding that the FCC "proceeding was illegal and beyond the authority of the commission."

Meantime, on March 27, in a letter to an attorney friend who was outside the government and operated within the entertainment industry, Leonard Posner mentioned, almost in passing, "Incidentally, I am bemused by the fact that MCA was apparently the only talent agency which got a *blanket* waiver from the talent unions. Am I correct in stating that this is a fact? And, if so, do you know why this happened?" This was the first reference to either the American Federation of Musicians or the Screen Actors Guild since the official investigation began. And Posner would follow up.

But the federal government was faced with the problem of having too many investigations of MCA. While the Justice Department and the FCC determined what to do with the defiant Taft Schreiber, the Antitrust Division's General Litigation Section was weighing the options of prosecuting Schreiber for either civil or criminal contempt. There would be major consequences if the government attempted to prosecute Schreiber at all. For instance, what would happen if Schreiber was again required to testify before the FCC hearing and then took the Fifth? Would he then be given immunity from prosecution and required to testify? Would such actions harm the Antitrust Division's investigation of MCA?*

As another complication, Posner received a telephone call from Nicholas Zapple, special counsel to the U.S. Senate Interstate and Foreign Commerce Committee, chaired by Senator Warren Magnuson. Zapple told Posner that the Senate panel had a subcommittee dealing exclusively with investigations into the television industry, and that

---

*Eventually, the Justice Department's Criminal Division decided *not* to press criminal contempt charges against Taft Schreiber, yielding instead to the FCC's efforts to proceed against the MCA vice-president in civil court. That case was later dropped.

several senators were interested in conducting a probe of MCA "if the Antitrust Division was not prepared to move effectively and promptly into the affairs of that organization."

"I told Zapple," Posner said, "that we were investigating MCA ... [but] that there were difficult problems connected with the investigation: witnesses appeared to be frightened; there were reports that MCA had prepared special reports designed . . . to prove they were innocent of antitrust violations. In addition, it was anticipated that it would be a very difficult case because we would get no evidence from MCA, and it would hence be necessary to lay a firm foundation of evidence from other sources."

Zapple said the senators would, thus, probably "not go into the matter themselves."[2]

A week later, MCA attorney Albert Bickford, who had replaced Cyrus Vance, talked to Posner and asked "whether there was any connection between the FCC hearing and its actions against Schreiber and our investigation . . . ," Posner wrote. "I told Bickford that so far as I knew the FCC was primarily seeking something different from our interest in the matter."[3]

Lee Loevinger called Posner on April 10 and demanded to know "where we stood on MCA." After giving him some background information, Posner replied that it would be important "to try to have a grand jury in the MCA matter because the witnesses were frightened to death and we wouldn't expect to be able to get any specific direct evidence without the cloak of secrecy of a grand jury."[4]

The following month, Posner wrote a lengthy memorandum on the MCA investigation. In explaining the case, Posner wrote, in part: "Even more crucial is the fact that our theories depend on proof of conspiracies between MCA and two talent unions (SAG and AFM) and between MCA and NBC. We propose to learn more about these conspiracies in the next month or two in as quiet a way as possible. For example, we propose to accept SAG's offer to examine their files while we are on the West Coast. We are very much afraid that if MCA and its alleged conspirators learn of our suspicions—which will be inevitable once the 'large' FBI investigation gets under way—this evidence will disappear and all information concerning these conspiracies will go underground. This, in itself, could mean loss of the case before we are fairly started."[5]

On May 22, Nicholas Zapple from the Senate Interstate Commerce Committee met with Posner and told him that the members of his subcommittee on television wanted to move on MCA. Posner wrote,

"We discussed fully with Zapple the reasons why the Antitrust Division would like two or three months in which quietly to conduct an investigation of MCA. Zapple said that he understood the problem. We did not, however, mention talent unions. We indicated to Zapple that we were afraid that if there were undue publicity on MCA, that MCA would attempt to contact potential witnesses and alter or suppress their testimony. We also indicated that it would be very difficult to obtain evidence on the case."

That same day, further complications arose when Paul Laskin, counsel to the Senate Subcommittee on Juvenile Delinquency, chaired by Senator Estes Kefauver, wanted to explore how crime and violence were portrayed on television. In order to do so, Laskin said, according to Posner, there was a definite possibility that they might find themselves immersed in developing evidence on MCA directly. We told Laskin that this would definitely prejudice our case. . . . He promised to do all he could to try to avoid going into MCA directly."[6]

The next day, the Antitrust Division formally requested from the IRS all of the income tax returns of MCA and all of its subsidiaries, including MCA Artists and Revue Productions.

On May 25, Posner began his investigation into the Justice Department's "conspiracy theory," involving NBC, SAG, and AFM. Posner's first industry source told him that "[NBC's Robert] Kintner could not possibly have been so dishonest as to have sold out his own company even though he had been given the job [as president of] NBC through influence exerted by MCA." Instead, the source thought that "NBC had entered into some sort of exclusive arrangement with MCA whereby it [NBC] got the first pick or first refusal on a number of programs . . . [but] that such an arrangement would, of course, have required NBC to take the bad programs along with the good."

Regarding the MCA-SAG relationship, the source said that he did not think the fact that MCA had been the only agency to receive a blanket waiver was significant. "MCA had foreseen this situation long before anyone else," he said, "and had therefore anticipated [it] by moving in quickly and asking for a blanket waiver."

Posner replied that he "considered this slightly far-fetched: any of the talent agencies would have realized that the biggest profits would come from program sales since they would have the opportunity to see the contracts that their actor-clients had signed. Furthermore, any talent agency which came across a script that looked like a promising deal for one of its clients would want to put together the package and produce it. . . . A blanket waiver was the only way that any company could effectively engage in continuous television production."

The source later clarified himself, saying that he agreed that there was a conspiracy between MCA and AFM. "Furthermore," Posner wrote, "on the basis of his knowledge of SAG, he thinks it only logical that exactly the same pattern is being repeated in television today. As soon as I began to describe the setup in radio days, [the source] exclaimed: 'That's it! That's it! It's exactly the same system that MCA used in radio days.' He said that he had been very familiar with MCA's radio and band practices, and he said, 'Now you have it. They are doing the same damn thing in television today.'"

The source said that James Petrillo—who had finally been replaced as national president of AFM by Herman Kamin in 1958 but kept control of his Chicago local—had been "tied in with Willie Bioff and racketeers. He said that he has absolutely no doubt but that our theory of the AFM contributing to the rise of MCA is correct. This would be reflected by the minutes of AFM . . . that it was his recollection that no big-band leader ever won a dispute against MCA. . . . He said that Stein and Petrillo were great buddies and they were the closest of associates. They always spoke very highly of one another. He is sure that Petrillo did favors for Jules Stein. He was not surprised to learn that Petrillo acquired a block of MCA stock."

Posner noted that his source "became quite excited as the interview progressed. He said he had had a vast amount of experience in the big-band field. He was sure we were correct in suspecting that AFM had contributed to the rise of MCA and to its eventual 'lock' on big bands." When asked to compare the ethics of AFM with those of SAG, the source replied that he felt that there were many dishonest people in leadership positions in SAG, and that he "had long believed they did not really try to represent the rank and file of actors in their union. He said that we would find that Ronald Reagan was president of SAG at the time that MCA was given the waiver. . . . He was absolutely convinced that the Screen Actors Guild blanket waiver had contributed to MCA's achieving dominance in the field of television film production."[7]

Other sources began to corroborate what Posner's industry source had told him about AFM and SAG. On June 7, he interviewed another top industry source, whom he described as "completely honest." Swearing the source to secrecy about their conversation, Posner asked about the MCA-SAG waiver. The source replied that "at least one other talent agency had asked for a blanket waiver and had been refused." He agreed with Posner that no company could become involved in film production without such a waiver and "thought it strange that only MCA had been granted this."

Posner asked about Ronald Reagan. "Ronald Reagan," the source said, "is a complete slave of MCA who would do their bidding on anything." He added that he "would not be surprised to find that some type of consideration had passed between the top people in SAG and MCA to [cement] the deal."

He then repeated that it was "extremely likely that SAG had contributed to MCA's rise in the television film production industry exactly as the AFM had helped MCA in its control of big bands."[8]

Another source told Posner on July 11, "[I]t is unconscionable for the Screen Actors Guild to continue permitting MCA a blanket waiver when it goes against all the rules of conflict of interest."

CHAPTER TWENTY-TWO

ON AUGUST 22, Nicholas Zapple asked Posner if the Antitrust Division's investigation would be harmed if his Senate subcommittee did one of two things: either called twelve to fifteen witnesses for a series of limited hearings on MCA, or called those people to testify who were already on the record about their feelings toward MCA. Posner felt that both of these alternatives would be harmful.

When Zapple asked why, Posner replied, "It would, at least, illustrate for MCA the main areas of thrust which they could expect to be exploited during an antitrust case. Hence, they would shore up their defenses against these areas, and seek ways of explaining away the testimony of these persons. . . . I told Zapple that in my estimation there was no possibility of using surprise as a means of catching MCA off base and that the only thing we could do was to prepare a very solid foundation for a case."[1]

Three days later, on August 25, Attorney General Robert Kennedy authorized a federal grand jury to be convened in the Southern District of New York to investigate the numerous charges against MCA. In his request for authorization, Lee Loevinger charged that "MCA's power has created fear of retaliation, including the 'blacklist' of talent and the boycotting of producers from access to 'name' talent. The alleged existence of boycotts, blacklists, predatory practices, and per se violations (such as 'tie-ins') may provide a basis for a criminal suit, and thus makes desirable the empaneling of a grand jury." Loevinger added that "no grant of immunity to any of MCA's top executives is planned."

On August 28, Paul Laskin from the Senate Committee on Juvenile Delinquency told Posner that soon "the lid would be off" on the Senate's proposed investigation of MCA. Posner pleaded with Laskin "that it was vitally important within the next few weeks that we get no publicity at all insomuch as we were going to the [West] Coast to try to unearth certain information with respect to practices of MCA."

"When are you going to indict MCA?" Laskin asked sharply.

Posner said, "I told Laskin that because of the type of action that he himself had indicated might be contemplated, it was vitally important that our witnesses not be disclosed, and that their testimony not be made known to MCA. I explained that in all criminal cases, defendants make strenuous efforts to obtain the minutes of the grand jury, and to obtain by inspection thereof the testimony of the chief witnesses who would be marshaled against them, and that such defendants also commonly make great efforts to obtain lists of witnesses."

Laskin finally said that he was sympathetic and saw the need for secrecy, asking, however, to be kept informed as to the progress of the case.

On August 28, rumors were flying from coast to coast in the wake of the decision to convene the grand jury. According to the Hollywood gossip, Revue Productions was planning to split off from MCA and merge with Paramount—and Paramount president Barney Balaban was going to yield his job to Lew Wasserman. Simultaneously, SAG was preparing to rescind its blanket waiver to MCA. Posner learned that "SAG is definitely pushing ahead. It will make new demands, and a waiver retraction will be one of these." In a memorandum to his files, Posner wondered whether it was "significant" that SAG was acting at the exact time that Revue appeared to be preparing to split from MCA.[2]

On Friday, September 8, the Screen Actors Guild jolted the television production industry when it announced that it had voted to eliminate the waivers enabling talent agencies to produce shows, effective December 31, 1961—although SAG stated that it could grant a six-month extension.

The question became: What would MCA do now? Would it try to divest itself in advance of the deadline? Would it apply for the six-month extension? How would it retain as much control as possible over its empire, even after it was broken up?

Four days later, Posner received information that "MCA has already moved a considerable amount of its personnel to Revue. . . . Wasserman has been in Europe but is due back about now." However, Posner also learned that SAG had no intention of policing the breakup—"so long as there is a legal separation, SAG will not care whether or not there is a practical separation." As far as Posner was concerned—from what he had learned from his sources—a mere cosmetic separation would keep MCA in violation of federal antitrust laws.[3]

Had SAG—which could have been charged with restraint of trade by virtue of its singular blanket waiver to MCA—simply bought itself out of legal jeopardy by its sudden action? SAG's good faith was immediately questioned, particularly considering the union's cozy past with MCA. Posner's sources speculated also that the whole waiver scenario between SAG and MCA had resulted from the fact "that certain actors had been instrumental in the granting of the MCA waivers, and that possibly this may have been due to promises by MCA to the actors that they would get a reward via certain tax-saver corporations."

Another prominent theory, based on some evidence, was "that an aggressive corporation like MCA would not be apt to split off cleanly but there would remain certain close rapport between their officials [in MCA and SAG] for a number of years after this supposed divestiture."[4]

Was there a secret deal? John Dales, the executive secretary of SAG, said, "Oh, no. Our attorney Bill Burger and my assistant, Chet Migden, and I met with Wasserman and [SAG counsel Laurence] Beilenson, and [we] told them that we were not going to renew the waiver."[5]

On September 18, Loevinger was told by his antitrust lawyers that "if the split-off were genuine, it might possibly eliminate the most important element of the case, and could possibly lead to abandonment."

Posner and his colleagues recommended that the Justice Department continue the FBI investigation and accelerate the grand jury by immediately calling witnesses. Loevinger agreed. "The way to keep pressure on MCA," he said, "was to push ahead with the grand jury as hard as possible," even though he realized that "the MCA split-off might seriously impair our case."[6]

The immediate problem was procedural, one of empaneling a grand jury. For this antitrust case, twenty-three jurors would be selected by a random drawing from a pool of 125–150 persons. (There is always a danger that some of the prospective jurors may have connections with the company under investigation.) October 10 would be the earliest date that a grand jury could be seated. In the interim, the Justice Department began compiling its witness list and subpoenas, and started reviewing FBI reports and its own interviews.

During a conference with the FBI on October 2, special agents lamented that the results of their interviews had been "disappointing." According to Posner, "They ran headlong into the principal problem of this investigation, i.e., fear of MCA."[7]

The FBI was given more time, and the Antitrust Division decided to postpone the grand jury and move it from New York to Los Angeles. They asked Robert Kennedy for authorization. The attorney general gave his approval but in a handwritten note on the memorandum stated, "However, I want a summary of info we have developed on this. . . ."

On October 31, Posner received an official copy of the recent special MCA-SAG agreement, which had been negotiated on October 24. According to the Justice Department's analysis of the document, "MCA will keep the same people in the talent agency as subagents. Moreover, MCA will keep in the same lieutenants who will be responsible to, and have loyalty to, the same MCA subagents. . . . There is little doubt that the new SAG-MCA agreement provides that MCA will spin off Revue. However, MCA personnel will still be manning the talent agency." The agreement also stated that MCA would have until September 30, 1962, to make a decision whether to divest itself of the talent agency or its film production company.

Under the agreement, MCA could buy the stock of a motion picture studio. There had been published reports in some newspapers that MCA was considering the purchase of either Paramount or Universal. Further, only the representation of screen actors was affected under the agreement. MCA could continue to represent producers, directors, and writers.

In a letter to its membership, dated October 31, 1961, the SAG board informed its members of its ultimatum to MCA but added, "The Guild board believes it to be a foregone conclusion that MCA will surrender the agency franchise and maintain and probably expand production activities."

The Justice Department report also stated that "the members of the Artists' Managers Guild [representing talent agents] were incensed because MCA, one of its members, was conducting secret negotiations with SAG without informing the rest of the members. The deal between SAG and MCA was conducted in strict secrecy, and many of the members of the Artists' Managers Guild are still apprehensive that there are elements of the negotiations which they do not know and that MCA in giving up its waiver may have gotten other considerations and privileges not yet announced by SAG."*

As the process of selection for the federal grand jury in Los Angeles began, the Antitrust Division summarized its case for Robert Kennedy in a long memorandum. Aside from the three hundred witnesses interviewed by the FBI, the antitrust attorneys had talked to another 150 industry sources. The memorandum to the Attorney General charged that a variety of antitrust violations had been engaged in by MCA, including:

1. Attempt to monopolize the trade in name talent;
2. Attempt to monopolize the production of TV film programs;
3. Conspiracy with the Screen Actors Guild to monopolize the trade in name talent;
4. Conspiracy with the Screen Actors Guild to monopolize TV film program productions; and
5. Restraint of trade in name talent and TV film program production by (a) contract with SAG, (b) tie-in sales and contracts with networks, (c) "shadow" or extorted payments for services not actually rendered, (d) foreclosure of independent producers from market, (e) discrimination between talent clients of MCA and producers represented by MCA in order to serve MCA's interests, and (f) predatory practices.

"It is likely that MCA saw in television the opportunity for an operation similar to that by which it had obtained control of bands and radio band programs," Loevinger wrote. "The union which parallels in TV film programming the operation of the AFM is the Screen Actors Guild.

"MCA obtained the only *blanket* waiver granted by SAG to a talent agency to engage in the production of television film on a permanent

---

*On October 10, 1961, SAG granted an "MCA-type waiver" to another member of the Artists' Managers Guild, GAC, which was represented by attorney Abe Fortas of the Washington, D.C., law firm of Arnold, Fortas and Porter—in the midst of rumors that GAC was preparing to purchase Desilu Studios. According to George Chandler, Reagan's successor as SAG president, "A request from General Artist Corporation for an MCA-type waiver, signed by Herbert J. Siegel, September 27, 1961, was received by the Guild shortly thereafter. This was his only request for such waiver. It was considered by the board of directors of the Guild on October 9, 1961, and granted. The actual waiver was dated October 10. . . . Whether this request had any connection with a purchase of Desilu Studios was never revealed to the Guild by Mr. Siegel."⁸

basis [with the exception of that provided to GAC a few weeks earlier]. . . . We also hope to prove that the grant of this *blanket* waiver was effectuated by a conspiracy between MCA and SAG."

Loevinger concluded his report by saying: "We expect to present witnesses to the grand jury as rapidly as possible."

By mid-November, the grand jury had started calling witnesses. Posner continued to conduct the investigation. John Fricano of the Trial Section of the Antitrust Division and E. C. Stone of its New York office handled the questioning of the witnesses, who included Cary Grant and Danny Kaye, as well as a variety of industry executives, agents, producers, directors, and writers.

The FBI received reports that MCA tried to intimidate at least one witness, warning actor Joseph Cotten that MCA officials would receive a copy of his testimony, and that his film career would be affected accordingly.

CHAPTER TWENTY-THREE

On February 5, 1962, John Fricano prepared to question the man whom he hoped would shed new light on the relationship between MCA and the Screen Actors Guild. That afternoon, Ronald Reagan, wearing casual clothes after spending the morning shooting a new episode on the set of *General Electric Theater*, stepped to the witness stand and took the oath.

The following is a verbatim transcript of Ronald Reagan's February 5, 1962, secret testimony before the federal grand jury in Los Angeles, investigating alleged violations of antitrust and criminal laws by MCA. The original transcript, taken down by certified shorthand reporter Lucille Girlow, contained occasional misspellings and typographical errors, which have been corrected by the author in brackets. This is the first time this document has been published in its entirety.*

"State your name and residence address," John Fricano asked.

"Ronald Reagan, 1669 San Onofre Drive."

"What is your profession, Mr. Reagan?"

---

*Excerpts have been published by *Daily Variety* reporter David Robb, who uncovered the document, and Dan E. Moldea and Jeff Goldberg in *City Paper*. (See bibliography, p. 365, under heading "On Ronald Reagan and MCA.")

"Actor, I think."

"I think the Grand Jury recognizes you, Mr. Reagan. We will dispense with the usual formalities. However, very briefly will you state for the record your history, as it were, [of] being in the entertainment industry."

"I graduated from college in 1933. I became a radio sports announcer in the Midwest. [Four] years later in 1937 I went under contract to Warner Brothers Studios here in Hollywood to make motion pictures, most of which are showing up on the late late show, and in 1954 [sic] while I was at Warner Brothers, with renewals of the seven-year contract until 1949 at which time we rewrote the last two years of a contract, the last three years of a contract to one picture a year for three years with no exclusivity. I had the right to go outside to make pictures for other companies. I did those three pictures and then was a free lance. In 1954 I took my present job with the *General Electric Theater*."

"In 1937, Mr. Reagan, when you were under contract to Warner Brothers, by whom were you represented?"

"MCA, oh, wait a minute."

"1937?"

"William [Meiklejohn]."

"Who was your next agent after Mr. [Meiklejohn]?"

"MCA. In a way, still both of them, William [Meiklejohn] Agency. MCA had never been in the motion picture representation field and they decided to come into the field and they did it by buying William [Meiklejohn] Agency and taking six of us who were clients as the first motion picture clients of MCA."

"Do you recall who the other five were?"

"Bill Demarest was one I know. Jane Wyman was one, I don't recall the rest beyond that. I know three of us. I think there were six. Could have varied one or two but I always referred to it as six."

"Do you recall when MCA acquired the William [Meiklejohn] Agency?"

"I think around 1939 or '40 but my memory is a little hazy there."

"Have you been represented by MCA since 1939 or '40 when William [Meiklejohn] was acquired by MCA?"

"Yes. Could I volunteer something here? I wouldn't want these ladies and gentlemen to think that I wouldn't wear a shirt and necktie to come down here. They caught me at the studio. I had no choice."

"Revue [Productions'] studio?"

"Yes."

"When was your first excursion into television, Mr. Reagan?"

"Well, that would have been in the period—oh, dear, that would be just prior to 1954. I would say in the year and a half or so prior to 1954 I did some guest shots. I did a few shows, both live and film, and I did them both here and in New York. It was new and you want to get your seat wet a little bit and find out what it is all about and at first it seemed like radio. We always did things like *Lux Radio Theater* and I did a few shows of that kind."

"Who was your personal agent at MCA when you first went to the organization?"

"Lew Wasserman."

"Have you ever had any other personal agent?"

"Yes, as Lew went more into the administrative end, becoming president of the company, Art [Park] has been my particular agent."

"And he has handled you more or less exclusively since Mr. Wasserman gave up his duties?"

"Yes, except in MCA, when you have been around this long, you still go to Lew Wasserman on some matters and with Art and also they have a system there, it seems to me, of having men assigned to particular studios and a man is assigned to particular studios and a man is assigned like Irving Salkow to television. So many times you are offered a guest shot and it will come through Irving Salkow because that is his department and he is assigned to that as a department, not to me as an individual. If I have any question about rates or whether I should do it or not, I would take it up with Art [Park] and discuss it with him in relation to any problems we might have."

"Returning once again, if we may, to the time when you went to MCA in 1939 or '40. What type of contracts did you sign with MCA?"

"Oh, I never read them but they were the regular contract that is provided for by the arrangement with the Screen Actors Guild, the regular agency contract which I have helped negotiate those contracts with the agents when I was an officer and board member with the Guild, and yet I can't remember where we made the changes. I know sometimes we shortened the time they were to hold you, that an agent company could hold an actor, but whatever it was it—"

"Well, did you sign an exclusive contract with MCA to the effect they would represent you in all media?"

"Yes."

"In which you appear?"

"Yes."

"I don't know if they had what was known as a package representation as early as 1939 or '40. Do you know if you had such a contract?"

"I wouldn't know. There were times back there every once in a while the things come in the mail and you sign it if you are satisfied with the agent. Sometimes there were, I remember, some period[s] in which I signed additional for representation in additional fields."

"Have you ever refused to sign any contract of representation by MCA?"

"No."

"Then we can assume that you at the present time have the regular SAG contract for talent representation with MCA, that they represent you in all media in which you might appear which might be television, radio, and motion pictures, and also that you have with them a package representation contract; that's correct, is it not?"

"I would say so, yes."

"Do you know of your own personal knowledge whether you have such contracts with MCA at this time?"

"Well, now, if my life depended on it, no. I just signed what was sent and sent it back."

"I think we can fairly assume that Mr. Reagan had such contracts. Did MCA ever condition representation by them of your signing of any contract?"

"No."

"What unions are you a member of, Mr. Reagan?"

"Screen Actors Guild and AFTRA. I have been a member, in addition, of the American Guild of Variety Artists for a brief time when I made personal appearances."

"How long have you been a member of AFTRA? When did you first become a member?"

"Well, it was just radio, the Radio Guild, and I imagine that was probably about the same time when I came out here and joined the Screen Actors Guild. In my early days of sports announcing in the Midwest, we didn't know about such things. We were all out in the open with no unions, no union representing, when this organization was created."

"Do you recall when you became a member of SAG?"

"Yes, when I came here and signed my contract with Warner Brothers."

"1937?"

"Yes."

"What positions have you held in SAG since you became a member in 1937?"

"Well, I have probably held twenty years of membership total as a board member. I briefly was a vice-president and I had six and a half terms as president."

"Do you recall the years that you were president?"

"Yes, I was appointed to fill out the term of a resigning president around 1946 or '47. I served five and a half years then and refused to run anymore but served on the board continuously until a couple of years ago, I guess 1959 or '60. I became president again for one year. Just shortly before the end of that year [I] resigned."

"Then you were president of Screen Actors Guild in July 1952?"

"Yes."

"And you were a member of the board of directors in June 1954?"

"Yes."

"What committees have you served on, Mr. Reagan, of the Screen Actors Guild?"

"Well, the negotiating committee for years back."

"Would that be negotiations with respect to both motion picture studios and television production companies?"

"Yes, and negotiations also—I have been on the negotiating committee to negotiate the basic agreement between the Artists' Managers Guild, the agent."

"Of June 30, 1954?"

"Yes. Then I have been on committees that had to do with trying to work out arrangements between ourselves and AFTRA over the question of jurisdiction of television."

"In what year was the jurisdictional dispute between AFTRA and SAG settled?"

"Oh—"

"That was with respect to TV film?"

"That went on for a great many years. I hope it's settled now. I think it was settled—I would have to say, isn't that awful, it's been about a year and a half or two years when we finally refused, the Screen Actors Guild refused any idea of a joint merger into one union."

"That's right, sir. I think you have misapprehended my question and I will rephrase it, if I may. There was in the early '50s, was there not, a dispute between AFTRA and SAG as to which union would have jurisdiction of TV films?"

"That's right."

"Was that dispute settled at that time?"

"Well, it was settled to the extent that we had jurisdiction of film, although AFTRA really never gave in. They always protested and claimed that we shouldn't have. We were the only one in the talent field, when television came we were the only ones that gave up jurisdiction of television. We were the only ones that found ourselves in trouble because when we gave up we didn't think we were giving up the right to negotiate for actors to negotiate with motion picture studios and making film[s]."

"Do you recall, sir, whether or not AFTRA and SAG went before the National Labor Relations Board to settle the jurisdictional dispute over TV film?"

"I think there were thirteen of those appearances. AFTRA I think filed about thirteen times."

"There were thirteen suits but I am referring specifically to the one in which the NLRB decided with respect to TV film. Was that in [1951]?"

"I think it was."

"In that year SAG received jurisdiction of TV film?"

"According to the NLRB in that suit, yes."

"When SAG received jurisdiction in TV film, what then did it have to do, what procedures did it follow to actually implement its jurisdiction?"

"We then had to negotiate for the working conditions and wages of films made for television. We also had to negotiate for motion picture distribution."

"Were these as such carried on?"

"Yes."

"Do you remember the year of such negotiations?"

"I know this seems silly but you are asking about an awful lot of years of memory."

"Let me try to refresh your recollection if I may, Mr. Reagan. I think we have already established that in [1951] the NLRB settled the SAG-AFTRA jurisdictional dispute, correct?"

"Yes."

"Then another followed closely?"

"I think in [1951] the negotiations—we would have ended these negotiations."

"Do you recall with what companies SAG negotiated at this time?"

"Well, again we had to negotiate with the major producers, major motion picture studios, even though many of them weren't engaged in television. We realized this, of course, was where the battle would have to be won or lost and then we negotiated with the group representing the ten independent motion picture producers of TV."

"Does the name 'Alliance of TV Film Producers' ring a bell with you?"

"Yes, that's right."

"So then negotiations took place with the major motion picture production companies and with the Alliance of Television Film Producers, correct?"

"Yes."

"Do you recall with which companies SAG negotiated in the motion picture film—for TV film production, of course?"

"Well, now I may be wrong in this but it seems to me, once having cleared the decks and negotiated, I think we negotiated with the motion picture producers as an association with the major studios in addition to the Alliance."

"Did these negotiations, to the best of your knowledge, sir, take place generally simultaneously?"

"That again—my memory would be pretty dim on. I would think, yes. Maybe—I don't honestly know."

"What was the big point at issue in the negotiations with TV film production companies in 1952?"

"Well, of course, the biggest point of all was to recognize the principle of residual payments for actors in films once made, that they would be paid again when those films were run."

"That was the dispute that was going on between SAG and this union at this time, correct?"

"Well, that was to get—naturally the studios after fifty years of operating on a basis of once they had the film in the can it was theirs, they resisted at this idea of anyone having a lien against that film and they did not have complete ownership of it. One studio head said, 'It's mine to throw off the end of the dock if I want.' I made some that I wish he had."

"In point of fact, television was a dirty word in the motion picture industry in 1952?"

"That's right."

"It's also a fact, is it, Mr. Reagan, that the first company to capitulate with respect to repayment for reuse was a TV production company?"

"I am sure that would have been the Alliance, yes."

"Which company, whether a member of the Alliance or not, was the first to capitulate with respect to repayment for reruns?"

"There you have me. I wouldn't know where we cracked that and if you tell me I'll have to take your word for it."

"Well, you were president of the Screen Actors Guild in 1952, were you not?"

"Yes."

"This was a very important matter which Screen Actors Guild was taking up and it was the most important point of the Guild?"

"Yes, and I don't want to appear as though I am trying deliberately to be vague, but, as I say, I would like you to realize in my history of holding an office with the Guild, my memory is like a kaleidoscope of meetings, that I am sure if I sat down with someone and started in, I could then recall the details. But I met for seven months twice a day five days a week in an attempt to settle the big jurisdictional question in 1946 and '47. I mean personally for more than eight or nine weeks almost every day in 19—before 1947 as a member of negotiating committees. I mean, it's the length of negotiations that led to the stopgap that led to the release of feature motion pictures to television and I went to New York and I met out here for countless meetings with AFTRA when they were attempting to evade what was our right and jurisdiction."

"I think the grand jury understands, sir, at this time you were very busy and the memory of man is not the greatest faculty he possesses. I will attempt to refresh your recollection with respect to this time period. In the first place, does the fact that I state to you now that MCA was the first, MCA-Revue, that is, was the first to acquiesce to the residual payments help you out in your recollection? Can you substantiate that statement?"

"No, I can't. I honestly can't. I know that many times Jack Dales reported to me as president, he is the executive secretary of the Guild, that he had talked off the record to Lew Wasserman about this problem and about the recognizing of this principle and so forth. When did this occur, when did you say?"

"July 1952. July 23, 1952."

"Well, maybe the fact that I got married in March of 1952 and went on a honeymoon had something to do with my being a little bit hazy."

"I'm glad you raised that point. If we might digress, who is your wife?"

"Nancy Davis."

"Was she a member of the board of directors of SAG in 1952?"

"Yes."

"Do you recall any other unusual or momentous events in 1952 with respect to SAG's relations with one or more TV film production companies?"

"Well, now what kind of events?"

"In 1952, when you were president of the Screen Actors Guild, did not the Screen Actors Guild grant to MCA what is known in the trade as a blanket or unlimited waiver to produce TV films?"

"Oh, we have granted—I don't know when it exactly started, we granted an extended waiver to MCA to be engaged in production as we had done with other people. Mr. [Feldman], who was an agent and produced feature pictures, we gave him a waiver also."

"That was a limited waiver, limited specifically to two or possibly three productions a year. It was not a blanket or unlimited waiver?"

"That's right."

"What is SAG's history with respect to granting waivers in either media, motion pictures [or] television prior to 1952?"

"Oh, well, I would have to say there must have been, I am sure, there must have been times when for some reason or another we refused but I am sure also—I can tell you what our general attitude was. Our attitude was where we could see no harm to one of our members, to our membership, that we should do everything we could to encourage production because the great problem we have had has always been unemployment. Even in times of prosperity actors are unemployed. They sit out and wait. If somebody comes to discuss and tell us they want to make pictures, we are inclined to go along with them."

"You would like to have as many production companies making pictures as possible?"

"Yes, in America."

"We have bandied the term 'waiver' about. Let's see if we can be a little more specific about it. Why would it be necessary for a talent agent to apply for a waiver to engage in film production or motion picture production?"

"Well, it was [some] years ago the artists' manager, the agent in our business, agreed voluntarily to let the Screen Actors Guild set up the standard and legitimize the relationship between agent and actor. Up until this time if a man wanted to represent an actor, he might find some young man, make him a star, he could take as much as fifty percent of what they were making. There was nothing to guide it. They voluntarily entered into this arrangement, so we always, in the transposition of negotiating a contract with our employers as employees, and we turned around in turn and then negotiated with the agents as employers."

"If I may summarize what you are saying, Mr. Reagan, that the necessity for the waiver and the rules which SAG has, requires that a waiver be open talk is because of the fear of a breach of fiduciary relationships which the talent agency has with its clients?"

"That's right."

"Prior to 1952 what talent agencies, if you recall, obtained waivers from Screen Actors Guild and we'll take this ad [seriatim]. First in motion pictures?"

"The only one offhand that I can say that [I] recall was Feldman with his limited waiver."

"But you do recall that it was a limited waiver?"

"Yes. Now, there may have been others. I don't recall them right now."

"Myron Selznick, does that ring a bell?"

"Oh, he was a little before my time."

"You are familiar, are you not, with the waiver granted to MCA in 1952 during your term as president?"

"Yes."

"Can you tell this grand jury why Screen Actors Guild gave to MCA a blanket or unlimited waiver?"

"Well, my own reasoning and one of the reasons perhaps why this doesn't loom so importantly to me is I personally never saw any particular harm in it. I was one who subscribed to the belief, and those were times of great distress in the picture business, I was all for anyone that could give employment. I saw no harm in this happening. Now, anything I would answer from there would be hearsay. I have been told that Revue grew out of MCA's efforts to enter the motion picture industry, in moving into the field of television, and they wouldn't touch it. And when Revue had in their hands the possibility of these packages and couldn't get anyone to produce them, that they set up shop to produce them themselves."

"Do you recall how early this was in point in time?"

"I don't know. I think it was prior to '52."

"It would have been either the latter '40s or 1950?"

"Yes."

"Because Revue had been in production since that time?"

"Yes."

"Do you recall the year Revue first went into production, Mr. Reagan?"

"No, I don't. Television at that time, you must recall, was mostly live and was mostly centered in New York and I knew there were shows called package shows, that you got a chance to do a guest shot. You went to do yours and it was a Revue package. I wasn't even familiar with the name too much. I just called it an MCA package but then that wasn't strange because we had the same thing in radio."

"You have given us your rationale behind your reasons for the blanket waiver to MCA in 1952. What was Screen Actors Guild's reason for granting this waiver?"

"Well, that is very easy to recall. Screen Actors Guild board and executives met in meetings and very carefully considered these things, weighed them at board meetings. I remember discussions taking place about it and usually the result of the discussion would be that we felt we were amply protected, that if any harm started from this, if anything happened to react against the actors' interests—we could always pull the rug out from under them. No great harm would be done before we could ride to the rescue, that our feeling was here was someone that wanted to give actors jobs and that is the way it would usually wind up."

"How many more waivers did Screen Actors Guild grant to talent agents subsequent to the blanket waiver to MCA in order to give actors jobs?"

"I don't recall. I don't know if we did to William Morris or not. When I say I don't know if we did, it was because I was more familiar with William Morris in the live field of packaging."

"Do you know whether any talent agents applied for blanket waivers subsequent to the time SAG granted one to MCA?"

"No, I don't."

"Did Screen Actors Guild attempt to induce agents to enter TV film production subsequent to the time it granted a blanket waiver to MCA?"

"No, I don't think we ever went out and asked anyone to do that."

"That would be consistent with the rationale behind the granting of a blanket waiver, would it not?"

"No, I don't think the Screen Actors Guild is an employment agency. I think we can well recognize our not putting out blocks in the way of anyone who wanted to produce but I don't think ours was the point of trying to go out and get someone to produce."

"In other words, had the blanket waiver been asked by talent agents subsequent to 1952 in July when SAG granted the blanket waiver to MCA, such requests would have been considered by the Guild and granted, correct?"

"If all of the circumstances were the same as, they would be."

"Did you ever hear it said, Mr. Reagan, that Screen Actors Guild granted a blanket waiver to MCA due to the fact that MCA was willing at this time to grant repayment for reuse of TV films to actors?"

"No, sir."

"I will show you a document marked Grand Jury Exhibit Number 41 from [Laurence] W. Beilenson; do you know who Mr. Beilenson is?"

"Yes."

[Fricano reading:] " 'To Mr. Lew Wasserman, MCA Artists Limited, re amended Revue-MCA-SAG letter agreement of July 23, 1952.' This letter is dated June 7 [1954]. I will ask you to read Paragraph 1 of this document and see if that doesn't refresh your recollection as to the reason why Screen Actors Guild granted a blanket waiver to MCA. May I read it for you, sir?

" 'Should the letter be a superseding letter or an amendment?' And I might add for your information that this dealt with the renewal of the blanket waiver which had been granted in 1952. The original agreement in 1952 extended to '59 but for some reason which we hope to elicit, in 1954 another year was tacked onto that waiver. Continuing, 'I prefer the latter because the letter of July 23, 1952, was executed under a specific set of circumstances where Revue was willing to sign a contract giving the guild members reuse fees when no one else was willing to do so.' "

[Reagan replied:] "Well, then I was wrong but, and I can understand that, but I certainly, I am afraid when I answered before that I was under the impression you were trying to make out that in negotiating a contract we made this as a [bargaining] point of giving a waiver."

"Isn't it conceivable from this language?"

"Mr. Beilenson is a lawyer and in charge of negotiations. It's quite conceivable then if he says it in this letter."

"Does that refresh your recollection, sir?"

"I don't recall it, no."

"In your capacity of president of SAG it was your belief at this time that a waiver should be granted MCA because it would give actors work, is that right?"

"Well, this was always our thinking, yes."

"Did you ever preside at board meetings when other waiver requests were discussed?"

"I am sure I must have."

"Do you recall any of them?"

"I don't really. There weren't too many of those people as I recall that were interested in producing. Feldman, I recall coming up."

"Any other talent agents for TV film production?"

"I wouldn't recall."

"So that you wouldn't know whether or not blanket waiver requests were made by talent agencies, is that correct?"

"I couldn't say whether they were or weren't."

[Fricano said:] "I'll ask that this document be marked as Grand Jury Exhibit 44 for identification. It is a document entitled Screen Actors Guild Board of Directors as of July 1952.

(Whereupon the document was marked Grand Jury Exhibit 44.)

[Still Fricano speaking:] "Mr. Reagan, I will show you Grand Jury Exhibit Number 44 which is Screen Actors Guild Board of Directors as of July 1952, and I will ask you to go down this list and indicate to the best of your information and belief the agent representing each and every [one] of the board of directors."

"Wait a minute. You have me there. I know my wife. When is this? '54?"

" '52, sir."

" '52. At that time my wife was represented by [Bert] Allenberg."

"She was not represented by MCA?"

"I don't recall the date she went over to MCA. She was not represented by MCA following [Bert] Allenberg's death. She went with a member who had been a member, had been with the [Allenberg] agency, Coryell, and nothing happened there although she wasn't really working at having a career after we got married. So I happened to be the one who suggested to her one day why she didn't talk to Art [Park] about representation. This was after Mr. Coryell had admitted to her, because she only wanted now and then to work when it wouldn't interfere with being a wife and mother, that he didn't feel that his agency was set up to handle her on that basis. They had to devote their efforts to actors and actresses who were out of work and wanted to work and she spoke to Art and went over. I don't know. A lot of people are always changing agencies. I am looking here, trying to see if I can see a name that rings a bell."

"Why don't we take them ad [seriatim] and I will read them. Ronald Reagan we know MCA. William Holden?"

"Bill Holden is with Feldman."

"Walter Pidgeon?"

"I don't know."

"John Lund?"

"I don't know. Never asked him."

"Paul Harvey?"

"I don't know."

"George Chandler?"

"I don't know George."

"Leon Ames?"

"No."

"Edward Arnold?"

"Look, let me save you some time here. You don't particularly talk to people about this or ask. It just never occurred to me to ask who someone's agency was."

"I understand that, sir, but we are hoping you can assist this grand jury and give some information. If we call upon your expertise, we would be most appreciative."

"Bill Holden happens to be my very close friend so we used to talk over our business problems and I would hear what he said to Feldman and he would hear what I said to Art [Park]. I knew Nancy, of course. Many of these supporting players are with agents that deal in that sort of thing. This could have been true of a Chandler, of Leon Ames. They are with agents that deal in that kind of work, in the kind of parts they get, and I never bothered myself with it. It didn't seem to make any difference. I could tell you, whether his name is on there, that Van Heflin is in and out of MCA like somebody going in and out of a department store. He was always falling in and out of love with them. You never know about him."

"Did Mr. Heflin have a few hard times?"

"He was always in hard times. He enjoys hard times."

"Let's digress for a minute. What complaints did Mr. Heflin have against MCA?"

"Oh, everything. That he played the wrong part and they should have stopped [him] from playing it, or he didn't get the right part and they should have gotten it for him. This was true of whoever he worked for. I like Van very much, don't get me wrong. He is just one of those fellows who enjoys being unhappy. When he was under contract to Metro they were the worst people in the world."

"Let's continue with the names here."

"It might come that I could recall."

"Gertrude Astor?"

"No."

"Ward Bond?"

"Oh, Ward Bond, I don't know. I don't know who he was with then. I think later he did go with MCA, whether before or after *Wagon Train* I will never know."

"Macdonald Carey?"

"I don't know."

"Richard Carlson?"

"I don't think he was with MCA but I don't recall."

"Chick Chandler?"

"No."

"Fred Clark?"

"No."

"Wendell Corey?"

"No, I wouldn't know."

"Ann Cornwall?"

"I would guess that Ann would be with one of those smaller agents that handle supporting players."

"Nancy Davis?"

"Well, I told you she went through a couple of them and by marriage—"

"I'm sorry, sir, I forgot the fact that she was your wife."

"Rosemary De Camp?"

"I don't know."

"William Demarest?"

"Well, Bill Demarest I would have to guess unless he changed was with them because, as I told you, he was one of the original clients that went with MCA."

"So he was MCA?"

"Yes."

"Frank Thielan?"

"No."

"Glenn Ford?"

"Glenn Ford it seems to me, and I could be wrong, but somehow it seems to me like Glenn Ford sounds like the Allenberg Agency."

"What about Tyrone Power?"

"Golly! I think Ty Power was with what used to be the William Morris office."

"Robert Preston?"

"I wouldn't know."

"Frank Lovejoy?"

"Frank Lovejoy I don't think was with MCA but I wouldn't know who he was with."

"At this time, sir, in 1952, did you have any discussions with anyone at MCA-Revue or any of its affiliated corporations or divisions with respect to the blanket waiver which it had requested from the Screen Actors Guild?"

"No, not that I know of."

"Do you recall at all discussing this matter with personnel from MCA?"

"No, although I can't recall about that seeing them as much as I do, meeting as we do, that this very possibly could have been discussed but any discussions as such, would be in the files of the Guild."

"Well, either official or otherwise?"

"Not out of the regular negotiations with the agent and so forth."

"Do you recall whether or not you participated in the negotiations held by MCA and SAG with respect to the blanket waiver in July of 1952?"

"No, I think I have already told you I don't recall that. I don't recall. There were times when I wasn't involved on a committee. Whether that is one of them or not I wouldn't recall. I must tell you that I always told Jack Dales in the Guild that I realized I felt a little self-conscious sometimes about that, lest there might ever be a misunderstanding because of the fact that I had been so long with MCA, and sometimes I kind of ran for cover and was very happy to duck a committee duty in these matters."

"Because of the possibility of some conflict of interest that might arise?"

"That's right."

"Inadvertently or otherwise?"

"That's right."

"Do you recall if in 1952 you made the statement to Mr. Dales in connection with the Letter Agreement of July 1952?"

"I don't recall. I know I have very frequently told Mr. Dales my own feeling, that I have never seen any harm in this and felt they had filled a great gap in giving employment at a time when unemployment was quite heavy."

"Do you recall, sir, whether or not you spoke at board meetings or other negotiating committee meetings as a director of the Guild in 1952 in favor of the blanket waiver to MCA?"

"I always placed myself in favor. As I told you, I was one of the group that could see no harm because if ever harm developed, we always saw the ability to pull ourselves out of it and we favored someone giving jobs."

"Did you participate in any negotiations in 1954 on SAG's behalf with respect to a waiver to MCA? I refer specifically to June 4 of 1954 when the Letter Agreement of July 23 was extended another year. Did you participate in any way in those negotiations?"

"I don't honestly recall. You know something? You keep saying [1954] in the summer. I think maybe one of the reasons I don't recall was because I feel that in the summer of [1954] I was up in Glacier National Park making a cowboy picture for [RKO,] Ben Bogeaus Productions, so it's very possible there were some things going on that I would not participate in but I have no recollection of this particularly."

"I would like to know, sir, if you can tell the grand jury why in June of 1954 the blanket waiver to MCA was extended and the negotiations which SAG held with MCA were private negotiations, whereas twenty-four days later, negotiations were held for other talent agencies who had also requested waivers and the waivers which those agencies [received] were limited waivers?"

"I wouldn't be able to tell you."

"Were you aware of the fact?"

"I will say one thing. I don't know what you are getting at with the question and I am certainly in no position to infer that I want to tell you what to do or not. I can only say this. I have tried to make plain why my memory could be so hazy on a great many things whether it had to do with this or not because of the long years and participation in all of these in which days of meetings would be devoted to one particular point in a producer's contract or something. I can only say this, that in all of my years with the Screen Actors Guild I have never known of or participated in anything, nor has the Guild, that ever in any way was based on anything but what we honestly believed was for the best interests of the actor and, however it may look now as to the point of private negotiations or anything else, if there was—"

"If I may say one thing, sir, we do not mean to cast any aspersions on Screen Actors Guild. I think at this point the grand jury would be inclined to agree with you. The Screen Actors Guild is looking out for its members as it should as a union. I would just like to see if you can shed any light with hindsight on negotiations which took place at this time between SAG and MCA."

"In view of what is shown in Mr. Beilenson's letter, it is very possible at that time, in spite of my not remembering, it is very possible that we saw an opportunity to break the solid back of the motion picture industry with regard to residuals and if we saw that kind of thing we moved in, as we did in the most recent strike when we found one studio, Universal, which would break the unit of the motion picture studios and we signed a separate contract with them. You can refer to those as secret negotiations. I met in an apartment in Beverly Hills—"

"I didn't use the word 'secret' in speaking of the negotiations that took place between SAG and MCA. That was your word."

"Well, I met privately with the president of Universal Studios and we walked out with the contract and were about to face the rest of the producers with one of their number had broken this rank and willingly signed a contract to pay repayments. This could very well have taken place. I can see where MCA would be in an untenable position. They wouldn't represent actors and deny actors the right to residual payments."

"But the fact remains that according to Mr. Beilenson's letter, he states that 'we gave you residuals when no one else in the industry would,' and you have already stated, sir, that residuals at this time were a very important bargaining point between the guild, not only the TV producers, but also the motion picture production companies, is that right?"

"Yes."

"I might begin by calling these facts to your attention and the fact alone that you recalled that residuals were important at this time, that it might ring a bell with you as to the reason why at this time Screen Actors Guild granted a waiver to MCA of the type that it did."

"No, it doesn't."

"Were you aware, sir, that in 1954 negotiations did take place between MCA and Screen Actors Guild with respect to the waiver which had been entered in 1952?"

"No. It's like saying what I was doing on October 25, the night of the murder."

"I don't care what you were doing October 25."

"I mean you pick a year that is going back eight years and you say, where were you. I have to try to picture what [hassle] the Guild was in at that time."

"Take your time and think about it. I don't expect an immediate answer."

"I don't know. The Guild—"

"Do you recall now, sir, whether or not you were aware in 1954 of the renegotiations of the Letter of Agreement of 1952 between Screen Actors Guild and MCA?"

"All I can say, usually these negotiations and things of that kind seemed to fall in the even years. So I would say probably 1954, yes, this would be. To tell you of my own memory, in my mind I can tell you whether we did or not, no, I can't. Serving with Screen Actors Guild long years of negotiating on meetings for a long time, just retaining things that happened, the lawyers' reports and then so forth, and then you find yourself in a battle like we had with the communists or with the strikes."

"Excuse me, sir, I don't mean to interrupt you, but we would like to focus on this one question. Is your answer—I don't quite understand it quite frankly but is it your answer at this time you do not remember whether or not you were aware of the 1954 negotiations between Screen Actors Guild and MCA?"

"That's right."

"In other words, my presentation to you this afternoon came not as a surprise possibly but—"

"Well, yes, you are asking me thing[s] I haven't thought about for a long time, as a matter of fact, I [didn't] think about too much then."

"The fact that you hadn't thought about it too much either now or then is somewhat immaterial to the purposes of our investigation. My only question is at this point whether or not you were aware of this 1954 renegotiation of the MCA blanket waiver?"

"If it was going on, I must have been aware of it."

"But you have no independent recollection whatsoever at this time?"

"No. And all of this, including the opinions of myself, is vague at the Guild on everything that took place for all those years all the way back including whether I was present or not."

"I assume, then, sir, you would not be able to answer my next question, but I will ask it in any event. The original Letter Agreement of 1952 extended the waiver to MCA until 1959. In 1954 when this was, if we may use the term, renegotiated, it was extended for another year to December 1960. Do you know why it was extended for another year?"

"No, although very probably it could have been to arrange our own setup. Very many times I know we discussed getting contracts, contract negotiations in sequences where we didn't find ourselves all at once going in three directions. Very possibly this could have been to arrange it with regard to when other contracts such as the producers' contract expired. I don't know."

"That was speculation on your part right now as a possibility of why it may have been extended?"

"Yes."

"Do you know for a fact whether or not this was the case?"

"No, I don't although I say this is a thing that frequently came up and our office staff would be turned loose to see if we couldn't arrange some way. I know—you are awakening a memory. Some place along the line I remember extending the Artists' Managers contract, I am sure, to get it out of the way because we were producer negotiators and we didn't want to have to meet the agency negotiations at this same time. We just don't have that much manpower."

"There was a contract between Screen Actors Guild and Artists' Managers Guild November 1 of 1949. It was amended June 30, 1954, and primarily to include the television supplement or rule 16-E?"*

"Yes, but don't you find we had a little opening there? Was that blanket waiver that we couldn't interfere with it?"

"There were certain conditions but they were minimal. The letter is addressed, by the way, to both MCA-Revue. The letter states that you will waive commissions and that type of thing but other than that it is very, very general and proceeded entirely from the limited waiver which was granted by Screen Actors Guild to other television film producers, to wit, there was a paragraph in the [former] waiver which states that if an agent receiving the waiver extended its production scope any degree, he may lose his franchise, as [contrasted] with the MCA waiver which was granting an unlimited, almost as many productions as they could possibly produce. There is a marked difference."

"There is a marked difference between an agent and an agency that has a subsidiary production company which is in the production business."

"It's my understanding from reading Rule 16-E that the primary obligation of the talent agency, whether or not it is also a television company, is acting as a talent agency not a production company."

"Yes, but how many of those other talent agents would have a subsidiary corporation?"

"We don't know how many would have set up a subsidiary had they received a blanket waiver."

"I think that might have—"

"Would that have been a condition precedent to granting a blanket waiver?"

"No, but I don't see how we could have refused them."

"Did you participate in negotiations leading to amended Rule 16-E which is the Screen Actors Guild rule dealing—actually it's the agreement between SAG and AMG. Did you participate in these?"

"I think I negotiated probably. What was the year of that first one?"

---

*Rule 16-E required all SAG members to use only agents and subagents franchised by SAG when seeking screen-acting employment. In a Justice Department memorandum, dated May 13, 1955, the Antitrust Division charged that the requirement was illegal, because SAG "does not have the right to establish a 'white list' of agents with whom its members can deal."

"The first one is November 1, 1949. It was amended on June 1, 1954."

"I know I participated in the 1949 ones. I am not sure that I was a member of that committee that went on to amend and negotiate the next. As a matter of fact, it seems to me maybe the minutes will show I am wrong but I think I kind of ran for cover and ducked on that."

"Do you recall any discussions with other members of Screen Actors Guild, be they members of the board of directors or just union members, with respect to waivers to talent agents?"

"This was always a subject of discussion among actors whether they should or shouldn't. As I told you, I always held the other view. There were actors who always believed there were no extenuating circumstances. An agent should be an agent."

"Who were those actors?"

"Oh, some of them on the board. It's sort of a general thing."

"Can you recall anyone specifically, in your many discussions concerning waivers on Screen Actors Guild, a member who voiced a dissenting opinion, didn't agree with yours?"

"This would be terribly unfair if I tried to name. A name comes to my mind but I can't be sure that he was. Chick Chandler I think had voiced his feelings, not that he would say 'no, I'm against it' and I don't doubt he would go along, but he would say, 'I think we are wrong and this shouldn't go on.' To pick out individuals—which tooth of the buzz saw cuts you?"

"Do you recall ever having any discussions with Mr. Wasserman concerning waivers?"

"If they were, they were, no, I don't really recall. I was going to say they would be social and so forth. I was always very conscious of my position in the Guild and also my relationship with Lew and he was very conscious of it also."

"My question is still, sir, do you recall ever having had any discussion or discussions, be they at a cocktail party or anywhere, where you discussed waivers?"

"It's possible we did, but I don't recall."

"You do not recall but it is possible?"

"Yes. It would not be beyond reason that I would express myself to him that I believed that this was right, although I don't recall [ever] doing it."

"But you held that opinion in 1952. Is it likely, sir, that you might have expressed it to Mr. Wasserman?"

"Might have, yes."

"Do you recall whether you did?"

"I do not recall."

"Do you recall whether you expressed your opinion to Mr. [Park]?"

"I doubt it."

"Do you recall whether or not either Messrs. [Park] or Wasserman asked you your opinion with respect to waivers?"

"That I am sure they never did."

"I will ask you the question very generally with respect to MCA, had you ever had such discussions with any other personnel at MCA?"

"No."

"Do you recall, sir, who was the leading TV production company as of 1952?"

"1952 I didn't interest myself particularly of how they rated or how they stood. I wasn't in television. I don't know. I don't know when Screen Gems started. Wait a minute, I'm sure they had to be started because I did some shows. I am dating everything from my marriage. I don't know who would be in the lead. I know Screen Gems was under way. Hal Roach, Jr., was making a great many television shows at the time."

"Was Revue in contention at this time?"

"They might have been."

"They were one of the biggest?"

"They were?"

"I am asking you, weren't they?"

"Oh, they could have been. As I told you, a great deal of television in those days was in New York and centered there."

"When did you first start with *GE Theater*?"

" '54."

"What were the terms under which you appeared in the *GE Theater*?"

"I was not to [exceed] six shows. That was my own contention because I didn't want to over-expose myself. I introduced all of the shows and closed them out. I specifically refuse to do commercials and I don't think an actor should, and I did a number of weeks of touring for the company, visiting plants and employees, meeting the employees and appearing publicly, speaking and so forth, speaking speeches as a part of General Electric's employee and community relations program, because our show is under the institutional program."

"This was as early as 1954?"

"That's right."

"This was part of the contract?"

"That's right."

"Who negotiated your contract for *GE Theater*, Mr. Reagan?"

"Well, my first approach—do you mean with me?"

"No. Who represented you?"

"Art [Park]."

"With whom did he negotiate?"

"Art [Park] would have negotiated—well, first of all, it was Revue through Taft Schreiber who approached me. I turned down regular television shows a great deal. I did not feel—most actors were a little gun-shy of a series. I had been approached and offered seriously by other people. I kept holding out for motion pictures. Taft Schreiber finally told me of this client that was leaving a musical show, which turned out to be *The Fred Waring Show*, and they had an idea if they could move in with a certain type of show, that this sponsor would listen and they outlined to me the plan. They were going to submit an anthology, which is our type of show. Anthologies had been singularly unsuccessful and they felt the reason was because there was no continuing personality on which to hang the production and advertising of the show. So they were going to solve it by having a host, me, if I would do the job. Well, it met all of my previous objections; first of all, I couldn't be over-exposed and it would be made economically possible to get a good enough income out of the show to tie myself up for that time, and following that time it rested there until, while they then went in through BBD&O, the advertising agency, to sell to General Electric. At this point now came the discussion about me and where I sit and then Art [Park] negotiated with Revue and I am sure with representation by BBD&O, because I ended up as an employee of Batten, Barton, Durstine and Osborn, the advertising agency."

"How did that happen?"

"Well, it happened because the agency did not want me to be an employee of Revue. They felt that this, as later I was told, they felt this would put Revue, if this thing clicked and if I were the principal character of the show, it would give Revue more bargaining power than they wanted them to have with regard to future production. So they wanted control of me as an employee. Usually it's done that way. The sponsor won't have us as an employee. The sponsor doesn't want to have to justify an actor to the stockholders but he can justify so much for advertising and you are part of advertising. So I was employed by BBD&O."

"How long are the terms of the contract?"

"Five years with [a] one-way option, meaning I have to work for five years but they can drop me any one of those five."

"You were salaried?"

"I was salaried."

"Had Art [Park] attempted to obtain any ownership interest for you in the *GE Theater*?"

"No, when the show started the show was basically live so this was not an issue. We did a few pilots because we knew there were actors who still work on live television. The bulk of the show was made of live television shows."

"Is it unusual for an actor, a performer as yourself, to have an ownership in a live program?"

"This is very possible also but you must recall the only thing I would have been able to bargain for at this point was with the few shows I was in because my opening and closing did not go on beyond *General Electric.* There was no residual in my introduction of the show. No one else can ever use that."

"Did you discuss the possibility of an ownership interest in *GE Theater* in 1954 with anyone?"

"No."

"You did not discuss it with Art [Park]?"

"No, the main point of contention, and this became a great point of contention between Revue and MCA, was over a little idiosyncrasy of mine. In all the time I had ever done guest shows when I had done them on film I had always refused to sell the foreign motion picture rights. Many actors who do film television, when it's on film, they give up for their television fee the right to show that picture in foreign theatres. As a practical point I never wanted my pictures, which I know are made at a different budget for television, to ever have to compete on a motion picture screen with motion pictures made at a cost of millions of dollars. I didn't think it was fair for me as a performer. Revue wanted, if I wanted any of the show, they wanted the right to show them as they did other actors in the motion picture theatre. It finally came to a point when Art [Park], on my behalf, wouldn't give in. So Art [Park] who is a vice-president and Taft Schreiber who is a vice-president in charge of Revue went and took the problem to the head school teacher, Lew Wasserman, who is the president of the whole works and Lew Wasserman asked Art [Park] which he thought in a decision of this kind what was best for me as a performer and both Taft and Art had to admit naturally it was best for me as a performer not to give up the motion picture rights and it was Wasserman who said then, there is no question he doesn't give up his motion picture rights."

"Mr. Wasserman arbitrated the dispute between [Park] and Schreiber?"

"And ruled in my favor."

"So then ownership never came into the picture in 1954?"

"No, television—it's hard to think those few years back—television was pretty new. I had been offered ownership in some series that had been offered to me in which I would play a continuing part but, you see, the main bargaining value that an actor has in getting that kind of ownership is on his service as an actor. We are talking about a thing in which at the moment I would only appear in three or four and the rest would be live shows and I would only appear in three or four of these. Also, it happened when this came along I didn't have much bargaining power and I practically sat for fourteen months without a day's work in the motion pictures. They weren't beating a path to my door offering me parts and this television show came riding along, the cavalry to the rescue."

"They were beating a path to your door with respect to other TV series, were they not?"

"I was offered several and that is a lot. Seems like a lot. I was offered several which I wouldn't accept. I didn't believe I wanted to live in New York."

"Limiting our investigation here to the TV media, any of the offers which you received prior to your acceptance of the *GE Theater* in 1954, did they have ownership interests to them?"

"The offers to me?"

"That's correct."

"Oh, yes, when you are offered a part and they want you to play every week for thirteen weeks, of course, they offer you an interest in the show."

"So you had experiences with being offered interest?"

"Yes."

"In television shows?"

"Yes."

"Yet in 1954 when you signed the contract to perform in *GE Theater,* the ownership interest angle never occurred to you?"

"No, because that was not the kind of show supplemented [*sic*] to that. As I told you, we didn't know if we were going to be successful. We had nothing to go on."

"Well, nothing is known to be successful. It's not known. You are taking a chance any time. My question is directed to whether it occurred to you in 1954?"

"No."

"That you should have one?"

"I was very satisfied with the money that was offered."

"You did not discuss it with Mr. [Park]?"

"No."

"Will you tell this grand jury what your salary was for *GE Theater* in 1954?"

"I think it started at $120,000."

"Was that a year?"

"A year."

"Break that down."

"A year."

"You were not paid by the number of shows."

"No. It was prorated, at my request, prorated to a fifty-two-week–year payment."

"Which would mean $10,000—no, you said $120,000?"

"$10,000 a month. I think that puts me in the eighty-percent bracket."

"Did the show appear fifty-two weeks in the 1955 season?"

"No, we re-run through the summer. We review old shows through the summer."

"In 1957, in one season, *GE Theater* was on the air two times?"

"Not quite. You always give up a couple pre-emptions. Every show does. The network has the right to put on another show if they take your Sunday night away from you."

"Loosely speaking, you made approximately $2,500 a show, is that correct?"

"It figures out to that."

"That is all the monies that you realized from 1954 to 1955?"

"No, there was a graduated salary. It went up a little bit each of those five years. I don't recall now just how many but there was an increase, but for the two years it stayed. Then, as it proved itself, there was a little premium for continuing."

"When did it first occur to you, sir, that you should have an ownership interest in the *GE Theater*?"

"Along the end of the five years. We had been moving up the number of pictures we were making instead of live, and I was very instrumental, I never missed a chance to bedevil General Electric, that they would do better on screen than live. We were moving up and we made the decision just about the last year or so of the five-year deal. We made the decision to go all film. Now, this deal did not increase. That was, it decreased the number of shows I was in. I was still doing only about four shows a year. But each year while I have had an option that could be taken up each year, each year Revue had to go to bat with the agency and General Electric to see whether they would produce the show. They received no credit for having produced a successful show. Their general business policy is we are going to talk to all the producing companies and see how they can do this."

"General Electric is a great believer [in] competition?"

"Yes, both within and without the company. As a matter of fact, they proved it by firing guys you gentlemen were engaged with recently. Each time I had to, sir, wait to see if my option was going to be taken up and finally as it was evidenced, that show was successful and as it was evidenced, this would be recognized. General Electric was having me go on tours. Each year I go on these tours all over the country and make speeches. This had a great impact. It was never done by anyone in the television business so it was apparent that I had a value, a relationship with General Electric that was probably sufficient over and beyond the show, that if the show wasn't successful they would still retain me. I was employed by BBD&O. As a matter of fact, Revue at my request tried to get General Electric and BBD&O to let me produce several of the shows because I wasn't getting credit as being a producer, actually being in back of the actual productions. They resisted. They didn't want me to ever have that much authority."

"When you say 'they,' you mean BBD&O and General Electric?"

"They liked it the way it was. So finally at the end of the five years at this point General Electric, the agency, went out to CBS. They went to Four Star. They went to Screen Gems. Even to some independent production companies and they weren't going to buy a new show. They went to these companies and I always frankly felt it was a little funny. It was kind of rough going. They used to go to them and say, 'We want the same kind of show which you have, now what kind of a deal can we get from you fellows if you produce these shows?' "

"What companies?"

"Four Star, Dick Powell, Screen Gems, CBS. CBS was always competing with Revue, trying to do the show. At the end of the five-year contract I had had MCA expiring with General Electric and BBD&O, if there wasn't some way I could cut down my senior partner, the Department of Internal Revenue, and start building something for the future, instead of taking everything in straight income."

"Was this your own idea or was this suggested to you by somebody else?"

"This was my own idea. We tried in every way and we ran into the fact that I wasn't a GE employee so I wasn't eligible for any of their pension plans and so forth. BBD&O didn't have anything like that. All they could think was maybe withholding some more and creating a pension fund but this didn't sound satisfactory to me. At the end of five years they wanted to come in and talk again and I wanted to keep one foot in the clear because if you wait until March, as they had made me wait for five years to talk about options, and they don't take up the option, you are out a year's employment. It's too late to launch yourself into another program if you should suddenly want to go into that kind of setup. I'd be working every five years whether they were going to take up an option. We'll let them worry about the other end, as to whether they are going to have me next year. Now, at the end of—it was at this time that they went out with the negotiation year coming up, the sixth year of the show, that they really came close to going in other directions and I got calls. For example, Dick Powell, he asked me, it had been made plain to everyone, CBS and everyone, that there would be no dealing and it did not look good that General Electric insisted that I be part of it and he asked if I had any relationship with Revue that makes this impossible, and I said, 'Dick, I have kept out of it completely, no, I am not employed by the advertising agency. I value my relationship with General Electric. I think I have established that.' I said, 'I have not entered into it,' and I told him, I said, 'Dick, you know, I would, of course, enjoy very much working for you.' I have known him for many years. We were veterans of the Warner Brothers battle and I told him—so I said, 'I stand pat.' I naturally had a loyalty to the fellows at Revue. We have been making a show and doing a good job. So I am out of it. Once they see who is going to make the show, then I will make my decision about where I do it. I said, 'You know, of course, I would love to work with you.' CBS, I have heard since, has talked around and gossiped that the reason they didn't get the show was because I refused to go along if they produced the show, and that is an out-and-out lie, and the only reason they are saying that is because they have to save their face."

"How did Revue compete successfully for each renewal contract with General Electric?"

"Well, I suppose they had a way of negotiating for them and had been successful."

"And the fact that this is an anthology and they could guarantee talent?"

"I don't think any more than anyone else could. Dick Powell is, for example, a fine anthology show. I did shows, single guest shots. I did a show for *The June Allyson Theater.* I have done guest shows for those other companies. Actors go where there is a good show. I think one of the things that happened was that MCA recognized there was no financial benefit because no one—this business costs the same wherever you make it. A show is a show and costs so much money. I think they personally came back to where they had success. Now, at this time in dealing with these companies I was told that they had said this, too, that I would have to go with them. They reassured me. They wanted me. They said they had asked these companies if they were prepared to do whatever was necessary to get me and Dick Powell and CBS had both said they would be willing to work out some arrangement involving ownership in the show. Now, all films—there are no secrets in the business. I know this. Dick Powell told me, as a matter of fact, told me what my situation would be. At the time I was amused because I knew BBD&O and GE didn't realize in this we were negotiating to produce the show. The thing they always resisted was my employment with the company. I called Lew Wasserman and I told him what I knew. I said, 'Lew, it's now apparent to me, as it must be to you, that I represent a certain measure of the success of the show. In other words, I am now in a bargaining position that I wasn't in when the show started. We are approaching negotiations so I have a question. I have known you many years. I want to know one thing.' I asked Lew Wasserman, 'In the show for General Electric what are my services worth to go on with General Electric?' and Lew said, 'That's a very good question and it deserves a very good answer.' He said, 'I'm going to the Springs and I'll let you know when I get back.'

"When he came back he called me. He said, 'The answer is,' and he gave it to me, and it was a salary comparable to what I was getting plus twenty-five percent in the films, even those films in which I am not engaged. This was more than any of the other fellows offered."

"Mr. Wasserman had guaranteed to you at this time, and if I misstate it in any way, please correct me, he stated at this time that you would receive from Revue Productions the terms which he had told you. In other words, he would assure that Revue gave you these terms, is that correct?"

"That's right."

"Is that what he told you?"

"Yes."

"Would you please relate again because I lost the thread. Directly what ownership interest did Wasserman say Revue would give you?"

"That it was comparable to the salary I was getting plus the fact, by now becoming an employee of Revue, I no longer paid MCA commission. So that automatically gave me a ten-percent raise in salary, and they gave me twenty-five-percent ownership in all films made in the *GE Theater,* not just those in which I appeared, but all of them."

"Did Mr. Wasserman in this call Mr. Schreiber or anyone else at Revue?"

"Mr. Schreiber was in the office."

"Mr. Schreiber was present at the time?"

"Yes."

"Did Wasserman advise Schreiber to make such a form available in a future contract by you and Revue?"

"Well, he didn't have to. They were sort of sitting like you two gentlemen are sitting so it was obvious one was speaking but they were both agreeing."

"In other words, Wasserman was speaking and Schreiber was nodding his head like a mare?"

"That's right."

"Have you been advised at any time during the period 1954 to 1959 by anyone that you should have an ownership in *GE Theater*?"

"Oh, yes."

"By whom?"

"Well, along toward the last year or so when it was obvious we were hot and successful, we were a top show, and we had become film, why, there were people then who thought, knowing the circumstances, the fact that I was on a five-year contract, were throwing up their hands in horror. One was an agent, Mr. Coryell, said this. I should be and so forth. Dick Powell, and, as I say, I am very fond of Dick, we are old friends. Yes, it had now come to the point, there was no justification for this and I was in such a bargaining position that this would be proper compensation. I did not feel—in the earlier years I thought I had a pretty good deal."

"Did you call an attorney or any type of advisor, Mr. Reagan, with respect to your contract with Revue which gives you part ownership of *GE Theater* or did MCA act completely with Revue in this regard?"

"Oh, no, when it got down to details of working out the actual terms of employment contract and so forth and we negotiated also a thing in the employment contract of extra money also into the buildup of a retirement fund for tax purposes, then I talked—I had to talk to a lawyer, of course, and—"

"Who?"

"I have a business manager and I talked to my business manager."

"Who is he?"

"David Martin. There was no question of talking to anyone as far as I was concerned about the terms. I know the business. I know what I think is fair and I was, frankly, very pleased and happy and thought that I had about all the traffic could bear and—"

"In other words, you feel MCA-Revue gave you the best possible deal?"

"Yes, because I will tell you something. My contention was I thought I only had a right to bargain for ownership of the films in which I appeared. I have been out on the road for several weeks now and they have made a few pictures. I haven't even read the pictures and I own twenty-five percent of them."

"When do you think you will realize the money from ownership?"

"I think several years."

"When the films that are being made now go into—"

"Distribution and they go out. I have had some slight percentage of residuals of guest shows I did on film before I went to work before. Some have brought in some money, some don't."

"The first one in syndication of the films which are presently being made will not give you any money, correct?"

"I doubt it because we run a little loss."

"Don't say 'we.' You are running that loss. Revue isn't."

"No. Of course, let me put it this way: the sponsor does not pay the full cost of producing our film. They cost more than the sponsor pays to get his first run of the film."

"You mean Revue sells them cut rate?"

"This is quite common with many companies. The ownership of the film belonging to the producing company and not to the sponsor is the profit in many of these. Now, there is always an extra benefit."

"Let's stick to the track, Mr. Reagan. Revue is selling the *General Electric Theater,* right now, each series below what it costs them to produce, both below- and above-the-line costs. Are they still in the black with respect to these films?"

"I'm sure the packaging fee and their distribution and so forth, I am sure that they must have."

"They will still be in the black?"

"Probably."

"And you won't go back into the black, as it were, for many years?"

"Wait a minute. In the meantime I am drawing a pretty handsome salary. I am not just working for an ownership."

"That's correct, sir, but in fact you do have an ownership that might not be realized for several years?"

"Yes, I don't want to get it for several years. Right now my senior partner claims all of it."

"The Internal Revenue again. In any event, you are personally satisfied with this arrangement?"

"Yes, so satisfied that I have, since the arrangement was made, told people I wasn't interested once or twice when they have proposed another series to me, leaving the *General Electric Theater* to do another series in which I would have even more ownership."

"Have you had any offers by other TV producers other than Revue over the last five years?"

"Yes, I have been sounded as to what my position was with regard to *GE Theater,* could I do another series and so forth, and I have had to say, no, I can't do another series. It's exclusive and I'm sorry."

"What other discussions or conferences has Lew Wasserman mediated in your presence aside from what you have already related?"

"Those were the only two I remember, the one about foreign film rights and the one about the terms."

"You can't recall ever having been in the presence of Lew Wasserman and Taft Schreiber before in which you were interested in what was being discussed?"

"No, I don't."

"Have you ever met anyone, sir, who has told you that they had sent a script or inquired about your availability from Mr. [Park] or some other MCA official and was informed that you were not available which fact was never conveyed to you?"

"No; as a matter of fact, Mr. Park is very, very sure that he always sees that I know of every inquiry made of my services, whether speaking to a luncheon club or show or not. Just from that point alone he has repeatedly assured me that he makes sure I know all. He lets me know even when he thinks that there are some things that are so ridiculous that I call him back and ask him if he was out of his mind for bringing them and then he tells me the reason he brought it to me was because—"

"Did you ever express any discontent or complaint or any ire, as it were, with respect to the contract which MCA negotiated with respect to BBD&O and GE in 1954 to MCA?"

"No."

"You never complained?"

"Oh, yes, I have had one complaint and it was solved very easily. We almost made a mistake. We didn't know BBD&O and General Electric asked for twenty weeks a year of my traveling when we first started. I refused to go for twenty and got it down to sixteen. This was supposed to be in two tours of eight weeks and it only took us seven, because GE sent a man with me on the tour so he could get as flat-footed and tired as I was. It only took us about five of the eight weeks to know we had bitten off more than we could swallow. No man lives to do the eight-week tour, and not give snarling lessons. So they asked me—I must say General Electric was quite nice about this. Wouldn't even bother with Revue or MCA. At the end of this tour General Electric asked me what I thought should be the amount of time we could handle and we boiled it down to about twelve weeks, not to [exceed] three or four weeks [at a time]."

"Did you state this to MCA as a complaint?"

"No, I didn't need to. I stated it to General Electric."

"My question was, sir, have you ever complained to MCA concerning the initial contract which they entered into?"

"Oh, no."

"For GE or BBD&O in 1954?"

"No. Then after the end of the twelve weeks or so as we began to make more film and less live shows, I then one day out here said to MCA or Revue, it could have been either one, said, 'Next year let's tell the fellows we can't handle this many weeks.' I finally got it down to six weeks a year and last year they got it up to eight again on me so eight weeks is the limit of the tour, not to [exceed] two weeks away at any time."

[Fricano then asked the grand jury foreman:] "Mr. Hauer, does the grand jury have any questions of this witness?"

[A juror asked Reagan:] "Are you still working for BBD&O or are you working now exclusively for MCA?"

"I am now on an employment contract within which I have a partnership interest with Revue."

[A juror:] "You are under contract to BBD&O, is that correct?"

"No, by doing this other thing they now had to take the thing they didn't want to do at first. BBD&O has had to—by the fact that I was their employee if they wanted me they had to take Revue. This had never before existed until I wanted this change of ownership of the films. There was some hassling between Revue and BBD&O about that. BBD&O resisted but they were in an untenable position because they didn't have anything comparable to offer me."

[A juror:] "Mr. Reagan, does your salary on these tours, I mean, do you get any extra salary for the tours you make or is it included?"

"It's included in the salary, although General Electric pro-rates a portion of my salary as being for those tours."

[A juror:] "And does MCA get a portion of that?"

"No. When I was a BBD&O employee, MCA took its usual commission of my salary. When this other arrangement was entered into, MCA lost the commission because under our actors' contract they can't take a commission."

[A juror:] "I was going to ask you, Mr. Reagan, did anyone from MCA know you were called in this afternoon?"

"No. Well, wait a minute. I laughed this morning and told a few of the fellows at Revue, we were rehearsing the start of a new show, and I told them they had to get me clear because I had an appointment down with you folks. So the only thing I told them before I came down, I would come back and let them know if they were still working for Revue or not."

[Fricano asked:] "With whom did you have these conversations?"

"Stan Rubin, the executive producer of the show, the director we have hired for this particular show we are doing, and Jeanne Crain. She is going to be the leading lady on the show. We had lunch together before I came down."

[Fricano continued:] "Did anybody from MCA tell you they knew you were going to appear before this grand jury?"

"No."

"The only discussions you had with MCA personnel were the ones you had today?"

"At lunch when I told them where I was going after I called and found out the time I was to come."

[A juror:] "Off the record, please."

(Off the record discussion.)

[Fricano asked:] "Just to clear up one point, sir, for my own benefit. At what time did Mr. Wasserman tell you what your terms could be with Revue, as having a percentage interest, that is, in the *General Electric Theater;* what year was this, do you remember?"

"It would take in all of last year's shows and as a matter of fact, it was retroactive because we had already started producing and so forth and so it included shows that had already been made."

"Do you recall the year, sir, when you first entered into the contract with Revue giving you a production interest?"

"Well, now, wait a minute. I was on the five years of salary. I did one year which would have been 1959 and '60 season, yes."

"It was either '60 or '61?"

"I am certain for the shows of the '60 and '61 season and now the '61–'62 season."

"Do you remember what year it was that you had the discussion with Mr. Wasserman concerning your ownership interest in the *GE Theater*?"

"Yes, that would have been when we were talking about the production of the shows for last season which would have been in the spring of '59."

"That was when you had the conversation with Mr. Wasserman?"

"Yes."

"And Mr. Schreiber?"

"Yes."

[The grand jury foreman said:] "No other questions, Mr. Fricano."

[Fricano added:] "Mr. Reagan, the grand jury is finished with you for the moment. Actually, you are still under subpoena, sir. If we require your presence again, we will so notify you."

CHAPTER
TWENTY-FOUR

WHEN RONALD REAGAN regained his memory, he would eventually recall the events of that afternoon on February 5, 1962. Three years later—in his 1965 autobiography, *Where's the Rest of Me?*, which he coauthored with Richard C. Hubler—Reagan wrote that he "had spent a long, unhappy afternoon being interrogated by a federal lawyer who'd seen too many *Perry Masons*. Feuding is a mild word to use when one is talking of our government's campaign against a private business concern. . . .

"Once on the stand, he launched into a series of questions such as, 'Do you recall a discussion at a Guild board meeting the night of August 16, 1950 (ten years ago), regarding a waiver. . . .' Well, of course, I was not only caught off-guard but . . . I'd lived a lifetime of meetings, and to pick out one for specific questioning was like asking a fellow in a sawmill accident which tooth of the buzz saw cut him first. Before the day ended I was pretty red-necked."[1]

On February 13, a week after Reagan's testimony, the Antitrust Division subpoenaed the Internal Revenue Service for the income tax returns of Ronald and Nancy Reagan for the years 1952–55, the same period that the MCA blanket waiver was approved and reaffirmed while both of the Reagans were on the SAG board. The income tax returns of John Dales and his assistant, Chet Migden, and four members of the 1952 SAG board were also subpoenaed. However, no charges were filed against anyone.

Two days later, Leonard Posner learned from one of his key sources that MCA was receiving information from the grand jury.

"You mean from witnesses who have appeared?" Posner asked.

"No," his source replied. "MCA has a means of obtaining information from the grand jury itself."

However, when Posner tried to track down the leak on the grand jury, he was unsuccessful.[2]

On March 7, Posner interviewed another industry source with inside knowledge of the MCA-SAG blanket waiver. When asked how the MCA waiver affected competing talent agencies, the source replied that "the effect was drastic" and that the other agencies "could not compete against a talent agency which could promise jobs in television shows. . . . The talent was assured that they would get network exposure if they appeared in a Revue production. They could only get into a Revue production by joining MCA."

Posner wrote that his source told him that "Reagan may have been given the role of host, a most desirable plum, in *GE Theater* in return for having lent his good offices to see that MCA got the blanket waiver. He explained it this way: Reagan in 1952 was at the end of the road as far as [his] motion picture career was concerned. He was having a rough time. . . . Within a short time later, the concept of *GE Theater* apparently developed and after some months of preparation, the series went into production. [The source] thought it likely that Reagan had been given a promise of the role as host of *GE Theater* as consideration for his keeping actors in line. He also said that it was possible that Reagan may have sincerely believed that he was helping actors get jobs. However, he said that undoubtedly . . . [the idea that] MCA was going to be able to go into production and get a lot of jobs for hungry actors in television was completely fallacious. He said that there were many independent producers who were then in the television film production films [*sic*] that would have been necessary to fill whatever needs the networks had for television production, and consequently to give actors jobs. He said that the only effect of the blanket waiver to MCA alone was to give MCA the dominant part in this television production. It did not increase television production—it merely assured MCA a larger share of whatever television film production there was to be."

At the end of his memorandum, Posner described his source by writing, "He is honest and is giving us every bit of information within his recollection. He appears to be trustworthy and is not apparently just trying to hurt MCA."[3]

However, Posner had become pessimistic about the government's chances to break up MCA. Convinced that the antitrust action had come too late, Posner felt that the government "was merely locking the barn door after the horse had been stolen."

MCA had already started diverting its operations into other enterprises, including nonentertainment ones. Wasserman had even turned a portion of the Universal backlot into a cemetery and had purchased a bank in Denver, Columbia Savings and Loan Association.

Many of MCA's clients no longer had representation contracts—the traditional agent-artist relationship—with MCA. Instead they had converted them to long-term "employment contracts" to accommodate MCA's television production interests, as well as omnibus contracts which covered foreign engagements and any field not covered by their clients' unions. These agreements stated that even if a client left MCA Artists—by personal choice or forced by the government's antitrust action—MCA would retain perpetual rights to the work done while the client was under contract at MCA. If the government forced the spin-off of MCA Artists, MCA agents were prepared to form their own separate agencies while keeping their business ties with MCA intact.[4]

No matter what the Antitrust Division tried to do, MCA was always a step ahead.

On April 5, Posner received a telephone call from Hy Raskin, an MCA attorney. Raskin said that he wanted to be of service to the Justice Department. "I understand that MCA is somewhat arrogant, and, because of this attitude, people might misunderstand its motives." Raskin added that his only function on behalf of MCA was to help the government "get the facts. If you really knew all the facts, I think you and the government would be satisfied."

Posner replied, "It would be helpful if we had all the facts. . . . Without the facts we won't be able to arrive at a truly valid determination as to our proper course of action."

"I promise you, Mr. Posner, that a change of attitude will be forthcoming in MCA, and that you will begin to get all the facts you really want and need."[5]

Six days later, Allen E. Susman, MCA's lead attorney on the antitrust case, contacted Charles Whittinghill of the Los Angeles antitrust office. Susman said that he wanted to "get together" with the Antitrust Division and "discuss the matter."

When Whittinghill asked what he wanted to discuss in particular, Susman replied that MCA would soon be making an offer to the shareholders of the Decca Record Company* for the purchase of that company and all of its subsidiaries, including Universal Studios. Before Whittinghill had a chance to catch his breath, Susman assured him that MCA would cooperate and supply the government with all information regarding the sale. While Whittinghill waited for Susman to send him a copy of MCA's registration statement filed with the Securities and Exchange Commission, regarding the proposed purchase of Decca and Universal, the Antitrust Division responded to the latest development —and, once again, MCA seemed to have the edge.

In a rare interview, with Murray Schumach of *The New York Times,* Lew Wasserman claimed that he had never submitted a talent package to the motion picture industry—which, the government knew, was utter nonsense.

"We have never made a package deal," Wasserman insisted. "The truth is that presidents of movie companies have asked me if I have a package. I laugh at them. They want us to do their job.

"I know that many of these executives and producers look upon themselves as creative people and upon us as flesh-peddlers. The truth is that one of the reasons agents are needed so badly is because clients cannot trust movie executives. I look upon our agency as a business and a profession."[6]

Sorting out what MCA's takeover of Decca and Universal would mean, Posner was told that "it would have a profound effect on the music business since MCA controls so many artists who do singing and band work that they will have a tremendous competitive edge in the recording field." In the film industry, "MCA will quickly forge to the front in the motion picture production field. . . . It has the best manpower and is acquiring tremendously good manpower from Universal."

Posner also learned that MCA planned "to break cleanly between its talent agency and film production company. . . . MCA will not try to hang on to the talent agency, but will jettison it."

"Wasserman," Posner was told, "will have power in the recording field, motion picture production field, television production field, and sales. Moreover, in Universal he is getting a good distribution organization. No motion picture production company can be successful without some means of distribution."[7]

---

*Decca had become the fourth-largest recording company in the United States and had a gross income of $90 million in 1961, as well as company assets totaling over $73 million.

Posner's fear was that if MCA simply sold MCA Artists to its own agents, nothing would be accomplished by the government's long antitrust investigation. The block-booking and tie-in situations would potentially remain through a newly formed sweetheart relationship between MCA and its former employees.

On June 18, MCA acquired eighty percent of the stock of, and thus the controlling interest in, Decca and Universal, which also included Universal's library of 250 post-1948 feature films—such as *Hamlet, Harvey,* and *The Glenn Miller Story*—and nearly 2,500 hours of filmed television programs. The sale had received approval from the company's stockholders two weeks earlier.

Ten days later, during a conversation between the Antitrust Division and MCA's lawyers, the government was notified that MCA would "dispose" of its talent agency on July 18, 1962. However, when the Antitrust Division received the MCA prospectus sent to the SEC on June 29, it referred to "an agreement between MCA and the Screen Actors Guild in which MCA agreed to terminate its activities either in representation of SAG members or in television film production [by July 18]." The government suspected that MCA was trying to stage another charade by simply shuffling its talent agency around but still keeping it under its aegis.

In a letter to Assistant Attorney General Lee Loevinger, the head of the Antitrust Division, from Allen Susman on July 5, MCA assured the government that its talent agency would be "transferred to various present employees of MCA who, upon the transfer being accomplished, will no longer be employed by or connected with MCA in any capacity." Susman added that the purchase price for the agency would be neither secured nor guaranteed, adding that the time and method of payment had not been agreed upon. Loevinger became totally skeptical of MCA's facade of good faith.

The front page of the July 9 issue of *Variety* carried a story entitled, "MCA Spin-off of Agency Set for July 18," explaining that MCA had notified the Screen Actors Guild that it was divorcing itself from direct control of its talent agency.

Wasserman personally announced that Larry Barnett, the fall guy in the 1946 *Finley* v. *MCA* antitrust case, was to be appointed as board chairman of the new spin-off agency, and George Chasin, a long-time MCA agent, was expected to be its president. Among the stars Chasin had personally represented were Marilyn Monroe, Marlon Brando, Gregory Peck, Gene Tierney, and Kirk Douglas. Arthur Park, Reagan's day-to-day agent, would also join the new agency. Wasserman said that he would continue to head the MCA parent company, that Universal would continue to be headed by Milton R. Rackmil, and that Taft Schreiber would continue as president of Revue Productions.

Ultimately, it was MCA's own predictable arrogance that led it into the government's web—when just a few months earlier the government had feared it had no case at all.

Seeing through MCA's smokescreen, the government—after several days of secret meetings and coast-to-coast telegrams—moved ahead, on Friday, July 13, filing a complaint, approved by Attorney General Robert Kennedy, in federal court, and charging that MCA and its subsidiaries had violated the Sherman Antitrust Act. Named as co-conspirators were the Screen Actors Guild for its July 1952 and June 1954 blanket waivers granted to MCA, and the Writers Guild of America, West (formerly the Screen Writers Guild), for its April 1953 MCA waiver. At the same time, the Justice Department filed for and received a ten-day temporary restraining order against MCA, in an attempt to prevent MCA from selling off its talent agency to its former employees on July 18.[8]

CHAPTER
TWENTY-FIVE

THE GOVERNMENT did not tell the MCA lawyers that a complaint was going to be filed. When Allen Susman and the other MCA attorneys arrived for their meeting with the Antitrust Division on July 13, they were handed a copy of the complaint at the same time it was being filed in court. They were stunned by the suit—and particularly by the temporary restraining order. The MCA attorneys immediately filed a motion with the court to deny the government's request.

When reporters asked MCA executives for comment on the government's litigation, nearly all of them replied, "Ask Lew."

Two days later, Lew Wasserman filed his affidavit with the court, bitterly protesting the complaint and the motion filed by the government, stating:

1. I deny that MCA has been guilty of any violations of law or any other alleged wrongful acts charged.
2. I deny that MCA has engaged in any conspiracies . . .

   As for the assertions . . . that the proposed divestiture may not be "bona fide," the fact is that bona fide negotiations have been taking place between MCA and the proposed owners [of the new talent agency] for several weeks in an attempt to effectuate an agreement. . . . [I]t has been my personal observation and experience that such proposed owners and employees are devoted men and women who have worked, and will continue to work, honorably, efficiently and with integrity and dedication to serve the best interests of their clients.

The government replied to MCA by filing a motion for a preliminary injunction against the corporation to block its takeover of Decca-Universal. Neither Jules Stein nor Wasserman would comment about the government's latest action.

On Monday, July 16, there was a hearing in the Los Angeles federal court on whether MCA—which had filed motions in opposition to the proposed restraining orders—could divest itself of its talent agency on July 18. In an exchange with Laurence Beilenson—who, along with Susman, was representing MCA—U.S. District Judge William C. Mathes asked, "But this divestiture is a form of merger, isn't it?"

Beilenson replied, "No, Your Honor. You see, the whole thing, everybody has got it backwards about who employs whom. It's the agent that employs the actor. Excuse me. It's the actor who employs the agent. . . ."

Later, still attempting to convince the judge to deny the government's motion, Beilenson said, "It really doesn't make any difference to us, because we are not going to get a nickel out of it, Your Honor. Because if we sell the corporation involved [MCA Artists], it will be stripped where it can be sold for a nominal sum. MCA is not trying to make any money.

"It is not trying to make money out of the transfer of this agency. But it is trying to preserve the orderly share of its talent which it represented for many years and, despite all the allegations of the complainant, have renewed their contracts again and again and stayed with the agency. It's for their benefit, and for the people who served it so long, that they would like the opportunity to make an orderly transfer of the business."

When Posner presented the government's case, Judge Mathes asked, "Let's assume it's a collusive arrangement [the sale of MCA Artists to its own employees]. It's not an arm's-length deal at all, it's a collusive arrangement to continue indirectly what they can't do directly. Wouldn't that all come out later?"

"Yes, Your Honor," Posner replied, "I think that there is some suggestion of that on the face of the documents, since here they are selling the business that grossed annually 8.4 million dollars for what Mr. Beilenson said that they weren't taking a nickel out of. And MCA, up to now at least, has not had the reputation of being an eleemosynary organization."

"All business concerns are in business to make money," Mathes continued, "and I think one of the great misrepresentations, I'll say, of the twentieth century is the notion that business concerns can be philanthropic. They have no business being philanthropic. Anytime a board of directors or an officer of a business corporation isn't doing everything he can to make every dollar he can for that concern, he is committing a breach of trust."

"I agree, sir," Posner replied, "and that is precisely why the government is suspicious of this transaction. . . . We say that this MCA Artists has been the crux of the leverage which MCA has used to build its violations of the antitrust laws. In effect, we claim that MCA has said, 'If you want this actor, then you must take this program.' MCA has told that to networks. And we have many instances of that. And we say that if this huge pool of name talent is transferred en masse to any other group, and particularly to the old MCA agents, this pool of name talent is going to provide the basis for a leverage for causing the same abuses we have had in the past. . . .

"What we really want is to dissolve this mammoth corporation and turn these actors free to whomever they want."

Judge Mathes granted the government a temporary restraining order against MCA—on the spin-off of its talent agency—until July 23, when a full hearing on all of the government's charges would be held, including the government-proposed injunction against MCA's takeover of Decca-Universal.

That same day, MCA's stock dropped 4⅛ points on the New York Stock Exchange.

In an attempt to settle the case, the corporation's attorneys—with their hats in their hands—made a proposal to the government on July 17, asking that MCA be permitted to terminate all of its talent contracts and to obtain a two-month postponement of a preliminary injunction blocking MCA's purchase of Decca-Universal.

Loevinger said that he wanted a provision "that MCA will abrogate any talent employment contracts that MCA has negotiated with itself as a talent agency for production activities of Revue, Decca, or Universal. This would be true if these contracts provide for employment of talent more than six months in advance." Loevinger added that he would be firm on matters concerning the talent agency, but that the

Antitrust Division would be "flexible" on Decca-Universal, permitting the two-month postponement.[1]

At 12:01 A.M. on July 19, MCA's franchise with the Screen Actors Guild to represent television and motion picture artists expired. MCA Artists was forced to set free its 1,400 clients, who were immediately descended upon and wined and dined by the other talent agencies.

Later that day, a California state labor commissioner called Stanley Disney in the Los Angeles antitrust office and informed him that he had just received an application for a license to operate as a talent agency from a California corporation, Management Associates, Ltd., which wanted to do business as International Management Associates, Ltd. Corporate officers included Herbert Brenner and Howard Rubin, both vice-presidents of MCA, who had resigned the previous day. The application also included the names of eight other MCA employees who had submitted their resignations as well and would become IMA personnel. Disney told the official that the application was not in violation of the temporary restraining order.

Heated, secret discussions between lawyers representing the government and MCA continued over the weekend before the court hearing set for Monday, July 23. Drafts of proposed agreements went back and forth.

Finally, on Monday, before the hearing, lawyers for both sides went to Judge Mathes's courtroom. When he arrived, they simply asked him to sign their settlement, stating that MCA would completely dissolve its talent agency without selling it or receiving anything for it. Further, MCA was forced to surrender all of its guild or labor union contracts and licenses regarding its talent agency throughout the world. The settlement did not include any decisions regarding MCA's takeover of Decca-Universal or allegations of MCA's block-booking or tie-in violations; both were to be made separately. The only solace for MCA was that it was not required to admit any civil or criminal guilt.

According to the July 23 Stipulation and Order: "Nothing contained in this order . . . is meant to be nor shall ever be construed or deemed to be an admission of any kind

"(1) that MCA Inc. admits any of the acts alleged in the complaint or that it admits it is guilty in any respect whatsoever of any violations of the law or that any allegations of the complaint are true or correct;

"(2) that plaintiff has abandoned any of the allegations of the complaint, or is estopped to pursue any violations alleged therein, or any other violations."

In his victory statement to the press, Posner said that the action "destroys the power base MCA Inc. used for leverage for its filmed television production."*

Lew Wasserman issued a short statement, saying, "MCA deeply regrets that circumstances beyond its control precluded the company from having the opportunity to discontinue its talent agency functions in a more orderly manner."

The hearing for the government's motion for a preliminary injunction against MCA's takeover of Decca-Universal was scheduled for July 30. However, MCA quickly asked the government for more time to prepare its case. Posner thought that "it would be to our interest to have the hearing on the motion postponed as long as possible to give ourselves more time to prepare properly, and, if possible, to defer any hearing on Decca-Universal until the trial. My reason for this position was that if that judge hears all the ugly facts about MCA's practices and becomes well acquainted with the beast, and further learns of the large number of MCA acquisitions, he might well resolve any doubts about MCA's having violated Section 7 in our favor."[2]

At a meeting at the Antitrust Division's offices in Los Angeles, Susman tried to negotiate another settlement with the government. Susman insisted that all MCA was trying to do "during the interim period before the trial is to conduct the businesses of MCA, Decca, and Universal in their ordinary way without restraint," adding that "MCA must be free to run its business as it saw fit without interference, and that Decca and Universal must be free to do the same thing."[3]

Since the purchase of Universal, one of the government's biggest concerns was the "competitive impact" of the studio's remaining post-1948 library of feature films and television programs, not earlier purchased by Screen Gems, if MCA indeed gained control of that backlist. The Antitrust Division did not want that to happen; instead they wanted another company, such as Screen Gems or Seven Arts, to obtain the rights to these packages.

However, during Susman's negotiations with the government, he

---

*Daily Variety's July 24 banner-headlined report of the final settlement, "MCA DISSOLVES ENTIRE AGENCY," written by reporter David Kaufman, must have been particularly painful for MCA loyalists to read:

"MCA Inc.'s talent agency, only a week ago the most powerful in the industry, is no more. . . . Obituary for MCA Artists Ltd., the talent arm, was written in U.S. Federal Court yesterday, when MCA and the U.S. government in a stipulation agreement spelled out terms for dissolution of the agency.

"Actual death of MCA occurred in such a prosaic, offhand fashion it was like the funeral of a long-forgotten star of yesterday."

Syndicated columnist Jim Bishop, the former director of MCA's literary department, simply described his old employer as "a dead whale."

took the hard line, saying that he could not accept "any limitation on the right of Universal to dispose of its feature film library in any way that it saw fit. . . . If Universal wanted to sell to MCA, that was their business."[4]

Understanding that the government would be opposed to this—but that it would need additional time to prepare its legal arguments—MCA reversed course and asked for the hearing on the government's motion for the preliminary injunction to be held as quickly as possible.

During a telephone conversation with Gordon Spivack of the Antitrust Division's New York office, Posner suggested that the government find some middle ground so that MCA could be permitted to operate Universal through, perhaps, an independent manager until the legal matters were resolved. But Posner also recognized the issue of Universal's backlist as being "the stumbling block . . . possibly the break-off point in our negotiations [with MCA]."

When the compromise was posed to Susman, his response was an angry one. "[N]either MCA nor I did or would agree for one moment that the film library of Universal Pictures Company, Inc., was subject to any restrictions whatsoever under the then existing stipulation, nor would I or my client agree so to restrict or limit the disposition of the Universal film library. That position has not changed one iota."[5]

Preparing for trial with MCA, Loevinger formally requested a full-field FBI investigation of MCA's attempted takeover of Decca-Universal on July 30, 1962. Meantime, over on Santa Monica Boulevard in Beverly Hills, the beautiful MCA citadel—the home of MCA Artists—stood nearly vacant as a handful of employees cleaned out their offices, stepping around the antique-filled cartons scattered about the marble floors.

As the FBI began its work, MCA attorney Hy Raskin visited Posner and Harry Sklarsky, chief of the Antitrust Division's field operations. Raskin said that his client was interested in "entering negotiations with the government for disposition of the entire action against MCA." However, Raskin reiterated that "one thing was not negotiable . . . the Decca-Universal acquisition by MCA."[6]

The government agreed to negotiate a possible consent decree—approval of a corporate merger—and on August 9 the talks began. Present for the government were Posner and Sklarsky; MCA was represented by Susman, Raskin, and Albert Bickford.

Sklarsky opened the negotiations by addressing the central problem of Universal's library. He argued that "even if an auction for this property is agreed upon and MCA is permitted to participate, the problem, as I see it, is that MCA could bid as high as it wanted to, because the money would, in effect, be returned to itself—since MCA is the biggest stockholder in Universal. It would be doing nothing more than transferring money from one company to another."

"It doesn't work that way," Susman replied. "MCA is extremely interested in money. And if someone from the outside bids higher than MCA thought it could realize from its distribution operation, then MCA would be happy to let someone else do it. You also have to remember that MCA owns only about seventy percent of Universal, and that the studio's vigorous minority stockholders will be acting as watchdogs, protecting their interests. . . . Also, Universal is now an independently operated company with a separate board of directors and officers."[7]

With little hostility in the discussions and with what appeared to be a sense of mutual good faith, both sides agreed that there was room for compromise. They decided to postpone the hearing on the preliminary injunction until October 15, allowing both sides to better prepare their cases—and leaving time for a possible settlement.

In reality, both sides were playing poker. MCA held its cards close to its chest, privately fearing that the government could rip the corporation apart in court and, perhaps, force MCA to divest itself of Decca-Universal. Across the table—debating whether to call, raise, or fold—the government knew that even if an outside distributor was brought in to handle the Universal library, it would undoubtedly be under MCA's direct or indirect control. But prosecutors would still have to prove that MCA's possession of the library would give it an overpowering position, particularly in the television industry.

In a Justice Department memorandum, written on August 9 after the first round of talks, Stanley Disney said that he "did not believe we could get divestiture, [so] I recommended that they [MCA] negotiate for the best order possible [concerning] the use of the library. Posner said that he also doubted that we could get divestiture of the film library."

On August 14, the second round of talks began. The same cast was present, along with the addition of Robert L. Wright, the Antitrust Division's chief negotiator.

"I understand that the basis for these negotiations is that the acquisition of Decca-Universal is non-negotiable," Wright said. "But I also understand that MCA is prepared to discuss an alternative arrangement with regard to the film library. Is this correct?"

"You are correct," Susman replied.

"Okay, then, gentlemen, what are you prepared to offer in the way of a proposal?"

After spending some time discussing which side was supposed to come prepared with a written proposal, Susman managed to get the conversation back on track. "There is something that could compound our problems," he said. "If, for example, Screen Gems—which already has a formidable backlog—wishes to purchase the Universal film library, they might not do so for fear of being sued by the government in an antitrust action of its own."

"I think that the bidders might well receive some assurances that if they purchase the films the government will not sue them," Wright replied. "I believe this is an important point, because divestiture to an outside source appears to be the only practical way in which this matter can be quickly resolved. If MCA is disposed to have Universal sell to outside companies, this might be the solution to the entire case."[8]

In response to Wright's remarks, the MCA attorneys asked if forty-four movies made after 1958 might be exempted and retained by MCA. Wright asked for details at their scheduled third round of talks the following day.

The issue regarding the post-1958 movies was based on the theory that motion picture films had to play in theatres around the country until they were "milked," after which there was generally a clearance of two to three years before the films were offered to television. Some of the jewels in this collection included *Psycho, Spartacus, Flower Drum Song,* and *To Kill a Mockingbird.* And two television networks, ABC and NBC, were committed to the broadcasting of weekly movies, paying as much as $300,000 each.

The next day, Wright asked what MCA's position was on the government's divestiture proposal.

"We will not negotiate on that basis," Bickford said, "even if we are permitted to keep a portion of the library. MCA is only willing to negotiate on the basis which it had originally stated: that MCA would have a right to participate in competitive bidding for the film library. MCA has indicated that no other position is negotiable."

Sklarsky replied, "No, we have always been under the impression that MCA's only non-negotiable position was the divestiture of Decca-Universal."

"Okay," Bickford asked, "where do we go from here?"

"My position is this," Wright said firmly. "Unless MCA divests itself of the Universal library, a concentration of power will exist that will be in violation of the antitrust laws. You may go over my head if you like and discuss this matter with Lee Loevinger, but I would recommend settlement on nothing less than this."

The meeting then ended abruptly, without any plans for further discussions.

The following day, President Kennedy and his brother, the attorney general, received telegrams from the Hollywood AFL Film Council, stating: "Hollywood craftsmen and technicians and creative artists [are] suffering grievously from unemployment caused by the flight of feature motion picture production to foreign countries." A coalition of Hollywood unions dominated by the Screen Actors Guild, the American Federation of Musicians, the Teamsters, and IATSE, the film council lauded MCA for its "plans to create still further job opportunities and continuity of employment for studio workers" and asked the government "to reexamine the advisability of the present attempts of the Antitrust Division of the Department of Justice to prevent MCA from engaging in feature film production."

Both the White House and the Justice Department were baffled by the film council's request since no one in the Antitrust Division had even suggested that MCA be barred from producing films.

On August 22, Raskin, on behalf of MCA, decided to accept Wright's offer and discuss the situation with Loevinger. After several conversations, Loevinger stood behind Wright but offered a variation of the compromise that the MCA attorneys themselves had offered: that a portion of the Universal library be retained by MCA.

Loevinger's intervention into the negotiations brought new life to them. The talks resumed and details were worked out.

Finally, on September 18, Attorney General Robert Kennedy announced that a proposed consent decree had been filed in the United States District Court in Los Angeles, and that the settlement would become effective in thirty days.

The final judgment ordered that Universal Pictures sell 215 of the 229 films in its library. The studio could select fourteen of those films for remakes or reissues. Also, consistent with the conditions of a consent decree, all criminal proceedings against MCA and its alleged co-conspirators were suspended. And the entire case was taken off the public record. Further, Jules Stein, Lew Wasserman, Taft Schreiber, Ronald Reagan, and others avoided having to appear in open court to answer messy questions about their financial relationships.

Two months earlier, MCA had appeared to be dead, but the Department of Justice could not find the means to ram a stake through its heart. MCA would live again.

III

THE RESURRECTION

CHAPTER TWENTY-SIX

INDEED, MCA and Lew Wasserman were alive and well*—so well, in fact, that on September 19, 1962, the day after the consent decree was announced, workers began razing the Revue-Universal studio just north of the Hollywood Freeway, in one of the biggest real estate developments in the history of Hollywood. The land was to be cleared for the new, $110-million home of MCA's production companies. Included among other structures planned for the site, known immediately as "Universal City," were a bank, a post office, the Universal Amphitheatre, and the new, modernized Universal Studios. Universal City would also be the site of MCA's fifteen-story, black-glass-and-marble administration building, the "Black Tower"—which, quite intentionally, stood like a black steel monolith: an ominous presence, at once imposing and intimidating.

MCA's only public comment in the wake of its settlement with the federal government was that it intended, "in complete coordination

---

*In *The New York Times,* Murray Schumach wrote: "Financially, MCA is probably in a stronger position than any movie company in Hollywood. Its assets exceed $80 million. It owns a savings and loan association with assets of more than $63 million.

"Despite MCA's enormous expenditures for expansion in recent years, its net income has risen steadily and last year [1961] reached a record of nearly $7.5 million. At the start of this year the retained earnings of the company exceeded $33 million. During 1961 its current assets of some $50 million were double its current liabilities."[1]

with the management of Decca and Universal, to proceed constructively and vigorously in strengthening the production of motion pictures."

Universal provided MCA with an incredible legacy in film production. Former nickelodeon owner Carl Laemmle had founded the Universal Film Manufacturing Company in June 1912; soon after, the studio started cranking out silent movies, including *The Hunchback of Notre Dame* and *The Phantom of the Opera,* starring Lon Chaney.

Academy Award–winning director William Wyler, who had come to the United States in 1920, when he was eighteen, recalled, "I have a great affectionate feeling for the old Universal. It was my school, my cradle in America. Carl Laemmle . . . brought over dozens of young people from Europe. And not all of them were relatives, although I was. Old man Laemmle gambled on people. Many times he was right. Opportunities were easier to get in those days. Movies were a small business, not overcrowded. Working in films was even a little disreputable, not a sound profession."[2]

In 1930, Universal won its first Academy Award for Best Picture with *All Quiet on the Western Front.* But, for the most part, Universal became known for its inexpensive Westerns, romantic dramas, and comedies—those films which Laemmle was convinced would attract Middle Americans to their neighborhood theatres. Laemmle was right, and the studio made big money. With the Depression, Universal found itself in financial trouble. Laemmle turned his studio over to his son, Carl Laemmle, Jr., who could do little to turn the family business around. Consequently, in 1936, the Laemmle family was moved out and replaced by Robert H. Cochrane and Nate J. Blumberg, who developed the "new Universal."

But the new Universal was much like the old, as the new owners continued to produce horror films like *Son of Frankenstein,* even after some success with teenage singer/actress Deanna Durbin's movies, like *Three Smart Girls* and *One Hundred Men and a Girl.* But as the country began to slip out of the Depression and into war, the horror films again began to make money. Soon, Universal started to branch out into musicals, such as *One Night in the Tropics,* and Bud Abbott and Lou Costello comedies, including *Abbott and Costello Meet Frankenstein.*

Universal's "golden years" culminated just after its November 1946 merger with International Pictures, headed by Leo Spitz—who had negotiated the payoffs in Chicago between Willie Bioff, after he was hooked into the Chicago Mafia, and Barney Balaban, before he became the president of Paramount.

Universal-International made a corporate decision to stop making the second-rate films it had become known for and to attract a classier audience. The studio bought the American distribution rights of J. Arthur Rank Productions, a first-rate English movie company, and thereby acquired such films as Laurence Olivier's Academy Award–winning production of *Hamlet,* for which Universal shared its second Best Picture Oscar, and *The Lavender Hill Mob* and *The Man in the White Suit,* both starring Alec Guinness. Universal followed with such A-movies as *Brute Force* and *Naked City.*

When Universal was bought by Decca Records* in 1952, it returned to its low-budget films, concentrating on science fiction dramas, like *This Island Earth* and *The Creature from the Black Lagoon,* and series comedies featuring Francis the Talking Mule and Ma and Pa Kettle. These box-office successes were followed by a long string of "women's movies," produced by Ross Hunter, ranging from tear-jerkers like *Imitation of Life* to the Doris Day–Rock Hudson romantic comedies like *Pillow Talk.*

While the Antitrust Division tied up the loose ends of its litigation against MCA, Wasserman and Allen Susman met with government attorneys Leonard Posner and Malcolm MacArthur for a general discussion on October 1, 1962. According to the report of the meeting, Seven Arts appeared to have the inside track on the Universal post–1948 film library and eventually bought it for $21.5 million, with a $7.5 million down payment. The controlling interest in Seven Arts had been purchased by a business syndicate controlled by Louis A. Chesler, a Canadian financier and a long-time associate of Meyer Lansky. Also, Wasserman hinted that MCA would concentrate on the production of major motion pictures and their distribution. Clearly, the meeting between MCA and the government antitrust lawyers was cordial and congenial.[3]

The day after his meeting with Wasserman, Posner resigned from his job with the Antitrust Division to join a prestigious Beverly Hills law firm, which specialized in protecting the components of the entertainment industry from government tax and antitrust regulations.†

---

*Decca Records had originally been founded in Great Britain and then moved to the United States after World War II. Among other artists, Decca signed Guy Lombardo, Louis Armstrong, and Bing Crosby. In 1954, Milton Rackmil, who had been responsible for boosting the careers of Bill Haley and the Comets and Buddy Holly and the Crickets, became the president of both Decca and Universal. He remained as the head of Universal after the studio was bought by MCA.

†Three months later, Leonard Posner was found dead in his apartment after being stricken by an apparent heart attack. Posner, who had no history of heart trouble, was survived only by his father. No foul play was suspected.

In the wake of the demise of MCA Artists, the biggest winner in the former MCA client sweepstakes was clearly the William Morris Agency, with its rolls climbing to seven hundred actors under contract. At its peak, MCA represented only six hundred actors among its fourteen hundred clients.

Many MCA agents went into business for themselves, including Dave Baumgarten, who set up his own Agency for the Performing Arts, and Herman Citron and Arthur Park, who formed the Artists Agency Corporation, also known as Citron-Park. Other former MCAers, like Irving Salkow and Henry Alper, joined GAC, whose board of directors selected MCA vice-president Larry Barnett as its new president in 1963. Mike Levee, Jr., went with Rosenberg-Coryell, and four of MCA's top New York agents—Bobby Brenner, Kay Brown, Phyllis Jackson, and Jay Sandford—brought nearly one hundred top artists into the stable of the fast-growing Ashley-Steiner Agency. All of these agents remained tight with MCA and were destined to have a significant impact on future MCA productions.

MCA-Revue's television lineup was none too shabby, as it again had a commanding impact for the 1962–63 season. It included such shows as ABC's *Wagon Train* (which had moved from NBC), *Leave It to Beaver, McHale's Navy,* and *Alcoa Theater;* NBC's *It's a Man's World, Laramie,* and *Wide Country;* and CBS's continuation of *The Jack Benny Show* and *The Alfred Hitchcock Hour* (which had returned from NBC). MCA's total contribution to network television was eleven hours of programming, led by ABC with five hours, NBC's four and one-half hours, and CBS's one and one-half hours.

However, one long-running MCA show was on the verge of biting the dust, CBS's *General Electric Theater,* featuring Ronald Reagan, then opposite the top-rated *Bonanza* on NBC.*

In his role as General Electric's celebrity spokesman, Reagan had become increasingly controversial, bitterly attacking the Kennedy administration for its policies toward big business. Reagan had been particularly incensed by the breakup of MCA, calling the government's action "a meat-ax operation." Reagan started quoting Thomas Paine ("Government is a necessary evil; let us have as little of it as possible") and Justice Oliver Wendell Holmes ("Strike for the jugular. Reduce taxes and spending. Keep government poor and remain free").[5]

---

*According to a Justice Department memorandum, when *GE Theater* started having problems, MCA quickly intervened. Wasserman went to Jimmy Stewart and said, "Jimmy, I need a favor. The *General Electric Theater* has been lagging lately. We need a name. We need you to do a show. Please do it for me." Because of the relationship between Wasserman and Stewart, the actor agreed to do the program, even though he did not want to perform on television.[4]

Barney Balaban *(The Academy of Motion Picture Arts and Sciences)*

Carl Laemmle *(The Academy of Motion Picture Arts and Sciences)*

James Caesar Petrillo, president of the American Federation of Musicians

Willie Bioff, head of the International Alliance of Theatrical Stage Employees, leaves the Federal Building in New York after pleading innocent to charges of violating the Federal Antiracketeering Law. Bioff was indicted with William Browne, president of the union, and charged with obtaining money from leading motion picture producers under threat of calling a strike of employees. (*AP/Wide World Photos*)

Four ex-convicts during a House Subcommittee hearing investigating their paroles from federal prison. Clockwise, seated around table (starting from left, rear) are: Charles Gioe, Louis Campagna, Attorney Eugene Bernstein, unidentified man, Paul Ricca, and Philip D'Andrea. (*AP/Wide World Photos*)

Charles Gioe, one of seven men convicted in 1943 of conspiring to extort money from the motion picture industry, lies sprawled across front seat of auto, in which he was found shot to death. *(AP/Wide World Photos)*

Willie Bioff, former Hollywood labor racketeer, lies before the wreckage of his pickup truck. Bioff was killed as he stepped on the truck's starter at his home in Phoenix in 1955. *(AP/Wide World Photos)*

Roy Brewer, Hollywood representative of the International Alliance of Theatrical Stage Employees

Ronald Reagan, president of the Screen Actors Guild, listens to testimony at the House Un-American Activities Committee Investigation. *(AP/Wide World Photos)*

Sidney Korshak testifies before the Senate Rackets Investigating Committee. *(AP/ Wide World Photos)*

Taft Schreiber, MCA vice-president, testifying at a 1961 FCC hearing.

Johnny Roselli, overseer of the Chicago Mafia's operations in Hollywood

Paul Ziffren, California Democratic Committee delegate and law partner of William French Smith

Governor Reagan joins Dr. and Mrs. Jules Stein. Stein recieved the Humanitarian Award of Variety Clubs International.

Lew Wasserman

Frank Sinatra is shown in his dressing room at Westchester Premier Theater in New York, 1976. Shown from left to right, standing, are Gregory DePalma, Sinatra, Thomas Marson, the late Carlo Gambino, and Jimmy "the Weasel" Fratianno; in front is Richard "Nerves" Fusco. *(AP/Wide World Photos)*

Senator Paul Laxalt places the name of Ronald Reagan in nomination during the 1976 GOP convention. *(AP/Wide World Photos)*

President Reagan shaking hands with Sonny Werblin, former MCA vice-president. *(AP/Wide World Photos)*

President Reagan signs documents authorizing Senator Paul Laxalt to establish a committee for his reelection campaign and appointing Laxalt as committee chairman. *(AP/Wide World Photos)*

Teamsters President Jackie Presser, right, and Labor Secretary Raymond Donovan shake hands prior to a luncheon hosted by Presser at the union's headquarters in Washington. This was Presser's first day at the helm of the Teamsters. *(AP/Wide World Photos)*

Teamsters President Jackie Presser, right, goes over papers with his attorney John Climaco during his appearance before the President's Commission on Organized Crime in 1985. Presser invoked the Fifth Amendment fifteen times, refusing to answer questions about violence, his leadership, and policies of the Teamsters union. *(AP/Wide World Photos)*

Labor Secretary Raymond Donovan leaves Bronx Criminal Court in New York after pleading innocent to criminal charges *(AP/Wide World Photos)*

Bea and Sidney Korshak

Sidney Sheinberg, left, president of MCA, Inc., and Lew R. Wasserman, chairman, stand atop one of the hills of Universal City. MCA's Black Tower and studio backlot are in background.

MCA headquarters *(Scaramouche)*

In 1962, influenced by MCA's Jules Stein and Taft Schreiber, Reagan officially switched political parties and became a Republican. Life-long conservative Republicans, Stein and Schreiber had watched Reagan closely on the "mashed-potato circuit" for General Electric and discovered that he was speaking their language. "Both on the air and in the GE plants," wrote Reagan biographer Lou Cannon, "Reagan exceeded even Schreiber's high expectations. . . . Reagan accepted the various published descriptions of himself as a 'prominent conservative spokesman,' although he always bridled when the word 'right-winger' was added to the description. He thought of himself as an orthodox and patriotic American who was drawing attention to a problem of government growth that would destroy the country if it wasn't corrected. While still a registered Democrat, Reagan realized he had become a Republican."[6]

His political views became so reactionary that they even started offending the conservative high command of General Electric—to the point where both GE and the BBD&O advertising agency began holding private meetings, considering whether to replace Reagan with a new, more moderate host.

Stanley Rubin, who was *GE Theater*'s executive producer from 1959 to 1962, said, "There was a time when I heard from the executives from MCA-Revue that Ronnie was unhappy with the kind of liberal content, liberal point of view of the stories. To me, they were studies of the human condition. . . . Suddenly, he got the right to come to me with a couple of stories and to produce them. . . . I didn't like his selection at all. His stories were extremely political—right-wing political. They were exposés of communists in America."[7]

Rubin later added, "There came a time in the making of *GE Theater* in early 1961—while I was preparing scripts—a major executive at GE called me. He said they were coming out to the West Coast before the beginning of the new season. And he said, 'What do you think about a new host for the new season, and who would you suggest for the role?' I was kind of stunned. I said, 'Why don't you talk to Taft Schreiber?'

"Then they called back a couple of days later and asked 'What would you think of multiple hosts? Maybe Ronnie could be the host for the dramas, and maybe someone else could do the comedies, another could do the romances.' I told them it was possible but again suggested that they talk to Schreiber. They said they would be the following week. But, when they arrived, they said, 'Forget it.' I assumed that they had talked to Schreiber, who killed the idea of replacing Ronnie.

"I got one of the executives to the side and asked what had happened.

He said, 'You know that Ronnie, as the spokesman for GE, has been going around talking to all kinds of groups. And his speeches to these groups have been so ultraconservative that he has become an embarrassment to the GE executive suite.' "[8]

Finally, at the end of the 1961–62 season, *General Electric Theater* was canceled and the former president of the Screen Actors Guild was without steady work. Once again, MCA stepped in.*

---

*One long-time MCA loyalist whom neither Jules Stein nor Lew Wasserman could help was James Petrillo, who had given up his position as national president of the American Federation of Musicians in 1958 but kept control of his home local in Chicago. Running for reelection in Local 10 on December 5, 1962, Petrillo was narrowly defeated 1,690 to 1,595 by a rank-and-file reform candidate, dance-band leader Bernard "Barney" F. Richards, who sought an end to Petrillo's reign of terror within the union. By the end of his career, Petrillo rarely shook hands with people, fearing that another's germs would be passed along to him. At the conclusion of his farewell speech to his AFM brothers and sisters, he tearfully collapsed in the arms of his close friend, comedian George Jessel.

CHAPTER
TWENTY-SEVEN

SIDNEY KORSHAK had become, by 1962, a full-time resident of California with a home in the exclusive Bel Air section of Los Angeles —although he never officially practiced law in the state and never applied for the California bar. However, he continued to maintain his legal practice and businesses in Chicago. A confidential FBI report stated that he "is somewhat of a mystery man. He makes regular plane trips to Las Vegas and on occasion to Chicago as well as other places. He reportedly has an interest in the Riviera Hotel in Las Vegas."[1]

Another FBI report stated that "negotiations were being carried on whereby the Chicago organization [Mafia] was to obtain a tighter grip on Las Vegas hotels and casinos and that allegedly negotiations were being made through Sidney Korshak," who was later described in that same report as "one of the most powerful individuals in the country."[2]

One FBI source identified Korshak as "possibly the highest-paid lawyer in the world. The source stated that Korshak primarily represented a group in Las Vegas . . . the 'Chicago group,' who were in the opinion of this source the biggest single factor on the Las Vegas scene."

When in Las Vegas, he usually stayed in the Presidential Suite of the Riviera. He would occasionally give his quarters to Teamsters general president Jimmy Hoffa when he came into town, looking for investments for the Teamsters Central States Pension Fund. According to a Los Angeles Police intelligence report, on October 12, 1961, Korshak came into Las Vegas unexpectedly while Hoffa was in the Presidential Suite at the Riviera. When Korshak arrived at the hotel, Hoffa yielded to Korshak, moving out of the suite to a smaller room across the hall.

In late 1961, Korshak was asked to represent the Nevada Downtown Hotel Association in a strike involving the Las Vegas local of the Culinary Workers Union. He was also frequently spotted by law-enforcement officials meeting with Harvey Silbert, who was a Beverly Hills attorney close to Allen Dorfman, the fiduciary manager of the Teamsters pension fund.

Hoffa and the Teamsters, via the Central States Fund, had been extremely generous to Las Vegas, loaning hundreds of millions of dollars to the gaming establishments in Nevada, especially to midwestern gangster Morris Dalitz.

Moe Dalitz had been a key figure in Detroit's Purple Gang during the early 1930s, leaving for Ohio after a bloody war with a rival mob group. While in Michigan, Dalitz had become an important ally to young Jimmy Hoffa, introducing him to major Mafia figures throughout the country. Settling in Cleveland, Dalitz locked in with Ohio jukebox czar William Presser, who soon became head of the Ohio Teamsters—with the support of Dalitz, Hoffa, and their underworld friends. He also helped the Chicago Mafia bring George Browne and Willie Bioff to power in IATSE.

In 1949, Dalitz left Cleveland and moved to Las Vegas, where he and some associates bought the controlling interest in the Desert Inn. Dalitz selected Duke University graduate Allard Roen to manage the casino. Later, Dalitz and his business associates purchased the Stardust hotel/casino as well. Dalitz received $24 million in loans from the Central States Pension Fund for his Las Vegas casinos and nearly $100 million from the pension fund for the construction and subsequent renovation of his La Costa Country Club in Carlsbad, California—all personally approved by Hoffa and Allen Dorfman.

Korshak, according to a confidential FBI report, "was to act as a 'go-between' between John Factor ["Jake the Barber"] and the Desert Inn group made up of Morris Dalitz and Allard Roen in the sale of the Stardust property in Las Vegas, Nevada, owned by Factor. . . .

"Korshak was to keep the signed option and agreements in his personal possession concerning this transaction."

John Factor, an owner of the Stardust, was a wealthy international swindler, according to a Los Angeles Police report, who had served six years in prison in a mail-fraud scheme involving $1.2 million. The report also identified him as a "long-time friend of [the] Capone group from Chicago."

According to another FBI document, the government had learned that Korshak "had advised Hoffa not to make any loans from the Central States, Southeast, and Southwest Areas Pension Fund to the operators of Caesar's Palace in Las Vegas. That he, Hoffa, already had too many loans to Las Vegas gambling interests . . . that if the Teamsters membership ever found out about Hoffa's handling and misuse of the pension funds, he, Hoffa, would never get out of jail."[3]

The FBI was also investigating Teamsters pension fund loans to finance the Skyway Hotel at Miami's International Airport. Korshak was said to be the intermediary between the hotel group and Hoffa.

Back in Chicago, Korshak and his brother Marshall hosted a dinner in honor of the Cardinal Stritch Medical School of Loyola University. Meantime, Bernard "Pepi" Posner—who was identified in a confidential FBI report as the Korshaks' cousin but was no relation of Leonard Posner—was placed in charge of the underworld's bookmaking operations in the city's Hyde Park area. At the same time, Herman Posner, a rank-and-file dissident from Chicago's IATSE local and no relation to either Leonard or Pepi, was found knifed to death after preparing to turn state's evidence on extortion schemes and kickbacks involving local union leaders.

In New York, Korshak's name cropped up during an investigation of the New York State Liquor Authority and Ralph Berger, an organized crime associate who had reportedly gained "control over certain officials of the State Liquor Authority in New York, and of the Illinois State Liquor Control Board in Chicago. . . .

"Berger was a close associate of both Sidney and Marshall Korshak and resided in the same apartment building as Marshall Korshak and spent considerable time in the law offices of the Korshaks at 134 La Salle [in Chicago], and . . . Berger was a contact man between Korshak and . . . the chairman of the Illinois Liquor Control Board."

Federal investigators thereby assumed that Berger was fronting for the Korshaks. "[I]f Berger was able to exert any influence with certain members of the State Liquor Authority . . . he undoubtedly would do so as a representative of the Korshaks and not in his own right," the Justice Department document stated. "It was believed that any conniving Berger might do with the [New York] State Liquor Authority or with the Illinois State Liquor Control Board would be done on behalf of and under the instructions of the Korshak brothers."[4]

At the time of this New York investigation, Marshall Korshak was an Illinois state senator. He was also the president of Windy City Liquor Distributors, Inc., in Chicago. Judith Korshak, Marshall's wife, was the vice-president of the firm, and Mary Oppenheim was the secretary-treasurer. Oppenheim was also a secretary in the Korshaks' law firm.

In Los Angeles, Korshak was into everything from representing a drive-in theatre chain to putting together international deals for corporations. Court records also showed that Joe Glaser of the Associated Booking Company had legally given Korshak all "voting rights, dominion and control" over his interest in ABC. Although Glaser continued to head the agency, the legal maneuver would eventually give Korshak full authority.[5] An FBI report alleged that he was part owner of the Bistro Restaurant, although his name appeared on none of the company's records. A fashionable spot with a French decor and ambience on North Canon Avenue in the heart of Beverly Hills, the Bistro had become one of the most popular restaurants among those on Hollywood's fast track. According to several sources, the Bistro has been the favorite restaurant of Ronald and Nancy Reagan. "They've been coming here for years," said a long-time employee of the restaurant, who added that the Reagans had been given their own table.

Korshak was also personally involved in the negotiations between the California Federation of Race Tracks and the Pari-Mutuel Clerks Union. According to Korshak, he became involved in the dispute when Mervyn Leroy—the one-time MGM director who had introduced Ronald Reagan to Nancy Davis—was president of the Hollywood Park Racing Association and asked Korshak for help to head off an employees' strike at Hollywood Park. Although there were twenty-eight other attorneys involved in the negotiations, Korshak received sole credit for ending the strike. Even though some thought the contract to be sweet—with the employees being forced to compromise their benefits —Korshak said that he "merely brought union and management into accord through some of his contacts."[6]

Yet another FBI report indicated that the threatened strike at Santa Anita Racetrack in Arcadia, California, had been averted after Korshak intervened. As a reward, an FBI source alleged, "Korshak apparently obtained a substantial fee or interest in the racetrack as a result of his efforts. This source stated . . . that Korshak was also making himself available to the Los Angeles Dodgers baseball team."[7]

Korshak's relationship with the Los Angeles Dodgers came through his involvement in the ownership and operation of parking lots in the Los Angeles vicinity, in which he was a partner with Las Vegas casino owner Beldon Katleman and other businessmen in Affiliated Parking, Inc. During the building of Dodger Stadium, Korshak, according to an FBI report, "was represented to Mayor Samuel Yorty of Los Angeles as the attorney for Walter O'Malley, president of the Dodgers. At a meeting between Yorty, O'Malley, and other city department heads, O'Malley denied that he was represented by Korshak, and it developed that Korshak and others associated with him were interested in offering an attractive bid for the parking lot concession at the stadium."

The FBI report stated that O'Malley had originally contracted another parking lot company, "but, as opening day for the stadium approached . . . O'Malley . . . was going to have to pay fantastic wages to the attendants, who would be required to join a Teamsters Union local operating in the entertainment field. However, the group to which Korshak belonged could provide [sic] workers out of a different Teamsters local having a contract which could be extended to include the Dodger facility.

"The offer from the Korshak group was accepted by O'Malley."[8]

O'Malley later said, "We did what any ordinary prudent businessman would do." He added that Korshak "had the reputation as having the best experience in this area. He provided us a little insulation. . . . As far as we're concerned, he does a good job. And unless he's been convicted of a crime, we're not going to do anything."[9]

Korshak also had an interest in another national parking concern, the Duncan Parking Meter Company, which "was controlled by the 'Outfit,' specifically Gus Alex . . . and Sidney Korshak." The FBI learned that the owner of the company, a Canadian millionaire, had been "muscled" out of the company by the Chicago mob—which then put in their own front men to run the business.[10]

In an interview with FBI agents, Korshak admitted that he was involved with Duncan—but as its "legal counsel." According to the FBI, the business had since been sold to legitimate interests.

In the January 27, 1963, issue of *Parade Magazine,* a reader asked: "I would like to know if a Chicago mouthpiece named Sidney Korshak represents both Jimmy Hoffa and the Chicago syndicate in Las Vegas. —F.L., Chicago, Illinois."

The reply was short. "Attorney Sidney Korshak reportedly represents the Cleveland interests in the Desert Inn and Stardust hotels of Las Vegas. He is reportedly the attorney for the Riviera Hotel in Las

Vegas. Korshak is also a friend of such theatrical personalities as Dinah Shore and Debbie Reynolds. His exact relationship with Hoffa is not known."

Dinah Shore had appeared at the Desert Inn on February 3, 1961. The FBI speculated that Korshak might have "handled her contract on behalf of the Chicago group with whom Korshak was associated." Soon after, Shore and her husband, actor George Montgomery, threw a birthday party for Korshak at their home.

Debbie Reynolds appeared at the Riviera in January 1963, and Korshak was present for her opening performance. Korshak and his wife had purchased their Bel Air home in 1959 from Harry Karl, the president of Karl's Shoe Stores, Ltd., and Reynolds's second husband after her divorce from singer Eddie Fisher. Karl was a close friend and traveling companion of Korshak's.*

On June 28, 1962, the dapper Karl, an expert gin rummy player, went to the Friars Club, where he was greeted by singer Tony Martin, who was to be Karl's second. Karl's opponent that day was real estate developer Maurice Friedman, a former part-owner of the New Frontier Hotel in Las Vegas.

Friedman had developed a scam for his game with Karl. A hole had been drilled in the ceiling, covered by an air vent, over Karl's shoulder. An accomplice of Friedman, George Emerson Seach, crouched flush against the peephole and, with the help of a zoom lens, would observe Karl's cards. Friedman was wired with a small receiver taped to his chest, through which he would receive a prearranged set of impulses in the pattern of a special code, indicating the status of Karl's hand. In one thirteen-hour session, Karl lost $18,000 to Friedman. Friedman continued his scheme over the next few weeks. In all, Karl was cheated out of nearly $80,000. Another club member, Ted Briskin, was taken for nearly $200,000. Karl and Briskin were followed by Tony Martin, who lost $10,000; Zeppo Marx, who was fleeced for $6,000; and theatrical agent Kurt Frings, who dropped $25,000. Actor Phil Silvers also lost but never revealed how much. Still others lost even more.

In the midst of Friedman's cheating operation, several others were brought in as part of the scam to play more sophisticated games,

---

*Debbie Reynolds was Karl's fourth wife, after two marriages to Marie McDonald and another to Joan Cohn, whose 1959 wedding was held in Korshak's Chicago apartment. Korshak had also advised Karl on his 1957 divorce from McDonald, after which McDonald was kidnapped—while she was having an affair with Michael Wilding, Elizabeth Taylor's second husband. On the night of McDonald's abduction, both Karl and Korshak were observed at her home. When she was safely returned, she and Karl were remarried. No reasons for the kidnapping were ever given, and no arrests were ever made.

including Benjamin Teitelbaum, the owner of Hollywood Film Service, a film-studio equipment company, and a partner of Korshak in Affiliated Parking. Another co-conspirator who cut himself in for twenty percent of the action was mobster Johnny Roselli, who had figured out what Friedman and his associates were doing.

The Friars Club cheating scandal lasted for five years—until Beldon Katleman learned what was going on and, for unknown reasons, told FBI agent George Bland, who later managed to convince Seach to turn state's evidence. Federal agents raided the Friars Club and made arrests. The government's principal interest was Roselli, who was later indicted and convicted of racketeering and sentenced to yet another prison term.[11]

While Roselli was frequenting the Friars Club—and being seen on occasion with Korshak—he was also working in cooperation with the Central Intelligence Agency in the CIA-Mafia plots to assassinate Cuban premier Fidel Castro. Roselli had been brought into the plots by Robert Maheu, a top aide to billionaire Howard Hughes, in August 1960, while Dwight D. Eisenhower was president. Roselli brought Chicago mob boss Sam Giancana into the CIA web, and Giancana solicited the services of Florida gangland boss Santos Trafficante.

Maheu had met Roselli in 1958 when he was sent by Hughes to Los Angeles. In California, Maheu had a meeting with Greg Bautzer, a Beverly Hills attorney, who occasionally represented Hughes. Bautzer offered Maheu an all-expense-paid trip to Las Vegas to serve a subpoena on Beldon Katleman. Unable to get a reservation at Katleman's El Rancho Vegas, Maheu called a lawyer friend, Edward Bennett Williams, of Washington, D.C., who had also been a college buddy of Maheu's at Holy Cross. Williams then called Roselli, who then telephoned Maheu. Roselli confirmed reservations for Maheu and his wife at the El Rancho Vegas on the appointed weekend. The reservations had been personally approved by Katleman—whom Maheu was to subpoena for Bautzer.

Maheu recalled that after he arrived and was given Katleman's first-class treatment, "I had a quick decision to make. Was I going to be a son of a bitch and serve the subpoena? Or was I going to go back and explain what happened? To me, it wasn't a big decision. There was no way in the world that I was going to compromise my friendship with Ed Williams and the man I had just met, Johnny Roselli, under those circumstances."

Maheu gallantly decided not to serve the subpoena and enjoyed his visit to the El Rancho. When he returned to Los Angeles, he explained to Bautzer what had happened in Las Vegas and returned the attorney's expense money.

"Bautzer laughed like hell," Maheu said, "and subsequently he told the story to Roselli. Then Roselli said he wanted to find out more about this guy Maheu. After that we became friends. . . . When he and I began discussing the Castro plots, I was straight up with him. I wasn't about to cross this guy or any of his friends."[12]

During a conversation with Los Angeles crime boss James Fratianno, Roselli warned, "Well, you watch that fucking Korshak. He's Gussie Alex's man. . . . One thing you've got to keep in mind with Korshak. He's made millions for Chicago and he's got plenty of clout in L.A. and Vegas. . . . Sid's really burrowed in. He's real big with the movie colony, lives in a mansion in Bel Air, knows most of the big stars. His wife plays tennis with Dinah Shore, and he's been shacking up with Stella Stevens for years. . . . He calls himself a labor-relations expert, but he's really a fixer. A union cooks up a strike and Sid arbitrates it. Instead of a payoff under the table, he gets a big legal fee, pays taxes on it, and cuts it up. All nice and clean. This guy ain't never going to the joint, believe me. . . . In other words, if you're going to fuck with this guy, you better watch your step."[13]

Sidney Korshak was also a silent associate of the cool, gravel-voiced Bautzer in his Beverly Hills law firm, Wyman, Bautzer, Finell, Rothman & Kuchel. Married to actress Dana Wynter, Bautzer made his reputation as a Hollywood divorce attorney for such stars as Ingrid Bergman before shifting gears and concentrating on corporate law. He also represented Joseph Schenck of Twentieth Century–Fox, as well as the Flamingo hotel/casino in Las Vegas.

Eugene L. Wyman, the senior partner in the firm, had succeeded attorney Paul Ziffren as California's representative to the National Democratic Committee. Wyman was also elected as California's Democratic state chairman.

An FBI report stated that "Korshak is allegedly a close friend of both [California governor] Edmund G. (Pat) Brown and Gene Wyman. They are said to be frequent breakfast guests at his home."[14]

Consistent with that, another 1963 FBI document stated that an underworld informant close to Chicago racketeer Murray Humphreys and Sidney Korshak told federal investigators that Korshak had become "one of the biggest guys in the country today who has a pipeline right to the government in Washington."[15]

CHAPTER
TWENTY-EIGHT

In its first year under MCA's control, Universal Pictures—with its $50 million expansion well under way—produced several critical and box-office successes under production chief Edward Muhl, including Alfred Hitchcock's *The Birds; Charade,* which starred Cary Grant and Audrey Hepburn; *A Gathering of Eagles,* featuring Rock Hudson; *The Thrill of It All,* with Doris Day and James Garner; and *The Ugly American,* starring Marlon Brando.

Although none of these films won any Academy Awards, the most highly publicized film of the year and most expensive production of all time—which won four Oscars—was *Cleopatra.* Despite the steamy off-camera romance between the movie's stars, Elizabeth Taylor and Richard Burton, and the international gossip this romance ignited, the $44 million *Cleopatra* was a financial disaster, causing heads to roll at Twentieth Century–Fox, which was later forced to sell its backlot in order to pay the film's creditors. Spyros Skouras was forced out as the president of the studio, which was taken over by Darryl Zanuck from New York while his son, Richard, became its production chief on the West Coast.

That same year a fate similar to Skouras's befell MGM chief Joseph

Vogel, whose Waterloo was the remake of *Mutiny on the Bounty*. It cost over $30 million and was also a box-office failure.

Paramount had also fallen on hard times, forcing Barney Balaban—who had been president of the studio since the days of the payoffs to Willie Bioff, George Browne, and IATSE—to be kicked upstairs as Paramount's chairman of the board.

But the tragedies within the top management of Hollywood in 1963 were nothing compared to the national tragedy that fall.

On November 22, 1963, President John F. Kennedy was shot and killed while riding in an open convertible in Dallas, Texas. His assassin, Lee Harvey Oswald, had close ties with the Carlos Marcello Mafia family in New Orleans, particularly with Charles Murret, a top man in Marcello's Louisiana gambling network. Oswald had also been seen by numerous witnesses meeting with Marcello's personal pilot just days before he murdered the president.

Within forty-eight hours after the shooting, Oswald, who panicked after the assassination and was captured by police, was killed by Dallas nightclub owner Jack Ruby, who had a long-standing relationship with numerous associates of the Chicago Mafia and had worked as an organizer at one time for Paul Dorfman, the stepfather of Jimmy Hoffa's associate Allen Dorfman, in the Chicago Wastehandlers Union. During the days and weeks before the Kennedy killing, Ruby was calling and being called by top aides to Marcello, Florida mobster Santos Trafficante, and Hoffa—all of whom were known to have discussed plans with their associates to murder either John or Robert Kennedy. A U.S. House select committee investigating the Kennedy assassination later concluded that "Carlos Marcello,* Santos Trafficante, and Jimmy Hoffa† had the motive, means, and opportunity" to murder the president.[1]

---

*In September 1962, Carlos Marcello allegedly threatened to kill President Kennedy, according to Pulitzer Prize–winning reporter Ed Reid in his 1969 book, *The Grim Reapers*. Reid's source for the information was Ed Becker, a Los Angeles private investigator who had been present when Marcello made the threat.

While Reid was writing his book, there was pressure on him not to implicate Marcello in the assassination. According to the U.S. House Select Committee on Assassinations, "FBI files . . . contain repeated references to the Bureau's use of allegations about Becker received from Sidney Korshak, an alleged associate of various organized crime leaders. The files indicate a high level of awareness at the Bureau's headquarters that the Los Angeles FBI office was using the information received from Korshak in an effort to persuade Reid not to publish the Marcello allegations. There was, however, no reference in the files to Korshak's own possible background and activities, nor to his possible motives in supplying the information at that time."[2]

†Jimmy Hoffa was convicted of jury tampering and defrauding the Teamsters Central States Pension Fund in 1964; he was sentenced to thirteen years in prison. In 1971, he was replaced as general president of the Teamsters by Frank Fitzsimmons.

"The mob did it," said G. Robert Blakey, the committee's chief counsel. "It is a historical fact."[3] The committee's final report put forth the theory that Kennedy was killed to end the U.S. Justice Department's relentless assault on the underworld. The official investigation by the Warren Commission that followed never addressed the underworld ties to Oswald and Ruby. Many of those on the panel had been directly involved with the CIA in the CIA-Mafia plots to murder Fidel Castro—which the Kennedy brothers had no knowledge of until May 1962, at which time they ordered them stopped.

Meantime, Lew Wasserman had tried to revive Reagan's failing movie career. His last starring role had been in 1957, when he appeared with his wife in Columbia's *Hellcats of the Navy*. In 1961, MCA managed to get him the token role of narrator in *The Young Doctors*, a hospital soap opera with a surprisingly good cast, including Fredric March, Ben Gazzara, Eddie Albert, and George Segal in his screen debut.

In 1964, Reagan made his last feature film appearance in Universal's *The Killers*, with Lee Marvin, John Cassavetes, and Angie Dickinson, which was adapted from an Ernest Hemingway short story. A remake of a 1946 film—starring Burt Lancaster and Ava Gardner—*The Killers* had originally been made for television but was considered too violent for home viewing. Consequently, it was dumped into second-rate theatres around the country, despite the fact that it was actually as good a picture as the original version. Reagan's last part was his first and only bad-guy role in his fifty-five films. He played an unrepentant mobster who refused to run away from two hit men.

Reagan was becoming increasingly involved in Republican politics, particularly in Barry Goldwater's campaign for president. As he saw a growing response to his brand of political conservatism, he became more politically motivated, and his political rhetoric began to gel. His years as General Electric's spokesman, delivering addresses across the country and molding his political philosophy, culminated on Tuesday night, October 27, 1964—a week before the general election. That night, Reagan gave what has become known as The Speech: "A Time for Choosing" during a half hour on network television. An emotionally charged defense of Goldwater's ultra-right-wing politics and American conservatism in general, The Speech helped raise $8 million in small contributions for Goldwater and catapulted Reagan into the national political limelight.

"You and I have a rendezvous with destiny," Reagan said that night.

"We will preserve for our children this, the last best hope of man on earth, or we will sentence them to take the last step into a thousand years of darkness."

Reagan had also been buoyed by the stunning 1964 victory in California of actor and song-and-dance man George Murphy in his bid for the U.S. Senate. Murphy, a conservative Republican and a former president of the Screen Actors Guild, had defeated Pierre Salinger—the former press secretary to President Kennedy, who had been appointed by Governor Brown to fill the unfinished term of Senator Claire Engel— by over 200,000 votes.

Jules Stein and Taft Schreiber were also enthusiastic Goldwater supporters, but, from past experience, MCA had learned its lesson. The antitrust problems the corporation had had would be eliminated in the future by maintaining good relations with both political parties. A television executive said, "Ever since the Justice Department busted them up, they play both sides of the political fence so they have a friend whatever party is in office."[4]

While Stein and Schreiber covered the GOP, Wasserman was busy making friends among the Democrats. He became a close friend of Lyndon Johnson, a relationship he has never discussed, and became a key fund-raiser for the Democratic Party.*

Wasserman was still interested in remaining a behind-the-scenes powerbroker and continuing to build the MCA empire. As the daily television viewing habits of the American public reached an average of over five hours, the MCA brass began to restructure their production company. Revue Productions was renamed and became Universal-Television, and Revue's studios became Universal City Studios, Inc. In its first year, Universal unveiled *The Virginian,* the first ninety-minute Western drama. The success of *The Virginian* in the television ratings was great enough for MCA to order *Wagon Train* to be expanded to ninety minutes as well.

MCA-TV continued to be the name of MCA's telefilm syndication company, but its president and long-time MCA vice-president, Sonny Werblin, had gone into professional football, buying twenty-three percent of the New York Titans in March 1963 and changing its name to the New York Jets of the American Football League. Werblin was named as the Jets' president and chief executive officer, and gave the team his favorite colors, green and white, the colors of paper money. Werblin would be best remembered for signing Alabama quarterback

---

*According to published reports, Wasserman had been offered and had rejected the post of Secretary of Commerce in the Johnson Administration.

sensation Joe Namath to a $427,000 package with the Jets—which included $150,000 of MCA stock.

At the end of the 1964–65 season, Werblin decided to spend his time concentrating on his sports investments and resigned as president of MCA-TV. Upon his departure from MCA, George Rosen, a reporter for *Variety,* wrote in January 1965: "Last week's resignation of Sonny Werblin from MCA (after thirty-five years with the entertainment complex), expected as it was, signaled the end of an era. For in those more than three decades, Werblin wielded more influence, made more money, made and broke more careers than perhaps any other show biz impresario in New York.

"If he was not broadcasting's greatest showman, he certainly qualified as its greatest promoter and salesman.

"No one had better contacts, knew more secrets, swapped more information, flew so many airline miles, ate more meals at '21,' made more deals, or sold so many hundreds of millions of dollars worth of programming."

In 1965, the U.S. Borax Company needed to find a new host for its television show, *Death Valley Days,* a Western anthology series, to replace Stanley Andrews, who had introduced each episode since the program started in 1952. Borax's advertising agency was McCann-Erickson, of which Reagan's brother, Neil Reagan, was a vice-president. "I wanted to sign him for a contract," Neil Reagan explained. "He didn't want any part of it. I rather suppose he didn't want to work."[5]

Nevertheless, Reagan was offered and accepted the job as the host for *Death Valley Days,* with the help of his brother and the considerable influence of Taft Schreiber. He received $125,000 annually.

MCA fortunes were further enhanced with the creation of a series of "World Premieres" for NBC—which, in 1965, had moved network president Robert Kintner to chairman of the board. Out of this concept —which was nothing more than making movies exclusively for television—MCA was able to sell several long-running dramas, including *The Rockford Files, Columbo, McCloud,* and *Emergency.* Of the 116 "World Premiere" movies MCA produced, thirty-one were turned into regular television series. MCA also made a record $60 million deal with NBC for the television broadcast of one hundred Universal pictures.

"One major executive in our industry told me at the time that I was an idiot to make the deal," Wasserman said. "He thought I'd sold the product for too low a price. We did spend a hell of a lot of our own money on it, but we wanted to be certain we'd have enough production to keep the facility fully occupied."[6]

More money was being made on other fronts. MCA's wholly owned Columbia Savings and Loan Association of Denver had become the largest state-chartered S & L in Colorado. Since MCA's takeover of Columbia in 1962, the S & L's assets had risen eighty-three percent and totaled $115 million. In order to attract customers, MCA had authorized Columbia to begin a flashy public relations campaign, spending over a half million dollars on advertising and promotion. As a result, revenues in 1964 were up forty percent over the previous year. Jack Benny, a member of Columbia's board of directors, had also been sent by MCA to open a new branch office in Fort Collins. "The line of people waiting for Benny's autograph on a deposit book," one report stated, "stretched for a block."[7]

After Barry Goldwater's presidential defeat, conservative financier Henry Salvatori, the founder of Western Geophysical Company, and two of his political associates—Los Angeles car dealer Holmes Tuttle and A. C. Rubel, the chairman of the board of Union Oil—began to view Ronald Reagan seriously as their hope for the future. Salvatori explained, "After that speech, we decided we better keep that fellow on TV. We realized that Reagan gave the Goldwater speech better than Goldwater. He had more self-control. He could say the same things but in a more gentle way."

In 1965, the three Los Angeles millionaires formed the Friends of Reagan committee, consisting of, among others, Taft Schreiber; Leonard Firestone, a top executive of the Firestone Tire and Rubber Company; drugstore magnate Justin Dart; and Reagan's personal attorney, William French Smith. Rubel, serving as the committee's spokesman, announced, "Ronald Reagan, out of a deep sense of duty and dedication, is willing to serve as Republican candidate for governor, providing a substantial cross section of our party will unite behind his candidacy. To this end, Mr. Reagan has agreed to exhaustively explore the depth of filing and the possible commitment to such an endeavor."[8]

When Reagan was convinced by his political supporters to run for governor of California against incumbent Pat Brown, who was seeking his third term, the Friends of Reagan became the Reagan for Governor Committee. Schreiber was Reagan's chief fund-raiser and co-chaired his campaign, which was arranged and financed by Jules Stein and a group of conservative southern California businessmen.

Reagan even published his autobiography, *Where's the Rest of Me?*, a sanitized, revisionist look by Reagan at his Hollywood past and his wars with communism during his years with the Screen Actors Guild. Published by Duell, Sloan and Pearce, a New York publishing house, the book was co-authored by Richard G. Hubler. The appendix of the book included statements by Reagan indicating his views on issues ranging from "Fiscal Irresponsibility" to "Youth Aid Plans," and "Appeasement or Courage" to "Karl Marx."

With his background in films, Reagan mastered the art of the television political campaign, capitalizing on his image as a totally honest man with an endearing "golly-gee" naivete about him. After easily brushing off former San Francisco mayor George Christopher in the Republican primary, Reagan and his backers set their sights for Governor Edmund G. (Pat) Brown.

Pat Brown faced major problems, not the least of which was his opponent in the Democratic primary, Los Angeles mayor Sam Yorty, who was a close friend of Henry Salvatori and supported Reagan after Brown defeated him. When Reagan charged that Brown had "looted and drained" California's economy, the voters listened—regardless of how baseless the charge was.

Running on a tough "law and order" platform, Reagan accused Brown and the Democrats of being "soft on crime." Reagan's emphasis was on street crime and violence. He made no known statements on California's organized crime problem. When Reagan spoke of "the mob," he was generally talking about "the mob of students" at the University of California at Berkeley.

Reagan whipped Brown with fifty-seven percent of the vote and left his job as the host of *Death Valley Days* to become California's chief of state; his running mate, Robert Finch, became lieutenant governor.* Less than three months after becoming governor, Reagan, upon being asked during a press conference about his legislative program, said he did not know what it was. "I could take some coaching from the sidelines," Reagan said only half-jokingly, "if anyone can recall my legislative program."

Considering all the help Reagan received from Stein and Schreiber, the standing joke in Hollywood was that "MCA even had its own governor."† The Justice Department's 1962 antitrust settlement with

---

*In California, each party's nominees for governor and lieutenant governor run as a ticket but are elected separately, making it possible for the governor to be a member of one party and the lieutenant governor to be a member of the other. Robert Finch had managed Richard Nixon's 1960 campaign for the presidency and George Murphy's 1964 campaign for the U.S. Senate.
†Reagan's millionaire friends did own the governor's home. After Nancy Reagan refused to live in the official but run-down governor's mansion, California's First Couple rented a home in Sacramento for $1,250 a month. In 1969, Reagan's wealthy backers bought the governor's residence for $150,000 and leased it back to Reagan for the same price he'd been paying for rent.

MCA and the inconclusive audit of Reagan might have ended speculation about Reagan's relationship with MCA—if it hadn't been for the
additional questions that had cropped up about Reagan's finances during his political career. Most of the relevant facts about these financial
dealings surfaced only *after* the Kennedy Justice Department, the IRS,
and the FBI had closed the books on the MCA investigation. In the
years after the 1962 consent decree, Reagan made more than seventy-
five percent of his personal fortune—which would later be estimated to
be more than $4 million. Most of this wealth was amassed through a
series of extremely shrewd real estate transactions in California—with
the help of his friends at MCA.

Aside from the Reagans' purchase of their principal residence on San
Onofre Drive in Pacific Palisades, Reagan was involved in another
lesser-known deal—secretly orchestrated by Jules Stein and Taft
Schreiber—which made him a millionaire.

As noted earlier, Ronald Reagan had purchased 290 acres of property in Malibu Canyon in 1951. Reagan paid $85,000 for the property,
or $293 per acre. Ronald and Nancy Reagan never lived at this site,
using it only as a weekend hideaway and for such activities as horse
riding, barbecues, and cattle raising. The Reagans made no substantial
improvements to this property, which contained only a small, fairly
run-down house.

A little over a month after Reagan's election as governor, he sold 236
of his 290 acres to the Twentieth Century–Fox Film Corporation. The
studio then owned 2,500 acres of adjoining land, which it sometimes
used as a background site to film some of its movies. The controlling
interest of Twentieth Century–Fox was still held by Darryl Zanuck and
his family, who had supported Reagan in his race for governor.

The arrangement between Reagan and Twentieth Century–Fox was
handled by Stein and Schreiber, with the legal work handled by Reagan's personal attorney, William French Smith, a Los Angeles labor
lawyer working for management since 1942 and senior partner in the
huge Los Angeles firm of Gibson, Dunn, and Crutcher.* "I've spent
thirty years dealing with the Teamsters Union and the construction
workers' union and a few others," Smith said.[9]

The Reagan-Fox transaction occurred on December 13, 1966. Twentieth Century–Fox—via its real estate company, Fox Realty—pur-

---

*Smith was a close personal friend of Beverly Hills attorney and former Democratic Party boss
Paul Ziffren, who had been linked to major organized crime figures during the late 1950s; Smith
was also at least acquainted with Sidney Korshak, according to several sources. Attempts to
interview Smith for this book were unsuccessful.

chased the 236 acres for $1,930,000, or $8,178 per acre. Reagan made more than a 3,000 percent profit on his purchase of fifteen years earlier.

According to a rider to the deed, signed the next day, Fox also received an option to buy the remaining fifty-four acres of Reagan's ranch at some later date—at the same price of $8,178 an acre.

It was unclear why Fox would have wanted any of the land at that price. According to published reports, Fox's own appraisers had judged the larger portion of land to have a market value of only $4,000 per acre. County appraisers estimated that the property was worth even less. The fifty-four optioned acres, all on very steep terrain, were actually worth only about $550 an acre. To explain the deal, the movie company announced that it planned to move its headquarters and studios to the property. But no such construction was ever undertaken.

One month later, on January 31, 1967, the Assignment of Deed of Trust for Reagan's property was filed with the Los Angeles County Recorder's Office. The paperwork showed that two of the trustees of Reagan's property sale to Fox were William French Smith and Jules Stein. Three days after the land sale, on December 19, 1966, the Reagans had signed over their power of attorney to Smith.

Reagan later told a reporter, "I could not have run for office unless I sold the ranch."[10]

Reagan added to his story later on, saying that he could not afford the property taxes for the ranch on his governor's salary of $44,000 a year. Nancy Reagan also said, "We had to sell our ranch at Lake Malibu when Ronnie became governor . . . [because] Ronnie had taken a large cut in income when he left television to become governor. We simply could not afford the luxury of a ranch."[11]

CHAPTER TWENTY-NINE

SINCE THE rise and fall of Bugsy Siegel, Nevada had become a haven for major organized crime figures throughout the United States. When the gaming industry—which already had a history of corruption—became popular in the postwar era, "the people who were available to run it when the decriminalization process began were the same people who were running it under the old illicit period," explained attorney G. Robert Blakey, who served in the Justice Department under Attorney General Robert Kennedy. "The public demanded regulation upon legalization—that is, the screening of ownerships, the licensing of casinos, and the subsequent oversight over these operations. The public pressure placed the power to regulate the gaming industry in the hands of the politicians. And it followed naturally that the politicians reached out to corrupt the industry."[1]

During the early 1960s, Nevada caught the attention of the Kennedy Justice Department, which had launched a major campaign to prosecute organized crime figures. For fifteen months, secret FBI wiretaps placed on the business telephones of five major casinos yielded an astonishing history of syndicate involvement in Las Vegas, including massive skimming operations that were being funneled into other

Mafia-backed activities, such as narcotics and payoffs to politicians.

While the intelligence collected from this FBI surveillance was unprecedented, the operation presented a very touchy problem, since all of the taps had been installed illegally. None of the data could be used in court. As a result of this nondisclosure bind, numerous public officials in Nevada—led by Democratic Nevada governor Grant Sawyer —were able to charge convincingly that the federal government had launched into nothing more than a campaign of harassment against the casino operators, whom Sawyer and his followers viewed as legitimate businessmen. "Give us your evidence," Sawyer insisted, "or call off your dogs!"

Without hearing any rebuttal from the Justice Department, Governor Sawyer continued to speak out against the FBI. His aim, naturally, was to protect his state's gaming industry, which in 1965 grossed $330 million, employed 35,000 people, and contributed thirty percent of all tax revenues to the state.

Sawyer's voice fell silent when crime reporter Sandy Smith of *The Chicago Sun-Times*—armed with leaked Justice Department documents—published evidence of the mob's Las Vegas skimming operations. Smith's exposé made a mockery of the state's gaming licensing requirements and enforcement practices.

In 1966, this situation, in addition to a depressed state economy, set the stage for the emergence of Governor Sawyer's 44-year-old opponent, Paul Laxalt.

Laxalt was born in 1922 in Reno, the oldest of the six children of Dominique and Theresa Laxalt. His father was a sheep herder who immigrated to Reno from the misty valleys of the French Pyrenees and later moved his family to Carson City, Nevada's capital but still a small, Ponderosa-like town. Working in the family's restaurant as a young boy, Paul Laxalt was able to obtain his political baptism by serving such people as long-time Nevada senator Patrick McCarran, the Democrat who ran Nevada's bipartisan political machine.

A star athlete in high school, Laxalt later attended Santa Clara University, a Jesuit school in California, receiving his undergraduate degree in 1943. At that point, his mother had wanted him to go to a seminary to become a Roman Catholic priest, but Laxalt had more ambitious plans for his future.

After a tour of duty in the U.S. Army, serving in the South Pacific, he went to law school at the University of Denver, graduating at the top of his class in 1949. Meanwhile, he married Jackie Ross, the daughter of John Tom Ross, a powerhouse in Nevada's Republican Party, who later became a respected federal judge. Fresh out of law school, Laxalt joined his father-in-law's law firm.

Ross was Laxalt's early mentor, introducing the young attorney to the intricacies of Nevada state politics. Wasting little time, Laxalt was elected district attorney of Ormsby County within a year of his graduation, but he left office after one term in 1954 to return to private practice. In 1962, he was elected lieutenant governor of the state, running on a ticket under the gubernatorial candidate, Rex Bell, a former cowboy movie star who had found Laxalt after approaching Judge Ross for advice on a possible running mate. During the campaign, however, Bell died. In the wake of his death, Laxalt, because of his inexperience, decided not to step up and seek the office of governor. He remained as the candidate for lieutenant governor and won by a large margin; the GOP's last-minute replacement for governor lost to Democratic incumbent Grant Sawyer.

The following year, while simultaneously running Barry Goldwater's presidential campaign in Nevada, Laxalt received the Republican nomination for the U.S. Senate. That November, he lost by just forty-eight votes to the incumbent Democrat, Howard Cannon, who was seeking his second term.

In 1966, while the embattled Sawyer, who was running for his third term, was waging his civil war against the Justice Department, Laxalt decided to challenge him for governor.

To launch a serious effort, Laxalt needed money for his campaign. He received help from Ruby Kolod, part-owner of the Desert Inn with Moe Dalitz and a member of the Cleveland Mayfield Road Gang, who became one of Laxalt's major fund-raisers.

Kolod was not the typical campaign worker. He had been convicted just a year earlier of threatening to kill a Denver attorney over a disputed investment deal. His situation was further clouded because the murder threat prompted the Nevada Gaming Control Board to file a complaint against him, challenging his gaming license. That complaint was pending at the time Laxalt was using him to raise funds for his campaign.

"My administration had taken away Kolod's gaming license," Sawyer said, "because he had been convicted of a crime. He took the position that we should wait until after his appeal had been settled. We said no. So he, therefore, became Laxalt's prime fund-raiser among the casinos. And he did a hell of a job."[2]

Laxalt later conceded that Kolod "did help us, tremendously."[3]

During the campaign, Sawyer's criticism of the FBI became an issue —with Laxalt supporting the Bureau.

"Laxalt indicated that he would want to make peace with J. Edgar Hoover," Sawyer explained. "He went to see him just before the election. That was a much-heralded meeting. Hoover wrote a letter condemning me, and it was printed on the front page of the *Las Vegas Sun* —just before the election. In those days, no one went against Hoover and came out alive."[4]

Later, Laxalt suggested that his position on the FBI was based more on politics than on conviction. "We had a rather peculiar situation here in the closing months of a gubernatorial campaign, attempting to assess whether the FBI was the good guys or the bad guys. I adopted a white-hat posture at the time, and I wonder if it wasn't a questionable political posture."[5]

Paul Laxalt's first and most important job upon becoming governor was to turn around the state's depressed economy. To do so, he had to change Nevada's gangster image and repair the damage done to the state's relationship with the federal government. At the same time, he had to be sure to balance his actions carefully by appeasing the gambling community.

Laxalt took office in January 1967—the same month as Reagan took over in California. The two governors both became active in the Western Governors' Conference. From this association, a close personal and professional friendship developed.

In February, billionaire Howard Hughes came to Nevada with $500 million in cash, hoping to buy up Las Vegas with the profits he had made from the sale of Trans-World Airlines.

Robert Maheu—Hughes's right-hand man and the 1960 liaison between the CIA and the Mafia in the Castro murder plots—said, "Considering the poor condition of the economy, the investigations of organized crime's involvement in the state's chief industry, and the consequent public relations problems they caused, Laxalt viewed Hughes's entry onto the Las Vegas scene as a blessing. Laxalt was convinced that Hughes and his 'nonmob' money—which could buy out 'suspected' casinos—would ultimately save Nevada's declining gaming industry."[6]

Laxalt has admitted to having given Hughes preferential treatment. "Let's face it," Laxalt told reporters, "Nevada has an image problem —the typical feeling is that sin is rampant here. Anything this man [Hughes] does, from the gaming industry all the way down the line, will be good for Nevada."

Regardless of Hughes's purported "Mr. Clean" image then, it is clear that he was encouraged and helped by members of organized crime when he came to Las Vegas—particularly by mobster Johnny Roselli, who had been Maheu's contact man in the CIA-Mafia plots against Castro. Roselli and his cohorts assumed that Hughes's presence would automatically take the heat off those casinos still operating illegally.

With Roselli's help—as well as that of Teamsters Union president Jimmy Hoffa, who was en route to Lewisburg Penitentiary—the Hughes Tool Company's first purchase was the Desert Inn, which it bought for $13.6 million from the Dalitz-Kolod syndicate in March 1967. Roselli and Hoffa's attorney, Edward Morgan of Washington, D.C., received a $150,000 finder's fee for greasing the sale by serving as liaison between Hughes and Dalitz.

Laxalt wanted to help the reclusive Hughes get his license without scrutiny from the Nevada Gaming Commission. Three days before the commission hearing, Hughes, in a brilliant public relations ploy to obtain the license, offered to donate over $200,000 a year for twenty years to a proposed state medical school.

Laxalt made the public announcement of the grant on Hughes's behalf, praising the billionaire for his unselfish generosity. The gaming commission apparently got the message. During the hearing, Hughes was not required to appear before the panel. In fact, he was granted the Desert Inn gaming license—without ever being subjected to a public investigation of his finances. With Laxalt's help, Hughes's privacy was strictly maintained in his subsequent purchases of the Sands, the Castaways, the Frontier, the Silver Slipper, and the Landmark in Las Vegas and Harold's Club in Reno. But he eventually needed help to run them.

"At first, Hughes brought in his own business people to run the casinos," said Tom Mechling, president of the National Gambling Information Center. "But they lost him money. He learned that you have to protect yourself against the people outside and inside the casinos who are trying to cheat you. So Hughes brought Dalitz back into his operations, naming him as a 'senior consultant.' Dalitz is the elder statesman for Las Vegas, and he speaks for the whole gambling community. He knows how to make a casino work."[7]

Sidney Korshak also came into the picture in 1967 as he increased his influence over the Associated Booking Company, by then the third largest talent agency in the country.* He took over the booking of acts

---

*Upon Joseph Glaser's death on June 4, 1969, Korshak gained full authority over the Associated Booking Company.

into Hughes's hotels. Among the big stars he brought in were Ann-Margret, Dean Martin, Tony Martin, and Barbra Streisand.

After the Justice Department's Antitrust Division threatened to take action against Hughes if he bought the Dalitz-owned Stardust hotel/casino, Laxalt protested directly to Attorney General Ramsey Clark. In a letter to Clark, Laxalt charged that, by blocking the $30.5 million Stardust transaction, the Antitrust Division had "jeopardized the employment of 2,000 people in the Stardust enterprise. . . . The end and only result of an antitrust action of this type that I can see is drastic and permanent damage to our economy."[8]

Laxalt also reminded the attorney general that the federal government owned over eighty-seven percent of the state's land, or 60,000,000 acres, implying that Nevada could cause the U.S. Department of the Interior and other government agencies jurisdictional problems. "If suit is instituted," Laxalt warned, "and this most assuredly is no form of threat but simply is offered as a factor in your legal evaluation of whether or not to proceed, we would be faced with no alternative other than to intervene and oppose the action with all the resources of the state."

Before the hot-tempered governor had a chance to declare war on the federal government, Hughes backed off from his attempts to purchase the Stardust. Hughes next attempted to acquire the Dunes hotel/casino, which was also blocked by the Antitrust Division. Consequently, Laxalt worked to change state law so that public corporations could purchase gambling casinos and be licensed by the gaming commission. Laxalt claimed that this "reform" would prevent hidden interests by mobsters in Nevada gaming establishments since corporations are required by the Securities and Exchange Commission to disclose their chief operating officers and major stockholders. However, organized crime figures continued to hold hidden interests in Nevada's casinos.

Perhaps the most interesting example of this was the Parvin-Dohrmann Company, primarily a hotel and restaurant equipment and supply company that was principally owned by Albert Parvin. In 1955, Parvin had purchased the controlling interest in the Flamingo and later in the Fremont and Aladdin hotels. Among Parvin's directors was his vice-president and treasurer, Harvey Silbert, who was Sidney Korshak's friend and business associate from the Riviera. In 1966, Parvin-Dohrmann became embroiled in a nationally publicized scandal when it was discovered that Supreme Court Associate Justice William O.

Douglas had been on the payroll of the Albert Parvin Foundation. Douglas, president of the tax-exempt foundation—which was primarily financed by profits from the 1960 sale of the Flamingo—had received $12,000 a year since 1962. At the time of the 1960 Flamingo purchase, Parvin paid mobster Meyer Lansky a $200,000 finder's fee for finding the buyer.

Despite these revelations about his business deals and associates, Parvin still managed to obtain approval from the Nevada Gaming Commission in 1968 to purchase the Stardust from Moe Dalitz—after Howard Hughes withdrew his bid. Dalitz was hoping to finally leave Las Vegas and retire to his La Costa Country Club. Sidney Korshak received a $500,000 finder's fee from the Dalitz group for arranging the Stardust sale.*

In 1969, weary of all the problems in Las Vegas, Albert Parvin decided he wanted out. Waiting to buy the corporation was a Korshak business associate, Delbert Coleman, a Harvard man and an attorney. Earlier, Coleman had purchased and sold a Chicago jukebox manufacturer, the J. P. Seeburg Corporation, for which Korshak had served as labor consultant. For $10.5 million, Coleman became the largest stockholder in Parvin-Dohrmann—and consequently, the Stardust, the Fremont, and the Aladdin.

At the time of Coleman's 300,000-share purchase, Parvin-Dohrmann was valued at thirty-five dollars a share on the American Stock Exchange. Within months, a bizarre and complex series of financial manipulations sent the stock skyrocketing to $141. When the corporation peaked, Coleman and his stockholders, through Korshak, tried to sell it to the National General Corporation, which owned a large theatre chain. However, the negotiations between National General and Korshak broke down. Harold Butler, the president of Denny's Restaurants, then stepped forward and bought out Coleman, Korshak, and three other investors at $150 a share when its market value had already started to drop below one hundred dollars a share. Then, suddenly, Parvin-Dohrmann's stock collapsed to a low of $12.50, forcing the Securities and Exchange Commission to suspend trading.

---

*Korshak had continued to remain busy. In 1966, while serving as the chief negotiator for Schenley Industries, the liquor company, Korshak settled a labor dispute between Schenley's president, Lewis Rosenstiel, and Cesar Chavez, the director of the United Farm Workers Union. Advised by Korshak, Rosenstiel broke with other grape growers, recognized the UFW over the Teamsters Union as the bargaining agent for California's migrant farmers and signed a one-year contract.

Rosenstiel's impetus to settle was Korshak's power within the Culinary Workers Union, which threatened a boycott of Schenley's products in bars and restaurants.

Coleman went to a close friend of Korshak, Washington lobbyist Nathan Voloshen, who was asked to help lift the suspension and to avoid possible prosecution. Voloshen went to Martin Sweig, the top aide to Democratic Massachusetts congressman John McCormack, the speaker of the House, and asked for Sweig's assistance to set up a meeting with the head of the SEC. After the meeting—in which the SEC refused to allow Parvin-Dohrmann to begin trading again—it was discovered that Voloshen had received $50,000 from Coleman, which was prohibited under SEC rules. After a lengthy investigation, Voloshen pleaded guilty for influence peddling and was sent to jail. Speaker McCormack, who was reportedly seen accepting a $15,000 payment from Voloshen but was not indicted, did not seek another term.

The SEC charged that Parvin-Dohrmann, under Coleman, had filed false reports with the SEC during its purchase of the corporation, concealed the true identity of certain participants in the control group, allowed this group to buy into the corporation at thirty-five dollars a share when it was trading for seventy-five dollars a share, and then fraudulently manipulated the worth of the company's stock. Among those named in the complaint were Sidney Korshak; his brother Marshall Korshak, who was then Chicago city treasurer; Las Vegas gambling boss Edward Torres; and actress Jill St. John,* who owned 1,000 shares and made $150,000 on the deal. Sid Korshak, who had had 12,500 shares of stock, made nearly $2 million.

Also charged by the SEC in the Parvin-Dohrmann scheme was Denny's Restaurants, a California-based restaurant franchise. At the time of the Parvin-Dohrmann purchase by Denny's, those holding Parvin-Dohrmann stock were promised four shares of Denny's for one share of Parvin-Dohrmann.

During Korshak's deposition to the SEC, he was asked what other corporations had come to him asking for his help in buying Las Vegas properties. Korshak replied, "There were half a dozen people talking to me at different times . . . about possible acquisitions in Nevada. They would have been companies I was close to, probably represented. There was a period immediately following Mr. Howard Hughes's acquisitions, where everybody became interested in making an acquisition in Nevada."

---

*Korshak had met St. John with Frank Sinatra during the early 1960s. Both men became interested in her and advised her to divorce her second husband, Woolworth heir Lance Reventlow, and pursue a movie career. Grateful for their advice, St. John, who dumped Reventlow and became a star, remarked, "Fortunately, all Frank's friends happen to be very influential."[9]

"Do you remember the name or names of any of those corporations in 1968, Mr. Korshak?" asked the SEC attorney.

"It is possible that the Gulf & Western people that I do general labor work for could have talked to me about the possibility of an acquisition in Vegas."

"Are there any other—excuse me—"

"I do work for the Hilton Corporation. It is possible that they talked to me. At this particular time, many hotels were interested in expanding their holdings into Nevada. And it is possible that the Hilton people talked to me about it. I believe it is possible that the Hyatt Hotel Corporation talked to me also about the possibility of their making an acquisition in Nevada. Maybe others, as I have stated; at this particular moment, I can't think of any."[10]

In the end, a settlement was reached with the SEC, in which the defendants had to neither admit nor deny the charges against them—although Coleman was forced to resign as the head of Parvin-Dohrmann. Parvin returned and again took control of his corporation but changed its name to Recrion, giving Korshak another $500,000 finder's fee for making the arrangements.

CHAPTER THIRTY

IN THE late 1960s, corporations were beginning to diversify, merge, or sell out—so much so that the word "conglomerate" and its application to the business world became part of the English language. Numerous corporations successfully added major entertainment companies to their empires.

Seven Arts bought out Warner Brothers, making Jack Warner board chairman. The National General Corporation had wanted to buy out Warner Brothers–Seven Arts but was thwarted by the Antitrust Division. Eventually, the film interest was sold to a funeral, parking lot, and cleaning services company, the Kinney Corporation, headed by Steven J. Ross, for $400 million. Kinney later changed its name to Warner Communications. Ted Ashley, who was bought out of Ashley–Famous Artists talent agency by Kinney, was picked to head Warner Brothers.*

Screen Gems merged with Columbia Pictures Industries, Inc., which

---

*As it had with MCA, the Antitrust Division forced Kinney to divest itself of Ashley–Famous Artists, which was then purchased by Marvin Josephson Associates, another talent agency. Ashley–Famous Artists was renamed International–Famous Artists, which later bought out the Chase-Park-Citron agency. Josephson had once been with the General Amusement Company— which became Creative Management Associates (CMA), headed by Freddie Fields. Eventually, International–Famous Artists merged with CMA to form International Creative Management (ICM), which rivaled William Morris as the most influential talent agency in the United States.

was being run by president Leo Jaffe, Abe and Stanley Schneider, and Mike Frankovich, who took over in the wake of Harry Cohn's death. Korshak's client Gulf & Western took over Paramount Pictures. Transamerica, an insurance and financing company, accumulated ninety percent of United Artists—which bought Warner Brothers' pre-1948 film library, giving it the largest such library in the business. Avco, which specialized in military and aerospace equipment, merged with Embassy Pictures, creating Avco–Embassy Pictures.

In the midst of hard times at MGM and the death of former board chairman Joe Vogel, the studio sold its controlling interest to Kirk Kerkorian. A tall, dark, and handsome man, Kerkorian was described by rivals as "a poor man's Howard Hughes." He was an eighth-grade dropout who, after working as a used-car salesman, bought a single World War II surplus airplane, beginning an airline company, which became Trans International Airlines, making runs from Los Angeles to Las Vegas after Bugsy Siegel built the Flamingo. In 1968, Kerkorian sold his firm to Transamerica—which had already bought United Artists—for stock eventually worth $104 million. With his profit, he managed to borrow another $73 million in unsecured loans and acquired a thirty-percent interest in Western Airlines and the Bonanza casino in downtown Las Vegas. He then bought the Flamingo in 1969 and merged it with his newly constructed International Hotel.

With his hotel and casino profits, Kerkorian bought MGM, naming James T. Aubrey, the former president of CBS, as MGM's president.*

Kerkorian was a long-time friend of Charles "The Blade" Tourine, a top New York mobster and an associate of Meyer Lansky. Federal investigators had wiretapped a telephone call Tourine had made to Kerkorian in Beverly Hills on October 5, 1961. During the conversation, Kerkorian said that he was going to give Tourine $21,300, and that actor George Raft would be his bagman.[1]

In 1966, Lew Wasserman was elected chairman of the Association of Motion Picture and Television Producers. The AMPTP was principally responsible for negotiating the studios' contracts with Hollywood's labor unions. The AMPTP's lobbying arm in Washington was the Motion Picture Association of America, which was headed in 1966 by Jack Valenti, a former aide to President Lyndon Johnson who was hand-picked by Wasserman. Louis Nizer, the prominent trial lawyer, became the MPAA's general counsel. By nearly everyone's standards,

---

*Kerkorian would eventually sell his casino and hotel interests in Las Vegas to Hilton Hotels, which was then represented by Korshak.

there was now no doubt that Wasserman had become the most powerful legitimate force in Hollywood.

To help the film industry, Governor Reagan pushed legislation through the California State Assembly, giving all Hollywood studios, including MCA-Universal and Twentieth Century–Fox, huge breaks on their film libraries. The tax savings at each studio was estimated to be worth a minimum of $3 million. Former California governor Pat Brown had previously vetoed the same bill.

"I've always been puzzled by it," Brown told reporter Jeff Stein. "All the assessors were opposed to it. It should never have been signed." Significantly, no other industry in California received such relief for its inventory.

MCA also further diversified, buying Spencer Gifts, a mail-order house based in Atlantic City, New Jersey—specializing in gifts, housewares, stationery, home decor items, notions, and novelties— which would later become a fixture in shopping malls around the country and a multi-million-dollar enterprise.

In 1966, MCA had grossed nearly $225 million from its movies, television productions, records, real estate investments, and other holdings. But, on account of a number of box-office disappointments—like *Thoroughly Modern Millie* in 1967, and *Counterpoint, The Loves of Isadora,* and *Secret Ceremony* in 1968—MCA found itself facing an $80 million debt, the biggest in the corporation's history.

"So Stein, Wasserman, and Schreiber made a number of moves to deal with the situation," one report stated. "Wasserman set up a three-person executive vice-presidents' group that included studio-tour head Al Dorskind, TV syndication operative Berle Adams, and former Lehman Brothers executive Dan Ritchie, who was put in charge of financial affairs."[2]

Then the Pittsburgh-based Westinghouse Electric Corporation— which in 1967 had $3 billion in sales of everything from light bulbs to nuclear reactors—got into the act. Already the owner of five television and seven radio stations, Westinghouse wanted to add MCA to its huge complex. The $365 million deal offered by Westinghouse stood to make Jules Stein a whopping $102 million and make him Westinghouse's largest stockholder. Wasserman stood to make a cool $50 million. Westinghouse also promised to continue the expansion of Universal City.

"Stein and Wasserman were in favor of the whole thing and wanted it to happen," said a former top MCA official. "Stein wanted out of the business to pursue his interests in eye research. He had just pulled all kinds of strings and raised and personally contributed a lot of money to get the Jules Stein Eye Institute built right on UCLA's campus. For Stein, that was everything. That was his red-marble monument. Wasserman wanted to remain autonomous in movie and television production—which the Westinghouse deal also guaranteed. For Lew, that's what made the whole thing so sweet. Stein wanted the immortality; Wasserman wanted the power."

Once again, the Justice Department's Antitrust Division sprang into action, threatening an investigation of the Westinghouse-MCA merger on the basis of Westinghouse's extensive investments in television and radio. Consequently, in April 1969, it was Stein and Wasserman who called the deal off.

A month before MCA terminated the arrangement, Stein, with the support of Taft Schreiber, had made plans to fire Wasserman as the president of MCA. The firing was to have been based upon Universal's dismal box-office receipts and the handling of the Westinghouse merger. "All Stein had to do was vote his shares at a meeting of the MCA board on March 31, 1969," said Hollywood columnist James Bacon, who was the first reporter to break the story. "But I got wind of what he was going to do and wrote a column on the Friday before the board meeting. . . . In my column, I wrote that it was Wasserman's guiding genius of MCA in its talent agency days that boosted Stein from a mere band-booker to a multi-millionaire tycoon of the entertainment industry. . . .

"The board meeting was held on Monday as scheduled and a few executives who had hoped to get Wasserman's job were disappointed: Jules, instead of firing Wasserman, handed him a new long-term contract."[3]

Reporter Bob Gottlieb interviewed another top MCA official, who quoted Wasserman before the board meeting as saying, " 'Either I'm in control or not.' And then, puff, it was gone—the idea that they could really move against him. Lew was in charge, because no matter what Stein and Schreiber thought about their stock or whatever, Lew *was* the company. It was like waking up from a dream and then saying, 'Now why did I ever feel that way?' "

According to published reports, in the wake of the attempted coup, MCA executive Berle Adams, who was loyal to Stein and Schreiber and Wasserman's heir-apparent, was forced out of the company. After a brief housecleaning, Wasserman firmly took charge and began to deal with the corporate debt, beginning with a reshuffling of priorities at

Universal. Ned Tanen, a Wasserman protégé who had started out in MCA's mailroom in 1954 and moved up through MCA's record company, was moved over to Universal, where he and thirty-two-year-old Daniel Selznick, the son of the legendary producer David O. Selznick, were placed in key executive positions.

As MCA began to get back on track, another merger negotiation emerged, this time with the $2 billion Firestone Tire and Rubber Company of Akron, Ohio, which owned no television or radio stations. The initial driving forces behind Firestone's attempted takeover of MCA were Schreiber and Leonard Firestone, both of whom had been active on Reagan's 1966 campaign committee.

"When MCA's merger with Westinghouse fell through," Firestone said, "I called Taft Schreiber, a good friend for many years, to say I was sorry. It occurred to me to ask, 'Why don't we talk?' I sent their annual statement to my brother [corporate board chairman Raymond Firestone] with a note saying we ought to take a look at this, and he showed it to the people there."[4]

Like Westinghouse, Firestone—which had offered $320 million for MCA—promised the entertainment complex complete autonomy over its movie and television productions and pledged to expand Universal City. Unlike Westinghouse, there was little chance of an antitrust suit being filed to block the merger. But in the end, it was Lew Wasserman who was unenthusiastic at the prospect of his company being taken over by a tire manufacturer. Firmly in command at MCA, Wasserman said no, and the Firestone deal simply collapsed.

In 1968, Ronald Reagan attempted but failed to win the Republican nomination for president of the United States, losing on the first ballot at the GOP convention to Richard Nixon. That same year, the California governor tried, without success, to sell the remaining fifty-four acres of his Malibu Canyon ranch, since Twentieth Century–Fox had decided not to exercise its option to purchase the property. Reagan's asking price for the property was set at $165,000—or five times the assessed value.

Acting on his behalf, Reagan's trustees—including William French Smith, Jules Stein, and real estate tycoon William A. Wilson—used the parcel of land as a down payment for a 778-acre ranch in Riverside County in a remote area between Los Angeles and San Diego. Reagan bought this second ranch from a partnership that included the Kaiser Aluminum Corporation. The total purchase price was $346,950. The Reagan trust paid $181,950 in cash and swapped the fifty-four acres for the $165,000 balance. Smith and Schreiber also purchased large tracts of land nearby as well.

However, there was a proviso on Reagan's sale agreement with Kaiser. If the Kaiser partnership could not sell the fifty-four-acre down payment within one year, then Reagan would be required to buy back the land at the same price, $165,000.

In July 1969, a year after the sale, Kaiser could still not sell the fifty-four acres, so Reagan had to take it back. Needing $165,000, Reagan was lucky enough to have generous friends and was able to rid himself of the property without putting up any of his own money. A mysterious company—the "Fifty-seventh Madison Corporation," which was chartered in Deleware—bailed Reagan out by slapping down the full $165,000 and buying the fifty-four acres.*

The Fifty-seventh Madison Corporation was created and owned by Jules Stein. Reagan's fifty-four acres were the company's only real estate holding outside of New York. The corporation's property manager, Ross Simpson, told *Washington Post* reporter Charles Babcock that Stein had "made the purchase because the land was close to property Fox had developed into housing and made a lot of money [on]. He said he was going to invest in that and cut up the land to make houses." But neither Stein nor Twentieth Century–Fox ever followed through with these plans.[5]

The month before Stein came to Reagan's rescue, Stein received the annual Humanitarian Award of Variety Clubs International, which was held in the Empire Room of the Beverly Hilton. Among the 1,500 guests were Governor Reagan and his wife. Reagan praised Stein as "a truly great humanitarian," and an "old and valued friend . . . I know that this man in his own business has carried his principles into the lives of those who were known as his young men."

As his first term as California governor closed, Reagan had surprised many of his early critics and proved himself to be a competent public office holder. "By any standard," explained Lou Cannon, Reagan's principal biographer, "after nearly four years in office, Reagan's achievements were modest ones. After his initial fling at across-the-board budget cutting, he had become a fairly orthodox governor who had restored funds for higher education and provided money for a community mental health treatment program. . . . The top appointments in the Reagan administration were faulted by some critics for a pro-business bias, but generally accorded high marks for compe-

---

*Reagan sold the Riverside property for $856,500 in December 1976.

tence. . . . [T]here was not the suggestion of taint in any aspect of the administration. Even Reagan's stern law-and-order rhetoric had been tempered by reality. . . . All in all, Reagan's record as governor had been moderate and responsible but undistinguished."[6]

His campaign for president in 1968 was viewed as a diversion from his first term because his campaign took him away from pending matters of state. Nevertheless, his closest friends and those whose counsel he trusted had encouraged him to seek the presidency despite his own dilemma as to whether to run or not. In his absence, the governor's duties were administered by his executive assistant Edwin Meese, who was the architect of the organization of the Reagan administration in Sacramento.

"Reagan took the loyalty of his staff members seriously," said one observer. "He cultivated their loyalty and used it as a means to hold the governor's office together. He charmed his staff. Whenever he returned from an extended stay out of town, he habitually went from one end of the office to the other asking [about] everyone's welfare. He insisted that everyone's birthdays, especially those of the clerical staff, be celebrated during office hours, and he always attended the party whenever he was in Sacramento. He distributed jelly beans as a means to set people at ease. He passed out acknowledgments of appreciation —his own doodles, pens used to sign bills, autographed pictures—to those who worked with him. He told jokes in cabinet meetings. . . . He took part in none of the office squabbles. Staff and cabinet members made special efforts to avoid any open show of animosity because everyone knew he did not like such conflict. As a consequence, Reagan's closest aides were the ones who did the dirty work of disciplining people, of discharging the worst offenders and sanctioning the rest. . . . He tried to leave work at five and told others to leave when he did."[7]

While Reagan prospered, personally and politically, Hollywood crashed. By the beginning of 1970, Universal wasn't the only studio experiencing hard times. Paramount and Twentieth Century–Fox were financially crippled.* Paramount was nearly sold by its parent company, Gulf & Western, to a nearby cemetery. Twentieth Century–Fox had to hold a public auction of its movie memorabilia, as did economically strapped MGM, which sold for $15,000 the magic shoes Judy Garland wore in *The Wizard of Oz*.

---

*Among MCA/Universal's difficulties were the medical problems of board chairman Jules Stein. Suffering from ventriculitis, affecting his intestines and stomach, Stein underwent exploratory surgery in December 1969, another operation in January 1970, and surgery for the third time the following month. However, the seventy-three-year-old Stein recovered.

Universal's problems, however, were short-lived. In 1970, Ross Hunter produced the star-studded *Airport,* based on Arthur Hailey's best-selling novel. Grossing $80 million in domestic sales alone, *Airport* became one of the biggest money-making films in history and placed Universal—and MCA—back on top. The studio followed up with the critically acclaimed *Diary of a Mad Housewife.* And in 1971 Universal came back with *The Andromeda Strain, Mary, Queen of Scots,* and *Play Misty for Me.*

At Universal-Television, Wasserman promoted his protégé, a thirty-five-year-old Texas attorney named Sidney J. Sheinberg, to be its new president in 1970. Sheinberg had joined MCA in 1959, starting out in its legal department before being discovered by Universal-TV president Jennings Lang and becoming a vice-president of Lang's fiefdom in 1968. Sheinberg computerized Universal-TV and kept production costs to a minimum, to the delight of MCA. In 1971, Sheinberg helped MCA make television history again, producing the first mini-series, *Vanished,* a two-part, four-hour, exclusively made-for-television movie about the kidnapping of a top adviser to the president of the United States.

MCA was facing financial losses from its prime-time series, even its successful programs like *Marcus Welby, M.D., It Takes a Thief, Adam-12,* and *Night Gallery.* Consequently, MCA began to sell the programs to foreign markets, which dubbed them into French, Spanish, and Japanese, among other languages. These sales helped make up previous losses. More profits came when MCA, after leasing programs to the networks for two prime-time showings, then syndicated them to local stations. A new and exciting age had begun for MCA—which knew the television market was becoming wide open.

In 1970, Reagan ran for a second term as California governor. His Democratic opponent was Jesse Unruh, the speaker of the California State Assembly and a nemesis of the Republican governor since he first took office. Unruh was the quintessential back-room politician. He was an ambitious deal-maker and a ruthless legislator, yet he was well-liked and respected.

As with Pat Brown, Unruh had to face party renegade Sam Yorty in the Democratic primary. While Yorty thrashed away at Unruh, the Assembly speaker tried to keep the party together and defeated Yorty with sixty-four percent of the vote. The strength of Unruh's victory was such that he was widely considered a formidable candidate to run against the still-popular Reagan.

Unruh raised the issue of Reagan's property deal with Twentieth

Century–Fox—but only gently. He preferred to concentrate his attack on Reagan's millionaire friends. Unruh charged that they "don't need a governor because they can buy the governor's house and probably even the governor."[8]

Seeing that Unruh's offensive was doing some damage to his campaign, Reagan called Unruh "a demagogue," "a hypocrite," "dishonest," and "a man who has no regard for the truth."[9]

The Reagan-Unruh battle for the California governorship quickly became a no-holds-barred political free-for-all.

Courted by partisans of both Reagan and Unruh* was Sidney Korshak, who was being viewed as among the most influential people in the state—perhaps even an institution himself. A former top official in the Justice Department explained, "During the Reagan-Brown campaign of 1966, Korshak pretty much stayed out of the fray. He was close to Brown, and he had a lot of friends who were working hard for Reagan. In 1970, things were a little different. He wasn't as close to Unruh—although they certainly knew each other well—and he already liked how close he was to the center of power at the governor's mansion in Sacramento. So, Korshak, instead of staying out of it, backed Reagan when he ran for reelection."

In November, Reagan edged Unruh, carrying fifty-three percent of the vote. The extent of Korshak's alleged support in Reagan's victory remains unknown, although Frank Sinatra, a life-long Democrat and a close friend of Korshak, bolted from the party to support Reagan and appear at several political fund-raising events on his behalf.

In Nevada, more than a year before the end of his first term as governor, Paul Laxalt announced that he would not seek reelection. He explained that he was retiring from politics because he wanted to spend more time with his family, particularly his wife, with whom he had had seven children, including four who were adopted.†

Upon leaving the governor's mansion, Laxalt returned to his Carson City law practice in 1971, with Howard Hughes among his firm's first clients. Within a matter of days, one of his first tasks was to carry out a high-level favor for the imprisoned Jimmy Hoffa.

On January 26, 1971, Laxalt wrote a "Dear Dick" letter to President Richard Nixon, asking him to release Hoffa, whom he described as "a victim of [Robert] Kennedy's revenge." The entire letter read:

---

*Attempts to interview Unruh for this book were unsuccessful. There is no evidence that either Reagan or Unruh personally solicited Korshak's support.
†Two years later, he and his wife were divorced.

Dear President Dick:

The other day I had an extended discussion with Al Dorfman of the Teamsters, with whom I've worked closely the past few years.

He described for me in detail the history of Jim Hoffa's difficulties with the Justice Department.

This discussion, which described in detail the personal vendetta that Bobby Kennedy had against Hoffa, together with other information provided me over the years, leads me to the inevitable conclusion that Jim is a victim of Kennedy's revenge. This, in turn, convinces me that through vindictive action he has been and continues to be a political prisoner.

Without going into the merits further, since I'm certain you have been fully informed, may I add my support to those who are requesting Executive Intervention so that he can be released in March.

While I don't know Mr. Hoffa personally, I have had occasion to have a great deal of contact with Mr. Dorfman and the members of the Executive Committee of the Teamsters. As you know, their loans to Nevada resort hotels represent by far the greatest investment in Nevada. Their activities here have been "aboveboard" at all times and they have made a material contribution to our state.

Several months ago I had the members of the board [of the Teamsters] at the Governor's Mansion for a briefing of our State Gaming heads. The candidness, the spirit of cooperation which they extended, impressed all of us greatly. I cannot believe that the man who organized this group is the criminal type so often depicted by the national press.

The more I move along in life the more impressed by the inaccurate and tragically false images that are created by our national press [sic].

Intervention by the White House would be highly sensitive and would undoubtedly result in severe criticism in certain segments of our country. However, I know that hasn't deterred you in the past. Action of this type would restore and reinforce a great deal of faith in our federal government. Millions of "little people" would applaud your concern for one of them.

Most executives wouldn't touch this case with a "ten-foot pole." It's simply too hot a "political potato"—but the Dick Nixon I know has the guts not only to make the decision which should be made but dramatically explain it to the satisfaction of fair-thinking Americans. I hope that you do.

My thanks to you for taking a few minutes of your time to read this plea from a friend of yours.

Sincerely,
Paul Laxalt

On December 22, 1971, Hoffa's prison sentence was commuted by Nixon. Hoffa was released the following day.

In 1972, Laxalt and his brother Peter built a new 237-room hotel/ casino on seven commercial acres two blocks from the state capitol in downtown Carson City and named the property Ormsby House. Opening in July 1972, the swanky casino featured two dice tables, one roulette wheel, eight blackjack tables, a $25,000-limit keno game, a bingo game, and three hundred slot machines.

Laxalt and his brother invested only a total of $1,851 of their own money in the venture that cost more than $5 million. The rest of the funding came from three Nevada banks, the First National Bank of Chicago, and several private investors—including Bernard Nemerov, a former front man for Allen Dorfman and a known associate of others in organized crime. Nemerov purchased $75,000 in stock and gave the Laxalts a $475,000 loan for the project. Peter Laxalt later described him as "the eyes and ears" of the business, as well as the person who had "a direct line of communication with Paul Laxalt."[10] Laxalt insists that he was unaware of Nemerov's shady past.

Paul and Peter Laxalt, the president and vice-president, respectively, of Ormsby House, were the only two shareholders with voting stock. Two other brothers, Robert and John Laxalt, were also directors of the corporation, but they held only nonvoting stock, like the other investors —including Nemerov, who was the "chief liaison officer."[11]

At the licensing hearing for Ormsby House before the Nevada Gaming Commission, the Laxalts expressed confidence that their funding was all in order. Peter Laxalt told the panel, "We feel at the present time that we have very adequate funding to carry this project forward through the tough winter months and for the expected future."[12]

Within a year, the Laxalts were having financial problems, which were complicated by Paul Laxalt's dispute with Nemerov over a matter that Laxalt has never publicly explained.

"The falling out was strictly over business," Nemerov claimed. "There were times when there wasn't enough money for the payroll, and I had to go into my own pocket and loan them the money. . . . When it comes to running a business, this guy's stupid."[13]

Paul Laxalt sought financial help by returning to the First National Bank of Chicago, where he had already received an initial $950,000 loan, secured only by a personal guarantee from him and his family. In May 1973, the First National loan officer, Robert Heymann—the son of former MCA executive board member and Korshak associate Walter Heymann, the vice-chairman of First National—authorized an additional $750,000 loan. This loan, secured only by pledges of casino stock, was partly used to buy out Nemerov the following month. First National later threw even more money into the pot, loaning Laxalt an additional $200,000 in November 1973 and another $200,000 in February 1974 to help keep the casino afloat.

Robert Heymann had a history of helping out Nevada casino owners. He explained that he had first met the former governor through one of Laxalt's clients, Delbert Coleman. Coleman had previously received millions of dollars in loans from the First National Bank of Chicago to help finance his earlier takeover of the Parvin-Dohrmann corporation, which had purchased the Stardust, Fremont, and Aladdin. These loans were administered by Heymann and were arranged by Sidney Korshak.

Heymann denied that either Coleman or Korshak had anything to do with the Ormsby House loans.

"My negotiations and dealings with Paul and his brother on the part of the First National Bank were strictly between their group and the bank," Heymann insisted. "The fact that he had been Coleman's attorney had nothing to do with the loans."[14]

Laxalt has also firmly rejected the suggestion that either Coleman or Korshak were involved in the First National deal. Laxalt specifically denied that Coleman "was responsible for assisting me in the obtaining of finances and loans for Ormsby House." Laxalt added, "I have never been associated in any manner with Mr. Korshak. . . . Mr. Korshak had no role in my conversations with Mr. Heymann."*[15]

Ormsby House continued having financial problems after Heymann's dismissal. Executives of the First National Bank of Chicago consolidated Ormsby's loans—including those to the three Nevada banks—in a $7.3 million package, accepting the hotel/casino as collateral. Laxalt legally avoided paying $155,000 in federal income taxes from 1970 to 1975, using the casino as a tax shelter. The final sale of Ormsby House cost Laxalt an additional $76,592 in taxes.[16]

Just when Laxalt was facing the most serious financial crisis of his career, Nevada Democratic senator Alan Bible announced that he was not going to seek reelection. Laxalt—who had previously given thousand-to-one odds against his ever returning to politics—immediately made his bid for the senate seat. His Democratic opponent was Nevada's lieutenant governor, Harry Reid. They were both challenged by a third-party candidate.

---

*In 1974, Heymann was fired from the Chicago bank after a federal investigation revealed that he had been on the payroll of a New Jersey company, which had received nearly $30 million in First National loans. Heymann was later indicted for his activities and has since pleaded guilty.

"It was a hotly contested election," said Reid. "Paul had an effective campaign. I brought up his personal finances and the Ormsby House matter as campaign issues, but, frankly, they went nowhere. He was just too strong in the northern part of the state [Carson City and Reno, among other towns], and that's where he beat me."[17]

In the end, after a recount, Laxalt's forty-seven percent of the total vote ensured him a victory by the narrow margin of 624 votes.

CHAPTER
THIRTY-ONE

IN DECEMBER 1972, Lew Wasserman announced that MCA would soon be marketing a new technological breakthrough in home entertainment. During a dramatic demonstration, motion pictures and other programs were placed on video discs and played on home machines hooked up to standard television sets. Like a long-playing record, the disc was thin and flexible, while the player resembled a stereo turntable which "read" discs with a laser-beam stylus. MCA had begun to explore this potential market in 1965 and was now looking for a manufacturer.

MCA's search for a partner/manufacturer for its "Disco-Vision" venture ended up at the doorstep of N. V. Philips, a large Dutch electronics firm and the thirteenth-largest corporation in the world, the third-largest outside the United States. It had also recently acquired Magnavox, the television company. The idea behind the prospective partnership was that Philips's responsibility was to manufacture the hardware, and MCA's responsibility was to produce the programs for the software.

The negotiations between the two companies were tough, particularly after MCA tried to put a leash on Philips. In a letter to Wasserman, Jack Findlater, the president of Disco-Vision, wrote, "Under no circumstances will Philips agree to limit their sales or other activities to Europe or anyplace else. . . . Philips operates globally and they intend to sell video-disc hardware world-wide in competition with other manufacturing companies to whom licenses are granted or who have systems of their own. If that is not possible, there can be no deal."[1]

After two years of hard bargaining, the problems remained but were slowly being worked out. Findlater told Sheinberg, "[T]he way the contract would read is that Philips can include its own issued patents in any such multi-product cross-license but no know-how or trade secrets; that if the cross-licensee wants any MCA-developed patents or technology they would have to come to MCA for that; and if they do, then MCA keeps one hundred percent of any licensing income it receives—Philips does not participate.

"The risk MCA would assume with this approach does not appear to be substantial. . . ."[2]

Finally, in September 1974, the MCA-Philips deal was finalized; the two corporations held equal shares from licensing agreements made through their new, joint operation. However, MCA would not share in Philips's revenues from the sale of players, and Philips would not share in MCA's revenues from the sale of discs. Ready to proceed, Lew Wasserman—who was driving around Los Angeles in a Mercedes roadster with California tags that said "MCA-1"—had high hopes that Disco-Vision would be the crowning glory of his incredible career.

In 1972, Henry Denker, a well-known New York writer, producer, and director, wrote *The Kingmaker,* a thinly disguised, fictional account of the rise of MCA. The Jules Stein character, Dr. Irwin Cone, is the founder of the Talent Corporation of America, TCA, which busily combats the Justice Department's Antitrust Division while attempting to make a popular has-been actor, Jeff Jefferson, into a legitimate political figure.

The book began with the inauguration of Jefferson as the governor of California. Denker wrote: "To take a man who had been an actor, a man without a single day's experience in government, and catapult him to the highest office in the state was an achievement. And nothing to feel guilty about.

"If there had to be blame, place it where it belonged. On the system which sanctioned it. On the people who permitted it. On the media which allowed themselves to be manipulated so easily.

"All the Doctor had done was to apply the same basic rule to politics as he had to developing TCA into the leading power in the entertainment industry.

"A lifetime ago he had been instructed by an expert, a man of primitive but deep insight: 'Never waste your muscle. Find out where the weakness is and put your muscle there.' "[3]

Interestingly, there was no Lew Wasserman character in Denker's book, but Wasserman found reason enough to call Denker's book a "piece of garbage."

Stein had remained involved in politics. He and Taft Schreiber had contributed $118,000 and $68,000 respectively to President Richard Nixon's 1972 reelection campaign. Schreiber was also a co-chairman of the finance committee of the Committee to Reelect the President.

According to an FBI document, Stein, who had been to Nixon's Western White House in San Clemente, had been asked for his contribution to the CRP by Schreiber, who then invited Stein to another meeting with the president. The FBI report stated: "On April 5, 1971, President Nixon had held a meeting at his San Clemente home which was attended by approximately thirty people who were interested in the movie and communications industry. It was attended by members of the Teamsters Union and other such individuals including several studio executives from the Los Angeles area. During this meeting the members furnished their views to the president regarding their belief that tax investment credit should be given to the movie industry, the prime-time access rule concerning television, support for the copyright laws regarding the recording industry, and their views concerning cable television."[4]

Although the report stated that Nixon "made no commitment whatsoever," Stein agreed to make his large contribution after this meeting.

Schreiber's name came up in another FBI report. "On 6/6/73," the document stated, "source advised that John Mitchell, former attorney general of the United States, was at a party for Pat Nixon at [Taft] Schreiber's house in Beverly Hills, California, on the night that word was received about the break-in at the Democratic Headquarters. Source advised that Mitchell had no drinks and appeared extremely nervous throughout that evening."*[5]

Governor Ronald Reagan was one of Nixon's chief defenders, insisting that the Watergate conspirators were "not criminals at heart."

---

*Mitchell—who had resigned as Nixon's attorney general to head the president's campaign committee—was later convicted of obstruction of justice and perjury in connection with his role in the planning and cover-up of the Watergate break-in.

Reagan had also been present at Schreiber's party—along with actors Jimmy Stewart and John Wayne, among others—and had held a joint press conference with Mitchell earlier in the day.

While Stein and Schreiber were busy helping Nixon, Wasserman had other matters on his mind. In December 1972, he named Sidney Sheinberg as the executive vice-president of MCA, opening up speculation throughout the entertainment industry and Wall Street that Sheinberg was being groomed to be Wasserman's handpicked successor. Wasserman also appointed H. H. Martin as the new president of Universal Pictures, succeeding Milton R. Rackmil, who became the studio's "president emeritus." The MCA president also signed a long-term contract with David Brown and Richard D. Zanuck—who had become an independent producer after losing a proxy fight against his father at Twentieth Century–Fox in 1971 and a subsequent battle with Warner Brothers, which had since been taken over by Warner Communications.

By the end of 1972, MCA had shattered all records with revenues totaling almost $350 million and profits of nearly $21 million.

On May 22, 1973—after Wasserman was given the Jean Hersholt Humanitarian Award at the Academy Awards ceremonies—seventy-seven-year-old Jules Stein shocked the entertainment industry by resigning as the chairman of the board of MCA. Just as quickly, the sixty-year-old Wasserman—who had made $250,000 during his twenty-seventh year as MCA president—was named to succeed Stein, and Sidney J. Sheinberg was selected as MCA's new president. And Frank Price replaced Sheinberg as the head of Universal-Television. Sheinberg, thirty-seven, who was immediately given a $156,000 annual salary, beat out thirty-year-old Thomas Wertheimer, an MCA vice-president for financial affairs, for the job. The corporate changes became effective as of June 5, 1973, at the MCA board of directors meeting, where Stein was officially given the title "Honorary Founder." Stein told reporters that he would continue as a director but would concentrate on his medical philanthropy causes, adding, "Mr. Wasserman has been the quarterback; he's been calling the plays."*

During the fall of 1973, MGM's Kirk Kerkorian decided to sell his studio's theatres and properties in its overseas markets. The immediate reason was a plan to construct the MGM Grand Hotel in Las Vegas.† The buyer of MGM's overseas assets was the Cinema International

---

*Stein left MCA holding 1,687,294 shares of stock, or twenty-one percent of the company. Wasserman held 869,083 shares, 10.4 percent of MCA.
†Kerkorian purchased from Moe Dalitz the land on which the MGM Grand was built; he paid Dalitz $1.8 million.

Corporation, which had been created jointly by MCA and Gulf & Western and its Paramount subsidiary. The CIC had been organized to expand the lucrative foreign distribution businesses of both corporations—and to avoid U.S. antitrust laws that had plagued MCA and G & W. Personally negotiating with Kerkorian were Wasserman, representing MCA, and Charles G. Bluhdorn, the chairman of the board of Gulf & Western. Sidney Korshak was selected to mediate the negotiations, which culminated with CIC's purchase of the overseas package for nearly $93 million.

"Mr. Korshak was very close to Wasserman and Kerkorian and played a key role as a go-between," Bluhdorn said. "It was a very, very tough negotiation that would have broken down without him."[6]

Korshak received $250,000 for helping to make the deal, which was signed at the Bistro in Beverly Hills.

Incredibly enough, Korshak, a multi-millionaire, needed the money. The previous fall, the Chicago office of the IRS had charged him with fraud and negligence, resulting from his alleged failure to pay $677,000 in federal income and gift taxes. The IRS also asked the U.S. Tax Court in Washington, D.C., to impose a $247,000 penalty on Korshak. According to IRS records, government auditors discovered that Korshak and his wife had only declared $4,481,703 in taxable income between 1963 and 1970, when his real taxable income was $5,080,987. Documents showed that Korshak had not paid $13,031 in gift taxes on stocks worth $115,124—from Parvin-Dohrmann, Pizza Hut, and City National Bank—that he gave to his two sons, Harry and Stuart. Also, the IRS charged that Korshak had falsely declared a $10,000 gift to Jill St. John as legal fees paid to her attorney. The IRS examiner auditing Korshak's taxes concluded that Korshak's actions were "intentional and substantial."[7]

The litigation was settled just before the case went to court, with the IRS dropping all charges against Korshak and agreeing to allow him to pay only $179,244, twenty percent of the initial demand.

In early 1974, after Wasserman named Sheinberg as MCA president, he stepped down as the chairman of the Association of Motion Picture and Television Producers.* He was replaced as chairman by Gordon T. Stulberg, the president of Twentieth Century–Fox; MCA's Sid Sheinberg was named vice-chairman. The move ensured Universal's

---

*The nine members of the AMPTP were Universal, Paramount, Columbia, Twentieth Century–Fox, Metro-Goldwyn-Mayer, Warner Brothers, United Artists, Avco-Embassy, and Allied Artists. All operated as production/distribution companies, with the exception of MGM, which had an exclusive distribution contract with United Artists.

continued influence over labor negotiations, especially with Wasserman serving as a behind-the-scenes powerbroker and deal-maker—sometimes with the help of his close friend, Sid Korshak. When a major problem arose, the Hollywood powers still turned to Wasserman for advice. Others, like American Airlines and the California Institute of Technology, sought his counsel by naming him to their boards of directors. At a testimonial dinner thrown for Wasserman in Beverly Hills by the entertainment industry in late 1974, he was even honored by IATSE*—whose president over the past thirty-three years, Richard Walsh, had retired earlier that year and was succeeded by Walter F. Diehl.

The year 1973 was a blockbuster for Universal Pictures. *American Graffiti,* producer Francis Ford Coppola and director George Lucas's rock-and-roll film about four teenagers growing up in the 1950s, earned $52 million against a production cost of $1 million. The film's soundtrack provided an additional bonanza for MCA.

In December 1973, Universal released *The Sting,* starring former MCA Artists clients Paul Newman and Robert Redford, who played two con men who try to swindle an Irish gangster who ordered the murder of a mutual friend, in the studio's biggest moneymaker for 1974 and one of the biggest grossers of all time. The film won the studio its third Academy Award for Best Picture, the first since MCA took over the company.

"You need to make a minimum number of films a year," said Universal executive Ned Tanen. "There are films you come across that look very safe. The downside risk is fairly minimal, so therefore we will take them on. You do enough of these films and out of that group will suddenly emerge a picture that is a huge hit."[8]

Universal had also produced Steven Spielberg's highly acclaimed *Sugarland Express,* as well as three big box-office smashes: *Earthquake,* with "Sensurround" providing realistic rumbles; *Airport 1975* in 1974, the latest in a series of star-studded disaster films trying to mimic the success of *Airport.*

Traditionally, MCA would wait until television series had been can-

---

*In February 1973, Wasserman was singled out by IATSE for his intervention in a stalemated labor dispute between the union and television producers. Called a "hero" by IATSE officials, "Wasserman was the guy who clinched the deal, really," an IATSE leader told Will Tusher of *The Hollywood Reporter.* "He was the only one that we listened to. The only one of that group we believed was Wasserman. He made two or three really brilliant talks. . . . You've got to hand it to Wasserman. I think he saved the day." Of his negotiating skills, Wasserman told Tusher, "you accomplish unanimity by locking people in various rooms—I might add, without any bathrooms. It's amazing how many deals have been finalized because of a lack of a washroom."

celed before it would syndicate them to local stations. That practice was abandoned in 1972–73. Even though programs such as *Columbo, McMillan and Wife,* and *McCloud* were still hot after three years of production, MCA's syndication rights division immediately began to sell them locally, capitalizing on the shows' current popularity—thus increasing the price of syndication. Later, MCA would go even further, offering 104 episodes of *The Six-Million-Dollar Man* if the buyer gave MCA an option to sell the buyer thirteen episodes of *The Bionic Woman.* Both programs had been broadcast on ABC.

An attorney in the Antitrust Division, who was monitoring MCA for possible antitrust violations, wrote, "In short, MCA is using the power of *Man* to make sure that it gets syndie money from *Woman* (in a deal that reportedly was set up before *Woman* went on the ABC [schedule])."[9]

Spencer Gifts mail-order and retail-store division had a record year in 1972. With plans being made to expand Spencer to over four hundred stores around the country, total revenues from Spencer's current outlets were $61,446,000, a thirty-four-percent increase over the previous year. Since MCA had purchased Spencer in 1968, sales had tripled.

MCA's Trans-Glamour tours—an open-air bus ride through Universal City, planned and executed by MCA vice-president Albert A. Dorskind and Cliff Walker, a renegade from Disneyland, Inc., in 1964—were being taken by nearly two million visitors each year. The tours produced millions of dollars of clear profit for only the cost of, among other items, bus and property maintenance and tour guides, who were usually attractive college students hoping to be discovered, who gladly worked for low wages. The money made from a few of the many souvenir stands covered these expenses.

For the price of admission, the curious saw Western gunfights acted out with stuntmen who fell off buildings after being "shot," how animal trainers prepared their pets for cameo film appearances, and a glimpse of Norman Bates's hilltop home in Alfred Hitchcock's *Psycho.* Occasionally, a star or two would be available to talk shop and sign autographs. A family could easily spend the rest of the day—as well as their vacation money—walking around and seeing the sights after the bus trip. The program was so successful that MCA had already expanded Trans-Glamour and added Landmark Services in Washington, D.C., where tourists received bus tours of the nation's capital and its monuments.

MCA had also developed the large-stage, 3,800-person capacity Universal Amphitheatre, which became a tourist attraction in itself, as well as a treat for natives of southern California. The new facility had been built to accommodate concert and theatre performances. At the end of 1972, MCA added Yosemite Park and Curry Company—encompassing the food, lodging, and transportation concessions at Yosemite National Park in the Sierra Nevada Mountains in central California—to its Recreation Services Division.

At the end of July 1974, Universal announced that during the first six months of 1974, its profits were higher than in any six-month period in the history of the company. And the news would only get better.

Universal hit the mother lode with the spring 1975 release of *Jaws*, a Steven Spielberg tale of a great white shark's invasion of Martha's Vineyard during the Fourth of July holiday. It costarred Lorraine Gary, Sid Sheinberg's actress-wife. Another record-breaker at the box office, *Jaws* became the biggest money-making film in motion picture history.*

Universal had become a movie factory, cranking out films like Congress cranks out legislation—but with better quality control and discipline. Few celebrities basking in the excitement and glamour of Hollywood thought of themselves as being workers on an assembly line. But under contract at Universal they were. Schedules and budgets were etched in stone, and no one fooled with them once they were decided.

"The assembly line . . . ," one description stated, "is organized into three phases. In preproduction, budgets are drawn up, personnel assigned, and sets designed and built. . . . Then comes production—what most people think of as moviemaking—where the actual shooting takes place. Once the cameras quit rolling, the raw film and soundtracks are delivered to film editors and dubbing specialists in the postproduction department. The entire process takes from eight weeks for a thirty-minute TV show to a year for a full-blown movie.

"To coordinate the whole operation MCA has developed some special techniques. At 1:30 every afternoon the technical-department heads meet in a 'war room' with the unit managers of all the production companies to talk over personnel and equipment allocations for the next day's shooting. The discussion gets down to such items as battle-

---

*According to *Variety*, the twelve all-time top-grossing films in 1976 were *Jaws, The Godfather, The Sound of Music, Gone With the Wind, The Sting, The Exorcist, The Towering Inferno, Love Story, The Graduate, Doctor Zhivago, Airport*, and *American Graffiti*. Soon after the release of *Jaws*, Jules Stein put a sign on his front gate, warning: "Beware of Guard Dogs and Sharks."

scene explosives and doughnuts for the crew. By paying attention to detail, MCA's managers have earned a reputation as the maestros of the bottom line."[10]

With MCA so incredibly attractive and corporate mergers becoming an everyday event, the MCA board of directors decided to insulate the company against a possible hostile takeover by amending MCA's by-laws. The new amendment required that seventy-five percent of MCA's stockholders had to approve of any attempt to absorb the corporation.

"I wanted to protect the future management and the board to the maximum degree possible," said Lew Wasserman. "If the board wants to make a deal, fine. They've got total authority, whoever is on the board at that time. I just don't want them to be sitting ducks, spending all of their time worrying about being raided."[11]

There was one area where MCA was enjoying less than success. It was having enormous technical problems with Disco-Vision. RCA had emerged as MCA and Philips's most serious competitor in the video-disc market, claiming that its system, SelectaVision, would be less expensive and easier to make and service than Disco-Vision. The individual discs for both systems were to cost two dollars to ten dollars. As the MCA-RCA race for control of the home video market was neck-and-neck, the Sony Corporation—which was developing its own system, using audio/videotape cassettes—was coming fast from behind. Other companies in the field included Matsushita-Panasonic, the 3M Corporation, Bell & Howell, TPC, Zenith, Telefunken, CSF Thomson, and Eastman-Kodak.

To add to MCA's growing concern for Disco-Vision, the Justice Department's Antitrust Division was again investigating MCA—because of "the possible anticompetitive affects" of its prospective uses of the pending patent of its system.[12]

On August 25, 1975, Willie L. Hudgins, the attorney in charge of the probe, recommended that charges be filed against MCA and Philips for violations of the Sherman Antitrust Act, specifically, among other things, for "forming a technology pool to handle all licensing of their video-disc technology," and because "MCA's programming will be used exclusively to support the joint Philips-MCA video-disc system." Hudgins believed that this situation would have the adverse effect of "eliminating competition between Philips and MCA in research and development," which would result in the "restricting and suppressing [of] competition in the purchase of patents and patent rights covering video disc technology."[13]

Hudgins asked that the MCA-Philips partnership be disengaged and "that the defendants be required to make available [all of their technology] on a royalty-free basis to any applicant interested in developing video-disc technology" created by both MCA and Philips.

There was still another complication on the home entertainment front. Almost twelve years after former NBC president Pat Weaver lost a 1964 statewide referendum, hoping to get approval for the establishment of pay TV in California, cable television came of age during the mid-1970s. Home Box Office, owned by Time, Inc., began offering subscription services to the general public. HBO, which distributed its programs via satellite, offered viewers movies from the studios' film libraries, as well as first-run specials produced exclusively for subscribers and a variety of sporting events.

The difficulties plaguing MCA did not stop Wasserman and his wife, Edie, from throwing a big Hollywood party at their Beverly Hills home in honor of Henry Kissinger, President Gerald Ford's secretary of state. The guests included: William French Smith, Paul Ziffren, Taft Schreiber, Jules Stein, and Sidney Sheinberg—along with Cary Grant, Kirk Douglas, Danny Kaye, Rosalind Russell, Alfred Hitchcock, and Gregory Peck. "Show business people and politicians aren't that dissimilar," Kissinger replied to a Wasserman toast, "except that politicians play only one role and have a shorter life."

"The Wasserman driveway and the house itself were jammed with Secret Service men as well as Superstars, Super-producers, Super-directors and Super-distinguished citizens," gushed Los Angeles Times gossip columnist Joyce Haber. "The living room was California-fresh with plants and flowers. Someone remarked correctly that Edie, the hostess, does parties so well that if she ever stopped, florist David Jones would be out of business. Each lady found a spring flower on her napkin at dinner. The dinner itself started off with a baked potato topped by Iranian caviar and ended with Dom Pérignon."[14]

Kissinger, who attended the party with his new wife, Nancy, had previously dated Jill St. John. During their romance, the press frequently speculated about the possibility of marriage between the two. When asked what he might do after he left the government, Kissinger replied, "I'm thinking about going into the movies. I've got the connections now."[15]

CHAPTER THIRTY-TWO

IN 1976, New Jersey voters approved a state referendum to legalize gambling in Atlantic City. Within two years, casino gambling would be in operation. However, what worried the Nevada gaming community was not the competition of Atlantic City or the 1976 death of billionaire recluse Howard Hughes but the forced end of all loan commitments to its casinos from the Teamsters Central States Pension Fund. After years of corruption and fiduciary mismanagement, the pension fund—which had loaned hundreds of millions of dollars to Nevada casinos—was placed by the federal government in the supervisory hands of private investment firms.

In 1976, Frank Sinatra bought five percent of the Las Vegas–based Del Webb Corporation along with his attorney Milton Rudin. Sinatra had had his interest in the Cal-Neva Lodge, a casino in Lake Tahoe, revoked in 1963 by the Nevada Gaming Control Board because of his ties to Chicago mobster Sam Giancana. The 1976 deal was an attempt by Sinatra to move back onto the Nevada gambling scene. But the Nevada Gaming Commission stepped in, insisting that Sinatra and Rudin be licensed since their share in the company was so large. Although Rudin was appointed to Webb's board of directors, Sinatra backed off from the company, not wanting another confrontation with law-enforcement authorities.

Soon after Nevada senator Paul Laxalt came to Washington in 1975, his Ormsby House was near financial collapse, forcing the Laxalt family to find a buyer. In 1976, its new owners simply assumed the $8.5 million debt the hotel/casino had amassed. Laxalt walked away from Ormsby House suffering a major loss, and preaching the gospel of the risky business of casino ownership.

"People have the mistaken impression that all you have to do is build a casino and open the doors and then reserve a vault in Fort Knox," Laxalt said. "It plain doesn't happen that way, and I say that from my own experience. . . . The lead time of almost every Nevada casino, almost without exception, is close to five years before it flies. And this requires continued financial subsistence."[1]

In the midst of the failure of Ormsby House and his new marriage to his long-time secretary, Carol Wilson, Laxalt quickly became involved in national politics, trying to convince his friend Ronald Reagan to challenge President Gerald Ford for the Republican nomination. In July 1975, with the support of some of Reagan's long-time backers, Laxalt formed the Citizens for Reagan Committee, which also included Holmes Tuttle, Henry Salvatori, William French Smith, William A. Wilson, and Jules Stein.*

"They've known each other since the mid-1960s, since the Goldwater campaign," said Reagan's 1976 campaign manager, John Sears. "After they were elected the governors of their states—Reagan in California and Laxalt in Nevada—they became closer. They principally got together during meetings of the Western Governors' Conference, where they discussed such issues as water rights and other functions in which politics and individuals interact. But they both loved the outdoors. They both liked horses and wore cowboy boots. . . . Reagan and Laxalt really became close during Reagan's first campaign for president [in 1968]. A lot of people were skeptical of Reagan's chances, and Laxalt was one of the few national elected officials to stand beside him."[2]

Reagan aide Jude Wanniski explained, "Laxalt was very anxious for Reagan to run against Jerry Ford, because he thought Ford was the Eastern-wing candidate, typifying business-as-usual Washington. Laxalt felt that Ford served the interests of the establishment rather than

---

*Reagan Kitchen Cabinet member A. C. Rubel died in 1967.

the free markets. This is what brought Reagan into the race. Laxalt, very early, kept pushing and yelling, 'Come on! Come on!' Reagan resisted until he finally realized, 'Yeah.' "[3]

Since leaving the governor's mansion in California, Reagan had started a daily radio commentary program, which was carried by nearly three hundred stations, and wrote a newspaper column that was syndicated by over two hundred newspapers. Even though the Republican Party had been hurt by President Nixon's resignation, Reagan's popularity remained undiminished. According to public opinion, Reagan was still "Mr. Clean."

Despite his challenge of Gerald Ford's bid for a full term as president, Reagan was supportive of his opponent, especially after Ford had pardoned Nixon. Reagan was among those who stated that Nixon "had suffered enough"; thus he felt that Ford's pardon of the former president was justified.

In the days preceding the 1976 Republican convention, Reagan shocked everyone by selecting his vice-presidential candidate in advance, Pennsylvania senator Richard Schweiker, a moderate who had been a member of the U.S. Senate Select Committee investigating the CIA-Mafia plots to assassinate Fidel Castro* and had been selected to co-chair, with Democratic senator Gary Hart, a special Senate inquiry into the assassination of President Kennedy. Schweiker was respected by both conservatives and liberals. Liberals were as shocked that he had accepted Reagan's offer as conservatives had been that Reagan made the offer in the first place. The controversy quickly became academic when Ford defeated Reagan on the GOP convention's first ballot.

Reagan's defeat was the second big blow he suffered that summer. The first came on June 14 when his long-time friend and political supporter, MCA vice-president Taft Schreiber, died after being admitted to the UCLA Medical Center for "minor and routine prostate surgery." Schreiber entered the hospital on June 3 and was operated on the following day. Schreiber was administered a mislabeled transfusion, causing a "hemolytic transfusion reaction, renal breakdown and other complications." However, Schreiber's cause of death was not known until the coroner's autopsy report was released on July 21. The report

---

*In 1975, a U.S. Senate Select Committee investigated the CIA-Mafia plots to assassinate Cuban premier Fidel Castro. Two of the suspected conspirators, Sam Giancana and Jimmy Hoffa, were murdered in the midst of the investigation. Johnny Roselli, who had continued being a familiar face in Hollywood, did testify before the committee—but was later found dismembered and badly decomposed in a fifty-five-gallon drum floating in Florida's Biscayne Bay. He had been last seen on a boat owned by Santos Trafficante, one of his co-conspirators in the Castro plots. (See Dan E. Moldea, *The Hoffa Wars*, chapters 18 and 19.)

showed that Schreiber had died "due to complications of a transfusion reaction due to incompatible blood after prostate surgery."

Using the coroner's findings, Schreiber's widow, Rita Schreiber, and her two children filed a "wrongful death" suit against the Regents of the University of California, charging "medical malpractice," according to court records. The case was later settled with the final terms undisclosed.

In late 1976, the Sony Corporation announced the production of the new Sony Betamax system, which used audio/videocasette tapes. MCA and Walt Disney Productions immediately sued Sony for copyright infringement, because home viewers could use the Sony Betamax to record television programs from a receiver and replay them over and over again. Obviously, Universal, Disney, and the rest of the studios preferred that viewers *not* be taping their programs and film libraries sold to television. Aside from recording television programs and playing prerecorded tapes, the Betamax offered the consumer an optional camera to film home movies. Disco-Vision only offered the viewer the ability to play prerecorded programs. The Sony technology had been tried and tested, and was ready to be marketed. On the other hand, the MCA-Philips effort, which was still having trouble with its patents and overall cost, was not. MCA hoped that its suit would delay Sony from gaining the lead in the potentially billion-dollar home entertainment industry.

In an expression of frustration, Sidney Sheinberg told reporters, "If Sony's Betamax prevails, I don't know if there will be a video-disc industry ultimately."

Earlier, a meeting was held in Los Angeles between the Antitrust Division and lawyers representing Philips; for unknown reasons, MCA's attorneys did not attend. After hearing the government's lead attorney, Willie Hudgins, explain the investigation, Sam Rossell, Philip's in-house counsel, protested that if Disco-Vision was stopped, RCA, which was already ahead of MCA-Philips, would completely dominate the video-disc market. He added that, because of all the problems MCA-Philips had faced, their program was a year behind schedule, and their products would not be available until late 1977. Without any resolution to the situation, Philips's attorneys simply asked that they be permitted to argue their case again before the government officially filed antitrust charges.[4]

A few weeks later, MCA lawyer Allen Susman wrote a letter to Thomas E. Kauper, the head of the Antitrust Division in Washington, insisting that there was no cause for an antitrust suit. "[A]ny action against MCA and Philips . . . would be not only unsustainable, it would have an immediate and long-term substantial anticompetitive impact."

Susman continued, "In 1974 top executives of MCA became convinced that MCA had developed the better [audio/visual playback system]; however, the world was not beating a path to MCA's door. Since millions of dollars had been spent by MCA on their new [system], this lack of enthusiastic response naturally led the company to question how it ended up in this position."[5]

While the problems with Disco-Vision continued, Wasserman became closer to former Georgia governor Jimmy Carter, who had become the presidential nominee of the Democratic Party for the 1976 general election. In an interview, with *W* magazine, Carter said of Wasserman, "I met him when I was still governor of Georgia. When I decided to run [for president], Mr. Wasserman was one of the first out-of-state people I told. People respected his judgment in business, international affairs, and political affairs. When he let his friends know he had confidence in me, it was extremely helpful." The MCA chairman threw a fund-raiser for Carter* in August. Among those in attendance was Sidney Korshak.

Two months before the party for Carter, the sixty-nine-year-old Korshak was the target of a major four-part investigative series from June 27 through June 30, 1976, in *The New York Times*. It was written by Pulitzer Prize–winning journalist Seymour M. Hersh. Along with his collaborator, Jeff Gerth, Hersh had spent six months doing research. Their report was the most penetrating and detailed analysis of Korshak and his power yet written. "To scores of federal, state and local law-enforcement officials," the *Times* stated, "Mr. Korshak is the most important link between organized crime and legitimate business." The series described him as "a behind-the-scenes 'fixer' who has been instrumental in helping criminal elements gain power in union affairs and infiltrate the leisure and entertainment industries."

Although Korshak refused to be interviewed, several who knew him did speak on the record. Wasserman said that Korshak was a "very good personal friend. . . . He's a very well respected lawyer. He's a man of his word and good company." When asked about the allegations of Korshak's ties to the underworld, Wasserman replied, "I don't believe them. I've never seen him with so-called syndicate members or organization members."

---

*After being elected, Carter appointed former MCA legal counsel Cyrus R. Vance as secretary of state.

Stating that Korshak was "entrenched in Hollywood's social and business structures," Hersh and Gerth reported that he was a close friend of Gulf & Western chairman Charles Bluhdorn. "Their meeting had been arranged in 1969 by Robert Evans, the successful Paramount executive and close Korshak friend [and client], shortly after Gulf & Western purchased Paramount.

"Mr. Korshak often used his influence and his skill as a mediator to solve problems for Gulf & Western.

"For example, Mr. Bluhdorn recalled that during early casting for *The Godfather,* one of the biggest successes at Paramount, his company's subsidiary, Mr. Korshak obtained for the production the services of Al Pacino, the actor, then under contract to MGM."

Hollywood columnist Joyce Haber added, "Sidney Korshak is probably the most important man socially out here. If you're not invited to his Christmas party, it's a disaster." Haber, in a January 1975 column, identified the "The Big Six" in Hollywood social circles as "the Paul Ziffrens, Lew Wassermans, and Sidney Korshaks."

According to the *Times*, although never indicted, Korshak had been named in no less than twenty organized-crime investigations and had been called as a witness before no less than a half-dozen grand juries.

The reaction to the Hersh series on Korshak was favorable in Chicago, generally unreported in Los Angeles, and hostile in New York. Columnist Nat Hentoff, a respected civil libertarian, was enraged. "To be crudely accurate about it, *The New York Times* . . . set out to get Sidney Korshak. . . . Tom Jefferson may not have had this mouthpiece precisely in mind when he envisioned the democratic populace two centuries hence but he could not have excluded even him from the Bill of Rights."

Objecting especially to the FBI inside information used in the report, Hentoff wrote that he saw "no First Amendment problems in punishing officials in the criminal justice system who have violated Sidney Korshak's rights by leaking protected information to Sy Hersh. I am assuming, by the way, that Hersh did not conduct his own black-bag jobs into the FBI to get the kind of material that has so badly damaged Korshak."[6]

Korshak had been hospitalized in Chicago for an intestinal disorder in the midst of Hersh's series, but he was still loved in Hollywood. Three days after the *Times* series, Korshak was among three hundred guests at the Wassermans' fortieth wedding anniversary party. According to published reports, when Korshak was getting ready to leave the affair, Wasserman embraced him. To no one's surprise, film producer

Harry Korshak, Sid's son, had his first film released for Universal—
Gable and Lombard, a fictitious rendering of the love affair between
film stars Clark Gable and Carole Lombard, starring James Brolin and
Jill Clayburgh. In August, Sid Korshak's wife, Beatrice, was Barbara
Marx's matron of honor at her wedding to Frank Sinatra, which was
held at Walter Annenberg's home in Palm Springs.* And the following
month, he was in attendance at a testimonial dinner honoring Charles
Bluhdorn, arranged by Barry Diller, Paramount's new chairman of the
board.

Despite the *New York Times* series, 1976 turned out to be another
banner year for Korshak. Instead of being viewed as a corrupt, Mafia-
backed lawyer, he was regarded as a Hollywood institution of legendary
proportions and continued to be feared, respected, and even revered by
those who brought the American public what they viewed on television
and at their local movie theatres.

---

*Ronald and Nancy Reagan took time out from his 1976 presidential campaign to be among the
130 guests at Sinatra and Marx's wedding.

CHAPTER
THIRTY-THREE

THE PHOTOGRAPH WAS REAL. After years of denying his associations with major Mafia figures, Frank Sinatra was pictured in his dressing room with several top mobsters, including New York syndicate head Carlo Gambino and Los Angeles Mafia boss Jimmy Fratianno.* The 1976 photograph was admitted as evidence in a New York grand jury fraud investigation, stemming from the bankruptcy and wholesale skimming of the Westchester Premier Theater—which would lead to the indictments of several Mafia figures, including three mob associates who also appeared in the picture with Sinatra: Gregory DePalma, Thomas Marson, and Richard Fusco. Adding to Sinatra's woes was the revelation that the telephone of his personal secretary had been wiretapped by federal investigators, because it was thought that she knew about the skimming operation. However, neither Sinatra nor his secre-

---

*Sinatra performed at the Westchester Premier Theatre three times in 1976 and 1977. Regarding the photograph, Sinatra insisted to Nevada gaming authorities, "I was asked by one of the members of the theatre. . . . Mr. Gambino had arrived with his granddaughter, whose name happened to be Sinatra, a doctor in New York, not related at all, and they'd like to take a picture. I said, 'Fine.'

"They came in and they took a picture of the little girl and before I realized what happened, there were approximately eight or nine men standing around me and several other snapshots were made. That is the whole incident that took place."

tary were charged with any wrongdoing. The bugging had begun while Sinatra and Dean Martin had been performing at the theatre.

In early 1977, during an investigation of corruption in Las Vegas, the FBI had tapped the telephones of Marson and DePalma. On one of the tapes, DePalma said that he and his business partners were planning "to siphon off money at an upcoming Frank Sinatra appearance at the Westchester Theater in New York to keep [the money] from bankruptcy officials."

Owned by DePalma, Fusco, and Eliot Weisman, the 3,500-seat Westchester Theater in Tarrytown, New York, which opened in 1975, was a popular entertainment center where celebrities performed before sellout audiences. Gambino, who had loaned the Westchester Theater $100,000 to help in its construction, died in 1976 before the indictments were handed down. Funzi Tieri, who headed the notorious Vito Genovese crime family in New York, and Fratianno were named as unindicted co-conspirators in the case. A Tieri associate, Louis Pacella, reportedly a close friend of Sinatra, was indicted for allegedly skimming $50,000 from the theatre.

Also implicated in the scheme were two top executives of Warner Communications: Solomon Weiss, Warner's assistant treasurer, and Jay Emmett, a top assistant to Warner boss Steven J. Ross. Both were accused of accepting a $50,000 bribe from the theatre's management, hoping to influence Warner Communications to buy Westchester stock. After the alleged bribe was made, Warner bought 20,000 shares at five dollars per share.

Fratianno, who later turned state's evidence, explained that after Sinatra agreed to perform at the theatre, the management thought, "Two days, four performances, with about two hundred unrecorded seats at fifty dollars a seat: that was $10,000. A thousand scalped tickets, the best seats in the house, going anywhere from fifty to a hundred dollars above cost. That was about $75,000. All the other stuff, the programs, the T-shirts, at least $3,000 per performance. Multiply everything by four and you got $400,000, split three ways: one third to DePalma for the theatre, one third to Louie Dome [Pacella], one third to [Fratianno]. Louie Dome was included for insurance, to make sure Sinatra fulfilled his obligation. Besides, Louie was Frank's good friend, which automatically earned him a cut."[1]

In 1976, for the first time in its history, MCA grossed $100 million in a single year, a forty-percent increase over the previous year. The following year, Universal-TV started making moves to become a fourth network in a project called Operation Prime Time. An effort to sell first-run movies to independent stations throughout the United States with world-wide syndication potential—thus bypassing CBS, ABC, and NBC—Prime Time also involved Paramount Pictures, which was also MCA's partner in the CIC overseas distribution venture. Initiating the project with a drama based on Taylor Caldwell's best-selling novel *Testimony of Two Men,* MCA-Paramount hoped to offer one night a week of quality programming to these independent stations.

After an unsuccessful attempt to buy Sea World in 1976, MCA's attempts to diversify continued.* MCA made a $140 million offer to purchase the Coca-Cola Bottling Company of Los Angeles; Wasserman personally called Coke's chairman, Arthur D. MacDonald, to inform him of the takeover bid. Upset with the offer, which they considered too low, Coke and MacDonald battled MCA in the courts and in the press while looking for a better bid. They found it when Northwest Industries topped MCA by $60 million. For its $200 million investment, Northwest later sold the Los Angeles Coca-Cola franchise for $600 million.

Simultaneously, MCA's problems with Disco-Vision continued. A federal court in Los Angeles heard testimony on MCA's copyright suit against Sony, which MCA was expected to lose. Meantime, MCA-Philips and Pioneer Electronics, a Japanese corporation, formed an equal alliance to distribute video-disc players all over the world, aiming first at industrial applications.

The Antitrust Division was still in pursuit, claiming that "MCA and RCA had tied up programming for video discs to such an extent that it was very unlikely that video-disc hardware other than theirs will be able to enter the consumer market. . . . [F]or any video-disc hardware to succeed in the consumer market it has to have programming available. No one will buy a video-disc player without some assurance that programming on compatible discs will be available. By controlling the programming a firm could control the hardware that comes on the market."[2]

In 1978, Jules Stein, who had become "the grand old man of Hollywood," was honored by the Motion Picture Pioneers, a philanthropic Hollywood group established to help needy people in the film industry. The dinner for Stein was held at New York's Waldorf-Astoria Hotel,

---

*MCA also became involved in the publishing industry, buying G. P. Putnam's Sons of New York, which owned Coward, McCann & Geohagan and Berkley Books, a paperback company. In 1978, MCA purchased *New Times,* a newsmagazine featuring investigative reporting, but allowed it to fold within a few months.

where Stein used to book big bands. Jack Valenti made the introductions; Danny Thomas was the master of ceremonies; Health, Education, and Welfare Secretary Joseph Califano was the keynote speaker; and Diana Ross sang "Reach Out."

"I'm here only by chance," a beaming Stein told his crowd of admirers. "If Johns Hopkins had accepted my application . . . but I lacked eighteen hours of work in organic chemistry and they said come back next year. I was in a hurry so I applied to the University of Chicago and it was while I was working my way through medical school that I started my second career—booking bands. If it were not for those eighteen hours in chemistry I might be an unknown eye doctor in the Midwest still saying do you see better this way . . . or this way."[3]

Meanwhile Wasserman and MCA filed suit against *Playboy* publisher Hugh Hefner because "videotapes of Universal motion pictures contained in *Playboy*'s private film library constituted copyright infringement."[4] MCA feared that Hefner's ownership of the films might establish a dangerous precedent, influencing *Playboy* readers, in MCA's opinion, to violate copyright laws as well.

Hefner was convinced that there had been a misunderstanding and tried to talk to Wasserman, who was still sensitive about the fate of Disco-Vision and combative about MCA's copyright lawsuit against Sony. Consequently, Wasserman refused to speak with him. According to court documents, Hefner contacted and hired "Sidney Korshak, an Illinois attorney with influence in the Hollywood, California, community, as an intermediary to deal with Korshak's friend, Lew Wasserman. . . . Hefner paid Korshak $50,000 [by check, dated March 16, 1978], seemingly simply for the purpose of having Korshak explain Hefner's position to Wasserman and to arrange a meeting with Wasserman, not Universal's attorneys, to discuss a possible settlement of the lawsuit."[5]

Korshak failed to arrange the meeting with Wasserman or to soften his position against *Playboy* but kept the $50,000 for trying. In the end, Hefner was forced to relent and surrender the Universal films in his personal library.

The following month, Korshak was in attendance at a political fundraiser for incumbent California governor Jerry Brown, who was being challenged in the Democratic primary. The party was held at Lew Wasserman's home in Beverly Hills. "We called Lew in the primary," said a Brown campaign staffer, "and we asked him to host a dinner that could bring $50,000. Well, sure enough, by the time we collected all the money it came to $50,000—almost to the penny."[6]

Brown said that it did not bother him that Korshak—who had reportedly given Brown a $1,000 contribution in 1974—was present. Wasserman—who chaired the Brown campaign's executive committee —personally gave $10,000 to the cause; there is no known record of a Korshak contribution in 1978.

Days later, California attorney general Evelle J. Younger, the Republican candidate for governor, released an eighty-eight-page report on the status of organized crime in the state, which had heavily contributed to the $6.8-billion-a-year California crime industry. Included was a list of ninety-two known organized crime figures operating in the state. Among the names listed was that of Korshak, who was described as "a senior adviser to organized crime groups in California, Chicago, Las Vegas, and New York."[7]

Edwin Meese, Governor Reagan's former executive assistant and vice-chairman of the eight-member commission that published the report, told reporters, "It's true that most of the information was in the hands of law enforcement prior to our hearings but now it is all pulled together in one place for everyone to see."

In a rare interview, Korshak told *Los Angeles Herald Examiner* reporter Mike Qualls, "He [Younger] can put up or shut up. . . . I've never been cited, let alone indicted, for anything. I've never been called before any bar association. As far as I know there's never been a complaint against me of any kind." Korshak added that he had contributed $3,000 to Younger's 1970 and 1971 campaigns for attorney general and had been asked to serve on Younger's campaign committee for his gubernatorial bid. "The damage this has caused me is irreparable," Korshak said, "because what can I do to combat it?"[8]

In the midst of charges that he had used the organized crime report as a publicity stunt for his campaign, Younger claimed that he had returned Korshak's contributions and had instructed his staff not to accept any money from him.

Korshak nearly became as central a campaign issue in the California race for governor as Proposition Thirteen, a state referendum for property-tax cutbacks, because both candidates had links to him. While the Republicans charged Brown with accepting $50,000 in contributions during his 1974 campaign from the Culinary Workers Union, in which Korshak exercised enormous power, the Democrats charged that Younger had met with organized crime figure Moe Morton—with whom Korshak was in business—while Younger was the Los Angeles district attorney in 1970. Morton had built a condominium unit in Mexico in 1967, called Acapulco Towers, known as a meeting place for top underworld figures. Involved in the Acapulco Towers project were Korshak, Meyer Lansky, Delbert Coleman, Beverly Hills attorneys and long-time Korshak associates Greg Bautzer and Eugene Wyman, Philip Levin of Gulf & Western–Paramount, and Eugene Klein, the owner of the San Diego Chargers professional football team.*

A Los Angeles superior court judge had been forced to disqualify himself from a trial in which Moe Morton was involved after it was learned that the judge had met Morton while on vacation in Acapulco. The judge later said that he had been introduced to Morton by Younger —who could not recall knowing Morton. "I can't deny it," Younger told the press, "but I don't know that I ever met him [Morton]."

MCA stayed out of the fray but contributed $2,500 to both candidates. Brown was reelected, but his lieutenant governor was Republican Mike Curb, the former president of MGM Records and owner of Warner-Curb Records. Within four months of his election, Curb signed with MCA to create an MCA-Curb label.

On the national political scene, Wasserman remained inactive but accepted an invitation to the White House for a luncheon with President Jimmy Carter. Although the event was not a fund-raiser, Wasserman contributed $100,000 to the Democratic National Committee to offset a long-term debt incurred by the party during the 1968 presidential campaign.

Later, an unidentified informant complained that Carter had solicited Wasserman's $100,000 contribution to the committee. If true, the alleged solicitation was a violation of post-Watergate campaign financing laws. The Justice Department opened an inquiry. In early February 1979, Attorney General Griffin Bell announced that the investigation —which could have led to a broader special prosecutor's probe—had been dropped.

In December 1978, NBC News reporter Brian Ross broadcast a story that Sidney Korshak had earlier served as an arbitrator between Wasserman and producer Dino DeLaurentiis in their fight over who would produce the remake of *King Kong,* which was released in 1976. At the meeting, which was held at Korshak's home in Bel Air, the decision was made to allow DeLaurentiis—who paid Korshak at least $25,000 for his help—to do the film. Pictures of Wasserman's telephone log demonstrated "frequent contact with Korshak. . . . The two men had been close for years. . . . Many people in the industry say one way to do business with Wasserman is to go to Korshak."[9]

---

*Acapulco Towers was eventually sold to the Gulf & Western Land Development Corporation in a deal engineered by Korshak and Levin.

CHAPTER
THIRTY-FOUR

IN JANUARY 1979, MCA bought ABC Records for $30 million. The sale price reflected the extent of losses ABC had had in 1977, which was rivaled by an equally bad year in 1978. MCA Records, on the other hand, had nearly doubled its earnings in 1978 over the previous year. The top MCA performers in 1978 were Steely Dan and The Who. Olivia Newton-John's music was also selling well, but in early 1979 she left MCA. Lynyrd Skynyrd's records were big sellers—especially in the wake of a plane crash in October 1977 that killed three members of the band.

There was good news on April 9 at the Academy Awards ceremonies at the Dorothy Chandler Pavilion in Los Angeles. Universal and EMI Films shared the Best Picture Oscar for the production of *The Deer Hunter,* beating out *Coming Home* and *Midnight Express.*

As MCA-Universal announced plans for a $27.5 million expansion of Universal City, MCA and Disney lost their lawsuit to Sony. A federal judge in Los Angeles ruled, in a landmark decision, that it was legal for videotape machine owners to copy television programs as long as they were for personal use, not for sale or for future viewings at which admission was charged. Wasserman and Sheinberg were reportedly shocked by the decision and immediately appealed.

IBM and MCA-Philips announced a joint venture to build and market video discs and video-disc players. IBM's involvement was to use its technology to place large quantities of programming on discs. Nevertheless, RCA's SelectaVision had already begun to dominate the video-disc market and was doing well against the Sony Betamax.

On March 2, Lew Wasserman threw another dinner for President Jimmy Carter and the Democratic National Committee—in the midst of a "dump Carter in 1980" campaign in Hollywood, which included such liberal Democrats as television producer Norman Lear and Joyce Ashley, the wife of Ted Ashley, the chairman of the board at Warner Brothers. The pro-Carter affair was a $1,000-a-plate dinner and was held at the Beverly Hilton Hotel. Governor Jerry Brown accepted Wasserman's invitation to introduce Carter.

The Sidney Korshak–Governor Brown relationship was again in the California spotlight in 1979 after Korshak became involved as the principal union negotiator for the Service Employees International Union, which was in the midst of a strike against the state's horse-racing tracks. However, the behind-the-scenes drama pitted Korshak against Marjorie Everett, the owner of Hollywood Park and a long-time Korshak nemesis. Korshak had formerly represented the Hollywood Park management as the chief labor relations negotiator until Everett bought the track in 1973; then he started working for the union.

Everett's father was Ben Lindheimer, the overlord of Chicago's racetracks. Korshak had been Lindheimer's personal attorney and chief negotiator for years. When Lindheimer died in 1960, his daughter assumed control of his racing empire and released Korshak.

"From his deathbed, Ben Lindheimer hired Sidney Korshak to head off a threatened strike at Washington Park [one of Lindheimer's tracks]," said one report. "That time Korshak failed, and the mutuel clerks at Washington walked out the night Lindheimer died. His daughter . . . blamed her father's death on Korshak's failure and fired him when she got control of the tracks."[1]

In 1970, Everett was bought out by Philip Levin, a wealthy real estate investor from New Jersey. Before buying Everett's racetracks, Levin—an associate of imprisoned New Jersey mobster Angelo DeCarlo, who was later pardoned by President Nixon—attempted a 1967 takeover at MGM but failed. Levin had been the studio's largest stockholder. The following year, he took his $22 million investment out of MGM and put it in Gulf & Western. G & W chairman Charles Bluhdorn then named Levin as president of the G & W real estate company. Among Levin's first purchases were Everett's two Chicago racetracks, which he merged with the Madison Square Garden Corporation, another G & W subsidiary. After that, Levin reappointed Korshak as counsel.

Marjorie Everett was given a long-term contract to remain as the executive director of the tracks. But early in the contract period she was pushed out by Levin, after complaining about Levin's purchase of nine percent of Parvin-Dohrmann stock and his involvement in Acapulco Towers, two deals in which Korshak was a party.

Through a private detective, Everett discovered that Levin's real estate company—which had been renamed Transnation—had been involved in the purchase of Acapulco Towers. The subsequent federal investigation of Acapulco Towers led to the arrest of mobster Meyer Lansky, who had been hiding out there, forcing him to flee to Israel. But Israel refused to provide him permanent asylum because of his criminal background, forcing him eventually to return to the United States, where he was apprehended. It was Korshak who had persuaded Levin initially to buy into Acapulco Towers as a private investor, and then Korshak advised him to buy it outright for Gulf & Western.

In 1971, Levin testified before the Illinois Liquor Control Commission about a decision he had made to contribute $100,000 to some Republican candidates for office, based on advice he received from Korshak about who should receive the money and how it should be delivered. Levin wrote nine checks, totalling $100,000, taking the money from several of his companies, such as Western Concessions, the Arlington Park Jockey Club, and the Washington Park Jockey Club, among others.[2]

Levin died later that year but not before Korshak personally engineered a $16 million loan for Levin from the Teamsters Central States Pension Fund for a Transnation construction project—which was also owned by G & W's Madison Square Garden Corporation—near O'Hare International Airport in Chicago. "Gulf & Western officials acknowledged . . . ," it was reported, "that Korshak had received a $150,000 finder's fee from Transnation for arranging the pension fund loan. But that fee, the Gulf & Western officials said, was apparently not recorded by Transnation."[3]

While the May 1979 strike negotiations between the service workers' union and California's racetrack management continued, Korshak, in a rare loss of cool, threatened to shut the track down. But after other unions crossed the Korshak-inspired picket line, Hollywood Park remained opened. Interestingly, at the time of the strike, Everett and Hollywood Park were in the midst of discussions for a possible takeover of the racetrack by Madison Square Garden Corporation, which was then being run by former MCA executive Sonny Werblin.

Suddenly, seemingly out of nowhere, Governor Jerry Brown stepped in and tried to shut Hollywood Park down, claiming that it posed a safety hazard. The California racing board, which heard the request, turned the governor down, even after its chairman received several telephone calls from Brown.

"I think he [Brown] was under tremendous pressure from Sidney Korshak as to the conduct of it," Marjorie Everett told NBC reporter Brian Ross.

"Governor Brown was under pressure?"

"Yes," she replied, "possibly disturbed but under tremendous pressure."

"Do you see the hand of Sidney Korshak in all of this . . . ?"

"Not only do I see the hand, I see the total image of Sidney Korshak."[4]

Charles Chatfield, the chairman of the California Horse Racing Board, told Ross, "We heard from both sides that Mr. Korshak was involved. . . . [H]e was the man behind the scenes directing the negotiations."[5]

The strike ended soon after Korshak took himself out of the negotiations.

That same month, Korshak was a topic of discussion among Teamsters insurance man Allen Dorfman, Mafia capo Joseph Lombardo, syndicate executioner Tony Spilotro, and two other associates; the exchange was secretly taped by the FBI. Dorfman was discussing the problems they were having with West Coast Teamsters leader Andy Anderson.* "You know, an' he's as absolutely an eighteen-carat cunt, but he belongs lock, stock, and barrel to Sidney."

"All right," Lombardo replied.

"That I can tell ya."

"How old is Sidney?"

"Ah, Sidney is 70. . . ."

"Sidney Korshak. Well, if Sidney dies, who's got Andy Anderson? Nobody?"

"Nobody," Dorfman replied. "Nobody. He belongs to him lock, stock, and barrel."[6]

Perhaps the worst humiliation for Korshak and Governor Brown came in mid-July when cartoonist Garry Trudeau did a satirical series on their association in his *Doonesbury* comic strip. Several California

---

*Andy Anderson was also the president of Teamsters Local 986, Los Angeles's largest Teamsters local, which is heavily involved in the entertainment industry.

newspapers, including *The Los Angeles Times,* refused to run Trudeau's work because they thought its contents were "unsubstantiated and possibly defamatory." Also referred to in the series was Lew Wasserman. In one of the strips, the Brown character said, "Okay, so I may have run into him [Korshak] a few times at Lew Wasserman's parties. . . . Lew Wasserman. He's a movie mogul. He has to deal with Korshak to get his movies made."[7]

Brown, who was actively challenging Jimmy Carter's reelection bid for president, shrugged the whole matter off, saying that he was "flattered" by Trudeau's attention, even though the series was "false and libelous." Unfortunately, Korshak's and Wasserman's reactions were not recorded.

In late July, Korshak associate Delbert Coleman and casino manager Ed Torres bid $105 million for the Aladdin hotel/casino in Las Vegas. Both had earlier been investigated by the SEC, along with Korshak, for their roles in the Parvin-Dohrmann affair. At the time of the Coleman-Torres offer, law-enforcement officials had been threatening to shut down the Aladdin after it was proven that Detroit mobsters had taken hidden control of the casino. Simultaneously, the U.S. Strike Force Against Organized Crime began looking into allegations of hidden mob interests at the Riviera. The targets of the investigation were Korshak, Coleman, and Torres, who had run the Riviera until 1978. Federal investigators believed that the Riviera was controlled by the Chicago Mafia, with Korshak acting as its conduit. Other casinos being looked into were the Dunes, the Fremont, the Stardust, and the Tropicana.

Back in California, Korshak's old friend from Chicago, Paul Ziffren, and his brother, Lester—the founders of Ziffren and Ziffren in Beverly Hills—had a serious split with their attorney/sons, who were also working in the family business, forcing the firm to dissolve. Paul Ziffren found a new home at Gibson, Dunn and Crutcher when senior partner William French Smith, Ronald Reagan's personal attorney, invited Ziffren* into the Los Angeles firm.

"Paul and I used to be on the political debating circuit together," Smith told *The Los Angeles Times.* "This goes back to the Eisenhower campaigns. We debated on radio, on TV, all around. It was during that period I developed a high respect for his talents."[8]

---

*Simultaneously, Ziffren and travel company chairman Peter V. Ueberroth were named by the U.S. Olympic Committee as permanent chairman and president–general manager, respectively, of the Los Angeles Olympic Organizing Committee for the 1984 Olympic Games.

CHAPTER THIRTY-FIVE

In March 1979, Nevada senator Paul Laxalt formed the Reagan for President Committee, saying that Ronald Reagan "is the man who pioneered the concept of putting responsible restraints on government —an idea whose time has come today with the public's resistance to excessive taxation, irresponsible spending, and oppressive regulation of our lives.

"We pledge our support and commit our efforts to Governor Reagan because we believe he is the most able man in America today to inspire our people, to deal with problems and not shrink before them, and to restore the United States to a respected role in the affairs of the world."

Financially, Reagan was in good shape. He was worth over $4 million and was making nearly $500,000 a year from his lectures, charging as much as $10,000 per booking, and radio and newspaper commentaries. To provide additional income during the campaign, Reagan sold off nearly $234,000 in stocks.

Jules Stein had also helped Reagan to obtain a tax shelter for his growing fortune while Reagan was still the governor of California. Stein introduced Reagan to Oppenheimer Industries, Inc., a little-known, Kansas City–based land and cattle-breeding company run by Stein's stepson, Harold L. Oppenheimer, a retired brigadier general in the

Marine Corps. The firm was owned by Stein, his wife, and his stepson, and catered to wealthy investors, like Reagan, who were seeking to shelter their money.

All Reagan had ever said about the transaction was that he had invested $10,000 in cattle on a ranch in Montana. "I knew this guy who does this, bought a herd of bulls," he said. "What do you do with them? They're out on lease for breeding. . . . I made a little money."

But as a result of the Stein-orchestrated shelter, Reagan paid no state income tax in 1970, nor had he paid virtually any state income taxes from 1966 to 1969. This unsettling fact was not disclosed voluntarily by Reagan. Throughout the late 1960s, Reagan had repeatedly refused to make public his tax returns, insisting that it was a private matter even though he had become a public official. The closest he came to a disclosure occurred in April 1968, when he stated at a press conference, "I just mailed out my own tax return last night, and I am prepared to say 'Ouch' as loud as anyone."

However, in 1970, an inquiry by *The Sacramento Bee* revealed that Governor Reagan had paid an average of only $1,000 per year in state taxes from 1966 to 1969, on annual earnings of more than $50,000, which did not include the separate capital gains taxes paid on the earlier sale of his ranch.

The disclosure created an enormous political flap in California. When Reagan was asked about his taxes, he claimed that he could not recall how much he paid. "I don't know what my tax status was," he said at another press conference. But, confronted with the *Bee* report, Reagan reacted angrily, calling it an "invasion of privacy" based on information that had been "illegally" obtained. When reporters continued to press Reagan for details, an aide instead explained that "he had paid no taxes because of business reverses on his investments."*

On November 13, 1979, at the New York Hilton Hotel—just ten days after the American hostages were taken in Iran—Reagan announced he was going to seek the Republican nomination for president. During his speech, Reagan said, "In recent months leaders in our government have told us that we the people have lost confidence in ourselves; that we must regain our spirit and our will to achieve our national goals. Well, it is true there is a lack of confidence, an unease with things the way they are.

---

*In 1974, when Reagan was again being considered as a likely future presidential candidate, his attorney, William French Smith, was asked by reporters to provide additional data on Reagan's taxes and real estate deals, but Smith declined to cooperate. "We'll worry about that when he becomes president," Smith replied.

"But the confidence we have lost is confidence in our government's policies. Our unease can almost be called bewilderment at how our defense strength has deteriorated. . . .

"I believe this nation hungers for a spiritual revival; hungers once again to see honor placed above political expediency; to see government once again the protector of our liberties, not the distributor of gifts and privileges. Government should uphold and not undermine those institutions which are custodians of the very values upon which civilization is founded—religion, education, and, above all, the family. Government cannot be clergyman, teacher, and parent. It is our servant, beholden to us. . . .

"I believe that you and I together can keep this rendezvous with destiny."

The overall chairman of Reagan's presidential campaign was William Casey, the head of the SEC under President Nixon. An intelligence officer during World War II, Casey had been founder, general counsel, and member of the board of directors of Multiponics, an agribusiness firm. Originally called Ivanhoe Associates, Inc., the company was created for the purpose of industrializing scientific farming and owned 44,000 acres of farm land in Mississippi, Arkansas, Louisiana, and Florida. By midsummer 1970, the company had suffered huge financial losses. Doing little more than changing the company's name to Multiponics, the corporation filed for bankruptcy in February 1971—owing $20.6 million to creditors, including Bernard Cornfeld, the head of Investors Overseas Services and an associate of international swindler Robert Vesco.*

One of Casey's partners in Multiponics was Carl Biehl, an associate of underworld figures in the Carlos Marcello crime family in New Orleans who had been attempting to penetrate waterfront operations on the Gulf Coast. Information on Biehl was based upon federal wiretaps in Washington and New Orleans which showed that Biehl had been working with the underworld since the early 1950s.

When revelations about Biehl and other Multiponics improprieties surfaced, Casey claimed that his relationship with the firm was from a distance. However, during the Multiponics bankruptcy hearing in New Orleans on September 15, 1975, Casey testified, "I think the record will

---

*During his tenure at the SEC, Casey had discussed a commission suit against Vesco with former attorney general John Mitchell, who was concerned about the political embarrassment of a $200,000 cash contribution Vesco had made to Nixon's reelection campaign. Casey made this admission during his testimony at Mitchell's Watergate trial.

show that I had a great deal to say and a fair amount of influence in the basic decisions that the directors made."[1]

Repeatedly accused of having questionable business ethics, Casey was particularly attacked by Senator William Proxmire in 1971. "Mr. Casey," Proxmire charged, "has cut corners when he considered it to be necessary to business profit. He has wheeled and dealed his way into a personal fortune, sometimes at the expense of his clients. . . . And he has made less than a complete and accurate disclosure of his activities to Congress."

In another case, Casey had represented SCA Services, a New Jersey–based waste disposal concern, in 1977 in an unsuccessful effort to head off an SEC action against SCA and some of its top officers. Although SEC attorneys proceeded with the complaint—which alleged the diversion of some $4 million in company funds for personal use by its officials—Casey negotiated a settlement of the case in which SCA neither admitted nor denied the charges.

Later, a government informant told congressional investigators that SCA had "been involved with organized crime in the garbage business and now they're moving into hazardous waste." New Jersey State Police intelligence had identified at least three recent SCA employees as having "strong, deep-rooted connections to organized crime." Thomas C. Viola, the president of SCA, had been forced out of the company by the SEC because of his own links to the underworld. Crescent Roselle, the manager of Waste Disposal, Inc.—which was taken over by SCA in 1973—had been personally involved with numerous Mafia figures and was later found murdered.[2]

Casey's assistant during the Reagan campaign was Max Hugel, an executive vice-president of the Centronics Data Computer Corporation of Hudson, New Hampshire. A portion of Centronics was owned until 1974 by Caesar's World, the casino gambling company, then under federal investigation for alleged hidden mob ownership, when Hugel's previous firm, Brother International Corporation, bought Caesar's World's holdings in Centronics. Also Centronics had had a consultancy relationship with mobster Moe Dalitz and his Las Vegas casinos. Hugel had also been involved in a pattern of improper or illegal stock market practices intended to boost the stock of the New York wholesale firm he had headed in the mid-1970s. He was alleged to have threatened to kill a former business associate and told another that he might be found "hanging by the balls."[3]

Hugel, who said that he had known Casey for twenty years, was in charge of organizing "ethnic, nationalities, occupational, religious, and other voting groups" for Reagan.

Reagan's principal competition during the Republican caucuses and primaries in 1980 was former CIA director George Bush. Although Bush spent over a month in Iowa, campaigning for the state caucuses, he edged Reagan by a mere 2.1 percentage points. Reagan had spent less than forty-eight hours there, concentrating on the New Hampshire primary instead—where he soundly defeated Bush by a two-to-one margin. Reagan continued to clean up in the primaries. By the time of the Republican National Convention, Reagan knew that he had the nomination in hand. The only mystery was the person whom Reagan would select as his running mate.

One of the names on the short list of politicians being considered was Paul Laxalt. The public explanation of why Laxalt was not chosen was that he, like Reagan, came from the West and, on top of that, Nevada was an electorally insignificant state, ranking forty-third in population and with only four electoral votes.

However, Reagan aide Jude Wanniski told a different story. "I was sitting having a beer at the Pontchartrain Hotel in Detroit [during the 1980 Republican convention]," Wanniski said, "and Chic Hecht, who is now the junior senator from Nevada but was then just a delegate, said, 'My God, I just heard from somebody sitting next to me that Paul Laxalt was about to be indicted by a federal grand jury.' And I said, 'Aw, come on, Chic, that's going on here because Reagan is picking his running mate.' "

Wanniski explained that "during the two or three super-heated days of the convention . . . the various candidates, who were trying to be running mates, were spreading rumors about each other. And Laxalt was easy to slam because he's from Nevada. No presidential nominee has ever picked a Nevada person because of the baggage you acquire when you pick one. Everyone in the whole world, the whole press corps, will swarm all over Nevada, writing about the Mafia."[4]

Whether Reagan would have chosen Laxalt is uncertain, but such talk about mob ties surely could not have helped the senator's chances. Laxalt was not in attendance at the Republican convention when George Bush was selected as Reagan's vice-presidential candidate. But even if the national GOP high command was unwilling to accept a divorced, former casino operator from Nevada as Reagan's running mate, the citizens of Nevada saw no problem with Laxalt's background.

Laxalt's 1980 campaign against Mary Gojack, a Las Vegas businesswoman whom he defeated handily with fifty-nine percent of the vote, was nothing less than a Laxalt love feast. The disappointed Gojack said, "The campaign against Paul involved a package of criticism that included taking big casino contributions and the fact that he had missed about a year's worth of votes—because he had been working on Reagan's campaign and at the same time was one of the highest earners on the speaking circuit. The gist of all of that was that he had really neglected the majority of Nevadans. There was an over-representation on his part of special casino interests here in Nevada.

"The only people who really cared when I raised these issues were a minority of intellectuals and more thoughtful newspaper editors. Most people in Nevada think that Paul is a nice guy, that he couldn't do anything wrong, and that outsiders are constantly trying to pick on him."[5]

Laxalt was easily returned to Washington in 1980 by the people of Nevada, who had agreed with his campaign slogan, "He's one of us." During the campaign, Laxalt raised a total of $1,126,826, outspending Gojack by nearly four to one. In addition to the tens of thousands contributed by legal casino operators, known associates of organized crime contributed nearly $50,000 to Laxalt's two senatorial campaigns. The most controversial of these were two separate $1,000 contributions from reputed mobster Moe Dalitz, according to Laxalt's own campaign records filed with the Federal Elections Commission.

Laxalt apparently gave no thought to returning any of these questionable contributions—as did some politicians like Texas wheeler-dealer John Connally, in his unsuccessful bid for the 1980 Republican presidential nomination. Connally received a $1,000 contribution from Dalitz, but returned it, "for reasons I'm sure can be understood," a Connally spokesman said.[6]

"Moe Dalitz is a friend of mine," Laxalt told *The New York Times Magazine.* "I'm not going to say to him now, 'Get lost, you're too hot.' I don't play it that way."

On August 27, 1980, Reagan kicked off his fall campaign by delivering a speech in Columbus, Ohio, before the Ohio Conference of Teamsters, which was run by Jackie Presser, an international vice-president of the union and the head of the Ohio Conference. Before his address, Reagan met in private for forty-five minutes with Presser and Roy Williams, another Teamsters vice-president.

That same morning, the wire services, newspapers, radio, and television carried stories about Williams's testimony before a Senate subcommittee the previous day, reporting that he had taken the Fifth Amendment twenty-three times when asked about his personal and financial dealings with top organized crime figures. Among the mobsters with whom Williams had been associated was New Orleans underworld boss Carlos Marcello, who had recently boasted, "We own the Teamsters," according to a tape recording made in the course of the FBI's BRILAB (bribery and labor racketeering) investigation.

Williams had been twice indicted for embezzlement of union funds. He was acquitted in the first trial after a key witness was found shotgunned to death; the second indictment in 1972 was dismissed by a federal judge who cited "procedural errors" during the investigation. In early 1974—in the midst of the sweetheart arrangement between the Teamsters and the Nixon White House—Williams was indicted for falsifying union records. But that charge, too, was aborted by the government.

Just a few weeks before Williams's testimony, a former Mafia figure turned government witness, Jimmy Fratianno of Los Angeles, stated before a federal grand jury that Presser had told him that he took his orders from James Licavoli, the boss of the Cleveland underworld. Presser, who started out as an organizer for the Culinary Workers Union, was the son of convicted labor racketeer William Presser—who was a close associate of Moe Dalitz, Allen Dorfman, and Sidney Korshak, all of whom Jackie Presser was now associated with.

Soon after Reagan's meeting with Presser and Williams, the Teamsters Union announced their support of Reagan's candidacy for president—after Presser delivered a passionate speech on Reagan's behalf before the union's general executive board. The Teamsters were the only major union to endorse Reagan.*

On Labor Day 1980, Reagan delivered another speech in Jersey City, New Jersey. Dressed in white shirtsleeves and with the Statue of Liberty casting a dramatic background, Reagan accused Carter of "betraying" American workers. "A recession is when your neighbor loses his job," Reagan said. "A depression is when you lose yours. Recovery is when Jimmy Carter loses his."

The Jersey City extravaganza was engineered by Raymond J. Donovan, the executive vice-president of the Schiavone Construction Company of Secaucus, New Jersey, who had been brought into the Reagan

---

*The Maritime Workers Union and the Air Traffic Controllers were two smaller unions endorsing Reagan for president.

campaign by Reagan's attorney, William French Smith. Donovan had also raised $200,000 at a dinner for Reagan. The featured entertainer at Donovan's dinner was Frank Sinatra. Through all of his fund-raising efforts, Donovan made $600,000 for the Reagan campaign.

The Carter reelection campaign was having its troubles. A Carter administration official told reporter Elizabeth Drew, "The fund-raising structure is not unlike the Mafia. If you want to do business in that area, there is one person you have to deal with [Lew Wasserman]." According to Drew's source, Wasserman "put Carter in a box. . . . If Wasserman doesn't return your phone calls, you can't do business in Los Angeles. Wasserman will put you through Chinese water torture before he'll raise money for you, and he won't let anyone else do it."[7] Also, it had been reported that Carter had had a falling out with Wasserman, who many suspected was really supporting Reagan.

Following his stunning victory, Reagan made his first trip to Washington on November 18. His first official stop—accompanied by Vice-President–elect George Bush—was at the headquarters of the International Brotherhood of Teamsters, where he attended a closed meeting of the union's executive board, which included the president, Frank Fitzsimmons, and vice-presidents Andy Anderson, Jackie Presser, and Roy Williams. According to reports of the meeting, Reagan invited the Teamsters high command to help him select his secretary of labor and other top administration officials.

A few weeks later, Reagan and Edwin Meese, the chief of the president-elect's staff, appointed Presser as a "senior economic adviser" to the transition team. An eighth-grade dropout who was then making over $350,000 a year as a union official, Presser boasted that he would screen potential appointees to "the Labor Department, Treasury, and a few other independent agencies." Those departments would have jurisdiction in any future investigations of the Teamsters Union.

Senator Sam Nunn of Georgia warned that the Presser appointment raised "serious questions of conflict of interest." He added, "The appointment of Mr. Presser . . . raises several significant questions which should be addressed at the highest levels of the incoming administration. . . . Is it a violation of fundamental principles of government ethics for Mr. Presser to help organize the very department that has brought suit against him?"

At the time, Presser and other former trustees of the union's Central States Pension Fund were targets of several civil suits brought by the Labor Department, seeking reimbursement to the fund of $120 million in illegal loans made to Las Vegas casinos and to organized crime figures and their associates. The trustees had been forced to resign in 1976 because of those loans.

Not long before Presser's appointment to the Reagan team, New Jersey State Police officers testified before the state's Commission of Investigations that Presser—who at that point had never been indicted, despite dozens of allegations of wrongdoing—was a contact for underworld bosses seeking loans from the union's pension funds.

When asked at a press conference about accusations that Presser had ties to organized crime, President-elect Reagan replied that he had not been informed of any such charges. "If that's true," he said, "that will be investigated and brought out." Later, Meese contradicted his boss, saying that Presser *had* been investigated prior to his appointment but that the charges of mob connections had been found to be "mostly innuendo."

While the controversy over Presser continued, Reagan nominated Ray Donovan as secretary of labor. According to a report in *The New York Times,* Meese was told by Presser in December 1980 that the Teamsters did not support Donovan and wanted Betty Murphy, a former chairwoman of the National Labor Relations Board, instead. After Meese conveyed that news to his boss, *The Times* reported, Reagan called Teamsters president Frank Fitzsimmons for verification. When the ailing Fitzsimmons said that Murphy was indeed the union's choice, Reagan decided to withdraw Donovan's nomination. No formal announcement was ever made, however, and Donovan's name went to the U.S. Senate for confirmation.[8]

What happened? According to a top Teamsters official, the union's support of Murphy was a charade, and *The Times* story the result of a deliberate leak. "After the Presser thing with the transition team," he explained, "there was a need to show that Reagan wasn't just rolling over for us. . . . Donovan was our man all the way. Betty Murphy was just the smokescreen."

Given Donovan's past dealings with the Teamsters, their support of him was no surprise. During his confirmation hearings, Donovan was accused of having made payoffs to a New York Teamsters official on behalf of his construction company. He was also accused of associating with top Teamsters racketeers like Salvatore Briguglio of Teamsters Local 560 in Union City, New Jersey. Briguglio—who, according to the government, was the killer of Jimmy Hoffa in 1975—had been murdered in 1978. Donovan was also charged with associating with William Masselli, a top Mafia leader in New York.

An FBI memorandum detailing Donovan's associations with organized crime figures and Teamsters toughs was hand-delivered to Reagan's transition team the day before Donovan's confirmation hearings began. It was addressed to Fred Fielding, Reagan's conflicts-of-interest adviser. The memorandum said that numerous charges against Donovan had been "corroborated by independent interviews of confidential sources." Also, Fielding was notified of a tape recording linking Donovan to organized crime figures. The FBI asked Fielding, "Do you want us to do any more?" Fielding said, "Not at this time."[9]

The information on Donovan's ties to the underworld was then concealed from the Senate panel investigating Donovan.

Other Reagan appointments included William French Smith as attorney general and William Casey as director of the Central Intelligence Agency. Casey later appointed his assistant during the presidential campaign, Max Hugel, as his deputy director of operations, which conducted sensitive covert actions and clandestine intelligence-gathering abroad.

Reagan also announced that he was going to appoint William E. McCann, a New Jersey insurance executive and a friend of Casey's, to become the ambassador to Ireland. The McCann confirmation hearings were held up because of the discovery of McCann's ties to organized crime, which eventually forced the White House to reluctantly withdraw the nomination. Specifically, McCann—who had co-chaired the $200,000 Reagan fund-raiser with Ray Donovan during the presidential campaign—had been an associate of convicted stock fraud and insurance swindler Louis Ostrer, who had been indicted with mob bosses Santos Trafficante of Miami and Tony Accardo of Chicago for bilking the health and welfare fund of the Laborers Union. McCann's firm, Foundation Life Insurance Company, was also being investigated by the New York State Insurance Commission for selling insurance without a license to Teamsters Local 295 in New York City.

Senator Paul Laxalt also had some of his people appointed to top administration posts. One was Reese Taylor, Jr., who was appointed chairman of the Interstate Commerce Commission. Common Cause, the citizens' lobbying group, charged that Taylor had been handpicked for the job by the Teamsters Union because of his opposition to the proposed deregulation of the trucking industry, which would hurt the organizing abilities of the Teamsters. A former law partner of both William French Smith and Paul Laxalt at different periods during his legal career, Taylor was helped in his successful confirmation bid by Nevada senator Howard Cannon—who was the earlier target of Teamsters bribe offers from Roy Williams and Allen Dorfman for his assistance in blocking total deregulation. Cannon's watered-down version did finally pass. Williams, Dorfman, and Chicago Mafia figure Joseph Lombardo were later indicted for their attempts to bribe Cannon, who was not indicted.

Another appointment brought about by Laxalt was that of James Watt as the secretary of the interior. Watt was the head of a "public interest" law firm, the Mountain States Legal Foundation. An anti-environmentalist group, Mountain States received major financial contributions from such Nevada gambling interests as Harrah's, Inc.; Bally Distributing Company; Harvey's Wagon Wheel; the Sahara Nevada Corporation; and the Union Plaza hotel/casino. Three of the lawyers in Watt's firm represented the Riviera; the Dunes hotel/casinos; the Horseshoe club/casino; the Pioneer Club; the Summa Corporation; Del E. Webb; Caesar's World; Circus-Circus; and Slots-a-Fun, Inc. Several of these businesses were connected to organized crime.

Perhaps the biggest party for Ronald Reagan's victory before his inaugural was held on December 12, 1980. The place was Rancho Mirage near Palm Springs, California, at the desert home of Frank Sinatra. The official occasion was Sinatra's sixty-fifth-birthday celebration. In attendance were two hundred guests, who included Walter Annenberg,* other members of Reagan's Kitchen Cabinet, and an array of Hollywood luminaries. Although the Reagans had been invited but could not attend, the president-elect's attorney general–designate, William French Smith, did attend. Smith—who had been named as attorney general the day before the affair—had known Sinatra since 1970 after being introduced to him by Reagan Kitchen Cabinet member Holmes Tuttle.

At the time of the party, Sinatra was still being investigated by a federal grand jury in New York which was trying to determine whether Sinatra was involved in the skimming operation at the Westchester Premier Theater during his appearances there in April and September 1976 and in May 1977. By the end of 1980, eight people had been convicted for their involvement in the Westchester scheme. Sinatra himself was not indicted.

Later Sinatra renewed his efforts to regain his gambling license from the Nevada Gaming Commission. He was hoping to "participate in

---

*Walter Annenberg's wife, Leonore Annenberg, was later appointed as chief of protocol at the Reagan White House. Mrs. Annenberg had been previously married to Beldon Katleman, the owner of El Rancho Vegas, and former bootlegger Lewis Rosentiel, the head of Schenley Industries. She and her third husband, Walter Annenberg—the owner of the *Daily Racing Form, Seventeen,* and *TV Guide*—were close friends of the Korshaks'.

management" of Caesar's World, Inc., in Las Vegas. Previously, the New Jersey Casino Control Board had rejected Caesar's admission into Atlantic City because its president was known to be associated with top organized crime figures. As a reference for his application in Nevada, Sinatra—who was organizing the entertainment for the new president's inaugural gala—used Reagan's name.

Later, in his glowing letter of recommendation on Sinatra's behalf addressed to the Nevada Gaming Commission, Reagan described his friend as "an honorable person, completely honest and loyal." When asked by a reporter about Sinatra's ties to the underworld, Reagan simply replied, "Yeah, I know. We've heard those things about Frank for years, and we just hope none of them are true." Sinatra* was granted his "key employee" license by the gaming commission.

Smith had the same reaction when the press questioned his judgment in attending the Sinatra party, adding that he was "totally unaware" of Sinatra's associations to the underworld. *New York Times* columnist William Safire chided Smith, writing, "[T]he involvement of the designee for attorney general in the rehabilitation of the reputation of a man obviously proud to be close to notorious hoodlums is the first deliberate affront to propriety of the Reagan administration."

Despite the uproar over Smith's association with Sinatra, Safire and the rest of the media—with the exception of *Washington Post* columnist Maxine Cheshire—missed the fact that a jubilant Sidney Korshak was also present at the party. A Smith aide said that if his boss talked to Korshak, "it was purely accidental."[10]

---

*Reagan later awarded Sinatra and Walter Annenberg with Presidential Medals of Freedom and appointed Sinatra to serve on the sixteen-member President's Commission on Arts and Humanities. Of Sinatra, Reagan said, "His love of country, his generosity for those less fortunate, his distinctive art . . . and his winning and compassionate persona make him one of our most remarkable and distinguished Americans . . . and one who truly did it his way."

EPILOGUE

LEW WASSERMAN

"Hollywood" is no longer in Hollywood. Few movies are now made there; few stars live in Hollywood Hills. The corner of Hollywood and Vine is just another rundown commercial area. There is little magic in the air, and the local glitter is mostly supplied by the motorcycles that line Hollywood Boulevard and the punk rockers who hang out in front of cheap T-shirt shops. With the exception of Paramount, most of the big movie and television studios—including Universal, Columbia, Warner Brothers, NBC, and Disney Studios—have moved from Hollywood to the San Fernando Valley, where, just on the edge of the valley, the MCA Black Tower remains the symbol of the awesome strength and power of the new Hollywood.

MCA's lobby is unglamorous, cold, and sparse. A uniformed guard, sitting at a large desk, is responsible for checking visitors in and out of the building and generally keeping the peace. To his right is a bronze bust of Jules Stein and beyond that several elevators. On the top floor, where the MCA high command works, "corridors have disappeared or widened into lushly carpeted indoor avenues, deep and soft enough to turn an ankle, so hushed that no one would hear [a] scream," wrote author Saul David. "The furnishings here are European antiques of immense value and astonishing discomfort. Everything is the wrong height—the great desks and ornate tables meant to serve people who either stood or perched on stools. There are wonderful cranky cabinets with doors, tall chests and short chests and doubled chests with twinkling rows of little drawers and pigeonholes. . . . Wasserman's office was large but not especially ornate—tending to the austere in shades of gray, black, and white, like Wasserman himself."[1]

Toward the end of the Carter administration, MCA and Lew Wasserman were seething after its new cable television network, named Premier—a consortium of Hollywood studios, including MCA-Universal, Twentieth Century–Fox, Columbia Pictures, and Paramount—was closed down, after an injunction was filed against it by the Carter Justice Department, less than four months after the joint venture was announced. With MCA still haunted by its nemeses, Antitrust Division attorneys charged that the project was "anticompetitive" and that it would be engaging in price-fixing and group boycotting. Premier had promised subscribers that it would offer motion pictures from its participating studios at least nine months before the same films would be offered to Home Box Office, Inc., or Showtime Entertainment—which were taking in twenty to thirty percent of the pay-TV subscription fees for distribution while the studios were getting only about twenty percent versus the forty-five percent they received from the box office. The studios stood to make an additional $450 million a year in the long term had Premier gone into operation. Those companies involved in Premier lost over $20 million as a result of the antitrust action while profits in cable television had jumped from $192 million in 1978 to $400 million in 1979.

More bad news came for MCA in mid-1980, when the Screen Actors Guild struck against the film industry over demands for actors' participation in revenues from cable television. The thirteen-week strike caused MCA-Universal's lucrative television programs to be postponed or cancelled. MCA lost millions of dollars in television revenues as a consequence of the strike. However, a Directors Guild of America strike was averted when Wasserman was called in by both the directors and the producers to mediate a settlement.*

Soon after becoming president, Ronald Reagan began moving toward deregulating the communications industry, proposing to strip the

---

*In 1981, Wasserman also intervened in the midst of a thirteen-week strike of the Writers Guild (formerly the Screen Writers Guild) and managed to negotiate a settlement between the screenwriters and the producers.

Federal Communications Commission of much of its authority. "Under Reagan era 'deregulation' of radio and television," wrote author Ronnie Dugger, "existing stations are to be protected from challenge by new competitors, and people are going to have to watch more and more commercials as the price for seeing and hearing the programs they like. [Mark Fowler,] Reagan's chairman of the Federal Communications Commission (FCC), is proposing to give present TV station owners permanent title to their licensed access to the publicly owned airways, immune from competitive challenge, and to remove limits on how many radio and TV stations one company can own. On the other hand, the Reaganized FCC is opening some new communications technologies [like cable television] to free competition."[2]

That same year, MCA, Paramount, and Time, Inc., bought a one-third interest in the USA Network, another part of the cable-TV broadcasting system. And later, MCA-Universal negotiated a deal with HBO, whereby HBO was required by contract to buy all of Universal's motion pictures.* There were no antitrust problems, and, under Reagan, none were anticipated.

Deeply affected by the antitrust problems experienced by MCA and General Electric, Reagan told *Business Week* in 1980, "We don't want to give up our protection against monopoly at home, but why can't we make it possible for American concerns to compete on the world market and not have it called collusion or restraint of trade?" Attorney General William French Smith chimed in, "Bigness in business does not necessarily mean badness. . . . The disappearance of some should not be taken as indisputable proof that something is amiss in an industry." To further the cause, one of the most outspoken critics of U.S. antitrust laws, William Baxter, a former law professor at Stanford, was appointed as head of the Justice Department's Antitrust Division. With the signals clear and a new Republican majority in the U.S. Senate, Republican senator Strom Thurmond, the new chairman of the Senate Judiciary Committee, completely abolished its once-effective antitrust subcommittee.

The Reagan Justice Department also began considering challenging the 1948 Supreme Court "divorcement" decision in the Paramount case, which forced the studios to divorce themselves of their theatre chains. Upon hearing the news, studio heads in Hollywood were described in published reports as being "enthusiastic." Baxter, who spearheaded the campaign, said that the review of the decisions made by the

---

*In March 1984, MCA negotiated six-year, nonexclusive contracts with HBO/Cinemax and Showtime–The Movie Channel.

Supreme Court against the major film companies had resulted from "the age, significance, and complexity of those judgments, their apparent success in destroying the cartel to which they were originally addressed, and the many profound changes in the motion picture industry since the judgments were entered." Just the previous year, a federal court in New York had denied a motion to vacate the decrees against the studios.

On Tuesday, April 28, 1981, at 5:00 P.M., eighty-five-year-old Jules Stein was rushed to UCLA Medical Center—where he had given millions of dollars for the internationally renowned institute to prevent blindness that bore his name—suffering from what was thought to be a badly inflamed gall bladder. At about midnight, while receiving treatment, Stein suffered a massive heart attack and was pronounced dead at 12:20 A.M. on April 29.

Nearly six hundred people, including some of the biggest names in show business, attended a celebration of Stein's incredible life on the east patio of the Jules Stein Eye Institute on UCLA's campus. Henry Mancini and a twenty-piece band were joined by former Tommy Dorsey singer Helen O'Connell in a tribute to Stein. Among those songs played was Stein's favorite, "Alexander's Ragtime Band."

Grief-stricken, Wasserman described Stein as "a singular being," adding that Stein's death had left him "bereft . . . in ways that defy the power of language to express. He was my mentor, my partner, and my closest friend for more than forty-five years."[3]

Among Stein's seventy-six honorary pallbearers were President Reagan, former American Federation of Musicians boss James Petrillo,* producers Mervyn LeRoy and Hal Wallis, actors Jimmy Stewart and Cary Grant, and talent agent Irving "Swifty" Lazar. Stein's wife, Doris, died in April 1984.

Stein's death had come in the midst of a rare corporate crisis for MCA. During the first quarter of 1981, MCA's operating income dropped by thirty-seven percent, which followed a twenty-two-percent fall in 1980. To deal with the problem, Wasserman and Sidney Sheinberg dramatically cut Universal's film budget by thirty percent, reducing its annual movie production to only a dozen films, compared to twenty-two in 1980. Several disasters at the box office had contributed heavily to the decision. *The Blues Brothers,* starring Dan Aykroyd and John Belushi of NBC's *Saturday Night Live,* skyrocketed over budget, costing the studio over $30 million. Dino de Laurentiis's *Flash Gordon,*

---

*James Petrillo died on October 23, 1984.

which cost nearly $20 million, also bit the dust soon after its release. The only bright spots were *Coal Miner's Daughter,* a film based on the life of country singer Loretta Lynn, and Steve Martin's *The Jerk.* Each had gross receipts in excess of $30 million.

With MCA's stock dropping, there was still little concern about a hostile takeover of the corporation. Wasserman still controlled 8.1 percent of its stock and, as executor of Stein's $150 million estate in the wake of his death, controlled the 15.8 percent owned by Stein. In view of the fact that seventy-five percent of MCA's stockholders still had to approve any takeover bid, Wasserman alone could almost singlehandedly block any unwanted takeover attempt.

MCA's problem, according to corporate analysts, was that it had failed to diversify aggressively, depending too much on its film production, which comprised 84 percent of MCA's profits in 1980. But Wasserman had already realized that and embarked MCA on massive real estate development, which would eventually be separated from MCA's other operations. First, MCA announced that it planned to build a $175 million, 312-acre theme park in Orlando, Florida,* near Disney World and Sea World, which would be a semi-clone of its Universal City tour.† It also planned to build the new $100 million headquarters of Getty Oil in Universal City and a second $65 million, 500-room Sheraton Hotel. The project was to yield MCA an additional $15 million annually for leasing arrangements when it was completed in 1984.

The following year, in August 1982, Universal, Paramount, and Warner Brothers, Inc., nearly purchased a twenty-five-percent interest each in The Movie Channel, a cable-television company valued at $100 million and owned by American Express and Warner Communications, which would retain the remaining twenty-five percent. Although there was hardly a threat of possible antitrust action from the Justice Department, the deal fell through when the studios failed to come to terms among themselves. "You try to get three movie companies to meet for lunch, and you're going to get arguments," said Thomas Wertheimer, an MCA vice-president.[4]

---

*MCA later acquired a $1.7 million option to purchase nearly eleven percent of the Major Realty Corporation, which owned over a thousand acres adjacent to MCA's proposed theme park. Federal and state law enforcement agencies had previously linked Major Realty to top organized crime figures, including Meyer Lansky.

†The MCA theme park project in Orlando suffered a severe setback in May 1985 when Disney World announced that it was planning to build its own studio tour and the Florida legislature killed a bill that would have given MCA $175 million from the Florida Retirement System Pension Fund to help finance construction. MCA accused Disney of lobbying against the measure; Disney denied that it had.

Meantime, MCA resumed its steady growth, with nearly $1.5 billion in assets. Universal-Television led all production companies with seven hours of prime-time programming while Universal Pictures began leasing studio space to outside producers as it raked in twenty percent of the total revenues of Hollywood's 1981 film releases. Universal's hits were *The Four Seasons* and *Bustin' Loose,* along with *Endless Love, An American Werewolf in London,* and *The Great Muppet Caper.*

To everyone's surprise, the box-office smash of the season was Universal's *On Golden Pond,* featuring Henry Fonda, Katharine Hepburn, and Jane Fonda. As the crowning achievement to a long and distinguished career in motion pictures, Henry Fonda won the Academy Award for Best Actor just prior to his death, although the film itself was beaten out for Best Picture by *Chariots of Fire.*

In February 1982, MCA announced that it was selling its Disco-Vision operations, which had cost the corporation nearly $100 million, to Japan's Pioneer Electronics Corporation. Despite all of its research and marketing, MCA had sold only 35,000 video machines. MCA refused to disclose the purchase price, but MCA president Sidney Sheinberg permitted himself to say, "Bargain basement you don't get from MCA." The sale of Disco-Vision ended MCA's biggest corporate nightmare and the company's biggest failure. Earlier, in September 1979, MCA had formed a joint venture with International Business Machines, Inc. (IBM) to build and market video discs. The move was a break from IBM tradition, because it had thrust the company into the consumer market rather than its usual business market. The Dutch-based N. V. Philips Corporation had remained a partner in the enterprise—although MCA had complained that Philips was not producing enough machines while Philips charged that MCA was not delivering on the video discs. In the spring of 1980, MCA and IBM found themselves facing more competition when General Electric and Japan's Victor Company (JVC) introduced their own video-disc products, which were incompatible with Disco-Vision. In the end, despite its investment and because videocassette recorders, particularly the Sony Betamax, were outselling video disc machines, MCA had no choice but to sell.

Getting the Disco-Vision monkey off MCA's back was just part of the good news in 1982–83 as Universal came up with the biggest winner of all, Steven Spielberg's relentlessly charming *E.T. the Extraterrestrial,* which shattered all box-office records, earning almost $3.5 million a day.

In Washington, D.C., the Motion Picture Association of America, still run by Jack Valenti, ran a blitz of Capitol Hill, trying to secure congressional approval for a percentage of the home video rental market for the film industry. The crusade began in February 1984, just one month after the U.S. Supreme Court ruled that home video recording was legal. Hired to lobby the Hill was Senator Paul Laxalt's thirty-year-old daughter, Michelle, who had previously been in the State Department's congressional relations office. Senator Laxalt sat on the Senate Judiciary Committee, which was debating the matter. Michelle Laxalt, who had been placed on staff the previous fall, told *The Washington Post,* "I don't touch Laxalt. That's been my modus operandi as long as I've been in this town."

At the end of 1984, MCA appointed former Republican senator Howard Baker to the MCA board of directors. Baker joined Robert Strauss, the former chairman of the Democratic National Committee, who had earlier been appointed to the board.

Going into the 1985 television season, MCA-Universal had several potential hits on its lineup, including *Miami Vice, Simon & Simon, Airwolf, Murder She Wrote, Knight Rider,* and *Magnum, P.I.*—and mid-season replacements shows such as *The Misfits, The Equalizer, The Insiders, Alfred Hitchcock Presents,* and *Amazing Stories.* In all, the company had eleven hours of prime-time television programming. Also, Universal Pictures was producing more blockbusters like *The Breakfast Club, Back to the Future, Mask, Fletch, Out of Africa,* and *Brazil,* which became a major embarrassment for Sidney Sheinberg.

Terry Gilliam, the director of two Monty Python black comedies, found that the American opening of his film *Brazil,* which played well in Europe, was being postponed by Universal, its U.S. distributor. The problem was the film's ending. In Gilliam's sophisticated and sometimes eerie update of George Orwell's *1984,* the film's central character, Sam Lowry, meets a horrible end. But Sheinberg, who reportedly liked the picture but thought it could be better, refused to distribute it in the U.S. without a happier ending. Gilliam drew the line and told Sheinberg and Universal that the ending "is not negotiable." Under the terms of his contract with Universal, Gilliam gave the studio approval over the final cut. Also, according to the agreement, Gilliam was not permitted to be critical of the studio. Instead, he purchased a full-page ad for $1,400 in *Variety,* asking, "Dear Sid Sheinberg, When are you going to release my film, *Brazil*?" Gilliam then held two unauthorized screenings of the film in Los Angeles. *Brazil* immediately received raves from reviewers and won Best Picture from the Los Angeles Film Critics Association, bringing more pressure on Sheinberg and Universal to relent. Soon after, Sheinberg, who, like Wasserman, loves success, backed off and released *Brazil*—with Gilliam's original ending.*

Toward the end of 1985, MCA had remained a steel monolith in the entertainment industry, untouched by the scandals and corporate shake-ups other studios had experienced. By the end of the year, it had achieved revenues of $2.1 billion and a net income of $150 million. Despite the fact that its stock was selling at least $10 a share below the company's asset value—at 64¾ at one point—no serious takeover bids had threatened the corporation.

The only potential challenge came from the Golden Nugget, Inc., a gambling concern in Las Vegas and Atlantic City owned by forty-two-year-old Stephen A. Wynn.† The Golden Nugget had quietly amassed 2.3 million shares or nearly five percent of MCA stock, valued at $95 million. Under SEC regulations, the purchase of more stock would then require public disclosure of the investment. Wasserman warned that if Wynn and the Golden Nugget did buy any more stock it would be viewed as a hostile act, and that MCA would do "what was necessary" to protect itself. Wynn eventually sold his shares and abandoned his takeover bid. "Since then," according to one report, "MCA has increased its credit line to $1 billion—a war-chest that could be used to block a takeover—and amended its bylaws to reduce the power of dissident shareholders. Sheinberg described these steps as 'anti–unfair takeover' measures.

"He refuses to discuss merger rumors, which include a report that MCA has held talks with RCA. Responding to gossip 'can be a full-time job,' Sheinberg said."[5]

The talk circulating about MCA's possible merger with RCA was more than mere gossip. On October 20, 1985, a month after Wasserman shared center stage with First Lady Nancy Reagan at a star-studded Los Angeles dinner, *New York Times* reporter Geraldine Fabricant wrote: "Now there is evidence that Mr. Wasserman's era is coming to an end. The first indication surfaced last summer with the disclosure that Mr. Wasserman had discussed the possibility of the RCA Corporation acquiring MCA [making it RCA's largest division]. The talks broke off in September, but given Mr. Wasserman's age and the current merger mania, many in Hollywood are guessing that MCA's chairman will soon sell out—even possibly to RCA."

---

*Both Wasserman and Sheinberg refused to be interviewed for this book.
†Wynn had signed Frank Sinatra to an exclusive entertainment contract for the Golden Nugget in November 1982; the two men had done television commercials together promoting the casino. Sinatra also owned two percent of the Golden Nugget's stock.

Fabricant estimated that the purchase price for MCA would be $3.6 billion, based upon MCA's stock alone, then valued at a low $48 a share. She added that just the previous month, communications mogul Ted Turner had bought MGM–United Artists for only $1.6 billion, "the most expensive entertainment industry acquisition to date." By 1988, MCA would make $750 million solely from the syndication of its more recent television series, with another 12,000 episodes of other, older series. Universal Pictures further boasted the second-largest film library in the industry, with over 3,000 motion pictures.

In the wake of the *New York Times* story, the RCA-MCA merger was believed to be not only possible but imminent. But then, on December 11, 1985, after over a month of negotiations, Ronald Reagan's former employer, General Electric, bought RCA for $6.28 billion—the biggest and most expensive non-oil purchase in American history. A member of the RCA board of directors who voted to approve the deal was former attorney general William French Smith.* In a joint statement, the chairmen of the boards of both GE and RCA, John Welch, Jr., and Thorton F. Bradshaw, declared that the merger is an "excellent strategic opportunity for both companies that will help improve America's competitiveness in world markets."

Welch added, "We don't envision any government [antitrust] problems that would stop this in any way." The Justice Department's Antitrust Division approved the purchase on May 21, 1986. Ironically, fifty-two years earlier, U.S. antitrust chief Thurman Arnold had forced GE out as RCA's principal stockholder because the relationship was viewed as "monopolistic." The Carter administration had blocked a proposed merger between General Electric and Hitachi, both major television manufacturers, because of possible violations of the Sherman Antitrust Act.

Predictably, Reagan's top advisers in his cabinet and at the White House advised him to seek fundamental changes in U.S. antitrust laws in an effort to bring these statutes in tune with the new "economic realities." Reagan press secretary Larry Speakes insisted that these "reforms" would be chiefly "to allow those companies in the United States who are severely affected by foreign competition to have a better opportunity to merge. We believe it would put U.S. commerce on a more competitive footing and in the long range be beneficial to consumers." Specifically, according to one report, "A key proposal would ask Congress to change the seventy-one-year-old Clayton Act, one of the

---

*Smith was replaced by Edwin Meese as attorney general on February 23, 1985.

two pillars of antitrust enforcement, to lessen uncertainty over the legality of mergers. The language in Section 7 of the Sherman Antitrust Act prohibiting mergers that 'may' lessen competition or 'tend to create a monopoly' is so vague that it inhibits some mergers that would improve competition and strengthen markets and industries, administration officials say. The goal would be to remove this barrier."*6

Meantime, as things looked up for MCA on the antitrust front, other matters were still hanging. One was a $22.5 million lawsuit filed against MCA–Universal-Television by actor James Garner, who charged in 1983 that the studio had defrauded him in its handling of *The Rockford Files,* Garner's popular television series. Even though the program had been in the national syndication markets for several years, Universal had claimed that the show had yet to become profitable. "If that didn't make a profit," Garner told *Washington Post* reporter Tom Shales, "*what* makes a profit? You've practically got to go get your money from these guys. You've got to go get it with a gun practically. . . . I feel like I worked with the Charlie Manson family working for Universal. They're a bunch of crooks, and they always have been, and they always will be."

Garner continued, "I feel like I'm in a business with the biggest bunch of crooks you could ever put together. The Mafia's not as big as these people. They don't hold a candle to them. They can do it with a pencil."7

Although the running dispute between Garner and MCA-Universal had been going on years before he filed his suit against them, the shooting war began on January 16, 1980. Garner was driving his car on Coldwater Canyon in the Hollywood Hills, near the intersection of Mulholland Drive, when another car, driven by a free-lance photographer, tried to pass him on the right-hand side. Because there was no right lane, the two cars collided. Garner sat in his car, stunned, as the photographer jumped from his vehicle and ran to Garner. Seeing Garner's window open, the photographer punched the still-dazed actor in the face. Garner struggled to get out of his car and defend himself, but the photographer was too fast and too tough. Garner was badly beaten. According to a close friend and fellow actor of Garner's, "Right after the fight, Jimmy was helped up by an aide to a top MCA executive, who just happened to be in the traffic at the scene of the fight."

---

*While the Reagan Justice Department was reconsidering its antitrust laws, MCA outbid Westinghouse Broadcasting and agreed to buy WOR-TV—an independent station in New York, broadcasting throughout the U.S. via cable television—from RKO General, Inc., for $387 million. It was the first time MCA had purchased a television station.

While he was recuperating from the assault in the hospital, MCA-Universal filed a $1.5 million lawsuit against Garner for failing to complete the entire season of *Rockford* episodes. The litigations between Garner and MCA-Universal are still unresolved, and the corporation has refused comment on Garner's charges while the cases are pending.

However, the dispute with Garner did not attract the attention that MCA Records did. At the end of 1979, MCA Records had suffered nearly $10 million in losses. After some corporate personnel shuffling, the new management turned the record division around, reporting nearly $16 million in total gains by the end of 1980. This was primarily due to drastic reductions in staff and an overhaul in the day-to-day operations of the division. Frills like big industry parties, and even general spending, were cut while prices on records rose. MCA Records also began making distribution deals with other record companies. In 1984, MCA took control of the distribution of Motown Records, helping Lionel Richie's "Can't Slow Down" shatter Motown's sales record for a single disc.

While MCA Records appeared to be riding high, another payola scandal, a throwback to the late-1950s scams, broke wide open. Once again, record promoters were paying to get their clients air time. According to an *NBC Nightly News* report in late February 1986, record companies, including MCA, had become involved with independent record promoters who had ties to major Mafia figures. MCA and the other companies quickly got off the hook by simply denying any knowledge of wrongdoing and divorcing themselves from certain independent promoters.

At the time the payola matter was revealed by NBC, there was no official federal investigation into either payola or the use of independent promoters—despite NBC's claims to the contrary. In fact, a congressional investigation into the matter in 1984 failed to find any evidence of such practices, and recommended against further investigation.

However, according to federal investigators in Washington, D.C., the official investigation of the record business concentrated on the practice of counterfeiting in the industry and the sale of five million cutout (out-of-date) albums from MCA to Out of the Past, Inc., a Philadelphia-based discount record company. The FBI and the IRS uncovered a major counterfeiting operation in which 20,000 phony record albums were discovered. The owner of Out of the Past, John LaMonte, began cooperating with the FBI after serving time in prison for record counterfeiting. He entered the Federal Witness Protection Program, telling government investigators that he was allegedly the victim of extortion demands by Salvatore Pisello and Morris Levy, the president of New York's Roulette Records. Both Pisello and Levy have been tied by federal documents to organized crime. Pisello, in particular, has been identified as "a 'suspected' member of the Carlo Gambino family of La Cosa Nostra" and an alleged narcotics trafficker.

According to a sentencing memorandum filed in April 1985, in which Pisello was sentenced to two years in prison for income tax evasion:

> Pisello convinced MCA Records of Universal City to distribute the Sugar Hill label. Sugar Hill Records of New Jersey specializes in soul and rock 'n' roll music, including the recordings of Chuck Berry. According to MCA, Pisello put the parties together and received the rights to 3 percent of the net proceeds due Sugar Hill. MCA states that Sugar Hill soon had "cash flow" problems and remains in arrears to MCA for $1.7 million. Pisello personally received $76,530 in 1984 from MCA in commissions on the Sugar Hill deal. It remains unclear what Sugar Hill paid Pisello for his efforts.
>
> Pisello also sold MCA a large quantity of breakdancing mats. After paying Pisello's company, Consultants for World Records, Inc., $100,000 for the mats, MCA took a $95,000 loss when they did not sell. MCA also advanced Pisello $30,000 in 1984 for expenses involving his expertise in delivering a Latin music line and $50,000 in 1985 for future income on the Sugar Hill deal.
>
> In a fourth deal Pisello arranged for MCA to sell two of his clients 60 truckloads of out-of-date record albums and cassettes worth $1.4 million. Although [these were] shipped a year ago, the clients have yet to pay. Most of the trucks left the records and tapes at a company called "Out of the Past, Ltd.," in Darby, Pennsylvania; much of the rest went to Arkansas and South America.
>
> In total MCA paid Pisello over $250,000 in the past year for various deals. Yet Pisello told the Probation office that he has but $2500 in the bank, has earned but $50,000, and owes MCA and Sugar Hill $330,000.

LaMonte and Out of the Past had complained to both Pisello and Levy that the truckloads of records sent him by MCA were nothing but "junk" and completely worthless. As a result, LaMonte refused to pay Pisello and Levy, through Pisello's Consultants for World Records, Inc. Consequently, Pisello and Levy could not pay MCA. Soon after LaMonte's refusal to pay, he was badly beaten by Gaetano Vastola, a New Jersey Mafia member and an associate of Frederick Giovanielo, who was also present at LaMonte's meeting with Pisello and Levy.

Giovanielo, a member of the Genovese crime family in New York, was charged in February 1986 with the murder of a New York Police detective. The FBI, which had LaMonte under surveillance at the time, was able to capture the attack on film. Federal investigators have indicated that they believe that the Mafia might have been attempting to infiltrate MCA Records.

An MCA spokesman told *Los Angeles Times* reporter William Knoedelseder,* who first broke the MCA/Pisello cutout story, "Sal Pisello is a representative of Sugar Hill Records, an independent record company that MCA distributes. Additionally, he represented a buyer who purchased records discontinued from the MCA catalogue. MCA had no prior knowledge of the circumstances leading to Mr. Pisello's conviction. . . . MCA has been in constant contact with the Justice Department during this investigation and has cooperated fully and will continue to do so."[8]

RONALD REAGAN

A report released by the U.S. General Accounting Office, the watchdog of the federal government, in December 1980 stated, "Organized crime is flourishing. . . . [It] is a billion-dollar business which affects the lives of millions of individuals and poses a serious problem for law enforcement agencies. The effects of organized crime on society are pervasive."

The underworld during the 1980s has continued to cost the public billions of dollars each year. Organized crime's grip on industries ranging from construction to food processing and trucking to record companies, among other legitimate businesses—as well as some of the unions representing their workers—has only increased. This is apart from its traditional illegitimate enterprises in gambling, narcotics, prostitution, and loan-sharking, among others, which yield billions more. The tremendous rise in mob-owned garbage companies, the underworld's illegal dumping of dangerous chemicals, and its virtual takeover of the

---

*Knoedelseder also reported on May 11, 1985, on a lawsuit filed against MCA by George Collier —the former West Coast regional director for MCA Distributing, the manufacturing arm of MCA Records—who had been fired in June 1984. Collier claimed that he was doing "detective work" about the activities of several company vice-presidents who . . . were improperly sending "thousands" of free records to two retail accounts in the Los Angeles area. Knoedelseder wrote: "Collier became suspicious of the shipments because the records supposedly were being given away for promotional purposes but, on the orders of the vice-presidents, they contained no markings prohibiting their sale through normal retail channels." When asked about the case, MCA attorney Allen Susman simply said, "He was fired for cause," and refused further comment. The case is pending.

toxic waste industry have made its activities literally a public health hazard.

In short, organized crime has become institutionalized in the United States. One organized crime expert explained, "Whenever some tribute [to the underworld] is paid financially, it's going to be passed on to the consumer. The public doesn't view the problem in terms of how it affects them."

Prosecutors battling against the mob have been aided by the Racketeer-Influenced and Corrupt Organizations Act, or RICO, which made it a crime to conduct or finance even a legitimate business through any form of racketeering. The RICO statute also gave the federal government jurisdiction when certain crimes including murder were committed under state law.

The use of such laws by the Carter administration—especially by Attorney General Benjamin Civiletti, FBI Director William Webster, and David Margolis, the head of the U.S. Strike Force Against Organized Crime—was responsible for the investigations and indictments, as well as the convictions in some cases, of several top Mafia bosses, including Tony Accardo of Chicago, James T. Licavoli and Angelo Lonardo of Cleveland, Nick and Carl Civella of Kansas City, Dominic Brooklier and Sam Sciortino of Los Angeles, Santos Trafficante of Miami, Frank Balestrieri of Milwaukee, Carlos Marcello of New Orleans, Carmine Persico and Funzi Tieri of New York, Russell Bufalino of Pittston, Pennsylvania, Raymond Patriarca of Providence, Rhode Island, and Joseph Bonanno of Tucson, Arizona.

Less than a month after President Ronald Reagan was inaugurated, Ryan Quade Emerson, the publisher and executive director of *Organized Crime Review,* reported in his February 1981 issue, "About six months before the presidential election I received word that certain individuals within the Reagan camp were negotiating with key people in Las Vegas, Nevada, who were involved in the casino industry, the Teamsters Union, and organized crime. The basis for the discussions was the acute desire of the Teamsters Union to obtain relief from the aggressive probes by the United States Department of Justice organized crime strike forces and the Federal Bureau of Investigation. There was also a continuing grave concern about the FBI's productive court-ordered wiretaps that had revealed the hidden interests in many Las Vegas hotels and casinos by some of the country's most powerful organized crime figures."

During the early months of President Ronald Reagan's first term,

Nevada senator Paul Laxalt met with Attorney General William French Smith no less than three times, specifically to discuss the possibility of minimizing the role of the Justice Department's Strike Force Against Organized Crime in Las Vegas. Laxalt had been loudly complaining that Las Vegas was "infested" with pesky FBI and IRS agents, and he pledged to use his influence on the U.S. Senate Appropriations Committee to get federal investigators off the backs of Nevada's casino operators. Laxalt had publicly taken the position that organized crime was no longer a factor in Nevada, which, he insisted, had established tight monitoring programs to keep out mobsters.

Neither Laxalt's associations with a variety of shady figures nor his brazen attempts to curb the government's investigations of the casino industry drew even a flicker of interest at the White House. Fred Fielding, President Reagan's special counsel, said, "The White House doesn't review elected officials, but I have never had one moment's hesitation to be concerned about Paul Laxalt [sic]."[9]

David Gergen, Reagan's then-director of White House communications, added, "The president regards Paul Laxalt as one of his most trusted confidantes, someone who has been of tremendous assistance to him in his political life—not only in campaigns, but in the time he's been president. He believes that Laxalt is a man of integrity and forthrightness. He welcomes his advice, and it's always proven to be valuable."[10]

Apparently, Laxalt's advice was taken.* At President Reagan's first opportunity to revise the federal budget, he imposed a one-third cutback of the FBI's investigations of gambling, prostitution, arson-for-profit, gangland murders, and pornography—along with a hiring freeze and dramatic staff reductions within the FBI. Reagan also indicated that no new undercover operations would be authorized in fiscal 1982 against organized crime or white-collar crime.[11]

The Reagan administration then severely curtailed the investigative and enforcement abilities of the Securities and Exchange Commission, the Internal Revenue Service, and the Justice Department's Strike Forces Against Organized Crime—as part of its program to get the government off the backs of the people. The administration also attempted but failed to dismantle the Bureau of Alcohol, Tobacco, and

---

*In a letter to *The Sacramento Bee* dated November 18, 1983, Laxalt wrote, "Since 1981 and after investigating the FBI situation in Nevada, I came to the conclusion that staffing in Nevada was reasonable and since that time I have supported full funding for the FBI in Nevada in the committees in which I have direct jurisdiction over its resources." Attempts to interview Laxalt for this book were unsuccessful.

Firearms of the Treasury Department, which had been extremely effective in the war against organized crime but had been opposed by the Reagan-allied National Rifle Association.

In one of its first legislative moves, the Reagan administration urged Congress to repeal two federal taxes on gambling, saying that it is "wasteful and inefficient" to try to collect them. An assistant to Secretary of the Treasury Donald Regan outlined Reagan's views at a Senate hearing on a bill proposed by Senator Howard Cannon to exempt legal gambling from taxes.

Attorney General Smith moved to eliminate the Ethics in Government Act and the Foreign Corrupt Practices Act, as well as major portions of the Freedom of Information Act. He then reshuffled the Justice Department's priorities away from investigations and prosecutions of organized crime figures to a new emphasis on "violent crime." State and local authorities were not promised any additional funds from the federal government—although ninety-four percent of all crime committed is within their jurisdictions. Other federal programs slated for severe budget cuts were those dealing with the problems of narcotics trafficking and juvenile justice.

Reagan blamed the rising crime rate on "utopian presumptions about human nature. We should never forget: the jungle is always there, waiting to take us over."

While the Reagan administration went through the motions of fighting crime, Secretary of Labor Raymond Donovan had again found himself in trouble. He was facing numerous hearings before the Senate Labor Committee and a variety of charges leveled against him by an array of respected government informants. The focal point of most of the investigations of Donovan revolved around his personal and professional relationship with mobster William Masselli. At the time of the Donovan investigation in 1981, Masselli was under a double indictment for hijacking food and for manufacturing synthetic cocaine.

On May 22, 1981, less than a week after taking over as general president of the Teamsters Union in the wake of Frank Fitzsimmons's death, Roy Williams was indicted for conspiring to bribe Senator Howard Cannon. Two days earlier, the U.S. Permanent Subcommittee on Investigations released an interim report on the Teamsters. It described Williams as "an organized crime mole operating at senior levels of the Teamsters Union. . . . A serious question has arisen as to whether or not Roy Lee Williams has any place in any position of trust in the labor movement." At the time of his appointment as Teamsters president,

Williams announced, "I'll never forget where I came from, and I'll never forget the people who helped me get here."

The subcommittee recommended that the Labor Department take action against Williams to have him removed as the general president of the union because he had taken the Fifth Amendment in lieu of testifying in August 1980, the day before he and Jackie Presser met privately with Reagan. Ray Donovan refused to take any action against Williams, claiming that he lacked the authority to do so. Senator Sam Nunn recalled that in 1976 the Labor Department had forced William Presser to resign as a trustee of the pension fund because, like Williams, he had taken the Fifth while appearing before the subcommittee. Nunn charged that Donovan was trying "to protect the interests of the union hierarchy [rather] than the rank and file."

On June 1, just ten days after Williams's indictment and twelve days after he was described by the Senate as "an organized crime mole," President Reagan addressed the delegates of the Teamsters convention in Las Vegas on videotape. During his talk, Reagan said, "I hope to be in team with the Teamsters." On June 12, despite the criticism he received for his praise of the Teamsters, Reagan invited Williams to the White House with other labor leaders to discuss his federal tax-cut proposals.

Peter B. Bensinger, the head of the Drug Enforcement Administration who had been originally appointed by President Ford and retained by President Carter, was ousted by the Reagan administration in favor of Francis "Bud" Mullen, the assistant director of the FBI. Members of the Senate Labor Committee questioned whether the job was a payoff to Mullen, who had been chiefly responsible for concealing Labor Secretary Raymond Donovan's organized crime ties from the committee during his confirmation hearings.

In response to Reagan's proposals that the FBI budget be cut by six percent and that the DEA budget be cut by another twelve percent (which would cause the dismissal of 434 DEA employees, including 211 agents), Ira Glasser, the executive director of the American Civil Liberties Union—characterized by Reagan's chief of staff, Ed Meese, as a "criminal lobby"—called Reagan's anticrime proposals a "fraud in terms of being serious proposals to reduce crime."

Attorney General Smith announced that the Justice Department was going to launch a "vigorous" war on crime without additional funding. In response, Senator Joseph Biden charged that while the Reagan administration was talking tough about crime, it was cutting the budgets of the FBI, DEA, U.S. attorneys, Immigration and Naturalization Service, and Coast Guard. Biden also noted that sixty percent of the cases handled by the attorney general's office were being dropped because its lawyers did not have enough time to deal with them.[12]

Attorney General Smith later shifted gears and announced that narcotics trafficking—not violent crime—was the nation's "most serious crime problem," and that the FBI would assume jurisdiction over the Mullen-led DEA. FBI Director William Webster opposed the idea for the same reason J. Edgar Hoover had spoken out against FBI agents being involved in drug-related investigations. Both Webster and Hoover had feared that FBI agents might be corrupted by drug work that involved large amounts of cash. Unlike Hoover, Webster also wanted to avoid the perception that the FBI was becoming a national police force.

On January 28, 1982, Reagan appointed a Cabinet-level task force to coordinate federal efforts to combat drug-smuggling operations in south Florida, a haven for narcotics traffickers. Vice-President George Bush was appointed as the head of the special unit. Other members of the task force included Smith, Meese, and the secretaries of state, defense, treasury, and transportation. Soon after, Bush announced that federal authorities would use radar planes in their "war against drugs," as well as 130 customs and 43 FBI agents.

In March 1982, the General Accounting Office was lodging complaints with the White House, Congress, and the Department of Justice about the secrecy within the DEA, and the GAO's inability to review the agency's progress against big-time drug dealers. The study had been requested by Senator Joseph Biden. Both the White House and Attorney General Smith refused to cooperate and release the documents necessary for the GAO's investigation. In a March 31, 1982, letter to Reagan, Comptroller General Charles A. Bowsher reported that "for the most part, access to the records was denied altogether" by DEA. "Although some records were provided, access to them was delayed, and not all of the records were complete."[13]

As a result of the mounting charges against Labor Secretary Donovan, the U.S. Court of Appeals selected Leon Silverman, a New York attorney, as a special prosecutor to investigate Donovan. Smith wanted to limit Silverman's power to probing only specific allegations raised during Donovan's confirmation hearings, but the appeals court broadened his authority to include investigation of any charges brought against Donovan. Almost immediately, Silverman was criticized for the narrow scope of his investigation despite the latitude he had been given.

As Silverman began his grand jury investigation on February 1, 1982, the Senate Labor Committee continued its probe into allegations of mob money being laundered through Donovan's construction firm, as well as the FBI's handling of information regarding Donovan's underworld connections prior to his confirmation hearings. In the spring, the committee asked the Justice Department for wiretapped conversations of mobsters who had discussed their dealings with Donovan. However, Attorney General Smith refused to cooperate with the committee and did not turn over the tapes.

When finally asked how he was viewing the entire Donovan matter, President Reagan replied, "Nothing I've heard has . . . reduced my confidence in Secretary Donovan."

In mid-June, as the Donovan probe intensified, a key government witness against him in the special prosecutor's investigation, Fred Furino, was found in the trunk of his own car in Manhattan with a bullet in his head.

On June 20, puzzled by Reagan's apparent apathy regarding Donovan, *The New York Times* wrote: "At a minimum, Mr. Reagan's aides showed a lack of curiosity in January 1981, when they were told that Mr. Donovan had 'close personal and business' ties to organized crime figures."

Soon after Furino's murder, when asked whether Reagan had changed his mind about Donovan, presidential spokesman Larry Speakes replied with two words: "No change."

On June 28, Silverman issued a 1,026-page report that stated, "In sum, there was insufficient credible evidence to warrant prosecution of Secretary Donovan on any charge." Donovan called a press conference and said happily that he was "extremely pleased and not surprised," adding that the report "vindicated" him. President Reagan said, "Certainly I'm sticking with him. . . . This case is closed."

However, on August 1, Silverman reported that two new "substantial" charges had been made against Donovan. Twenty-four days later, William Masselli's son, Nat Masselli, was shot to death. Masselli had also been a key witness for Silverman, who stated after the killing, "I am disturbed that anybody who is involved in my investigation should be murdered, and I have asked the FBI to conduct an intensive investigation to see whether that murder is linked to this investigation."

Nevertheless, on September 13, Silverman, for the second time, announced that there was "insufficient evidence" against Donovan to prosecute him. But Silverman permitted himself to describe the lingering allegations about Donovan as "disturbing."* Larry Speakes said, "It was not unexpected. Case closed again."

In response to the Reagan administration's cosmetic anticrime measures, attorney Paul Ziffren's old friend, Judge David I. Bazelon, a member of the U.S. Circuit Court of Appeals for Washington, D.C., claimed that Reagan's anticrime actions would endanger civil liberties. "Nothing could have given Reagan's war on crime more legitimacy than an attack from Bazelon," said an FBI agent in Washington, D.C. "The liberals, taking their lead from Bazelon, would follow suit, saying that Reagan was being too tough on crime. In fact, Reagan had one of the softest attacks on crime we'd seen in years."

The Reagan administration reaped the rewards of President Carter's effective anticrime attack. William Webster, the FBI director, and Benjamin Civiletti, whom Carter had appointed attorney general in 1979, proved themselves to be the best crimefighters this country has had since Robert Kennedy was attorney general. But because of judicial due process, the success of the Carter administration's investigations and prosecutions of organized crime figures was not known until the early years of the Reagan administration.

By September 1982, of those organized crime cases initiated, investigated, and prosecuted by the Carter Justice Department, an amazing 1,100 convictions were won. This figure included over three hundred Mafia members, including top mob kingpins in New York, northern Pennsylvania, Philadelphia, the Buffalo-Rochester area, New Orleans, Chicago, Milwaukee, Cleveland, Detroit, and Kansas City.

The Reagan administration immediately took credit for these cases, adding them to its list of accomplishments to be heralded at election time—while continuing to attack the Democrats for being "soft on crime."

On October 14, 1982, to dramatize the administration's purported commitment, Reagan declared "war on organized crime," announcing that "the time has come to cripple the power of the mob in America."

---

*Bronx prosecutor Stephen R. Bookin testified at a federal court hearing on December 13, 1984, that Silverman had limited the scope of the Donovan inquiry, telling grand jurors that a probe into the business link between the Mafia-controlled Jopel Contracting Company and Donovan's Schiavone Construction Company "was not within their mandate," according to Bookin. Donovan was later indicted with nine others on charges stemming from his relationship with Jopel. After the special prosecutor's second report on Donovan, the press, for all intents and purposes, stopped covering the charges against Donovan. The lone exception was George Lardner from *The Washington Post,* who kept the story alive.

The president announced that he was going to create twelve special task forces around the country, composed of nine hundred new agents from a variety of federal agencies, in addition to two hundred new assistant U.S. attorneys and a support staff of four hundred. The program, Reagan said, would cost between $130 million and $200 million, and would be patterned after the special task force being conducted by Vice-President Bush in south Florida.*

The New York Times was skeptical about Reagan's announcement and published an editorial on October 18 saying, "Announcing a new White House drive against organized crime prior to a national election looks, well, political. There are no new funds for the program, and it offers no additional resources for what may be the most effective strategy: attacking the drug crops in other countries."

Immediately after the president's declaration of war and his early-November appointment of Paul Laxalt as the general chairman of the Republican National Committee, a budgetary dispute erupted among the heads of the ten federal agencies slated to be involved in Reagan's war against drugs. When Reagan was asked to intervene and settle the question of who would control the bulk of the funding as well as the prosecutions, the White House promised answers after the midterm elections.[14]

Reagan had few answers for the agencies after the elections, but did have time for a photo opportunity in south Florida on November 17. Photographers flashed cameras at Reagan and Smith while they inspected a cache of $4.5 million worth of marijuana and $5.9 million worth of cocaine that had been seized by federal agents. Later in November, Smith went to Pakistan and Landi Kotal, a tiny town in the Khyber Pass—which had been a major drug smuggling center for hundreds of years. In another photo opportunity that backfired, Smith and a small army of Pakistani soldiers became fearful for their safety as they walked through the town, filled with locals who were rumored to be well-armed and dangerous.

Back in Washington, Reagan announced that he would ask Congress to approve his $155 million antidrug package, including $25 million for south Florida alone, and to transfer the necessary funding from other government programs. On December 7, *The New York Times* once again published an editorial critical of Reagan's crime program. "Was

---

*The night before Reagan declared war on organized crime, top Reagan administration officials —Attorney General Smith, CIA Director Casey, and Presidential Chief of Staff Meese, among others—attended a fifty-dollar-a-plate "Tribute to Raymond J. Donovan" dinner. Guests wore buttons reading, "I'm a friend of Ray Donovan."

this just another bold anticrime proposal surfacing in the thick of a campaign and destined to sink from sight after the votes were counted? The skeptics now seem vindicated. The administration duly asked Congress to pare the needed money funds from other budgets. But when this met opposition, the White House backed off. The Office of Management and Budget now says it cannot find enough money in other programs, and offers no alternative. . . . Not to fund the program, now that the election is over, turns an admirable plan into a cynical ploy. In the matter of crime-busting, that is disgraceful."

Two days after the *Times* editorial, Smith went to the Senate Appropriations Subcommittee for an additional $130 million to help bail out Reagan's antidrug program. Senator Ernest Hollings charged, "We're behind the eight-ball in crime," adding that the number of employees in the FBI, DEA, Coast Guard, Customs, INS, ATF, and IRS had dropped by 19,609 since Reagan took office.

In response to the Reagan administration's pleas for help, Congress passed an anticrime bill, which, among other reforms, called for the creation of a Cabinet-level "drug czar" to oversee the federal crackdown against drug dealers. The administration immediately opposed the bill solely because of the drug czar clause, which the White House said would add another layer of bureaucracy.

Senator Joseph Biden of Delaware wrote an Op-Ed piece for *The New York Times* on January 4, 1983, insisting: "Turf wars among government agencies responsible for federal control of narcotics, long a major obstacle to such control, would finally be eliminated by a bill that is awaiting President Reagan's signature. If he succumbs to bureaucratic arguments to veto it, he will invite a severe setback to his own commendable efforts to control drug trafficking and the crime it spawns in every corner of this country."

In response, Smith claimed, "We have taken unprecedented steps to combat the widespread lawlessness in America." The war against crime in America continued to be a war of words.

Within the underworld, there was still plenty of action. On January 20, 1983, Allen Dorfman was shot eight times in the head by two ski-masked killers while walking across a parking lot in Chicago.* The

---

*The principal target of the Dorfman murder investigation was Anthony Spilotro, the chief enforcer for Chicago Mafia boss Joey Aiuppa and his underboss Jackie Cerone. Believed to have engineered the killing at the behest of Aiuppa and Cerone, Spilotro was also alleged to be the Chicago underworld's point man in Las Vegas, overseeing all of its gambling, narcotics, and prostitution operations. Also suspected to be a stone killer, Spilotro was a convicted gambler who had been arrested over twenty times and once indicted for murder. Although his alleged accomplice testified against him at that trial, describing how Spilotro mutilated the victim's body with

previous month, Dorfman and Teamsters general president Roy Williams were convicted of attempting to bribe Senator Howard Cannon. Informed sources said that Dorfman was considering plea-bargaining his way out of a long prison term at the time of his murder.

As Reagan pondered the fate of the congressional anticrime legislation, the General Accounting Office—which had finally pried loose the necessary documents from the DEA and the Justice Department—issued a status report regarding the war on drugs. The GAO report stated that the price of heroin had fallen from $2.25 a milligram in 1979 to $1.66 in June 1982, while cocaine dropped from sixty-five cents to fifty-two cents. The report added that while the price was going down, the purity of both drugs had also increased, indicating a larger supply. The GAO blamed the failure of the drug war on the lack of a central coordinator to direct those federal agencies involved. In south Florida alone, the report said, $66 million had been spent during the previous year with little result because of this lack of coordination.

Despite the official pressure to sign the anticrime bill, Reagan vetoed it in mid-January 1983 because of the drug czar clause. Soon after, William Webster said that the illegal flow of drugs into the U.S. without an effective response had caused Americans to lose faith in the government's ability to protect them. "It is the inundation of drugs—some of which are grown here—that is eroding public confidence and corrupting public officials," Webster said.

The convicted Roy Williams was succeeded by Jackie Presser as general president of the Teamsters Union on April 21, 1983. Presser promised to operate "an open, honest administration." When asked whether organized crime still had influence in the Teamsters, Presser simply replied, "Not to my knowledge." At the time of his selection as president, Presser was the target of a Labor Department probe, investigating his role in a union embezzlement scheme in Cleveland.

On April 25, after receiving a telegram of congratulations from Reagan, Presser had lunch with Secretary of Labor Ray Donovan. After the meeting, Presser said that Donovan "extended the hand of friendship . . . and gave me some advice . . . about which direction he would like to see this International go. He also gave me a couple of boots here and there, but I'm big enough to take that, and I understand what he's saying."

Donovan simply said, "I want to work closely with him [Presser] to

---

a knife, Spilotro was later acquitted. Federal investigators believe that during his career, Spilotro has either ordered or participated in the murders of a dozen people. Dorfman's murder was the 1,081st *unsolved* gangland murder in Chicago since 1920.

accomplish the ends that he has promised this union and the public that he would do. I have confidence that this relationship will . . . benefit all Teamsters throughout this country and I look forward to the relationship with Mr. Presser."

Three weeks later, Presser was invited to the White House for a June 7 state dinner. The move was viewed as part of an administration plan to use the Teamsters' support again this time for Reagan's 1984 reelection campaign. Fred Fielding, who advised Reagan against close ties with Presser, said that he was told by another top administration official that "the Teamsters are always under investigation. Presser hasn't been indicted, and there are good reasons for inviting him to the White House."[15]

Presser chose not to attend the White House dinner on June 7. However, earlier that day, he appeared before a Senate committee to testify against an antiracketeering bill pending before Congress.

After Reagan issued baseless public statements in June 1983, declaring victory for his antidrug program, columnist Jack Anderson wrote, "President Reagan has pronounced his war on drugs a raging success. But the truth is that the war has been long on ballyhoo and short on results. The price of illegal drugs [continues to be] down across the country, a sure sign that the supply is up."[16]

On July 28, 1983, Reagan continued his public relations war against organized crime by establishing a twenty-member President's Commission on Organized Crime, headed by U.S. federal judge Irving R. Kaufman of New York's Circuit Court of Appeals. After signing the executive order creating the commission, Reagan again declared war on the underworld, repeating that it was "time to break the power of the mob in America," which he said "infects every part of our society." Like the Kefauver Committee, the commission was expected to travel to cities across the country, gathering information and testimony about local organized crime problems. Its findings would be contained in a final report due by March 1, 1986.

The same day that Reagan signed the executive order, Attorney General Smith was on Capitol Hill defending Reagan's attendance ten days earlier at the convention of the organized crime–infested International Longshoremens Association, where he called its president, Thomas Gleason, a man of "integrity and loyalty." Smith also defended Reagan's appearance on videotape at the Teamsters convention in Las Vegas. Referring to the convictions of congressmen and a senator in the FBI's ABSCAM sting operation—conducted during the Carter administration—Smith said, "If the suggestion here is that we should boycott an organization because there may be individuals connected with that organization who have been convicted of some criminal activity, if that is the suggestion, it has remarkable ramifications because I assume, based on what has recently happened, there might be circumstances under which we would then have to terminate our relationships with Congress."

As the selection process for members of the president's commission was under way, John Duffy, the sheriff of San Diego County, who had been sponsored for a commission seat by Ed Meese, was forced to withdraw his name from consideration after his friendship with mobster Morris Dalitz was revealed.

Comparing Duffy's situation with that of Paul Laxalt, who had openly admitted his personal and financial relationship with Dalitz, a member of the commission said, "The controversy over Duffy arose, because, one, Duffy had been hurt by the revelations and, two, it could have led to a political embarrassment having him continue to serve on the commission. . . . Laxalt hasn't been hurt by any of the revelations about him, and he certainly hasn't become a political embarrassment to anyone. The only people who really seem concerned by all of this information are those who study the problem of organized crime—those in law enforcement and the media."

Back in New York, a cellmate of one of the men arrested in the gangland slaying of Nat Masselli stated under oath in court that he had been told the murder was committed to prevent Masselli and his father from cooperating with Silverman's investigation of Donovan. The informant neither asked for nor received any benefit for his testimony.

Meantime, the Senate Government Affairs Subcommittee disclosed that during the Reagan administration, federal judges had cracked down on white-collar criminals and drug traffickers, often imposing large fines to prevent them from profiting from their crimes. However, the federal government had failed to collect more than fifty-five cents on the dollar of those fines levied, and 22,532 criminal fines, worth over $185.6 million, had not been paid.

Associate Attorney General D. Lowell Jensen, who had been endorsed for his post by Ed Meese, insisted that it would "take time" for the Reagan administration's drug program to show results. "Our drug effort is like running a marathon," Jensen said. "And you shouldn't be timing a hundred-yard dash." He said that the drug war had already produced 183 indictments involving over 1,000 defendants, adding that 425 cases had been initiated against drug rings. Tom Lewis, a Republican congressman from Florida, criticized Reagan's drug war in his state, saying, "We're just arresting ponies, the little people. Why aren't we getting the big guys?"[17]

The President's Commission on Organized Crime battled the White House and the Justice Department over the questions of general independence, access to information obtained through electronic surveillance, and the power to subpoena witnesses. These measures were opposed in the Congress by Senator Paul Laxalt, who sat on both the Judiciary and Appropriations Committees, and by the American Civil Liberties Union—which wrote a letter to the Judiciary Committee warning that "it is essential that the fundamental civil liberties not be sacrificed in our zeal to attack" organized crime.

On November 29, during his testimony before the organized crime commission, Attorney General Smith told its members that a "new phase in the history of organized crime" had been created by the growth of motorcycle gangs, and foreign-based, drug-rich crime organizations, like the Hell's Angels, the Bandidos, the Outlaws, and the Pagans, as well as the Mexican Mafia, La Nuestra Familia, the Aryan Brotherhood, the Black Guerrilla Family, and the Chinese, Japanese, and Vietnamese crime groups. Smith had little to say about the traditional Italian/Sicilian Mafia.

Once again, on December 3, Reagan declared war on organized crime at a White House meeting of federal prosecutors, saying, "I've always believed that government can break up the networks of tightly organized regional and national syndicates that make up organized crime.

"So I repeat, we're in this thing to win. There will be negotiated settlements, no détente with the mob. It's war to the end with the mob. It's war to the end where they're concerned. Our goal is simple. We mean to cripple their organization, dry up their profits, and put their members behind bars, where they belong. They've had a free run for too long a time in this country."

Reagan, in his State of the Union Address on January 25, 1984, declared, "Already, our efforts to crack down on career criminals, organized crime, drug pushers, and to enforce tougher sentences and paroles, are having an effect. In 1982, the crime rate dropped by 4.3 percent, the biggest decline since 1972. Protecting victims is just as important as safeguarding the rights of defendants."

Reagan had earlier submitted his own forty-four-point anticrime package to Congress—deleting the drug czar concept and asking approval for, among other things, wider latitude for use of the death penalty, the submission of illegally obtained evidence in court, and bail and sentencing provisions. Reagan called for major budget cuts in the Treasury Department's anticrime programs, forcing Treasury Secretary Donald Regan to reduce funding for the Customs Service almost by half. Then, in his weekly radio address to the nation on February 18, 1984, Reagan attacked House Democrats for holding up passage of his anticrime proposals. "Nothing in our Constitution," Reagan said, "gives dangerous criminals a right to prey on innocent, law-abiding people."

In response, Representative Glenn English said, "The White House war on drugs is being bombed by its own troops. . . . I am appalled by the lack of cooperation and coordination at the highest levels of this government to put teeth into the nation's war on drugs. While Vice-President Bush is the titular head of the White House effort, the secretary of the treasury [Donald Regan] has all but thwarted the effort."[18]

In an effort to overcome the negative reaction to virtually cutting the Customs Service out of the war against drugs, the Treasury Department proposed regulations requiring U.S. financial institutions to furnish government agencies with records of their transactions with certain foreign banks that had been known to be laundering drug money for American dealers. Gambling casinos, like banks, would be required to report any and all financial transactions over $10,000 to the IRS.

Although the new Treasury regulations were enthusiastically endorsed by the President's Commission on Organized Crime, Nevada's Paul Laxalt opposed the measures and led an intense but unsuccessful lobbying effort in the Senate against it. Laxalt explained that he felt that the reporting requirements would be an unwarranted intrusion into the major industry of his state.

In May 1984, an internal report written by DEA Administrator Bud Mullen charged that Reagan's antidrug program was a "liability." Mullen commented that the campaign's "alleged grandiose accomplishments" will "become this administration's Achilles' heel for drug enforcement." Also critical of Vice-President Bush's south Florida effort, Mullen said that the task force had done little more than take credit for the work other agencies had done. A Coast Guard lieutenant commander on the front line of the antidrug campaign called the entire program "an intellectual fraud." Florida congressman Claude Pepper added, "I can't see a single thing [the south Florida task force] has accomplished. The lack of coordination among the various agencies charged with waging the war on drugs is disgraceful."[19]

Replying to Mullen's report and in the midst of demands by Congress

that the entire program be scrapped, Coast Guard Captain L. N. Schowengerdt, the head of Bush's program, simply said that the south
Florida unit was experiencing "growing pains."

Testifying before the Senate Budget Committee on May 25, Attorney
General Smith, when asked about Reagan's anticrime war, replied that
"the coordination and cooperation is outstanding" among those federal
agencies involved. Senator Dennis DeConcini, a member of the panel,
retorted, "General, you're not in touch with what's going on."

As criticism of the president's war on crime and drugs continued to
mount, Reagan simply blamed the national crime rate on "years of
liberal leniency," adding that the "liberal leadership" of the Congress
had bottled up his anticrime legislation.

That same month, Reagan appointed his old Hollywood ally, seven-
ty-four-year-old IATSE executive Roy Brewer, as the chairman of the
Federal Service Impasse Panel, which arbitrated disputes between federal agencies and the unions representing federal workers. A strong
anti-communist and a friend of Ray Donovan, Roy Brewer had been
the keeper of the Hollywood blacklist during the late 1940s and early
1950s. He blamed America's drug problem not on organized crime but
on the Russians. "The danger is that we cannot permanently exist with
the Soviet Union. They will either destroy us, or they will have to be
destroyed. See, the dope traffic—and our inability to control it—has
been brought about by a subtle program. They are undermining the
facilities by which we can resist things that are happening."[20]

As the 1984 presidential election approached, none of these issues—
the failed or even sabotaged war on crime and drugs or the president's
organized crime–connected appointments and associations—ever
emerged as major campaign issues. Despite the warnings of White
House counsel Fred Fielding, the Reagan-Bush team happily accepted
the endorsement of Jackie Presser and the 1.9 million-member Teamsters Union. Vice-President Bush attended the annual meeting of the
Ohio Conference of Teamsters in Columbus. Bush and Presser walked
into the convention hall literally arm in arm, sporting broad smiles.
"We couldn't be more pleased," Bush told the cheering Teamsters.
"We're very, very grateful, I'll tell you, and we will work, work hard
to earn the confidence of your members. We're proud to be here." When
asked about the federal investigations revolving around Presser, Bush
replied sharply, "We have a system of justice in this country that people
are innocent until proven guilty. There have been a lot of allegations;
the endorsement has nothing to do with that."

The closest the Democratic Party came to making an issue out of

Reagan's appointments was to compile a paper entitled "Unethical Conduct by Reagan Administration Officials," prepared by Congresswoman Patricia Schroeder, chairwoman of the House Subcommittee on Civil Service. The list—which contained 101 names of public officials serving in the administration who had been "involved in instances of criminal wrongdoing, abuse of power and privilege, and improper behavior"—became part of what the Democrats called "the Sleaze Factor."

The whole issue suddenly disappeared after press accounts began to detail the New York underworld ties of Democratic presidential nominee Walter Mondale's running mate, Geraldine A. Ferraro. Among other charges, Ferraro was said to have used a known underworld associate to help her raise money for her campaign for Congress in 1979. Her husband, a real estate executive, was accused of fronting for members of the Gambino crime family in New York. Reporter Sid Blumenthal later wrote in *The New Republic:* "Despite her personal attractiveness, her support of worthy causes, and her admirable compassion, [Ferraro's] story can be understood only by taking the Mob milieu into account. Ferraro may be a paragon of legality, but this reality has been crucial to her life." Among those mobsters linked to Ferraro was alleged Ray Donovan associate William Masselli, who had been "one of the largest contributors to the Ferraro campaign debt retirement fund."[21]

Although Ferraro characterized such reports as "lies," the evidence against her mounted and severely crippled any chance Mondale had of unseating the popular incumbent.*

The Republican Party, headed by Senator Paul Laxalt† and his Nevada protégé, Frank J. Fahrenkopf, never made an issue out of Ferraro's links to the Mafia. That decision might have been more self-serving than politically tasteful, because the refusal to make Fer-

---

*In May 1986, after a twenty-one-month investigation and Ferraro's announced decision not to challenge New York Republican incumbent Alfonse M. D'Amato for his seat in the U.S. Senate, the Justice Department closed its probe into the finances and disclosure statements of Ferraro and her husband.

†Laxalt was the target of two competing stories by *ABC World News Tonight* and CBS's *60 Minutes,* which were scheduled to have been aired on September 21 and 23, 1984, respectively. The stories detailed allegations of Laxalt's connections to organized crime. However, both stories were killed after *60 Minutes* reporter Mike Wallace, who was also a personal friend of Laxalt's, determined that the key source in both the ABC and CBS stories had lied to him about whether he had already been interviewed by ABC (which he had, when he claimed to Wallace he had not). After being told by Wallace about the lie, Laxalt had his attorney send both networks letters, threatening libel actions if the stories were broadcast. After being briefed on the matter by Wallace, Don Hewitt, the executive producer of *60 Minutes,* telephoned Roone Arledge, the president of ABC News. On the basis of their source's lie to Wallace about being interviewed by ABC, the two executives from the competing networks jointly decided to kill each of their stories.[22]

raro's associations a campaign issue also made such ties to Reagan and members of his administration moot.

"There was an unspoken understanding," said a top aide to the Mondale-Ferraro campaign, who refused to go into any further detail. "It was just one of those 'I'm okay and you're okay' things."

After the Congress passed Reagan's anticrime package on October 10, Reagan's attack on the Democrats for foot-dragging on that issue also became moot. To demonstrate that Reagan was doing something about the Mafia, the Justice Department indicted the entire leadership of the Colombo crime family in New York. The fifty-one-count indictment, naming eleven leaders of the group, was timed just a week before the national election.

The cavalier treatment by the Reagan administration of the serious national organized crime problem, as well as the blatant underworld ties of several of the president's top advisers, casts a long shadow over the sincerity and the willingness of this administration to combat organized crime in America. The end result will likely be a further tolerance of these activities by the general public.

The questions raised here do not necessarily allege guilt by association within the Reagan administration. However, there are legitimate reasons to question these patterns of association, particularly when President Reagan claims to be taking the hard line on the organized crime problem in America.

SIDNEY KORSHAK

Based in Washington, D. C., and a home for scholars, the American Enterprise Institute is a conservative think tank used extensively by the Reagan administration. In 1973, the Institute published an anthology of essays on the problem of crime in America. Entitled *The Economics of Crime and Punishment,* it included the chapter "A Defense of Organized Crime?" written by James M. Buchanan, a professor of economics at the Virginia Polytechnic Institute and State University.[23] Buchanan argued that organized crime was preferable to disorganized crime because a degree of control and discipline was implicit with organized crime. Conceding that such a suggestion could be misunderstood, the author wrote:

Emotions may be aroused by the thought that one implication of the whole analysis is that governments should "deal with the syndicate," that law enforcement agencies should work out "accommodations" or "arrangements" with those who might organize central control over criminal effort. ... It merely suggests that there may be social benefits from the monopoly of organized crime. Policy implications emerge only when we go beyond this with a suggestion that government adopt a passive role when they observe attempts made by entrepreneurs to reduce the effective competitiveness of criminal industries. In practice, this suggestion reduces to an admonition against the much-publicized crusades against organized crime at the expense of enforcement effort aimed at ordinary, competitive criminality.

A very strong argument can be made that this belief was shared by the Reagan administration, supported by Reagan's personal history and those of his top aides, as well as his administration's shabby performance in this area. Although no official close to the president had admitted it, the Reagan administration appeared to have divided people associated with organized crime into two categories: tolerable mobsters and intolerable mobsters. Those gangsters' associates who had relationships with Paul Laxalt, Ray Donovan, Jackie Presser, Roy Williams, William Casey, Frank Sinatra, Walter Annenberg, and the members of Reagan's Kitchen Cabinet were apparently viewed as tolerable mobsters. Those with no political connections to this administration were intolerable.

From all indications, Sidney Korshak* was a tolerable organized crime figure to the Reagan administration. Since Reagan was inaugurated, no one in the Justice Department or any other federal agency has laid a glove on him. Although the President's Commission on Organized Crime scheduled hearings to be held in Los Angeles, where Korshak was sure to be a major target, the planned trip was aborted at the behest of the Justice Department, which ostensibly did not want to prejudice the drug trial of auto executive John DeLorean, who was later acquitted.

According to charges brought by Jerry Van, a former mob legbreaker turned federally protected witness, members of the Los Angeles Strike Force Against Organized Crime "delayed or quashed grand jury action" against underworld figures in California. The investigation of Van's charges had been prompted by Congressman Charles Rangel (D-NY), who had received information about the alleged fixes while serving as the chairman of the U.S. House Select Committee on Narcotics Abuse and Control. According to one report, Van "made allegations of wrongdoing in the administration of cases by the organized crime strike force in Los Angeles. ... The allegations were general in nature,"

*Attempts to interview Korshak for this book were unsuccessful.

but it was determined by mid-level Justice Department employees "that there was smoke there."[24]

Many frustrated law enforcement observers who have realized the damage he had already done and how dangerous he continued to be feared Korshak was being protected. "It's not like Korshak operates in some specific area, like one particular business or labor union," said a former Justice Department official. "If that was so, the government could move in on that target and disrupt his interests. Korshak is unique, because he has the ability to deal with anybody, to fix anything. For that reason, Korshak himself has to become the target. And this administration doesn't seem to be interested in that idea at all. I honestly believe that their punch is being pulled."

Former California mobster turned government witness Jimmy Fratianno was deposed in Los Angeles on behalf of *Penthouse* on January 15, 1981.* The magazine had been sued by organized crime figure Moe Dalitz for a 1976 story published about Dalitz's La Costa Country Club, which has been frequently referred to as a playground for the top figures in organized crime.

"Are you familiar with a man by the name of Sidney Korshak, a lawyer?" Fratianno was asked.

"Yes, sir."

"Through which [crime] family?"

"The Chicago family."

"You have told us today that the present head of the Chicago family is Joey Aiuppa and under him is Jack Cerone. Now, in the hierarchy of that family and how it works, is Korshak a member of LCN [La Cosa Nostra]?"

"No, he is not, sir."

"How would Korshak deal with Joey Aiuppa? Who would control whom to get to Korshak?"

"Well, he has a man he goes to."

"Who is that?"

"Gussie Alex. . . . "

"So Korshak would deal with Gussie Alex. Who would Gussie Alex deal with?"

"Well, he deals with Joe Batters."

"That is Joey Aiuppa?"

"No. Joe Batters used to be the boss, [Tony] Accardo. You see, that

---

*A year earlier, in January 1980, during a meeting of the Mafia's national crime commission, the Chicago mob was given control over the underworld's interests in Las Vegas after the decision was made to keep Chicago mobsters out of Atlantic City.

is his man for years, Gussie Alex. This is what I was told. Now, I don't know if it is true or not."

"Who told it to you?"

"[Johnny] Roselli said something like that, him and Joe Batters. In fact, Joe Batters brought Gussie Alex into the picture when he was the boss of the LCN, sir. . . ."

"Who in turn controlled Korshak?"

"The Chicago family. Gussie Alex and the Chicago family."

The Chicago Crime Commission reported that Alex was still in "a key position of leadership . . . who has served his organization well and now desires to put some distance between himself and the ordinary problems of his group. Alex still maintains his condominium on Lake Shore Drive in Chicago, but spends most of his time at his other condo on Galt Ocean Mile in Fort Lauderdale, Florida. There is really no way the mob is going to let Alex simply fade away. His contacts among politicians, public officials, labor leaders, and members of the judiciary are simply too valuable to waste."[25]

Fratianno explained that he had met Korshak in 1975 at the Bistro restaurant in Beverly Hills, where they tried to work out a dispute between two Teamsters that was causing Fratianno some business problems. When the problem was not resolved, Fratianno returned to Korshak with reputed syndicate hitman Mike Rizzitello. At that second meeting, there was no attempt to intimidate Korshak beyond the presence of Rizzitello. Later, however, Rizzitello accidentally ran into Korshak on the street. According to Fratianno, the chance meeting scared Korshak, and he complained to Gus Alex that he was being muscled. Alex then told Accardo, who told Aiuppa.

Mafia figure Tony Spilotro, who oversaw the Chicago underworld operations in Las Vegas, then called Fratianno and asked to meet with him and Rizzitello. The three men had a sitdown with Accardo, Aiuppa, and Cerone, the underboss. Fratianno was told in no uncertain terms that he was no longer to have any further contact with Korshak —"because it is putting heat on him," Aiuppa explained. "Now, if you had anything that you want from Sid Korshak, come to us. He . . . has been with us thirty years. We don't want him loused up."

"Had Korshak reported that a dead fish had been left in his mailbox?" the *Penthouse* attorney asked Fratianno.

"Yes, sir."

"Does a dead fish have a special meaning in the world of the LCN?"

"Well, it means that somebody is going to kill him."

Korshak later came back to Fratianno and asked him if he knew who had left the dead fish. When Fratianno said he did not know, Korshak asked him to find out, which Fratianno never did.

On January 11, 1982, *Playboy* publisher Hugh Hefner was questioned under oath by the New Jersey Casino Control Commission about his 1978 fee of $50,000 to Korshak for the purpose of making peace with Wasserman over a copyright suit Universal had filed against *Playboy*. Hefner was trying to get a license for his new hotel/casino in Atlantic City. Dressed in a dark blue suit, a white shirt, and even a tie, Hefner said that he thought Korshak would be a good mediator between him and Wasserman. Although he said he regretted the entire matter, he thought there had been "nothing inappropriate" about it. New Jersey Deputy Attorney General James F. Flanagan III described Hefner's $50,000 as a payment to Korshak to "whisper in Lew Wasserman's ear."

Although three of five commissioners voted to grant Hefner and Playboy Enterprises, Inc., a gaming license, the law required approval of four of the commissioners. The commission found that Hefner was "unsuitable for licensure and association with a licensed New Jersey casino." However, the commission—which did not consider the Korshak incident alone the disqualifying factor—indicated that it would grant a license to Playboy's partner, Elsinore, with the condition that Hefner be disassociated from the project.*

In April 1983, the U.S. Senate Permanent Subcommittee on Investigations received evidence that the international presidents of the Culinary Workers Union (also known as the Hotel Employees and Restaurant Employees International Union) and the Laborers were "handpicked" by Chicago Mafia leader Tony Accardo. The information was provided by Joseph Hauser, a convicted insurance swindler who had flipped and turned state's evidence. After being convicted with former U.S. attorney general Richard Kleindienst in a multimillion-dollar insurance swindle involving the Teamsters Central States Pension Fund, Hauser had allowed himself to be used as the hub of several FBI sting operations during the Carter administration that yielded a pending indictment against Santos Trafficante of Florida and the bribery conviction of Carlos Marcello of Louisiana. Hauser had also received thinly veiled admissions on tape from Marcello during the FBI's

---

*The major disqualifying factors in Playboy's license application were the corporation's bribing of an official from the New York State Liquor Authority during the early 1960s, and the improprieties that led to the loss of Playboy's casino license in England in 1981. Also, the Elsinore Corporation, Playboy's partner, was part of the Hyatt hotel chain, owned by the Pritzker family, which had also been represented by Korshak.

BRILAB sting operation that he had been directly involved in the assassination of John Kennedy twenty years earlier.

During his testimony before the subcommittee, Hauser stated that Korshak was Accardo's contact to these corrupt union bosses from the Culinary Workers and the Laborers. Hauser explained, "Organized crime leader Tony Accardo, who I have known for many years as Joe Batters, told me on several occasions that he had sent Korshak to Los Angeles to represent the mob there."[26]

Prior to Hauser's testimony, Korshak had been sent a letter from the subcommittee, informing him that the Senate wanted him as a witness. Responding for Korshak was his attorney, Harvey Silets, who wrote: "After consultation with Mr. Korshak and a careful review of the contents of your letter, we wish to advise you, on behalf of Mr. Korshak, that he will not provide testimony, with or without a subpoena, based upon his constitutional privilege against self-incrimination."[27]

Hedging his bets between labor and management, Korshak had done legal work for the Hilton Corporation since the early 1960s on a case-by-case basis. After Conrad Hilton's son, Barron Hilton, took control of the business, Patrick Hoy, a vice-president of the General Dynamics Corporation,* who was a close friend of both Hilton and Korshak, recommended that Korshak be kept on retainer by Hilton.

Hilton took Hoy's advice and retained Korshak. Between 1971 and 1984 Korshak had made over $700,000 from Hilton alone. Korshak was chiefly responsible for handling some tax and real estate matters, as well as Equal Opportunity cases. Because of Korshak's association with the Culinary Workers Union in Las Vegas, Hilton claimed to have considered Korshak an adversary in Las Vegas labor relations cases.

Hilton had begun construction on a $270 million hotel/casino in Atlantic City, scheduled to open in May 1984. Hilton applied for its casino license from the New Jersey Casino Control Commission. During the commission's preliminary inquiry, state investigators discovered Hilton's links to Korshak. In a report filed with the commissioners, the staff stated, "It is quite evident that over the years [Korshak] has made good contacts with very powerful politicians. . . . Korshak's list of past

---

*Interestingly, General Dynamics, the nation's largest defense contractor, was owned by Colonel Henry Crown, for whom Korshak had done some unspecified legal work. While Hoy was a vice president of General Dynamics and Korshak was working for Crown, General Dynamics had engaged in fraudulent cost-overrun claims to the U.S. Navy. In 1984, when the Senate Judiciary Subcommittee began to investigate General Dynamics, it subpoenaed the Justice Department's internal records on the company. When Attorney General William French Smith repeatedly defied the committee, refusing to give it the requested documents, the subcommittee cited Smith for contempt of Congress. It is not known whether Hoy—who had earlier pleaded guilty to mail fraud in connection with a $2 million bank fraud case—or Korshak appears in those secret reports.

and present associates reads like a who's who of prominent southern Californians. . . ."

The previous March, after Hilton officials realized that their Korshak connection could cause them some licensing problems, Hilton fired Korshak. Hilton, through its legal counsel, sent Korshak a letter, stating: "I appreciate very much your understanding regarding the action we feel we're forced to take in dissolving the longstanding relationship between you and Hilton Hotels Corporation. As I stated in our telephone conversation, we very much regret this situation. We feel, however, that we cannot risk jeopardizing in any way the huge investment we have committed to New Jersey. . . .

"You can rest assured that you continue to be held in high esteem and affection by those of us at Hilton who have had the privilege of having you as a friend and adviser."

In the midst of the opening round of testimony in July 1984, Barron Hilton received a barrage of hostile questions from the commission on his association with Korshak. Hilton said, "I wish to hell we would have never hired him, because I can see it's a very distinct problem here in the minds of you gentlemen about this fellow's integrity."

Questioned again about Korshak in November, Hilton stated, "I want to say that I certainly appreciate the concern that this commission has that any applicant be free of any type of association [with] an individual such as Mr. Korshak, and I can say that today we would not be involved in any fashion with Mr. Korshak, and as you are aware, we, this latter year, discontinued our relationship with the individual, and I have to agree with you that it should have been done before, rather than now."

Corporate officials added that had they known that Korshak was going to take the Fifth before the Senate Subcommittee on Investigations they "would have fired him on the spot."

Korshak, who was feverishly loyal to his friends and expected to be treated in kind, was livid when he heard about Hilton's statements about him. In retaliation, the secretive Korshak, who rarely puts anything in writing, wrote Barron Hilton a letter, dated November 29, 1984.

Dear Sir:

I find it extremely difficult to address you in any other fashion.

I read with interest your disparaging remarks about me to the New Jersey Gaming Commission. When did you discover that I was unworthy of being an attorney or that I was associated with characters that shocked your most decent sensibilities?

I have in my possession a number of letters from your staff extolling my virtues as an attorney and telling me how happy the hotels were with my representation of your corporation. Those letters were also sent to your office for your personal perusal.

I am sending them to you again today.

Was I in a sorry plight with you when I met you in New York and worked out a deal with Charlie Bluhdorn of Gulf & Western [who died in February 1983], giving you their airport hotel and the Arlington hotel to manage without you investing one penny, despite your offer to pay Gulf & Western some $10,000,000 for a one-half investment in these hotels? If you recall, you will remember that I never billed you for my services in these matters. My fee ordinarily would be a very high one. Do you remember calling me in Las Vegas at 6 one morning while you were with Kirk Kerkorian and Frank Rothman [Kerkorian's chief executive officer at MGM–United Artists] for me to ask the [Las Vegas] unions involved not to strike you, namely Dick Thomas of the Teamsters and Bob Fox of the Engineers? As you well know, there was no fee involved.

You have caused me irreparable harm, and as long as I live I will never forget that. When did I become a shady character? I imagine when you were having difficulty getting a license in Atlantic City.

Very truly yours,
Sidney R. Korshak

At the conclusion of the hearings, New Jersey gaming commissioner Joel R. Jacobson said, "In my judgment, the thirteen-year-long relationship of the Hilton Hotels Corporation with Sidney Korshak is the fatal link upon which I primarily based the conclusion that this applicant has not established its suitability for licensure in New Jersey.

"In September of 1971, Hilton retained Sidney Korshak as outside counsel, an association which lasted until March 1984, when it was finally terminated under conditions that themselves raised questions of suitability.

"Throughout that thirteen-year period, during which Mr. Korshak received over $700,000 in fees and expenses, the publicity and notoriety about Mr. Korshak's unsavory reputation and associations with organized crime figures repeatedly swirled around his and Hilton's head."

Jacobson also raised *The New York Times* series on Korshak written by Seymour Hersh and Jeff Gerth. The commissioner asked, "How did Mr. Korshak respond to such scurrilous allegations? Did he mount a vigorous challenge? Did he descend upon *The New York Times* by rightly demanding a retraction and apology? Did he launch a $50 million libel suit? No, he didn't. He did nothing. And, in fact, Hilton Corporation executives responded to the information contained in the articles with a corresponding equanimity.

"Mr. Barron Hilton telephoned Korshak to offer sympathy for the bad publicity."

Hilton had said that after reading the series on Korshak, he sent his lawyer a letter of condolence. "Knowing that he was depressed about this publicity . . . ," Hilton testified, "I dropped him a note. I personally am not aware about his guilt or association with the underworld. This is something that really I have no opinion about."

The commission rejected Hilton's bid on February 28, 1985. The refusal was solely based on Hilton's association with Sidney Korshak —whom the commission charged as being "a key actor in organized crime's unholy alliances with corrupt union officials and its pernicious efforts to frustrate the rights of working men and women by infecting legitimate unions, to rob their members' future by stealing the benefits they have earned in the past from honest labor."

Barron Hilton could only say, "I am shocked and stunned at the decision." He also vowed to appeal, adding that he was "confident that the overwhelming evidence in support of licensing of the Hilton organization will ultimately prevail."

When asked to discuss the difference between the Playboy and Hilton cases—and their associations with Korshak—Jacobson said that three of the five members of the New Jersey commission had voted to license Hefner, because they found "nothing sinister or improper in the one-time retention of Sidney Korshak" by Hefner.

Jacobson continued, "Hefner paid Korshak $50,000 seemingly simply for the purpose of having Korshak explain Hefner's position to Wasserman, and to arrange a meeting with Wasserman, not Universal's attorneys, to discuss a possible settlement of the lawsuit. However, Korshak's mission failed. He apparently kept the $50,000, a high price . . . for simply trying to arrange a meeting and deliver a message. No commissioner drew the inference this was a venal influence-peddling scheme. Hefner testified that he engaged Korshak's services only because he thought Korshak could influence Wasserman. . . .

"Hilton clung to its relationship with Korshak until March 1984, long after everyone was fully aware of Mr. Korshak's reputation and associations, and after warnings had been issued by both the Nevada Gaming Board and the Appellate Division of the New Jersey Superior Court."

On January 22, 1984, William French Smith announced that he was resigning as attorney general. Almost immediately, the White House announced that Smith would be replaced by Reagan's chief of staff, Ed Meese, who had co-chaired the California Attorney General's Organized Crime Commission that named Korshak as one of ninety-two underworld figures operating in the state.

Viewed as a "tough cop," Meese proved during the transition period to be more of a politician. His support of Jackie Presser's appointment as a "senior economic advisor" to the Reagan transition team was viewed as nothing less than a political payoff for Teamsters support for Reagan during the 1980 election campaign. And, on December 5, 1980, before any charges had been alleged, Meese had met personally with FBI director William Webster, asking whether the bureau had any information that Ray Donovan was associated with organized crime.*

Archibald Cox, the incorruptible chairman of Common Cause, who was fired as the Watergate special prosecutor by President Nixon, said that Meese was "blind to the ethical standards and obligations required of a public official," and thus was "not fit" to be attorney general.

Meese's appointment was held up while special prosecutor Jacob Stein investigated charges that Meese had obtained federal jobs for friends who had helped him out of financial trouble. In particular, Meese had failed to disclose a $15,000, interest-free loan he received from a close friend. Another lingering concern was a $15,000 investment by the Meese family in a firm that invested $100,000 in a Nevada slot machine business. Because the company received funds from the Small Business Administration, it was prohibited by law from investing in any gambling enterprise.

Meese was eventually cleared by Stein of any criminal wrongdoing and was confirmed by the Senate, 63–31, to become attorney general on February 23, 1985—over a year after Smith had announced his resignation.

Earlier, in late 1983, Meese met with Teamsters president Jackie Presser—who, like Korshak, was also receiving hands-off treatment by the Reagan administration—to discuss the union's problems with the deregulation of the trucking industry.†

At the time of the Meese-Presser meeting, Presser was the target of a federal investigation in a $165,000 union embezzlement case in Cleve-

---

*The Meese-Webster meeting was held eleven days before Donovan's nomination. Meese asked Webster to inform him as to whether "checks [on Donovan] reveal any allegations relating to organized crime"—before the bureau conducted its Full-Field investigation of Donovan.

†In June 1983, Meese had attended a celebration for Presser at the Georgetown Club in Washington. Also in attendance at the party for Presser were Secretary of Labor Ray Donovan, former Reagan political adviser Lynn Nofziger, U.S. senators Robert Dole and Ted Stevens, and Congressman Jack Kemp, a presidential hopeful.

land. Two of Presser's associates, Allen Friedman and Jack Nardi, either had been convicted or had pleaded guilty for their roles in the scheme. Friedman was also Presser's uncle and was plea-bargaining with the government in return for his testimony against his nephew.

On May 31, 1984, federal attorneys in Cleveland decided to ask approval from the Justice Department for a criminal indictment against Presser. A week later, it was revealed that Presser had been an informant for the FBI since the 1970s. Suddenly, the case against Presser stalled.

On October 1, 1984, Ray Donovan was indicted by a New York grand jury on charges of grand larceny and fraud in connection with the city's subway project, on which his construction company was a major contractor. Donovan pleaded innocent but immediately took a leave of absence from his Cabinet position.

On February 26, 1985, William Webster and the FBI—working in cooperation with the New York Organized Crime Task Force, headed by Ronald Goldstock—arrested the heads of the five Mafia families in New York, as well as four of their top aides. The nine mobsters were charged with fifteen counts of conspiracy and operating "through a pattern of racketeering activity," which included murder, labor racketeering, and extortion, according to the indictment.

On April 23, 1985, two months after Meese's confirmation and a month after Ray Donovan resigned as Secretary of Labor,* Presser— who had promised to lead the Teamsters into a new era of responsible unionism—took the Fifth Amendment fifteen consecutive times before the President's Commission on Organized Crime, refusing to answer questions about his personal finances, his ties to organized crime, his union goon squads, and an array of other activities. That same day, a federal judge in Chicago ordered former Teamsters general president Roy Williams to begin serving time in a federal prison hospital† for conspiring to bribe Senator Cannon.

In late July, Justice Department officials testified before a federal grand jury in Cleveland, which was investigating Presser. They convinced the grand jury to cease its investigation of Presser on the basis of his role as a federal informant. The decision not to prosecute Presser

---

*After a five-month leave of absence from the Labor Department awaiting trial, Donovan decided to resign after his pretrial motion to dismiss the 137-count indictment against him and his nine co-defendants was rejected. President Reagan, upon receiving Donovan's resignation, issued a statement saying that Donovan "has not been convicted of anything" and that he "leaves the cabinet with my friendship and heartfelt gratitude."

†Williams was suffering from severe emphysema and heart problems.

was made by the chief of the Justice Department's Criminal Division, Stephen S. Trott, a former deputy district attorney in Los Angeles, who had later become the U.S. attorney in Los Angeles.

Attorney General Meese insisted during an appearance on ABC's *Good Morning America* on August 6, 1985, that he had not taken part in the decision to drop the case against Presser, "because we wanted to avoid any possibility of anyone claiming that there was any political interference," Meese said. "It's very clear [that] at no time was there any political influence or any undue influence."

On August 25, *The Washington Post* reported that the FBI had authorized Presser "to make payments to 'ghost employees' on the union payroll and did not inform the Justice Department of the arrangement, thereby dooming the department's thirty-two-month investigation of Presser." The report added that FBI Director Webster was "not told that the FBI was not only using Presser as an informant, but was also allowing him to engage in criminal activity. . . ."*

As a consequence, Presser's uncle was released from prison—without ever testifying against Presser as he had offered to do. Later, the charges against co-conspirator Jack Nardi, as well as his guilty plea, were also dropped.

Another surprise came when former Teamsters president Roy Williams flipped and turned state's evidence against several former colleagues in the underworld. Williams's testimony came during the trial in Kansas City of fifteen mobsters accused of skimming at several casinos in Las Vegas. The indictments had come as a result of an FBI investigation that began in 1978. Williams, who had been the third Teamsters president imprisoned for corruption in office, was the first to testify against his former cohorts.

Before his testimony at the trial, Williams was interviewed by Stephen M. Ryan, deputy counsel of the President's Commission on Organized Crime, on September 16. Ryan asked Williams about Presser's ties to the underworld. Ryan asked, "Would you describe your conversation with Jackie Presser that indicated to you that at times he had either a relationship or a problem with the mob?"

"He was in San Francisco one time after he became vice-president,"

---

*In early April 1986, a new grand jury was convened in the Presser case. The investigation concentrated on whether three FBI agents had made false statements to the Justice Department about Presser's role as an FBI informant. Consequently, Presser faced renewed federal charges about his activities, particularly those stemming from the Cleveland fraud case. Under extreme political pressure, Jackie Presser was indicted on May 16, 1986; on May 21, he was reelected president of the Teamsters Union.

Williams replied, "and I was getting a lot of static, as the president of the union. 'Why all of the big thugs around Jackie Presser?' And I'm not arguing that they were good guys. I don't know whether they was [sic] connected with anything or not, other than they were members of the Teamsters. And I got Jackie in a corner and asked him, because at least I was trying to find an answer for some of these questions.

"And he told me that the Mob was split in Cleveland, and he's afraid that he picked the wrong side."

During the interview, Williams also confirmed Fratianno's previous statements that Sidney Korshak controlled Teamsters vice-president Andy Anderson. "And Sidney Korshak is an individual who was believed, by you, to be a person associated with the Mob?" Ryan asked.

"Yes," Williams replied.

"Or a member?"

"Yes."

When asked by *The Washington Post* in mid-November 1985 whether Presser would continue to have a relationship with the Reagan administration,* Edward J. Rollins, the Reagan/Bush campaign director in 1984, replied that Presser was "a very good friend and will remain that." He added that Presser "put his money where his mouth was."[28]

On November 27, the Las Vegas skimming trial continued in Kansas City with the testimony of former Mafia boss Angelo Lonardo of Cleveland, who, like Williams, had also become a federal witness. Lonardo told the court that he had helped persuade Chicago's top Mafia leaders Joey Aiuppa and Jackie Cerone to support the Presser bid for the union presidency in 1983. When the Chicago mobsters balked at the idea, another Cleveland mob leader, Maishe Rockman, responded, "Jackie Presser is okay, and I can handle him."

According to an FBI summary report, dated October 28, 1983, "Rockman told Lonardo a story that was related to him by Presser. Presser was in Washington, D.C., at a gathering attended by Roy Williams, the President of the United States, the First Lady, Jackie Presser, and Presser's wife. When the President greeted Williams, he was merely cordial to him. When the President greeted Jackie Presser, both he and the First Lady hugged Presser and showed a great deal of personal attachment to Presser. The First Lady kidded Presser about

---

*On October 21, 1985, during a speech before a meeting of U.S. attorneys, Reagan said, "I'd like nothing more than to be remembered as a president who did everything he could to bust up the syndicates and give the mobsters a permanent stay in the jailhouse."

his need to lose weight. This was all done in full view of Roy Williams, who, according to Presser, was visibly hurt."

Presser was to be subpoenaed to testify at the skimming trial but told the court through his attorney that he would take the Fifth Amendment if forced to take the stand.

Two weeks later, President Reagan appointed a top associate of Presser, Charles L. Woods, a California Teamsters official, to fill a vacancy on the National Mediation Board at a salary of $72,300 a year. The board was responsible for settling labor disputes in the railway and airlines industries. Presser had personally recommended Woods to Reagan.

A 977-page pretrial deposition by Senator Paul Laxalt* in October 1985 was leaked to the press during the discovery process in Laxalt's $250 million libel suit against the McClatchy Newspapers of California. In 1983, Pulitzer prize–winning reporter Denny Walsh of McClatchy's *Sacramento Bee* accused Laxalt's casino, Ormsby House of Carson City, of being involved in a skimming operation with organized crime figures. Refusing to be intimidated, the McClatchy Newspapers countersued. Under questioning by McClatchy's attorneys, Laxalt admitted to be either associated with or to have accepted campaign money from Delbert Coleman, Morris Dalitz, Allen Dorfman, and Ruby Kolod.

On Sunday, January 12, 1986, an article appeared under President Reagan's byline in *The New York Times Magazine* entitled "Declaring War on Organized Crime." Written by Reagan aide Tony Dolan, the article celebrated the "success" of the Reagan administration's war on the underworld. Reagan recounted some of his own experiences:

> [Organized crime's] essential characteristics [are] not all that different from the face of organized crime a generation or two ago—a point on which I can cite personal experience. Like all too many Americans, I've seen the mob at work.
>
> In the early 1940's, along with many members of the Hollywood community, I watched with deep concern as organized crime moved in on the motion picture industry, largely through a takeover of the stagehands' and projectionists' union, the International Alliance of Theatrical Stage Employees and Motion Picture Operators [IATSE], and an attempted move on the union to which I belonged, the Screen Actors Guild. . . . But through the commitment and efforts of people like my friend Robert Montgomery, then president of SAG, the mob's attempted infiltration failed.

---

*In late August 1985, Laxalt announced that he would not seek a third term to the U.S. Senate. According to published reports, Laxalt had simply come to the conclusion that he would make more money working in the private sector.

Without ever mentioning the Teamsters Union or Las Vegas, Reagan added, "There will be no détente with the mob. It's war to the end. We mean to cripple their organization."

Two days after the article was published, the President's Commission on Organized Crime issued an interim report criticizing the Reagan administration for its close ties to the Teamsters Union, writing that "the appearance of impropriety" had been created. *The Washington Post,* in an editorial the following day, wrote, "The commission did not charge—and no evidence has been produced to show—that this administration has been corrupted by its ties to Mr. Presser. . . . [However,] it creates . . . the appearance of wrongdoing that leads to an erosion of public confidence in the government's commitment to fight organized crime. The Presser case will hound the administration until a full explanation of this episode is made."

The commission report shook up the White House and the Justice Department so badly that Attorney General Meese called a press conference to defend the White House–Teamsters relationship, saying that he did not see anything improper about it. Meese added that "at no time have I, nor, to my knowledge, any member of the administration, done anything which was designed to assist or aid anyone involved with organized crime. The fact that people did meet with labor leaders was certainly not designed or intended to in any way interfere with the proper investigation of organized crime."

Despite the commission's criticism of the White House ties to the Teamsters, its 222-page final report, entitled "The Impact: Organized Crime Today," was a disappointment when it was released in April 1986. Over half of the eighteen commissioners filed supplemental views or dissenting opinions on the report. In its defense, Chairman Kaufman said that the commission had "directed its searchlight on a few dark places, which will receive more attention than in the past." However, dissenters on the commission charged that too many "dark places" had been ignored. "Poor management of time, money, and staff has resulted in the commission's leaving important issues unexamined. . . . The true history of the commission . . . is a saga of missed opportunity."

One commissioner was asked why Korshak's name had not appeared in the final report. He replied, "That's a sensitive area. Korshak did come up in a couple of interviews and in one of the staff reports. But there was dissension about him throughout the life of the commission. . . . Several of us wanted to highlight him, particularly since he played such an important role in the Hilton hearings in Atlantic City. But it was just not meant to be. There were forces that didn't want Korshak touched. So the commission just rounded up the usual suspects."

Another commissioner went further, citing a nine-hour meeting prior to the release of the final report. "Leaving Korshak out of the final report was no accident. A conscious decision was made to leave out any reference to him, and we were told about it at that meeting. It was too late to do anything about it. We [the commissioners] really never had a chance to see the final version of the report before it was released. . . . I felt that there was pressure to keep Korshak out. And where that pressure came from, well, your guess is as good as mine."

As American conservatives become more and more disenchanted with the prospects of a George Bush or a Jack Kemp as their next presidential candidate, the search continues for another Ronald Reagan. No less than three prominent newspaper columnists agreed that Paul Laxalt is being seriously considered to champion the Republican Party in 1988. Lou Cannon wrote, "There are conservatives who see Laxalt as a potential successor to Reagan, despite the inherent difficulties of being a senator from Nevada."[29] Mary McGrory revealed that Laxalt "has told those urging him to get into the race that he will address the question when he gives up the chairmanship of the Republican Party [in 1987]. But he's thinking about it, and the right is yearning."[30] George F. Will stated that Laxalt was "waiting in the wings—not just waiting, actually pacing restlessly and pawing the dust."[31]

Perhaps Reagan himself supplied an answer for his right-wing colleagues on March 3, 1986, when he spoke of his "best friend," Senator Paul Laxalt, at a $1,000-a-plate dinner given in Laxalt's honor by conservative Paul Weyrich's Free Congress Political Action Committee:

"As most of you know, Paul [Laxalt] and I were elected governors of our respective states at about the same time. They say we started even. I had California, with one of the biggest economies of the nation. Paul had Nevada and Howard Hughes . . . There were those who said a straight shooter like Paul could never make it in Washington. But sure enough, Paul has disposed of problems here just as [easily] as he disposed of them in Nevada. He had the best possible training for Washington—as a rancher and a herder: They have exactly the same sort of disposal problems that we have."

Then, seemingly in an emotional plea, Reagan beckoned to his followers, "Look to the son of the high mountains and peasant herders, to the son of the Sierra and the immigrant Basque family. Look to a man, to a friend, to an American who gave himself so that others might live in freedom."

President Paul Laxalt? Ronald Reagan, Lew Wasserman, and Sidney Korshak would probably be the first to say that stranger things have happened. And, somehow, there would be a symmetry to it all.

Dan E. Moldea
Washington, D.C.
May 22, 1986

POSTSCRIPT

Ronald Reagan is a very loyal man. That is his special gift. He is loyal to those who protect him and his interests. He takes care of those who protect him. That is the story of his life. That is what has kept him alive politically.

In early November 1986, a small magazine in Beirut revealed that the United States had engaged in a secret deal to sell weapons to Iran, in return for American hostages held in Lebanon. The arrangement violated the expressed Reagan policy against making concessions to terrorists. While operating this plan, Reagan had been referring to Iran as "Murder, Inc." The revelation by the Beirut publication caused a public outcry against the Reagan Administration in the United States.

On November 17, Reagan lied during a press conference about the extent of his knowledge on this matter, saying, among other things, that no third country had been involved in the arms deal. When it became evident that Reagan was concealing the truth, his aides scrambled to provide clarification and cover. His lies were portrayed by them simply as innocent misstatements. They protected Reagan, who was loyal to them when their resignations were demanded by congressional leaders in the aftermath.

As during his 1962 appearance before the federal grand jury, when asked tough questions about possible wrongdoing by him or his friends, Reagan claimed that he couldn't remember, or simply refused to tell the truth. Reagan had again used the illusion of his ignorance of—or his inability to recall—important events as weapons for his personal survival.

On November 25, Attorney General Edwin Meese announced that as much as $30 million in profits from weapons shipped to Israel and sold to Iran were deposited in Swiss bank accounts (laundered through a network of dummy corporations), and "made available to the forces in Central America" at war with the Sandinista government. However, Contra leaders denied having had access to any Swiss bank accounts. In the wake of Meese's statement, and after numerous documents about the matter had been destroyed, Reagan dismissed his chief National Security Council advisor, John M. Poindexter, and Colonel Oliver L. North, an NSC aide, who had been implicated in the scheme.

When Poindexter and North were called to testify before Congress and took the Fifth Amendment, they did so with the President's support. Ironically, when members of the Screen Actors Guild had been called to testify before the House Un-American Activities Committee while Reagan was SAG president, as described in Chapter Nine of this book, Reagan had insisted, "It is every member's duty to cooperate fully."

On December 12, in the midst of a suspected cover-up, two members of MCA's board of directors, former senator Howard Baker* and former Democratic national chairman Robert Strauss, met with Reagan at the White House and implored him to take stronger actions to rescue himself from further damage.

Because of their far-reaching national and international consequences, the charges stemming from an arms scandal, of course, are more serious than those discussed in *Dark Victory*. But when all the facts about Contragate have finally been chronicled, they will dovetail with what has been described in this book.

When there is an issue involving missing millions of dollars, laundered money, dummy corporations, and Swiss bank accounts—all in the same breath—the real subject is drugs and organized crime. I am convinced that much of the Contragate affair is going to wind up as a series of multimillion-dollar drug deals involving right-wing ideologues who sold drugs to raise money for the Contras as part of their eleemosynary activities. But more prominently, there were those who were even

---

*Howard Baker replaced White House Chief of Staff Donald Regan on February 27, 1987.

more mercenary, selling drugs for profit, using the Contras as a cover for their illicit operations. Planes containing arms for the Contras landed in friendly Central American countries, unloaded these weapons, and instead of deadheading to the United States, they were loaded with drugs, particularly cocaine. I have been calling this "Coke-Run."

According to a January 20, 1987, report in *The New York Times,* "When crew members, based in El Salvador, learned that Drug Enforcement Administration agents were investigating their activities, one of them warned that they had White House protection." In October, Colonel North asked the FBI to cease its investigation of one of the air-freight companies involved in the Contra arms supply operation. On October 30, Meese ordered the FBI to delay the probe. Meese claimed that he had acted for "legitimate national security reasons."

If all this is true, how will the American public respond to a massive government-authorized program to conduct a covert war, which is funded, at least in part, by drug money? How will the public be able to believe that the Reagan Administration's war on crime and drugs is a sincere one? Will the public believe the fact that the same thing has been going on for years, not only in Central America but in Southeast Asia and the Near East?

The evidence supporting all of these items is mounting. On January 13, 1987, *The New York Times* reported, "Some senators say that any official inquiry [into Coke-Run] and how much if anything American officials knew about it, at this time would create such an uproar that it could derail the main thrusts of the Senate inquiry: to sort out the Reagan Administration's secret arms sales to Iran and diversion of profits to the Contras."

In an interview published in the August 11, 1986, issue of *Newsweek,* President Reagan said, "The polls show that [drugs are], in most people's minds, the No. 1 problem in the country. It is not only necessary to step up our efforts to make it difficult to get drugs, but the main thrust has got to be to get the people themselves to turn off on it."

After Ronald and Nancy Reagan appeared on national television on September 14 to announce their "Drug-Free America" program, the White House called for additional funding in the new federal budget to further combat the nation's drug problem. The theme of the project was embodied in the slogan "Just Say No."

On September 19, a week after the U.S. House passed a sweeping antidrug bill, ten Senate Republicans, who were seeking re-election in November, unveiled a federal antidrug package at a news conference.

"I don't think there is any turning back," said Majority Leader Robert J. Dole of Kansas. Senator Strom Thurmond of South Carolina added, "This bill is going to separate the talkers from the doers on the issue of drugs." After passage by Congress, President Reagan signed the $1.7 billion antidrug package on October 27, declaring that this was a "major victory" in the war against drugs. "The American people want their government to get tough and go on the offensive, and that's what we intend with more ferocity than ever before." But after the Democrats took both the House and the Senate in the midterm elections, President Reagan said little more about his drug campaign.

On January 7, 1987, Reagan proposed dramatic cuts in the war against drugs, asking that more than $913 million be eliminated from drug education, enforcement, and prevention. These funds had been stipulated in the antidrug bill cheered and signed by Reagan. Grilled about the cuts on Capitol Hill, White House budget director James C. Miller said, "No one in this administration is in favor of drug abuse." Representative Charles B. Rangel lamented that the cuts proposed by Reagan and the White House "seriously call into question the depth of their commitment to an effective drug-abuse strategy." House Speaker James Wright said that Congress would not approve the reductions.

On February 3, the Reagan Administration announced that the President would issue an executive order combining all of the federal government's antidrug programs under the National Drug Policy Board. Selected by President Reagan to head the board—which would be charged with developing budget priorities for every federal agency involved in the war on drugs—was Attorney General Edwin Meese.

As described in the Epilogue of this book, Reagan has been playing this game with the public ever since he was elected. He declares war on organized crime with all the tough rhetoric—and then creates a task force against drugs in south Florida, or a presidential commission against organized crime. After offering him accolades for being a crimefighter, the public's interest soon fades, while the task forces and commissions evaporate and are never heard from again.

In the past, red scares and terrorism have always successfully managed to get the public's mind off organized crime and public corruption. It happened during the mid-to-late 1940s, when the Hollywood studios diverted national attention away from the Mafia's penetration of, and cooperation with, the film industry, which is also discussed earlier in the book. Ronald Reagan, as the president of SAG, was a principal character in that charade, along with mob-connected unions, like IATSE, the Teamsters Union, and the American Federation of Musicians. The Kefauver Hearings of 1950–51 were eclipsed by the second round of hearings by the U.S. House Un-American Activities Committee and Senator Joseph McCarthy's witchhunt. The Senate Rackets Committee, which operated from 1957 to 1960, was replaced on the front pages by the fear of nuclear war with the Soviet Union and Cuban premier Fidel Castro, who had thrown the underworld out of his country and was consequently the target of the CIA–Mafia plots to murder him. During the late 1970s —after the disappearance of Jimmy Hoffa, which sparked numerous probes of the underworld's subculture—our attention was diverted by the Soviet invasion of Afghanistan and Iran's taking of American hostages. We have never been afraid of the national crime syndicate— even though organized crime, which Robert Kennedy once declared "the enemy within," is clearly the most serious threat we have to our national security.

Americans see nothing wrong with making a bet on a football game with the neighborhood bookmaker, or even just smoking a joint. The acceptance of these seemingly harmless vices can undermine the American public's disapproval of more serious forms of underworld activities. When diversions put money in the pockets of organized crime, some of it ends up in the hands of public officials on the federal, state, and local levels. And when one level of government has been corrupted, the system simply doesn't work right.

There are other reasons why organized crime is such an unpopular issue politically. The Left balks at any suggestion of electronic surveillance, which unfortunately is the only effective means of gathering intelligence against organized crime. In my thirteen years of investigating the underworld, I have never met a Mafioso or one of his associates who isn't against wiretapping and in favor of strong personal privacy laws. And I have been bored for hours, listening to them whine about the alleged impingements on their rights and freedoms by the FBI and the IRS. On the other hand, the Right decentralizes power, bringing it down from the federal government to state and local levels where mobsters can corrupt public officials, with newfound power and with whom they are on a first-name basis, within common jurisdictions. Consequently, organized crime figures can be civil libertarians and support right-wing causes simultaneously.

Organized crime figures, regardless of legal or moral considerations, are the quintessential capitalists. Their goals are simple: to acquire power, to make money, and to stay out of jail. Because of the nature of their operations and their means of enforcement, they are able to move from Point A to Point Z, in any given project, in a straight line. Legitimate businessmen—who are expected to proceed by the letter of the law, and are subject to competition, government regulations, taxation, and other obstacles—often make deals with underworld figures to help cut some of this red tape. These businessmen are accountable only to their boards of directors and stockholders, who demand that they make money. Corporate leaders like Wasserman, who do business with underworld figures (such as Sidney Korshak, the link between the legitimate business world and organized crime), will be tolerated as long as they are making money and their associations are not becoming an embarrassment.

To be sure, since becoming the president of MCA in 1936, and its chairman of the board in 1983, Lew Wasserman has never been anything less than a Hollywood institution. Yet MCA's association with organized crime figures still makes news headlines. On September 23, 1986, federal indictments of Morris Levy—the president of Roulette Records—and twenty business associates, including several top East Coast Mafia figures, were handed up in an extortion case described in my Epilogue. MCA—particularly the head of its record division, Irving Azoff—was directly linked to this scheme, although no one at MCA has been indicted. At this writing, the federal grand jury is continuing its investigation of MCA and of the mysterious relationship it has maintained with Mafia figure Sal Pisello, who was not indicted with the others but remains in jail for his previous tax evasion conviction.

The federal grand jury is also investigating MCA's earlier purchase of three small companies owned by Azoff and his associates, who received 500,000 shares of MCA stock, worth $25 million at the time of the sale. Federal investigators say that none of these companies was worth more than $5 million.

Ironically, one of these Azoff companies, Front Line Management, was a talent agency. Among its clients were rock 'n' rollers Jimmy Buffett, Boz Skaggs, Stevie Nicks, and Dan Fogelberg. For the first time since 1962—when the federal government forced MCA to divest itself of MCA Artists—MCA is again representing talent which it also employs.*

Azoff's growing power in MCA also manifested itself after bad blood developed between MCA president Sidney Sheinberg and Frank Price,

---

*As the Reagan Administration took further steps to weaken the Justice Department's Antitrust Division, MCA purchased the Cineplex Odeon Corporation, a theater chain, for $158 million. It also nearly purchased the World Champion New York Mets and Motown Records.

the chairman of the Universal Motion Picture Group. Price resigned after the $34.5 million film *Howard the Duck* was devastated at the box office. Named in late September to replace Price as Universal's head was Azoff's forty-three-year-old attorney Thomas Pollock, on whose behalf Azoff had waged a vigorous campaign.

On December 14, Wasserman celebrated his fiftieth year at MCA with a huge party. Held on Stage 12 at the Universal lot, the event brought a black-tie audience of more than 1,300 of the top names in politics and show business to honor Wasserman. Johnny Carson emceed. Frank Sinatra, appearing on videotape, sang "Lew's the Champ," to the tune of "The Lady Is a Tramp." Ronald and Nancy Reagan sent their greetings from the White House. *The Hollywood Reporter* gushed over Wasserman, saying, "His leadership has brought MCA and its many operations to great heights. Lew's deal-making and creativity are renowned in the industry. . . . Hollywood would be an entirely different place were it not for this man. He restructured the motion picture industry and led it into television. His alumni are leaders throughout the industry today."

The only thing certain at the time of this writing is that all bets are off for the 1988 Presidential election. Nobody knows for sure how George Bush will be affected by the Iranian arms sales and Coke-Run. Paul Laxalt, who has retired as the general chairman of the Republican National Committee, has kept a low profile and distanced himself from the fray. He resisted overtures to replace Donald Regan as Reagan's chief of staff. Laxalt is still the man to be watched for the Republican Presidential nomination. He has indicated that his decision to run will not depend on the public view of his "Nevada problem,"—Nevada politicians often find it hard to avoid the taint of being associated with organized crime—but on his ability to raise $8 million to $10 million for his campaign. Until something breaks, Laxalt has become a partner in the Washington office of Finley, Kumble, Wagner, Heine, Underberg, Manley, Meyerson & Casey, one of the largest law firms in the United States. At the firm, Laxalt has been joined by Russell B. Long, the recently retired, long-time Democratic senator from Louisiana.

Another factor in Laxalt's decision to run or not will be the final resolution of his libel case filed against the McClatchy Newspapers of California and reporter Denny Walsh, which is explained in the Epilogue. McClatchy has dropped its attorney, James Brosnahan, and retained Gibson, Dunn and Crutcher, the law firm of William French Smith and Paul Ziffren. The signal sent was that both sides were searching for a settlement.

With Gary Hart's most visible competitor, Mario Cuomo, out of the race for the Democratic nomination, the field is filled with names unfamiliar outside their home states and Washington, D.C. Clearly, however, the Democratic politician who has taken the hardest line in Congress against organized crime—and who is a serious contender but has announced that, for the time being, he is not running—is Georgia Senator Sam Nunn, the new chairman of the Senate Permanent Subcommittee on Investigations, and a member of the Senate select committee investigating the arms–Contra aid scandal.

Meyer Lansky, the financial wizard of organized crime, knew perhaps better than anyone else that the successful annihilation of organized crime's subculture in America would rock the "legitimate" world's entire foundation, which would ultimately force fundamental social changes and redistributions of wealth and power in this country. Lansky's dream was to bond the two worlds together so that one could not survive without the other. Those of us who recognize the vast power of the underworld in our nation today also understand how close that dream—and our nightmare—is to coming true.

February 27, 1987

NOTES

I. THE RISE

Chapter One

1. Dave Dexter, Jr., *The Jazz Story: From the Nineties to the Sixties* (Englewood Cliffs, New Jersey: Prentice-Hall, 1964), p. 31.
2. Albert R. Kroeger, *Television Magazine,* September 1961.
3. Michael Pye, *Moguls: Inside the Business of Show Business* (New York: Holt, Rinehart and Winston, 1980), pp. 20–21.
4. Justice Department memorandum, November 23, 1960.
5. *The New York Times,* December 6, 1962.
6. Justice Department memorandum, June 6, 1961.
7. Justice Department memorandum, June 9, 1961.

Chapter Two

1. Ovid Demaris, *Captive City: Chicago in Chains* (New York: Lyle Stuart, 1969), pp. 120–21.
2. Pye, p. 23.
3. Hank Messick, *The Beauties and the Beasts* (New York: David McKay and Company, 1973), p. 87.
4. Al Stump, *The Los Angeles Herald-Examiner,* January 27, 1980.
5. Testimony of John Roselli, "Investigation of Organized Crime in Interstate Commerce," October 7, 1950, p. 396.
6. *Annette Carvaretta Nitti* v. *Commissioner of Internal Revenue Service,* United

States Tax Court at Chicago, Illinois (Docket Nos. 8840, 8841, 8842), September 27–October 4, 1948.

7. Author's interview with Roy M. Brewer (tape-recorded with permission).
8. Bob Thomas, *King Cohn: The Life and Times of Harry Cohn* (New York: G. P. Putnam's Sons, 1967), p. 199.

Chapter Three
1. David Gelman and Alfred G. Aronowitz, "MCA: Show Business Empire," *New York Post Daily Magazine,* June 9, 1962.
2. Justice Department memorandum, October 14, 1941.
3. Re-created conversation based upon George Maury's report on his interview with Spike Jones.
4. Telegram from Arnold to Waters, October 22, 1941.
5. Justice Department memorandum, March 28, 1941.
6. Telegram from Hollywood attorney Martin Gang, October 22, 1941.
7. Justice Department memorandum, June 16, 1961.
8. Justice Department memorandum, May 25, 1943.

Chapter Four
1. Open letter from Kibre to IATSE membership, September 15, 1938.
2. Nancy Lynn Schwartz, *The Hollywood Writers' Wars* (New York: Alfred A. Knopf, 1982), p. 125.
3. Testimony of William Bioff, *U.S.* v. *Campagna, et al.,* 146 F.2d.524 (2nd Cir. 1944).
4. Ovid Demaris, *The Last Mafioso* (New York: Times Books, 1983), p. 272.
5. IRS report, May 7, 1962.
6. Chicago Crime Commission report, June 6, 1962.
7. Messick, p. 235.

Chapter Five
1. Justice Department memorandum, May 12, 1945.
2. MCA contract with the Pacific Square Corporation, November 4, 1941.
3. Justice Department memorandum, May 12, 1945.
4. Re-created conversation based on Justice Department memorandum, May 11, 1945.
5. Re-created conversation based upon Justice Department memorandum, May 12, 1945.
6. Pye, p. 26.
7. Justice Department memorandum, February 10, 1961.

Chapter Six
1. Memorandum from Billy McDonald to Tom Kettering, January 16, 1946.
2. *Finley* v. *MCA,* District Court of the United States for the Southern District of California, Central Division, Civil Action No. 4328-M (1946).
3. Pye, p. 34.

Chapter Seven
1. Verbatim conversation between Charles Wick and attorneys for the Los Angeles office of the Justice Department's Antitrust Division, March 5, 1946.

2. Letter from Fred Weller and Herman Bennett to Assistant Attorney General Wendell Berge, March 7, 1946.
3. *Finley* v. *MCA,* June 24, 1946.
4. Letter from George B. Haddock to William C. Dixon, August 12, 1946.
5. Martin A. Gosch and Richard Hammer, *The Last Testament of Lucky Luciano* (Boston: Little, Brown and Company, 1975), p. 312.
6. David G. Wittels, "Star-Spangled Octopus," *Saturday Evening Post,* August 24, 1946.
7. Schwartz, p. 239.

Chapter Eight
1. Ronald Reagan and Richard G. Hubler, *Where's the Rest of Me?* (New York: Dell Publishing Company, 1965), p. 154.
2. Lou Cannon, *Reagan* (New York: Perigee Books, 1982), pp. 47–48.
3. Clark R. Mollenhoff, *Strike Force: Organized Crime and the Government* (Englewood Cliffs, New Jersey: Prentice-Hall, 1972), p. 39.
4. Reagan and Hubler, p. 91.
5. Bill Boyarsky, *The Rise of Ronald Reagan* (New York: Random House, 1968), p. 64.
6. Reagan and Hubler, p. 121.
7. "Fifty Years in Motion," *Screen Actor,* August 1984.
8. Tichi Miles and Marcia Borie, *The Hollywood Reporter: The Golden Years* (New York: Coward-McCann, 1984), pp. 200–205.
9. David Thomson, *A Biographical Dictionary of Film* (New York: William Morrow and Company, 1976), p. 466.

Chapter Nine
1. Author's interview with Richard Walsh.
2. Interview with Roy Brewer.
3. Schwartz, p. 221.
4. Interview with Brewer.
5. David Caute, *The Great Fear* (New York: Simon and Schuster, 1978), p. 489.
6. Author's telephone conversation with Roy Brewer.
7. Interview with Brewer.
8. Reagan and Hubler, p. 179.
9. George H. Dunne, *Hollywood Labor Dispute: A Study in Immorality* (Los Angeles: Conference Publishing Company, n.d.), pp. 40, 44.
10. Reagan and Hubler, p. 208.
11. Dunne, p. 32.
12. Reagan and Hubler, pp. 199–200.
13. Reagan and Hubler, p. 167.
14. Seymour M. Hersh (with Jeff Gerth), *The New York Times,* June 28, 1976.
15. Interview with Irving Allen.
16. Interview with Brewer.
17. Dunne, p. 19.
18. Reagan and Hubler, p. 229.
19. Arthur Miller, "The Year It Came Apart," *New York,* December 30, 1974, pp. 43–44; quoted in Victor Navasky's *Naming Names* (New York: Viking Press, 1980), p. 213.

20. Interview with Brewer.
21. Vance King, *The Hollywood Reporter,* October 26, 1953.
22. Navasky, p. 165.

Chapter Ten
1. Lou Cannon, *Reagan* (New York: Perigee Books, 1982), p. 64.
2. Scott Herhold, *San Jose Mercury News,* August 25, 1985.
3. Justice Department memorandum, December 27, 1943.
4. Justice Department memorandum, April 4, 1947.
5. Justice Department memorandum, December 3, 1947.
6. Reagan and Hubler, p. 243.
7. Justice Department memorandum, March 22, 1962.
8. Nancy Reagan (with Bill Libby), *Nancy* (New York: William Morrow and Company, 1980), p. 110.
9. Mervyn LeRoy, *Take One* (New York: Hawthorn Books, 1974), pp. 192–193.

Chapter Eleven
1. U.S. Senate Special Committee to Investigate Organized Crime in Interstate Commerce, Third Interim Report, April 17, 1951, p. 51.
2. Chicago Crime Commission memorandum, June 6, 1962.
3. Demaris, p. 109.
4. Demaris, p. 46.
5. *The New York Times,* June 27, 1976.
6. FBI report, September 17, 1963.

Chapter Twelve
1. Leonard Katz, *Uncle Frank: The Biography of Frank Costello* (New York: Drake Publishers, 1973), p. 140.
2. *Hearings of the U.S. Senate Special Committee to Investigate Organized Crime in Interstate Commerce* (hereafter referred to as *Kefauver Committee Hearings*), October 6, 1950, p. 369.
3. Ibid., October 7, 1950, p. 394–395.
4. Ibid., September 9, 1950, p. 106.
5. *The New York Times,* June 27, 1976.
6. Lester Velie, "The Capone Gang Muscles into Big-Time Politics," *Collier's,* September 30, 1950.
7. *Kefauver Committee Hearings, Third Interim Report,* April 17, 1951, p. 2.
8. James Bacon, *Made in Hollywood* (Chicago: Contemporary Books, 1977), p. 105.
9. Letter from Herbert A. Bergson to William C. Dixon, May 31, 1950.

II. THE FALL

Chapter Thirteen
1. Pye, p. 53.
2. Author's interview with Laurence Beilenson.
3. *FCC Hearings on Programming,* Volume 24, October 13, 1960.

4. Justice Department memorandum, March 9, 1962.
5. Letter from George Chandler to Frank Gibney, publisher of *SHOW Magazine,* March 6, 1962.
6. Interview of John Dales by David Robb, unpublished, n.d.
7. Edward T. Thompson, "There's No Show Business Like MCA Business," *Fortune,* July 1960.
8. FBI report, September 28, 1961.
9. Justice Department memorandum, March 20, 1962.
10. Martin Kent, Ray Loynd, and David Robb, "Hollywood Remembers Ronald Reagan," unpublished series of interviews between 1981 and 1982, pp. 58–61.
11. Interview with Lew Wasserman by David Robb, February 24, 1984.

Chapter Fourteen
1. Kent, Loynd, Robb, pp. 54–55.
2. Reagan and Hubler, p. 284.
3. Reagan and Hubler, p. 285.
4. Laurence Leamer, *Make-Believe: The Story of Nancy and Ronald Reagan* (New York: Harper and Row, 1983), p. 176.
5. Kent, Loynd, and Robb, pp. 52–53.
6. Reagan and Hubler, p. 286.
7. *FCC Hearings on Programming,* Volume 24, October 13, 1960.
8. Letter from Maurice Silverman to William D. Kilgore, January 26, 1954.
9. *U.S.* v. *Shubert, et al.,* 99 Adv. U.S. Sup. Ct. Rep. 213, February 14, 1955.
10. *The Film Daily,* November 28, 1956.
11. Letter from Bernard M. Hollander to Marcus A. Hollabaugh, March 24, 1955.
12. Letter from Stanley E. Disney to James M. McGrath, acting chief of the Los Angeles Antitrust Division, May 13, 1955.
13. Letter from James M. McGrath to Stanley N. Barnes, Assistant U.S. Attorney General, May 17, 1955.
14. *Hover* v. *Music Corporation of America, et al.,* U.S. District Court, Southern District, Central Division, Civil Action No. 18159-HW.
15. Ibid.
16. *The Hollywood Reporter,* November 14, 1955.
17. David Robb, *Daily Variety,* April 18, 1984.

Chapter Fifteen
1. FBI report, April 23, 1969.
2. Walter Sheridan, *The Fall and Rise of Jimmy Hoffa* (New York: Saturday Review Press, 1972), p. 31.
3. Michael Dorman, *Payoff: The Role of Organized Crime in American Politics* (New York: David McKay and Company, 1972), pp. 197–201.
4. Letter from Pierre Salinger to Robert F. Kennedy, June 12, 1957.
5. *Hearings of the U.S. Senate Select Committee on Improper Activities in the Labor or Management Field* (hereafter referred to as *McClellan Committee Hearings*), October 30, 1957, pp. 6275–6276.
6. FBI report, September 17, 1963.

7. Ibid.
8. Ibid.
9. *McClellan Committee Hearings,* p. 13123.

Chapter Sixteen

1. FBI report, September 27, 1961.
2. Justice Department memorandum, March 6, 1958.
3. Dun and Bradstreet, "Analytical Report," May 21, 1957.
4. Justice Department memorandum, March 5, 1958.
5. Justice Department memorandum, April 22, 1958.
6. *Fortune,* July 1960.
7. *New York Post Daily Magazine,* June 6, 1962.
8. Justice Department memorandum, November 3, 1960.
9. Justice Department memorandum, June 22, 1961.
10. Justice Department memorandum, November 29, 1960.
11. Bill Davidson, *SHOW,* February 1962.
12. Justice Department memorandum, April 22, 1958.
13. Justice Department memorandum, August 7, 1958.

Chapter Seventeen

1. *TV Guide,* November 14, 1959.
2. Peter J. Schuyten, "How MCA Discovered Movieland's Golden Lode," *Fortune,* November 1976.
3. Justice Department memorandum, July 28, 1959.

Chapter Eighteen

1. IRS report on Sidney Korshak, February 1962.
2. FBI report, September 17, 1963.
3. Lester Velie, "Paul Ziffren: The Democrats' Man of Mystery," *Reader's Digest,* July 1960.
4. Ibid.
5. Hersh, *The New York Times,* June 27, 1976.
6. Los Angeles Police Department report, April 23, 1969.
7. FBI report, September 17, 1963.

Chapter Nineteen

1. Reagan and Hubler, p. 314.
2. Ellen Farley and William K. Knoedelseder, Jr., *The Los Angeles Times,* August 24, 1980.
3. Reagan and Hubler, pp. 317–318.
4. Author's interview with Richard Walsh.
5. *The Wall Street Journal,* October 29, 1980.
6. Ibid.
7. Kent, Loynd, Robb, pp. 19–20.
8. David Robb, *Variety,* April 18, 1984.
9. Raymond Strait, *James Garner: A Biography* (New York: St. Martin's Press, 1985), p. 374.
10. Reagan and Hubler, p. 323.

Chapter Twenty
1. Justice Department memorandum, October 20, 1960.
2. Ibid., Part II.
3. FBI report, April 16, 1962.
4. FBI report, September 25, 1961.
5. Justice Department memorandum, October 24, 1960.
6. FBI report, November 13, 1961.
7. Justice Department memorandum, October 25, 1960.
8. *Post Daily Magazine,* June 5, 1962.
9. Justice Department memorandum, November 24, 1960.
10. Justice Department memorandum, October 27, 1960.
11. Justice Department memorandum, March 23, 1962.
12. Justice Department memorandum, July 14, 1961.
13. *SHOW,* February 1962.
14. FBI report, April 22, 1960.
15. Justice Department memorandum, November 4, 1960.
16. Justice Department memorandum, December 5, 1960.
17. FBI reports, January 8, 1962, and January 10, 1962.
18. Howard Kohn, "Sinatra: The History Behind the Rumors," *Rolling Stone,* March 19, 1981.

Chapter Twenty-one
1. Justice Department memorandum, March 21, 1961.
2. Justice Department memorandum, March 31, 1961.
3. Justice Department memorandum, April 6, 1961.
4. Justice Department memorandum, April 10, 1961.
5. Justice Department memorandum, May 12, 1961.
6. Justice Department memorandum, May 22, 1961.
7. Justice Department memorandum, May 25, 1961.
8. Justice Department memorandum, June 7, 1961.

Chapter Twenty-two
1. Justice Department memorandum, August 22, 1961.
2. Justice Department memorandum, August 28, 1961.
3. Justice Department memorandum, September 12, 1961.
4. Justice Department memorandum, September 12, 1961.
5. Interview with John Dales by David Robb, unpublished.
6. Justice Department memorandum, September 18, 1961.
7. Justice Department memorandum, October 2, 1961.
8. Chandler letter to Gibney.

Chapter Twenty-four
1. Reagan and Hubler, pp. 325–326.
2. Justice Department memorandum, February 21, 1962.
3. Justice Department memorandum, March 7, 1962.
4. Justice Department memorandum, March 22, 1962.
5. Re-created conversation based on Justice Department memorandum, April 5, 1962.

6. *The New York Times,* April 22, 1962.
7. Justice Department memorandum, May 16, 1962.
8. *U.S.* v. *MCA,* District Court of the United States for the Southern District of California, Central Division, Civil Action No. 62–942–WM.

Chapter Twenty-five
1. Justice Department memorandum, July 18, 1962.
2. Justice Department memorandum, July 25, 1962.
3. Justice Department memorandum, July 26, 1962.
4. Ibid.
5. Letter from Susman to Posner, July 27, 1962.
6. Justice Department memorandum, August 6, 1962.
7. Re-created conversation based on Justice Department memorandum, August 9, 1962.
8. Re-created conversation based on Justice Department memorandum, August 16, 1962.

III. THE RESURRECTION

Chapter Twenty-six
1. *The New York Times,* May 10, 1962.
2. *The New York Times,* June 10, 1977.
3. Justice Department memorandum, October 1, 1962.
4. Justice Department memorandum, March 9, 1962.
5. Reagan and Hubler, p. 337.
6. Cannon, pp. 94 and 97.
7. Interview with Stanley Rubin by David Robb, unpublished.
8. Author's interview with Stanley Rubin.

Chapter Twenty-seven
1. FBI report, May 8, 1962.
2. FBI report, September 17, 1963.
3. FBI report, n.d.
4. FBI report, September 17, 1963.
5. *The New York Times,* June 29, 1976.
6. FBI report, October 23, 1963.
7. FBI report, September 17, 1963.
8. FBI report, September 17, 1963.
9. *The New York Times,* June 28, 1976.
10. Ibid.
11. John Kobler, "The Million-Dollar Sting at the Friars Club," *New York,* July 21, 1975.
12. Dan E. Moldea, *The Hoffa Wars* (New York: Paddington Press, 1978), p. 129.
13. Demaris, p. 272.
14. FBI report, n.d.
15. FBI report, September 17, 1963.

Chapter Twenty-eight
1. *Report of the Select Committee on Assassinations,* 95th Congress, 2nd Session, House Report No. 95–1828, Part 2, pp. 169–179.
2. Ibid., "Staff and Consultant's Reports on Organized Crime," Volume IX, p. 86.
3. Author's interview with G. Robert Blakey.
4. Earl C. Gottschalk, Jr., *The Wall Street Journal,* July 18, 1973.
5. Leamer, p. 193.
6. Peter J. Schuyten, *Fortune,* November 1976.
7. *Business Week,* May 1, 1965.
8. Boyarsky, p. 106.
9. *The Washington Post,* May 31, 1982.
10. Lou Cannon, *Reagan* (New York: Perigee Books, 1982), p. 354.
11. Nancy Reagan, p. 127.

Chapter Twenty-nine
1. Author's interview with G. Robert Blakey.
2. Author's interview with Grant Sawyer.
3. *Miami Herald,* January 25, 1981.
4. Interview with Sawyer.
5. Testimony of Paul Laxalt before the Commission on the Review of National Policy Toward Gambling, August 19, 1975.
6. Author's interview with Robert Maheu.
7. Author's interview with Tom Mechling.
8. Letter to Ramsey Clark from Paul Laxalt, July 25, 1968.
9. Messick, p. 223.
10. Deposition of Sidney Korshak, *SEC* v. *Parvin Dohrmann Company, et al.,* Southern District of New York, 69 Civ 4543, June 23, 1970.

Chapter Thirty
1. Messick, pp. 226–227.
2. Bob Gottlieb, "How Lew Wasserman Foiled the Wicked Witches and Became the Wiz of MCA," *Los Angeles,* January 1979.
3. James Bacon, *Made in Hollywood* (Chicago: Contemporary Books, 1977), pp. 155–156.
4. *Forbes,* September 1, 1969.
5. *The Washington Post,* September 20, 1984.
6. Cannon, p. 166–167.
7. Gary G. Hamilton and Nicole Woolsey Biggart, *Governor Reagan, Governor Brown: A Sociology of Executive Power* (New York: Columbia University Press, 1984), pp. 46–47.
8. Cannon, p. 173.
9. Ibid., p. 175.
10. Minutes of the Nevada Gaming Commission, June 22, 1972.
11. Ibid.
12. Ibid.
13. Author's interview with Bernard Nemerov.
14. Author's interview with Robert Heymann.
15. Laxalt's letter to *The Sacramento Bee,* November 18, 1983.

16. Edward Pound, *The Wall Street Journal,* June 20, 1983.
17. Author's interview with Harry Reid.

Chapter Thirty-one
1. Letter to Lew Wasserman from Jack Findlater, March 1, 1973.
2. Letter to Sidney Sheinberg from Findlater, July 19, 1974.
3. Henry Denker, *The Kingmaker* (New York: David McKay Company, 1972), p. 10.
4. FBI report, August 8, 1974.
5. FBI report, July 26, 1973.
6. *The New York Times,* June 29, 1976.
7. IRS report on Sidney R. Korshak, March 22, 1972.
8. *Fortune,* November 1976.
9. Justice Department memorandum, February 25, 1976.
10. *Fortune,* November 1976.
11. Ibid.
12. Justice Department memorandum, May 9, 1975.
13. Justice Department memorandum, August 25, 1975.
14. Joyce Haber, *The Los Angeles Times,* January 27, 1975.
15. Messick, p. 242.

Chapter Thirty-two
1. Laxalt's testimony before the Commission on the Review of National Policy toward Gambling, August 19, 1975.
2. Author's interview with John Sears.
3. Author's interview with Jude Wanniski.
4. Justice Department memorandum, April 12, 1976.
5. Letter to Assistant Attorney General Thomas E. Kauper from Allen E. Susman and Jeffrey L. Nagin, June 11, 1976.
6. Nat Hentoff, *The Village Voice,* July 19, 1976.

Chapter Thirty-three
1. Demaris, pp. 339–340.
2. Justice Department memorandum, March 15, 1977.
3. Jody Jacobs, *The Los Angeles Times,* October 18, 1978.
4. *In the Matter of the Application of Playboy-Elsinore Associates, et al.,* Superior Court of New Jersey, Appellate Division, A-4188-81T1, August 31, 1983.
5. Ibid.
6. *Los Angeles,* January 1979.
7. State of California, Evelle J. Younger, Attorney General, "Organized Crime Control Commission: First Report," May 1978, p. 61.
8. Mike Qualls, *Los Angeles Herald Examiner,* May 7, 1978.
9. *NBC Nightly News,* "Segment Three," December 14, 1978.

Chapter Thirty-four
1. Paul McGrath, "Horsing Around with Off-Track Betting," *Chicago,* November 1978.
2. *The Chicago Tribune,* July 21, 1971.

3. *The New York Times,* June 29, 1976.
4. *NBC Nightly News,* June 19, 1979.
5. Ibid.
6. FBI transcript of conversation among Joseph Lombardo, Red Strate, Anthony Spilotro, Allen Dorfman, and William Webbe, taped in Webbe's office on May 1, 1979.
7. Garry Trudeau, *Doonesbury, The Los Angeles Herald Examiner,* July 13, 1979.
8. *The Los Angeles Times,* May 26, 1979.

Chapter Thirty-five
1. Jack Anderson, *The Washington Post*, August 14, 1981.
2. Jack Anderson, *The Washington Post*, July 18, 1981.
3. *The Washington Post,* July 14, 1981.
4. Interview with Wanniski.
5. Author's interview with Mary Gojack.
6. *Miami Herald,* January 25, 1981.
7. Elizabeth Drew, *Politics and Money: The New Road to Corruption* (New York: Macmillan Publishing Company, 1983), p. 124.
8. *The New York Times,* December 14, 1980.
9. *The Washington Post,* June 10, 1982.
10. *The Washington Post,* December 17, 1980.

Epilogue
1. Saul David, *The Industry: Life in the Hollywood Fast Lane* (New York: Times Books, 1981), p. 215.
2. Ronnie Dugger, *On Reagan: The Man and His Presidency* (New York: McGraw-Hill Book Company, 1983), p. 149.
3. *The Los Angeles Times,* April 30, 1981.
4. *The Los Angeles Times,* September 26, 1982.
5. *The Los Angeles Daily News,* July 21, 1985.
6. *The Washington Post,* November 22, 1985.
7. *The Washington Post,* September 27, 1984.
8. *The Los Angeles Times,* April 23, 1985.
9. Author's interview with Fred Fielding.
10. Author's interview with David Gergen.
11. *The Washington Post,* November 20, 1981.
12. *The Washington Post,* October 24, 1981.
13. *The Washington Post,* April 9, 1982.
14. *The Washington Post,* October 29, 1982.
15. *The Washington Post,* May 9, 1983.
16. Jack Anderson, June 17, 1983.
17. *The New York Times,* October 13, 1983.
18. U.S. House Committee on Government Operations press release, March 23, 1984.
19. *The New York Times,* May 13, 1984.
20. Author's interview with Roy Brewer.
21. Sid Blumenthal, *The New Republic,* January 6 and 13, 1986.
22. Robert I. Friedman and Dan E. Moldea, *The Village Voice,* March 5, 1985.
23. James M. Buchanan, "A Defense of Organized Crime?" in *The Economics of*

Crime and Punishment, Simon Rottenberg, editor (Washington, D. C.: The American Enterprise Institute, 1973), pp. 119–132.

24. *The Washington Post,* August 2, 1984.

25. Chicago Crime Commission Report, March 4, 1983.

26. Hearings on the Hotel Employees and Restaurant Employees International Union, U.S. Permanent Subcommittee on Investigations (PSI), April 27 and 28, 1983, p. 29.

27. Letter to S. Cass Weiland, chief counsel of PSI, from Harvey M. Silets, January 18, 1983.

28. *The Washington Post,* November 14, 1985.

29. *The Washington Post,* March 3, 1986.

30. *The Washington Post,* March 6, 1986.

31. *The Los Angeles Times,* April 10, 1986.

BIBLIOGRAPHY

On Organized Crime and Labor Racketeering

Allen, Steve (with Roslyn Bernstein and Donald H. Dunn). *Ripoff: A Look at Corruption in America.* Secaucus, New Jersey: Lyle Stuart, Inc., 1979.

Blakey, G. Robert, and Richard N. Billings. *The Plot to Kill the President.* New York: Times Books, 1981.

Brill, Steven. *The Teamsters.* New York: Simon and Schuster, 1978.

Demaris, Ovid. *Captive City: Chicago in Chains.* New York: Lyle Stuart, Inc., 1969.

———. *The Last Mafioso: The Treacherous World of Jimmy Fratianno.* New York: Times Books, 1981.

Dorman, Michael, *Payoff: The Role of Organized Crime in American Politics.* New York: David McKay Company, 1972.

Dunne, George H. *Hollywood Labor Dispute: A Study in Immorality.* Los Angeles: Conference Publishing Company, n.d.

Fried, Albert. *The Rise and Fall of the Jewish Gangster in America.* New York: Holt, Rinehart and Winston, 1980.

Gosch, Martin A., and Richard Hammer. *The Last Testament of Lucky Luciano.* Boston: Little, Brown and Company, 1975.

Hutchinson, John. *The Imperfect Union: A History of Corruption in American Trade Unions.* New York: E. P. Dutton & Co., Inc., 1972.

Katz, Leonard. *Uncle Frank: The Biography of Frank Costello.* New York: Drake Publishers, Inc., 1973.

Kobler, John. *Capone: The Life and World of Al Capone.* New York: G. P. Putnam's Sons, 1971.

Messick, Hank. *The Beauties and the Beasts: The Mob in Show Business.* New York: David McKay Company, Inc., 1973.

———. *The Silent Syndicate.* New York: Macmillan, 1967.

Moldea, Dan E. *The Hoffa Wars: Teamsters, Rebels, Politicans and the Mob.* New York: Paddington Press, 1978.

Mollenhoff, Clark R. *Strike Force: Organized Crime and the Government.* Englewood Cliffs, New Jersey: Prentice-Hall, 1972.

Peterson, Virgil. *The Mob: Two Hundred Years of Organized Crime in New York.* Ottawa, Illinois: Green Hill Publishers, Inc., 1983.

Reid, Ed, and Ovid Demaris. *The Green Felt Jungle.* New York: Trident Press, 1963.

————. *The Grim Reapers: The Anatomy of Organized Crime in America.* Chicago: Henry Regnery Company, 1969.

Sheridan, Walter. *The Fall and Rise of Jimmy Hoffa.* New York: Saturday Review Press, 1972.

Smith, Dwight C., Jr. *The Mafia Mystique.* New York: Basic Books, 1975.

Turner, Wallace. *Gamblers' Money: The New Force in American Life.* Boston: Houghton Mifflin Company, 1965.

On Sidney Korshak

Hersh, Seymour M. (with Jeff Gerth). *The New York Times,* June 27–30, 1976.

Steiger, Paul E. *The Los Angeles Times,* September 15, 1969.

Velie, Lester. "The Capone Gang Muscles into Big-Time Politics," *Collier's,* September 30, 1950.

On the Reagan Administration and Organized Crime

Friedman, Robert I. "Senator Paul Laxalt, the Man Who Runs the Reagan Campaign," *Mother Jones,* August–September 1984.

————, and Dan E. Moldea. "Networks Knuckle Under to Laxalt," *The Village Voice,* March 5, 1985.

Goldberg, Steve. "Reputed Shady Figures Prominent in Laxalt's Backers," *Winston-Salem Journal,* November 14, 1982.

Gottlieb, Bob, and Peter Wiley. "The Senator and the Gamblers," *The Nation,* July 24–31, 1982.

Hamill, Pete. "With Friends Like These," *The Village Voice,* August 21, 1984.

McGee, Jim, and Patrick Riordan. "Laxalt Friends Allegedly Linked to Crime Figures," *The Miami Herald,* January 25, 1981.

Moldea, Dan E. "More Than Just Good Friends," *The Nation,* June 11, 1983.

———— "Reagan Administration Officials Closely Linked with Organized Crime," *Organized Crime Digest,* February 1982.

———— "The Reagan Administration, Organized Crime, and the Left." Seminar paper delivered at the Institute for Policy Studies, May 28, 1981.

———— "Paul Laxalt and His Connections," *Crime Control Digest,* May 28, June 4, and June 11, 1984.

Pound, Edward T. "Las Vegas Links," *The Wall Street Journal,* June 20, 1983.

Walsh, Denny. "Agents Say Casino 'Skimmed' During Sen. Laxalt's Ownership," *The Sacramento Bee,* November 1, 1983.

On Ronald Reagan

Anderson, Janice. *The Screen Greats: Ronald Reagan.* New York: Exeter Books, 1982.

Babcock, Charles R. *The Washington Post,* September 20, 1984.

Boyarsky, Bill. *The Rise of Ronald Reagan.* New York: Random House, 1968.

————. *Ronald Reagan: His Life and Rise to the Presidency.* New York: Random House, 1981.

Brown, Edmund G. (Pat), and Bill Brown. *Reagan: The Political Chameleon.* New York: Praeger Publishers, 1976.

Brownstein, Ronald, and Nina Easton. *Reagan's Ruling Class: Portraits of the President's Top One Hundred Officials.* Washington, D.C.: The Presidential Accountability Group, 1982.

Cannon, Lou. *Reagan.* New York: G. P. Putnam's Sons, 1982.

————. *Ronnie and Jesse: A Political Odyssey.* Garden City, New York: Doubleday & Company, 1969.

Dugger, Ronnie. *On Reagan: The Man and His Presidency.* New York: McGraw-Hill Book Company, 1983.

Harris, Roy J., Jr. "Old Friends May Play a Very Important Role in Reagan Presidency," *The Wall Street Journal,* December 12, 1980.

Hamilton, Gary G., and Nicole Woolsey Biggart. *Governor Reagan, Governor Brown: A Sociology of Executive Power.* New York: Columbia University Press, 1984.

Herhold, Scott. "Reagan Acted as Informant for FBI," *San Jose Mercury News,* August 25, 1985.

Leamer, Laurence. *Make-Believe: The Story of Nancy and Ronald Reagan.* New York: Harper and Row, 1983.

Kneeland, Douglas E. "Reagan More Than a Millionaire but Extent of Wealth Is Hidden," *The New York Times,* October 6, 1980.

Kent, Martin, Ray Loynd, and David Robb. *Hollywood Remembers Ronald Reagan.* Unpublished manuscript.

Miller, James Nathan. "Ronald Reagan and the Techniques of Deception," *The Atlantic Monthly,* February 1984.

Reagan, Nancy (with Bill Libby). *Nancy.* New York: William Morrow and Company, Inc., 1980.

Reagan, Ronald, and Richard G. Hubler. *Where's the Rest of Me?* New York: Dell Publishing Company, 1965.

Reid, T. R. "Reagan: A Life Built on Performing," *The Washington Post,* October 22–24, 1980.

Steffgen, Kent H. *Here's the Rest of Him.* Reno, Nevada: Foresight Books, 1968.

On Ronald Reagan and MCA

Farley, Ellen, and William K. Knoedelseder, Jr. "Ronald Reagan in Hollywood," *The Los Angeles Times,* August 24, 1980.

Moldea, Dan E., and Jeff Goldberg. "That's Entertainment: Ronald Reagan's Four Decades of Friendship with World Showbiz Colossus MCA," *City Paper,* October 5–11, 1984.

Robb, David. "New Info on Reagan, MCA Waiver Probe," *Variety,* April 18, 1984.

On Jules Stein, Lew Wasserman, and MCA

Beck, Roger, and Howard Williams. "MCA," *The Los Angeles Mirror-News,* November 11, 12, and 13, 1958.

Davidson, Bill. "MCA: The Octopus Devours the World," *SHOW,* February 1962.

Deutsch, Susan. "Lew!," *California Magazine,* March 1985.

Fabricant, Geraldine. "A Movie Giant's Unfinished Script," *The New York Times,* October 20, 1985.

Gelman, David, and Alfred G. Aronowitz. "MCA: Show Business Empire," *New York Post Daily Magazine,* June 4–10, 1962.

Harris, Kathryn. "MCA Takes the Cautious Road as Competitors Plunge Ahead," *The Los Angeles Times,* November 22, 1981.

Hentoff, Nat. "The Octopus of Show Business," *The Reporter,* November 23, 1961.

Gottlieb, Bob. "How Lew Wasserman Foiled the Wicked Witches and Became the Wiz of MCA," *Los Angeles,* January 1979.

Gottschalk, Earl C. "If It's Show Business, Chances Are MCA Inc. Is Deeply Involved in It," *The Wall Street Journal,* July 18, 1973.

Kroeger, Albert R. "The Winning Ways of Sonny Werblin," *Television Magazine,* September 1961.

Schumach, Murray. "Interview with Lew Wasserman," *The New York Times,* April 22, 1962.

Schuyten, Peter J. "How MCA Rediscovered Movieland's Golden Lode," *Fortune,* November 1976.

Thompson, Edward T. "There's No Show Business Like MCA's Business," *Fortune,* July 1960.

Wittels, David G. "Star-Spangled Octopus," *The Saturday Evening Post,* August 10, 17, 24, and 31, 1946.

On Hollywood and the Motion Picture Industry

Adams, Joey. *Here's to the Friars: The Heart of Show Business.* New York: Crown Publishers, Inc., 1976.

Atkins, Dick. *Hollywood Explained.* Livingston, New Jersey: Prince Publishers, 1975.

Bacon, James. *Made in Hollywood.* Chicago: Contemporary Books, 1977.

Balio, Tino, ed. *The American Film Industry.* Madison, Wisconsin: The University of Wisconsin Press, 1977.

Behlmer, Rudy, ed. *Inside Warner Brothers: 1935–1951.* New York: Viking, 1985.

David, Saul. *The Industry: Life in the Hollywood Fast Lane.* New York: Times Books, 1981.

Dunne, John Gregory. *The Studio.* New York: Touchstone Books, 1979.

Fitzgerald, Michael G. *Universal Pictures: A Panoramic History in Words, Pictures, and Filmographies.* New Rochelle, New York: Arlington House Publishers, 1977.

Goodman, Ezra. *The Fifty-Year Decline and Fall of Hollywood.* New York: Simon and Schuster, 1961.

Green, Abel, and Joe Laurie, Jr. *Show Biz: From Vaude to Video.* New York: Henry Holt and Company, 1951.

Gussow, Mel. *Darryl F. Zanuck: Don't Say Yes Until I Finish Talking.* New York: Da Capo Press, 1971.

Hampton, Benjamin B. *History of the American Film Industry: From Its Beginnings to 1931.* New York: Dover Publications, Inc., 1970.

Hayward, Brooke. *Haywire.* New York: Alfred A. Knopf, 1977.

Higham, Charles. *Hollywood at Sunset: The Decline and Fall of the Most Colorful Empire Since Rome.* New York: Saturday Review Press, 1972.

Hirschhorn, Clive. *The Warner Bros. Story.* New York: Crown Publishers, Inc., 1979.

Jobes, Gertrude. *Motion Picture Empire.* Hamden, Connecticut: Archon Books, 1966.

Lasky, Betty. *RKO: The Biggest Little Major of Them All.* Englewood Cliffs, New Jersey: Prentice-Hall, 1984.

LeRoy, Mervyn. *Take One.* New York: Hawthorne Books, 1974.

Marx, Arthur. *Goldwyn: A Biography of the Man Behind the Myth.* New York: W. W. Norton and Company, 1976.

McClintick, David. *Indecent Exposure: A True Story of Hollywood and Wall Street.* New York: William Morrow and Company, 1982.

Michael, Paul. *The Academy Awards: A Pictorial History.* New York: Bonanza Books, 1964.

Mosley, Leonard. *Zanuck: The Rise and Fall of Hollywood's Last Tycoon.* Boston: Little, Brown and Company, 1984.

Pye, Michael. *Moguls: Inside the Business of Show Business.* New York: Holt, Rinehart and Winston, 1980.

Rivkin, Allen, and Laura Kerr. *Hello, Hollywood.* New York: Doubleday & Company, 1962.

Rosow, Eugene. *Born to Lose: The Gangster Film in America.* New York: Oxford University Press, 1978.

Strait, Raymond. *James Garner: A Biography.* New York: St. Martin's Press, 1985.

Summers, Anthony. *Goddess: The Secret Lives of Marilyn Monroe.* New York: Macmillan Publishing Company, 1985.

Thomas, Bob. *King Cohn: The Life and Times of Harry Cohn.* New York: G. P. Putnam's Sons, 1967.

————. *Selznick.* Garden City, New York: Doubleday & Company, 1970.

Thomas, Tony. *Howard Hughes in Hollywood.* Secaucus, N.J.: Citadel Press, 1985.

Thomson, David. *A Biographical Dictionary of Film.* New York: William Morrow and Company, 1976.

Wiley, Mason, and Damien Bona. *Inside Oscar: The Unofficial History of the Academy Awards.* New York: Ballantine Books, 1986.

Wilk, Max. *The Wit and Wisdom of Hollywood: From the Squaw Man to the Hatchet Man.* New York: Atheneum, 1971.

Wilkerson, Tichi, and Marcia Borie. *The Hollywood Reporter: The Golden Years.* New York: Coward-McCann, Inc., 1984.

Wilson, Earl. *The Show Business Nobody Knows.* Chicago: Cowles Book Company, 1971.

Zierold, Norman. *The Moguls.* New York: Coward-McCann, Inc., 1969.

Zukor, Adolph (with Dale Kramer). *The Public Is Never Wrong: The Autobiography of Adolph Zukor.* New York: G. P. Putnam's Sons, 1953.

On Television and Radio History

Barnouw, Erik. *The Image Empire: A History of Broadcasting in the United States. Volume III: From 1953.* New York: Oxford University Press, 1970.

Bergreen, Laurence. *Look Now, Pay Later: The Rise of Network Broadcasting.* Garden City, N.Y.: Doubleday & Company, 1980.

Brooks, Tim, and Earle Marsh. *The Complete Directory to Prime Time Network TV Shows: 1946–Present.* New York: Ballantine Books, 1981.

McNeil, Alex. *Total Television: A Comprehensive Guide to Programming from 1948 to the Present.* New York: Penguin Books, 1984.

Mankiewicz, Frank, and Joel Swerdlow. *Remote Control: Television and the Manipulation of American Life.* New York: Times Books, 1978.

West, Robert. *The Rape of Radio.* New York: Rodin Publishing Company, 1941.

On Big Bands and Music History

Bane, Michael. *Who's Who in Rock.* New York: Everest House, 1981.

Chapple, Steve, and Reebee Garofalo. *Rock 'n' Roll Is Here to Pay: The History and Politics of the Music Industry.* Chicago: Nelson-Hall, 1977.

Chilton, John. *Who's Who of Jazz: Storyville to Swing Street.* Philadelphia: Chilton Book Company, 1972.

Dexter, Dave, Jr. *The Jazz Story: From the Nineties to the Sixties.* Englewood Cliffs, New Jersey: Prentice-Hall, 1964.

Gammond, Peter, and Peter Clayton. *A Guide to Popular Music.* London: Phoenix House, 1960.

Keepnews, Orrin, and Bill Grauer, Jr. *A Pictorial History of Jazz: People and Places from New Orleans to Modern Jazz.* New York: Crown Publishers, 1955.

Simon, George T. *The Big Bands.* New York: Macmillan Publishing Company, 1967.

Whitburn, Joel. *The Billboard Book of Top 40 Hits.* New York: Billboard Publications, 1985.

On General Media

Bagdikian, Ben H. *The Media Monopoly.* Boston: Beacon Press, 1983.

Compaine, Benjamin M. *Who Owns the Media? Concentration of Ownership in the Mass Communications Industry.* New York: Harmony Books, 1979.

Thomas, Dana L. *The Media Moguls: From Joseph Pulitzer to William S. Paley, Their Lives and Boisterous Times.* New York: G. P. Putnam's Sons, 1981.

Whiteside, Thomas. *The Blockbuster Complex: Conglomerates, Show Business, and Book Publishing.* Middletown, Connecticut: Wesleyan University Press, 1981.

On Red-Baiting and Blacklisting

Caute, David. *The Great Fear: The Anti-Communist Purge Under Truman and Eisenhower.* New York: Simon and Schuster, 1978.

Ceplair, Larry, and Steven Englund. *The Inquisition in Hollywood: Politics in the Film Industry, 1930–1960.* Garden City, New York: Anchor Press/Doubleday, 1980.

Cole, Lester. *Hollywood Red: The Autobiography of Lester Cole.* Palo Alto, California: Ramparts Press, 1981.

Kahn, Gordon. *Hollywood on Trial: The Story of the Ten Who Were Indicted.* New York: Boni and Gaer, 1948.

Navasky, Victor S. *Naming Names.* New York: Viking Press, 1980.

Schwartz, Nancy Lynn (completed by Sheila Schwartz). *The Hollywood Writers' Wars.* New York: Alfred A. Knopf, 1982.

Miscellaneous Works

Barlett, Donald L., and James B. Steele. *Empire: The Life, Legend, and Madness of Howard Hughes.* New York: W. W. Norton & Company, 1979.

Cantor, Bert. *The Bernie Cornfeld Story.* New York: Lyle Stuart, Inc., 1970.

Denker, Henry. *The Kingmaker.* New York: David McKay Company, Inc., 1972.

Fonzi, Gaeton. *Annenberg: A Biography of Power.* New York: Weybright and Talley, 1970.

Garrison, Omar V. *Howard Hughes in Las Vegas.* New York: Lyle Stuart, Inc., 1970.

Kohn, Howard. "Sinatra: The History Behind the Rumors," *Rolling Stone,* March 19, 1981.

Leuchtenburg, William E. *Franklin D. Roosevelt and the New Deal.* New York: Harper and Row, 1963.

Ostrander, Gilman M. *Nevada: The Great Rotten Borough, 1859–1964.* New York: Alfred A. Knopf, 1966.

Velie, Lester. "Paul Ziffren: The Democrats' Man of Mystery," *Reader's Digest,* July 1960.

Wilson, Earl. *Sinatra: An Unauthorized Biography.* New York: New American Library, 1976.

Zimmerman, Paul. *The Last Season of Weeb Ewbank.* New York: Farrar, Straus and Giroux, 1974.

Litigations

Brady v. *MCA,* U.S. District Court of Nevada, Civil Action No. 374, 1962.

Finley v. *MCA, et al.,* U.S. District Court, Southern District of California, Central Division, Civil Action No. 4328-M.

Hover v. *MCA, et al.,* U.S. District Court, Southern District of California, Central Division, Civil Action No. 18159-HW.

U.S. v. *Campagna, et al.,* 146 F. 2nd. 524 (New York, 2nd Cir. 1944).

U.S. v. *MCA, et al.,* U.S. District Court, Southern District of California, Central Division, Civil Action No. 62-942-WM.

U.S. v. *Paramount Pictures, Inc., et al.,* 334 U.S. 131, 92 L ed 1160, 68 S Ct. 915.

U.S. v. *Parvin Dohrmann, et al.,* U.S. District Court of New York, Southern District, 69 Civ. 4543.

U.S. v. *Schubert, et al.,* 99 Adv. U. S. Supreme Court. Rep. 213.

Official Documents

Committee on Governmental Affairs, U.S. Senate (Hotel Employees and Restaurant Employees International Union). Washington, D.C., 1983.

Committee on Governmental Affairs, U.S. Senate (Oversight of Labor Department's Investigation of Teamsters Central States Pension Fund). Washington, D.C., 1980.

Commission on the Review of the National Policy Toward Gambling, "Testimony of Senator Paul Laxalt," August 19, 1975.

General Accounting Office, Report by the Comptroller General of the United States, "Stronger Federal Effort Needed in Fight Against Organized Crime," December 7, 1981.

Nevada Gaming Commission Minutes, "Licensing Hearing on the Ormsby House," June 22, 1972.

President's Commission on Organized Crime, "The Impact: Organized Crime Today," April 1986.

Select Committee to Study Governmental Operations with Respect to Intelligence Activities, U.S. Senate. Washington, D.C., 1975.

Select Committee on Improper Activities in the Labor or Management Field, U.S. Senate, Washington, D.C., 1960.

Select Committee to Investigate Organized Crime in Interstate Commerce, U.S. Senate, Washington, D.C., 1951.

Select Committee on Assassinations, U.S. House of Representatives, Washington, D.C., 1979.

State of New Jersey Casino Control Commission, "Plenary Licensing Hearing of Hilton New Jersey Corporation," 1984.

Newspapers and Magazines
The Atlantic
Business Week
Chicago

The Chicago Tribune
Collier's
Daily Variety
Film Daily
Forbes
Fortune
The Hollywood Reporter
Los Angeles
The Los Angeles Herald Examiner
The Los Angeles Times
Newsweek
New York
The New York Times
Organized Crime Digest
Reader's Digest
The Sacramento Bee
The San Jose Mercury News
The Saturday Evening Post
SHOW
Television
Time
Variety
The Village Voice
The Wall Street Journal
The Washington Post
The Washington Star

INDEX

Accardo, Anthony, 24, 38, 83, 91*n*, 118–19, 134–35, 301, 336–39
Airport, 258
Aiuppa, Joey, 326*n*, 336–37
Alex, Gus, 38, 116–17, 121–22, 229, 232, 336–37
Alexander, Willard, 32
Allen, Irving, 70–71
Alliance of Television Producers (ATP), SAG vs., 99–100, 173–74
American Broadcasting Company (ABC), 98, 152, 215
American Enterprise Institute, 334
American Federation of Labor (AFL), 24, 25, 60, 67–68
American Federation of Musicians (AFM), 28, 33, 44, 75, 100
antitrust investigation of, 52–53
MCA's relation with, 4, 17–19, 31–34, 53, 55, 102–103, 156–59, 165
American Federation of Television and Radio Artists (AFTRA), SAG vs., 144, 170, 171–73
American Graffiti, 269
American Guild of Variety Artists (AGVA), 58
American Musicians Union (AMU), 17
American Veterans Committee (AVC), 63
Ames, Leon, 102
Anderson, Andy, 290, 346
Anderson, Jack, 328
Andrews, Dana, 103–104
Annenberg, Leonore, 302*n*
Annenberg, Moses, 84–85, 135
Annenberg, Walter, 84–85, 280, 302, 303*n*
Armstrong, Louis, 12, 14

Arnold, Thurman, 32–33, 313
Artists' Managers Guild (AMG), SAG and, 110, 113, 164–65, 171, 186–87
Arvey, Jake ("Colonel"), 116–17, 135
Ash, Harry, 84
Associated Artists, 30–31
Associated Booking Corporation, 14, 117, 228, 246
Association of Motion Picture and Television Producers (AMPTP), 252, 268

Babcock, Charles, 256
Bacon, James, 92–93, 254
Balaban, Barney, 23–24, 26, 28, 80, 160, 222, 234
Balaban and Katz, Inc., 23
Baldridge, Holmes, 54–55
Barnes, Stanley N., 111
Barnett, Larry, 41–42, 48–49, 50, 206, 222
Basie, Count, 32, 43–44
Bautzer, Greg, 231–32
Baxter, William, 307–308
Bazelon, David I., 324
Beck, Johnny, 30–31
Becker, Ed, 234*n*
Beckerman, Edith, 51
Beilenson, Laurence, 79, 99–100, 101, 110, 178, 183–84, 209–10
Bell, Griffin, 286
Bell, Rex, 244
Bennett, Walter K., 123
Benny, Jack, 149, 238
Berger, Ralph, 227
Bergman, Ingrid, 150–51
Bergson, Herbert A., 93
Bernstein, Eugene, 83
Bickford, Albert, 157, 213, 215

Biden, Joseph, 321–22, 326
Biehl, Carl, 294
Billings, Carter, 147
Bioff, Willie, 23–24, 26
  IATSE and, 4–5, 24–28, 35–37, 65, 67, 69, 89–90, 112, 226
  political associates of, 118–19
Bishop, Harold Eames, 41–42, 48–49
Blacker, Fred ("Bugs"), 23
blacklist, 73–75
Blakey, G. Robert, 235, 242
Bland, George, 231
Bluhdorn, Charles G., 268, 279, 280, 288, 341
Blumberg, Nate J., 26, 220
Blumenthal, Sid, 333
Brazil, 311–12
Brewer, Roy, 65–68, 71–75, 332
Bridges, Harry, 67
Briguglio, Salvatore, 300
Broderick, Helen, 60
Brown, Edmund ("Pat"), 136–37, 232, 238–39, 253
Brown, Jerry, Korshak and, 284–86, 288–91
Browne, George, 23–24
  IATSE and, 24–28, 35–37, 65, 67, 69, 89–90, 112, 226
Buchalter, Louis ("Lepke"), 24, 37n
Buchanan, James M., 334–35
Bureau of Alcohol, Tobacco, and Firearms, 319–20
Bush, George, 296, 299, 322, 331–32
Butler, Paul, 137

cable television, 273, 306–307, 309
California:
  organized crime in, 285–86
  Reagan as governor of, 1, 7, 239, 245, 256–57, 258–59, 266–67, 293
  Reagan's 1970 gubernatorial campaign in, 8, 258–59
Cannon, Lou, 223, 256, 349
Capone, Al, 12, 15, 20–24, 121
Carbo, Frankie, 85–86
Carey, Estelle, 37n
Carter, Jimmy, 8, 291, 306
  organized crime attacked by, 318, 324, 328–29
  Wasserman and, 278, 286, 288, 299
Casey, Pat, 25, 70, 85, 89
Casey, William, 294–95, 301
Castro, Fidel, CIA-Mafia's planned assassination of, 231–32, 235, 246, 276
CBS Artists Bureau, 33, 55

Cermak, Anton, 21–22
Chandler, George, 101, 165n
Chasin, George, 206
Cheshire, Maxine, 303
Chesler, Louis A., 221
Chicago, Ill., organized crime in, 12–15, 20–24, 336–37
Chicago Crime Commission, 39, 84, 337
Chicago Sun-Times, 243
Chicago Tribune, 136
Cinema International Corporation (CIC), MCA as joint owner of, 267–68, 283
Circella, Nick, 23, 25, 37n
City Paper (Moldea and Goldberg), 167n
Civiletti, Benjamin, 318, 324
Clark, Ramsey, 247
Clark, Tom C., 33–34, 58, 66
Clegg, Hugh, 78
Cleopatra, 233
Clift, Montgomery, 132, 152–53
Coca-Cola Bottling Company of Los Angeles, 283
Cochrane, Robert H., 26, 220
Coffey, Gordon, 53
Cohn, Harry, 26, 28, 74, 88–90, 138
Cole, David L., 144
Coleman, Delbert, 248–50, 262, 291
Collins, Harold F., 49
Colosimo, "Big Jim," 20
Columbia Broadcasting System (CBS), 33, 97–98, 126, 128, 130–31, 149–50, 193–94
Columbia Pictures, 26, 46, 88–89, 138
Columbia Savings and Loan Association, MCA's ownership of, 238
Committee to Reelect the President (CRP), 266–67
Commonweal, 69, 72
communications industry, deregulation of, 306–307
Condon, Eddie, 12, 13
Conference of Studio Unions (CSU), IATSE vs., 65–73
Connally, John, 297
Costello, Frank, 87–88, 105, 117
Covey, T. R., 48–49
Cox, Archibald, 343

Dailard, Wayne, 42–43, 48–49, 56
Daily Variety, 35–36, 153–54, 167n, 212n
Dales, John, 101, 102, 141–42, 163, 174, 182

Dalitz, Morris (Moe), 24, 226, 244, 246, 248, 297, 336
D'Andrea, Philip, 24n, 88
Danny Dare Review, 33–34
Dare, Danny, 33–34
Dark Victory, 62
David, Saul, 305–306
Davis, Bette, 30, 62n
Davis, Loyal, 81
Death Valley Days, 237, 239
Decca Record Company:
  MCA's purchase of, 6, 205–206, 209, 210–15, 219–20
  Universal purchased by, 104, 131, 205, 221
"Declaring War on Organized Crime" (Reagan), 347–48
"Defense of Organized Crime, A?" (Buchanan), 334–35
DeLaurentiis, Dino, 286
Democratic National Committee, 5, 136–37, 286, 288
Democrats, Democratic Party, 38, 87, 135, 236, 239, 258, 332–33
Denker, Henry, 109, 265–66
DePalma, Gregory, 281–82
Des Moines Register, 61n
Deverich, Nat, 45
Dewey, Thomas, 39
Disney, Stanley, 113, 211, 214
Disney, Walt, 66, 69–70
Doherty, Frank P., 49
Dolan, Tony, 347
Dome, Louis (Pacella), 282
Donovan, Ray, 298–301, 320–23, 327–29, 343–44
Doonesbury, 290–91
Dorfman, Allen M., 116–17, 226, 260, 290, 326–27
Dorfman, Paul ("Red"), 116–17
Dorsey, Tommy, 17, 45, 53, 57–58
Douglas, William O., 247–48
Drew, Elizabeth, 299
Drug Enforcement Administration(DEA), 321–22
Duchin, Eddy, 16
Duffy, Ben, 108–109
Duffy, John, 329
Dugger, Ronnie, 306–307
Dunne, George H., 69, 72

Eagle-Lion Studios, 83, 88, 99
Economics of Crime and Punishment, The, 334
Edwards, Blake, 151
Eisenhower, Dwight, 231

elections:
  of 1964, 235–36
  of 1966, 238–39
  of 1968, 255, 257, 275, 286
  of 1970, 8, 258–59
  of 1972, 266
  of 1976, 275–76, 278
  of 1980, 8, 292–99
  of 1982, 325–26
  of 1984, 328, 332–34
Ellington, Duke, 13, 32, 43–44
Emerson, Ryan Quade, 318
English, Glenn, 331
Everett, Marjorie, 288–90

Fabricant, Geraldine, 312–13
Factor, John ("Jake the Barber"), 120, 226–27
Max Factor Company, 120–21
Federal Bureau of Investigation (FBI), 2, 74, 117, 315–17
  CRP investigated by, 266–67
  Korshak investigated by, 121, 134, 137–38, 225–29, 232
  MCA investigated by, 33–34, 54–56, 93, 103, 132–33, 146n, 147–48, 154, 163–65, 213
  organized crime investigated by, 242–44, 281–82, 290, 301, 318–19, 321–23, 344–45
  Reagan as informant for, 5, 78–79
Federal Communications Commission (FCC), 33, 128–29, 146, 155–57, 306–307
Feldman, Charles, 100
Ferraro, Geraldine A., 333–34
Fielding, Fred, 301, 319, 328
Fifty-seventh Madison Corporation, 256
film industry:
  Communist influence in, 36–37, 66–67, 70, 72–75, 78–79, 81–82
  conglomerates in, 251–55
  financial disasters in, 233–34, 257–58
  HUAC investigation of, 72–74
  MCA as artist representative in, 30–32, 45–46, 81, 92–93, 131, 148–54, 164, 206
  MCA as producer and distributor in, 3, 5, 7, 8, 148–50, 176, 205–206, 219, 221, 233, 258, 269–71, 310, 311
  monopolistic practices of, 46–47
  organized crime's infiltration of, 4–5, 24–28, 73, 86
  Reagan as actor in, 5, 61–64, 79–80, 109n, 183, 235

film industry (*cont.*)
Reagan's gubernatorial decisions beneficial to, 7, 253
strikes in, 26, 67–71, 89–91, 306
see also specific studios
Finch, Robert, 239
Findlater, Jack, 264–65
Finley, Larry, 41–44, 48–49, 56, 113
Finley v. *MCA,* 48–50, 56, 114, 206
Firestone, Leonard, 238, 255
Firestone Tire and Rubber Company, 255
Fitting, Paul, 42–44
Flanagan, James F., III, 338
Fonda, Henry, 310
Ford, Frederick W., 146
Ford, Gerald, 275–76
Ford Star Time Show, 150–51
Formosa, Johnny, 154
Fowler, Mark, 306–307
Fox, William, 27
Foy, Brian, organized crime connections of, 61–62, 83, 88
Foy, Eddie, Jr., 62
Fratianno, James, 85, 232, 281–82, 298, 336–38
Frederick Brothers Agency, 43–44, 48
Freedom of Information Act, 2, 320
Friar's Club cheating scandal, 230–31
Fricano, John, 166, 167–201
Friedman, Allen, 344
Friedman, Maurice, 230–31
Furino, Fred, 323

Gambino, Carlo, 281–82
Garner, James, 143–44, 314–15
General Accounting Office (GAO), U.S., 317, 322, 327
General Amusement Company, 32, 42–43, 57–58
General Electric Theater, 7, 108–109, 149, 167, 203
cancellation of, 222–24
in conflict of interest controversy, 6, 139–40, 143
MCA-Revue deal for, 194–98, 200–201
Reagan's article on, 114–15
in Reagan's grand jury testimony, 188–201
Reagan's speaking tours for, 188, 193, 199–200, 223–24, 235
Genis, Samuel, 135–36
Gergen, David, 319
Gerth, Jeff, 278–79, 341
Giancana, Sam, 154, 231, 274

Gilliam, Terry, 311–12
Gioe, Charles, 5, 24*n,* 37–38, 61*n,* 83–84, 91, 117*n*
Glasser, Ira, 321
Glaser, Joseph G., 14, 40, 117, 228
Glimco, Joey, 116–17, 121
Goetz, Bill, 92–93
Gojack, Mary, 296–97
Goldberg, Jeff, 167*n*
Goldblatt, Joel, 71*n*
Goldstock, Ronald, 344
Goldwater, Barry, 7, 118–19, 235–36
Goodheart, William R. (Billy), 4, 15–16, 29–30
Goodman, Benny, 12, 13, 45
Gottlieb, Bob, 254
Grable, Betty, 30
Gradle, Harry, 15
Grant, Cary, 153, 166, 273, 308
Green, William, 68
Greenbaum, Gus, 118–19
Greenberg, Alex Louis, 135–36
Grim Reapers, The (Reid), 37*n,* 234*n*
Guiness, Alec, 150, 221
Gulf & Western, 250, 257, 268, 279, 286, 288–89
Guzik, Jake ("Greasy Thumb"), 21, 38, 118–19, 121

Haber, Joyce, 273, 279
Haddock, George B., 56
Halley, Rudolph, 87–88
Hansen, Victor R., 125, 132
Harding, Warren G., 25
Harlow, Jean, 24
Hauser, Joseph, 338–39
Hays, Will, 25–26
Hayward, Leland, 45, 50
Hayward-Deverich Agency, 32, 45, 55
Heflin, Van, 180
Hefner, Hugh, 284, 338, 342
Heidt, Horace, 45
Hentoff, Nat, 279
Hersh, Seymour M., 278–79, 341
Heymann, Robert, 261–62
Heymann, Walter, 71*n,* 145, 261
Hill, Virginia, 85–86
Hilton, Barron, 339–42, 348
Hitchcock, Alfred, 148–49, 270
Alfred Hitchcock Presents, 149–50
Hodges, Joy, 61
Hodkinson, W. W., 25
Hoffa, James R., 246, 300
J. F. Kennedy's assassination and, 234

Korshak and, 116–17, 118n, 134, 225–27, 229–30
Laxalt and, 259–60
Hollander, Bernard M., 112–13
Hollings, Ernest, 326
Hollywood Independent Citizens Committee of Arts, Sciences and Professions (HICCASP), 78
Hollywood Reporter, 36, 63–64, 75, 114–15, 153–54
Holmes, Oliver Wendell, 222
home video rentals, 310–11
Hoover, J. Edgar, 33–34, 132, 245, 322
Hope, Bob, 142
House of Representatives, U.S.:
    Select Committee on Assassinations, 234n, 235
    Special Subcommittee on Labor, 71–72, 73
    Un-American Activities Committee, 5, 72–75, 132
Hover, Herman D., 113–14
Hubler, Richard C., 202, 238–39
Hudgins, Willie L., 272–73, 277
Hugel, Max, 295–96, 301
Hughes, Howard, 104–105, 231, 274
    in Las Vegas, 245–48
    Laxalt and, 245–47, 259
Humphreys, Murray, 116–17, 232

Illinois Liquor Control Board, 227, 289
"Impact: Organized Crime Today, The," 348
Internal Revenue Service (IRS), 21, 23, 27, 35, 39, 106, 134, 158, 268, 315, 319
International Alliance of Theatrical Stage Employees (IATSE), 6, 23, 100, 141
    CSU vs., 65–73
    organized crime's control of, 4–5, 24–28, 35–37, 65–67, 69, 72, 112, 226–27
    Wasserman honored by, 269
International Business Machines, Inc. (IBM), 288, 310
International Management Associates, Ltd., 211
International Pictures, 26, 220

Jackson, Donald L., 75
Jacobson, Joel R., 341, 342
Jaffe, F. Filmore, 48
Jaffee, Henry, 126
James, Harry, 17, 30, 57

Jaws, 271
jazz, organized crime's interest in, 12–13, 15
Johnson, Lyndon B., 236
Jones, Jerry, 48–49
Jones, Lindsey ("Spike"), 31–32, 34
Justice Department, U.S., 33, 106, 242
    Antitrust Division of, 31–33, 57–58, 93, 103, 110, 117, 125–26, 132, 145–47, 149, 151, 155–58, 161, 202, 204–206, 210–16, 247, 254, 270, 277–78, 283, 306–307, 313
    documents of, 18–19, 22, 23, 33, 46, 78, 81, 101, 133, 153, 186n, 222n
    MCA investigated by, 2–3, 6, 31–34, 42–44, 52–58, 111, 113, 117, 123–29, 145–54, 155–60, 161–63, 270, 272
    SAG investigated by, 113–14

Kallen, Kitty, 30
Kalver, Roy L., 112
Karl, Harry, 138, 230
Karl, Joan Cohn, 138
Katleman, Beldon, 107–108, 229, 231
Katz, Michael, 120
Katz, Sam, 23–24, 26, 28
Kaufman, David, 212n
Kaufman, Irving R., 328, 348–49
Kazan, Elia, 74
Kearns, Carroll D., 72, 73
Kefauver, Estes, 87, 90–92, 135, 158
Kennedy, John F., 6, 154, 216, 222, 276
    organized crime implicated in assassination of, 234–35, 338–39
Kennedy, Joseph P., 26
Kennedy, Robert F., 6, 119–20, 155–56, 161, 164–65, 207, 216, 259–60
Kenneworth Music, 15
Kerkorian, Kirk, 252, 267–68
Kibre, Jeff, 35, 67
Killers, The, 235
Kingmaker, The (Denker), 265–66
Kintner, Robert, 126–27, 147, 158
Kissinger, Henry A., 273
Kleindienst, Richard, 338
Knoedelseder, William, 317
Kolod, Ruby, 244
Korshak, Harry, 279–80
Korshak, Judith, 228
Korshak, Marshall, 38, 91, 134, 227–28
Korshak, Sidney R., 2, 6, 91–92, 141–42, 240n, 303, 334–50
    in CIC negotiations, 268
    Fratianno's testimony on, 336–38
    government investigations of, 7,

Korshak, Sidney R. (*cont.*)
    38–40, 91–92, 119–21, 134–35,
    137–38, 225–29, 232, 268
  Hilton and, 339–42, 348
  Hoffa and, 116–17, 118*n*, 134,
    225–27, 229–30
  J. Brown and, 285–86, 288–91
  in Las Vegas, 225–27, 229–30,
    246–50, 262, 291
  Los Angeles Dodgers and, 228–29
  New York Times series on, 8, 278–80,
    341–42
  organized crime connections of, 1–2,
    5, 7–8, 37–40, 61*n*, 70–71, 84, 86,
    116–17, 119–21, 225–27, 232,
    278–80, 285–86, 290, 339, 343, 346
  political connections of, 5, 8, 137,
    285–86, 288–91, 348–49
  Reagan's 1970 gubernatorial bid and,
    8, 259
  in RKO purchase, 104–105
  Stein and, 40
  Teamsters and, 116–18, 134, 290, 346
  as a tolerable crime figure, 335, 343,
    348–49
  Wasserman and, 278, 279, 284–85,
    286, 291, 338, 342
Korshak, Ted, 38–39
Kostelanetz, Boris, 38
Kramer, Karl, 99, 110
Kramer, Stanley, 152–53
Krim, Arthur B., 83
Kruse, Leslie ("The Killer"), 86

Labor Department, U.S., 321, 327
Laemmle, Carl, 25, 26, 220
LaMonte, John, 315–17
Lamour, Dorothy, 30
Lansky, Meyer, 20–21, 85–86, 221, 248,
    289
Laskin, Paul, 158, 162
Lastfogel, Abe, 14
Las Vegas, Nevada:
  "Chicago group" in, 225, 229
  Korshak's activities in, 225–27,
    229–30, 246–50, 262, 291
  organized crime's activities in,
    242–50, 282, 318–19, 337, 345, 346
  Reagan's job offers in, 5, 107–108
Las Vegas Sun, 245
Laurel and Hardy, 34
Lawford, Peter, 121, 154
Laxalt, Jackie Ross, 243–44
Laxalt, Michelle, 311
Laxalt, Paul, 243–47, 311, 325, 331

casino of, 261–63, 275, 347
gubernatorial campaign of, 244–45
Hoffa and, 259–60
Hughes and, 245–47, 259
libel suit of, 347
Nixon and, 259–60
organized crime and, 7, 244, 261,
    297, 318–19, 329, 347
Reagan's friendship with, 245,
    275–76, 349–50
Reagan's presidential appointees and,
    301–302
Reagan's presidential campaigns and,
    7, 292, 296, 301–302
as Reagan's successor, 349–50
senatorial campaigns of, 262–63,
    296–97
Laxalt, Peter, 261–62
Lea Act, 52
LeRoy, Mervyn, 81–82, 228
Levin, Philip, 288–89
Levy, Morris, 315–16
Lewis, Jerry, 3, 132, 152
Lewis, Tom, 329–30
Lindheimer, Ben, 288
Linsk, Eddie ("Killer"), 30
Lipsey, M. B., 50
Loevinger, Lee, 155–57, 161–66, 206,
    210–11, 213, 215–16
Loew, Marcus, 27
Lombardo, Guy, 13, 16, 30
Lonardo, Angelo, 346
Long, Baron, 31
Los Angeles Dodgers, 228–29
Los Angeles Herald Examiner, 285
Los Angeles Strike Force Against
    Organized Crime, 335–36
Los Angeles Times, 273, 290–91, 317
Luciano, Charles ("Lucky"), 20–21,
    24*n*, 57, 85–86
Luckett, Edith, 81

McCann, William E., 301
McClellan, John L., 119, 121–22
McCormack, John, 249
McCormick, Paul J., 49–50, 56, 114
McDevitt, Barney, 42
McDonald, Billy, 44
McGrath, James M., 113
McGrory, Mary, 349
Mafia, *see* organized crime
Magnuson, Warren, 112–13, 156
Maheu, Robert, 231–32, 245–46
Maloy, Tom, 24, 39
Marcello, Carlos, 234, 298, 338–39

Martin, David, 197
Martin, Dean, 132, 152, 154, 282
Masselli, Nat, 323, 329
Masselli, William, 320, 323, 329, 333
Mathes, William C., 209–11
Maury, George, 31–34
Mayer, Louis B., 27n, 60, 79
MCA:
  agents of, 4, 51, 127–28, 222
  anonymity of, 3–4
  bands represented by, 16–19, 31–34,
    41, 43–45, 48–49, 53–56
  competition of, 32, 51, 127–28, 133,
    148
  as conglomerate, 3, 49, 53, 56–57,
    204
  corporate reorganization of, 145,
    162–64
  defenders of, 153
  early employees of, 29–30
  "employment contracts" of, 204
  exclusive contracts of, 15–16, 31–34,
    42–45, 48, 55, 169–70
  failures of, 7–8, 264–65, 272–73
  fictionalized account of, 265–66
  film libraries of, 124–25, 140, 142–43
  financial situation of, 110, 125–26,
    127, 219n, 253, 267, 271, 282,
    308–310, 312
  founding and rise of, 4, 15–18
  grand jury investigations of, 6, 55,
    161–66, 167–201
  lawsuits filed against, 2–3, 6, 41–42,
    48–50, 55, 113–14, 163–65, 204,
    207, 208, 239–40, 272–73, 314–15
  other agencies raided and absorbed
    by, 30–31, 45, 54, 55, 62, 168
  "package deals" of, 111, 124–25, 147,
    150, 169–70, 176–77
  Reagan represented by, 1, 5, 62–63,
    79–80, 101, 139, 143, 168–70, 182,
    187–90, 196, 198–99
  Reagan's financial ties with, 1, 2, 5–6,
    105–106, 199–201, 239–40
  studio real estate deals of, 131–32,
    148–49
MCA Records, 315–17
MCA-SAG agreements, Reagan's role
  in, 2, 5–6, 101–104, 105, 139–43,
  159–60, 167–201, 202–203
Meany, George, 141
Mechling, Tom, 246
Meese, Edwin, 257, 285, 299, 300, 321,
  342–45, 348
Meiklejohn, William, 61–62, 147

William Meiklejohn Agency, 55, 168
Metro-Goldwyn-Mayer (MGM), 26, 27,
  141–42, 233–34, 252, 268–69
Miller, Arthur, 74, 75
Mitchell, John, 266–67
Moldea, Dan E., 167n, 276n
Mollenhoff, Clark, 61n
Montgomery, George, 230
Montgomery, Robert, 36, 60, 64, 71,
  114
Moretti, Willie, 57n
William Morris Agency, 13–14, 29, 32,
  33, 43–44, 52–54, 103, 123–24,
  127–28, 133, 221
Morton, Ferdinand ("Jelly Roll"), 11
Morton, Moe, 285–86
Motion Picture Alliance for the
  Preservation of American Ideals,
  66–67, 74
Motion Picture Operators Union, 24, 39
Motion Picture Producers and
  Distributors of America
  (MPPDA), 25–27, 70, 85, 88
Motion Picture Producers Association,
  27, 35
Motion Picture Technicians Committee,
  35
Muhl, Edward, 233
Mullen, Francis ("Bud"), 321–22,
  331–32
Murphy, Betty, 300
Murphy, George, 64, 69, 70, 72, 125,
  236, 239n
Murret, Charles, 234
Mutiny on the Bounty, 233–34

National Broadcasting Company
  (NBC), 13, 32–33, 97–98, 130–31
  MCA's sweetheart relationship with,
  126–27, 147, 149–50, 157–58
National Gambling Information Center,
  246
National Labor Relations Board, 35, 69,
  144, 172, 300
National Mediation Board, 347
Nelson, Harmon, 30
Nemerov, Bernard, 261–62
New Jersey Casino Control
  Commission, 338, 339–42
Newman, Paul, 269
New Republic, 333
New York Jets, 236–37
New York Organized Crime Task
  Force, 344
New York State Liquor Authority, 227

New York Times, 8, 29–30, 71*n,* 91,
205, 219*n,* 278–80, 300, 303,
312–13, 323, 325–26, 341
New York Times Magazine, 297, 347
Nitti, Frank, 21, 24, 37, 83, 135
Nixon, Richard M., 72, 136, 255
Laxalt and, 259–60
Reagan's defense of, 266–67, 276
Stein and, 266
Nunn, Sam, 299, 321

Oliver, Joe ("King"), 12
O'Malley, Walter, 229
Operation Prime Time, 282–83
Oppenheimer, Harold L., 293–94
organized crime:
business interests of, 12, 15, 20–22,
317–18
disorganized crime vs., 21, 334–35
history and rise of, 20–28
institutionalization of, 317–18
Reagan administration's policy on,
317–34, 335–36, 347–48
Reagan's 1980 presidential campaign
and, 8, 294–98
Reagan's presidential appointees and,
300–303
Organized Crime Review, 318
Osterberg, Clyde, 24
Oswald, Lee Harvey, organized crime
and, 234

Paramount studios, 128, 148–49, 162,
234, 283
film library of, 125–26, 140
history of, 25, 26, 46
Stein and, 80–81, 124, 159
Park, Arthur, 107, 109, 169, 188–92,
198
Parsons, Louella, 64*n*
Parvin, Albert, 247–48, 250, 262
Parvin-Dohrmann Company, 247–50
payola scandals, 131*n,* 315
Penthouse, 336–37
Pepper, Claude, 331
Petrillo, James Caesar, 33, 40, 52, 75,
100, 224*n,* 308
organized crime connections of, 22,
28
Stein and, 17–19, 22, 33, 102–103,
159
N. V. Philips, MCA's venture with,
264–65, 272–73, 277–78, 283,
310
Pidgeon, Walter, 100, 102, 144
Pisello, Salvatore, 316–17

Playboy, MCA's suit against, 284, 338
Posner, Bernard ("Pepi"), 227
Posner, Herman, 227
Posner, Leonard, 113, 123–24, 147–51,
156–60, 161–65, 203–206, 209–14,
221
Powell, Dick, 194–96
President's Commission on Organized
Crime, 328, 330, 335, 344–45,
348–49
Presser, Jackie, 321, 327–28
government investigations of, 343–47,
348
Reagan's presidential campaigns and,
297–98, 332
Reagan's transition team and,
299–300, 343
Presser, William, 226, 298
Proxmire, William, 295
Psycho, 148–49, 270

Qualls, Mike, 285
quiz shows, government investigation
of, 130–31

Rackmil, Milton, 141
Radio Corporation of America (RCA),
13, 32–33
MCA's merger negotiations with,
312–13
radio industry, 13, 18, 32–33, 98
Rangel, Charles, 335
J. Arthur Rank Productions, 221
Raskin, Hy, 204, 213, 216
"Rat Pack," FBI Surveillance of, 154
Reagan, Jack and Nelle, 60–61
Reagan, Nancy, 5, 6, 107–10, 114, 174,
179, 181, 312
Reagan's first meeting with, 81–82,
228
Reagan, Neil, 237
Reagan, Ronald:
actors' criticisms of, 103–104, 142–44
autobiography of, 202, 238–39
birth and early career of, 60–62, 166
on communism, 63–64, 72–73, 75
divorce of, 77–78, 79, 81, 99, 107
finances of, 1–2, 5–7, 62, 105–106,
240, 292
grand jury testimony of (Feb. 5,
1962), 6, 167–201, 202
income tax records of, 6, 202–203,
293
military service of, 62–64, 78
political beliefs of, 7, 75–76, 222–24,
235–36

popularity of, 276
press coverage of, 293, 300, 307
published articles of, 114–15, 347–48
real estate deals of, 240–41, 255–56,
  258–59
speeches of, 293–94, 297–98, 321,
  349–50
record industry, 13, 17, 98, 287, 315–17
Redford, Robert, 269
Regan, Donald, 320
Reid, Ed, 37n, 234n
Reid, Harry, 262–63
Republican National Committee, 7, 325
Republicans, Republican Party, 5,
  235–36, 307, 349
Revue-MCA-SAG letter agreement
  (July 23, 1952), 178, 182–86
Revue Productions, 115, 126
  formation of, 99–101, 176–77
  General Electric Theater and, 109,
    115, 143, 194–98, 200–201
  MCA's split off from, 162–64
  Reagan's partnership interest with,
    189–90, 199–201
  see also television industry, MCA as
    producer and distributor in
Reynolds, Debbie, 230
Rio, Frankie, 23
RKO Pictures Corporation, 26, 42, 46,
  104–105
Robb, David, 167n
Robinson, George S., 88
Robinson, Hubbell (Hub), 150
Rockford Files, The, 314
Rockman, Maishe, 346
Roen, Allard, 226
Rogers, William P., 112
Rollins, Edward J., 346
Roosevelt, Franklin D., 21–22, 32, 97
Rose, David, 30
Roselli, Johnny, 83–86, 108, 337
  CIA plot to assassinate Castro and,
    231–32, 246
  Hughes and, 246
  IATSE and, 4, 25–26, 37, 70
  as Senate hearing witness, 88–91
Ross, Brian, 286, 290
Ross, John Tom, 243–44
Rubel, A. C., 238
Rubin, Stanley, 223–24
Ruby, Jack, 234–35
Rudin, Milton, 274–75
Ryan, Stephen M., 345–46

Sacks, Manny, 126–27
Sacramento Bee, 293, 347

Safire, William, 303
SAG, see Screen Actors Guild
St. John, Jill, 249, 268, 273
Salvatori, Henry, 238–39
San Diego Exposition, 42
San Jose Mercury News, 78
Saphier, Jimmy, 30
Saturday Evening Post, 56–57, 81
Sawyer, Grant, 243–45
Scalise, George, 39
Schenck, Joseph, 60
  CSU vs. IATSE and, 67–68
  organized crime and, 27, 28, 35–38
Schenck, Nicholas, 27, 28
Schowengerdt, L. N., 331–32
Schreiber, Taft, 1, 4, 29, 48–49, 50, 61,
  236
  death of, 276–77
  FBI on, 266–67
  FCC and, 146, 155–57
  in Reagan's gubernatorial campaigns,
    238, 239, 255
  Reagan's political philosophy and, 7,
    223
  television production and, 101,
    108–109, 190–91, 196, 201, 237
Schroeder, Patricia, 332–33
Schumach, Murray, 205, 219n
Schweiker, Richard, 276
Screen Actor, 140
Screen Actors Guild (SAG), 36, 64, 306
  AFTRA vs., 144, 170, 171–73
  AMG and, 110, 113, 164–65, 171,
    186–87
  antitrust investigation of, 113–14, 207
  ATP vs., 99–100, 173–74
  CSU vs. IATSE and, 6, 69–70
  history of, 59–60
  labor-management relations of MCA
    and, 100–104, 108, 110, 156–60,
    162–66, 167–201, 202–203,
    206–207, 211
  MCA's residuals settlement with,
    139–43, 171–73, 178–201
  Reagan as president of, 1, 2, 5–6,
    71–72, 75, 77–80, 98–99, 101–104,
    139–41, 143, 159, 171, 174–78
  Reagan on board of, 64, 65, 109–110,
    114–15, 171
  rule 16-E of, 186
Seach, George Emerson, 230–31
Securities and Exchange Commission
  (SEC), 248–50, 294–95, 319
Myron Selznick Agency, 32, 45, 100
Senate, U.S.:
  Appropriations Subcommittee, 326

Senate, U.S. (cont.)
  Budget Committee, 332
  Government Affairs Subcommittee, 329
  Interstate and Foreign Commerce Committee, 156–57
  Judiciary Committee, 307, 311
  Labor Committee, 320, 321, 323
  Permanent Subcommittee on Investigations, 338–39, 340
  Select Committee on Improper Activities in the Labor or Management Field, 119–22
Seven Arts, 125, 221, 251
Special Committee to Investigate Organized Crime in Interstate Commerce, 87–92
  Subcommittee on Juvenile Delinquency, 158, 162
Shales, Tom, 314
Shefferman, Nathan, 118, 119
Sheinberg, Sidney, 258, 267
  embarrassments of, 311–12
  video discs and, 7–8, 265, 277, 287, 310
Sherman Antitrust Act (1891), 32, 42, 46, 47, 112, 126, 207, 272, 313–14
Shore, Dinah, 138, 230, 232
Siegel, Bugsy, 20–21, 25, 37n, 85–86, 118, 242
Siegel, Herbert, 103, 165n
Silbert, Harvey, 226, 247
Silverman, Leon, 322–24, 329
Silverman, Maurice, 111
Simpson, Ross, 256
Sinatra, Frank, 57–58, 141, 154–55, 259, 299
  organized crime and, 274–75, 281–82, 302–303
Sirigano, John, Jr., 128–29
Sklarsky, Harry, 213–15
Skouras, Spyros, 36, 140, 233–34
Smith, John, 39–40
Smith, Sandy, 243
Smith, William French, 7–8, 238, 240, 273, 275, 291, 293, 298–99, 301–303, 307, 339n, 342–43
  Reagan's war on crime and, 318–23, 325–26, 328–30, 332
Sony Betamax, 277, 283, 287, 310
Sorrell, Herb, 67, 72, 73
Speakes, Larry, 313, 323–24
Speech, The (October 27, 1964), 235–36
Spencer Gifts, MCA's purchase of, 253, 270
Spielberg, Steven, 269, 271, 310

Spilotro, Anthony, 290, 326n–27n, 337
Spitz, Leo, 26, 28, 220
"Star-Spangled Octopus" (Wittels), 56–58
State of the Union Address (January 25, 1984), 330
Stein, Doris, 22, 308
Stein, Jacob, 343
Stein, Jeff, 253
Stein, Jules, 1, 5, 7, 125, 142–43, 145, 236
  awards and honors of, 256, 283–84
  bands booked by, 4, 14, 15–18, 22, 30
  death of, 308
  general talent sought by, 29–30, 132
  Korshak and, 40
  MCA's antitrust suits and, 42, 49–50
  Nixon and, 266
  organized crime connections of, 22–23
  Paramount stock held by, 80–81, 124, 159
  Petrillo and, 17–19, 22, 33, 102–103
  in Reagan's gubernatorial campaigns, 238, 239
  Reagan's political philosophy and, 7, 223
  Reagan's tax shelters and, 292–93
  real estate deals of, 256
  resignation of, 267
  on television, 98
  Westinghouse offer and, 253–54
Stempel, Herbert, 130–31
Stewart, Jimmy, 92–93, 222n
Sting, The, 269
Stone, Al, 33–34
Stone and Lee, 33–34
Stordahl, Alex, 58
Strauss, Robert, 311
Strike Force Against Organized Crime, U.S., 291, 318, 319
Sullavan, Margaret, 45
Sullivan, Ed, 153
Supreme Court, U.S., 47, 52, 80, 111–12, 114, 125, 307–308, 311
Susman, Allen, 204–206, 208–209, 212–15, 277–78
Susskind, David, 148
Sweig, Martin, 249

talent bureaus, 4, 117
  history of, 13–19
  MCA as, 2, 6, 14–19, 75, 205–207, 208–12
Taylor, Reese, Jr., 301–302

Teagarden, Jack, 44–45
Teamsters Union:
  cabinet selections and, 299–301, 347
  casino industry and, 246, 274, 318
  Korshak and, 116–18, 134, 290, 346
  organized crime's infiltration of,
    320–21, 327
  Reagan's presidential campaigns and,
    297–98, 328, 332, 348
Teitelbaum, Benjamin, 230–31
television industry, 80, 98
  early history of, 97–99
  government investigations of, 156–58,
    165–66
  MCA as producer and distributor in,
    3, 5, 93, 99–104, 108–109, 114–18,
    124–29, 131–33, 146–53, 156–60,
    188, 222, 236–37, 258, 310, 311
  MCA as syndicator in, 269–70, 313
  Reagan as actor and producer in, 6,
    109, 114–15, 139–40, 143, 149,
    168–70, 188–201, 203, 222, 223,
    237
  strikes in, 141–44
  see also Schreiber, Taft, television
    production and; Wasserman, Lew,
    television production and
Thomas, J. Parnell, 72, 73n, 79
Thompson, Edward T., 145–46
Thurmond, Strom, 307
Tieri, Funzi, 282
Tobey, Charles W., 87
Torres, Ed, 249, 291
Torrio, Johnny, 20–21
Touhy, Roger, 22, 120
Tourine, Charles ("The Blade"), 252
Trafficante, Santos, 231, 234, 276n, 301,
  338
Trans-Glamour tours, MCA's success
  with, 270
Treasury Department, U.S., 331
Trott, Stephen S., 344–45
Trudeau, Garry, 290–91
Truman, Harry, 58n
Trumbo, Dalton, 153
Tuohy, Joe, 68
Tuttle, Holmes, 238, 275, 302
TV Guide, 131
Twentieth Century–Fox Film
  Corporation, 27, 36, 46, 140
  Reagan's real estate deal with,
    240–41, 255–56, 258–59
Twenty-One, 130–31

Ungar, Arthur, 35–36
United Artists, 25, 46, 83

U.S. v. Paramount, 46–47, 80, 112,
  125, 307–308
U.S. v. Shubert, 111–12, 114
United Studio Technicians Guild, 25
Universal Amphitheatre, 270–71
Universal City, 219
Universal Pictures Company, Inc., 25,
  26, 46, 80, 92
  Decca's purchase of, 104, 131, 205,
    221
  history of, 25, 26, 220–21
  MCA's backlot purchase from,
    131–32, 148–49
  MCA's purchase of, 3, 6, 7, 205–206,
    209, 210–15, 219–20
  as movie factory, 271–72
  post-1948 film library of, 212–16, 221
  see also film industry, MCA as
    producer and distributor in
Universal-Television, see Revue
  Productions
Unruh, Jesse, 258–59

Valenti, Jack, 252, 284, 311
Van, Jerry, 335–36
Vance, Cyrus R., 128–29, 146, 157, 278n
Van Doren, Charles, 130–31
Vanished, 258
Variety, 115, 237, 311
Vastola, Gaetano, 316
Velie, Lester, 92, 137
video discs, 4–5, 7–8, 264–65, 272–73,
  277–78, 283, 287–88, 310
Virginian, The, 236
Vogel, Joseph, 142, 233–34, 252
Voloshen, Nathan, 249

Wall Street Journal, 104–105
Wallace, Mike, 333n
Walsh, Denny, 347
Walsh, Richard, 65–66, 100, 141
Walton, Kearney, Jr., MCA's contract
  with, 31–34
Wanniski, Jude, 275–76, 296
Warner, Jack L., 3, 25, 83, 85, 87–88
Warner Brothers, 25, 27, 46, 61–62,
  68–69, 79–80, 152, 168
Warner Communications, 282
Warren, Earl, 112
Warren Commission, 235
Washington Post, 256, 303, 311, 314,
  345, 346, 348
Wasserman, Lew, 29, 50–51, 92–93, 145
  attempted firing of, 254
  on attempted takeovers of MCA, 272,
    309, 312

Wasserman (*cont.*)
  awards won by, 267
  Carter and, 278, 286, 288, 299
  Korshak and, 278, 279, 284–85, 286,
    291, 338, 342
  parties thrown by, 273, 279, 284–85,
    288, 291
  as powerbroker, 236, 252–53, 268–69
  as Reagan's agent and confidant, 1, 5,
    62–63, 79–80, 101, 107, 139, 143,
    168, 187–88, 235
  Reagan's 1980 presidential candidacy
    and, 8
  SAG and, 110, 162
  on talent agency divestiture, 208–209,
    212
  on talent packages, 205
  television production and, 99–101,
    104, 108–109, 127–28, 131, 190–91,
    195–96, 200–201, 222*n*, 237–238
  video disc project of, 4–5, 7–8,
    264–65, 272–73, 288
  Westinghouse offer of, 253–54
Waters, Victor, 33
Watt, James, 302
Wayne, John, 74
Weaver, Sylvester ("Pat"), 126, 127,
  273
Webster, William, 322, 324, 327, 343,
  344–45
Welch, John, Jr., 313
Weller, Fred, 54–55
Werblin, David ("Sonny"), 4, 29–30,
  50, 126–27, 236–37, 289–90
Westchester Premier Theater, organized
  crime connected with, 281–82, 302
Western Governors' Conference, 245,
  275

Westinghouse Electric Corporation,
  MCA merger offer of, 253–55
Where's the Rest of Me? (Reagan and
  Hubler), 202, 238–39
Whittinghill, Charles, 126, 146, 204–205
Wick, Charles, 52–54
Wilkerson, Billy, 36*n*, 63–64
Will, George F., 349
Williams, Edward Bennett, 231
Williams, Roy L., 297–98, 320–21,
  326–27, 344–47
Wilson, William A., 255, 275
Wilson, Woodrow, 13*n*
Wittels, David G., 56–58, 81
Wonders, Ralph, 42–44
Wood, George, 87–88
Woods, Charles L., 347
Wright, Robert L., 214–16
Writers Guild of America, West, 110,
  207
Wyler, William, 220
Wyman, Eugene, 232
Wyman, Jane, 30, 64, 77–79, 99, 107
Wynn, Stephen A., 312

Yorty, Samuel, 229, 239, 258
Younger, Evelle J., 285–86
Young Lions, The, 132

Zangara, Giuseppe, 21–22
Zanuck, Darryl F., 27, 233, 240
Zanuck, Richard D., 267
Zapple, Nicholas D., 156–58, 161
Ziffren, Paul, 5, 8, 135–37, 232, 240*n*,
  291
Zukor, Adolph, 25
Zwillman, Abner ("Longy"), 24, 88,
  135–36, 137